M000236624

Adam Howell has produced an informative, highly useful, and visually attractive guide to the Hebrew text of Ruth. The book of Ruth is a great choice for students looking to improve their Hebrew reading skills after they have finished their first year of the language, and this text will be an invaluable resource. It will remind them of what they already learned, give them new insights into the language, and encourage them to persevere.

Duane A. Garrett, professor of Old Testament,
The Southern Baptist Theological Seminary

Adam Howell has produced an excellent resource for students of biblical Hebrew. Through a clause-by-clause analysis of the Hebrew text of Ruth, Howell reinforces the fundamentals while guiding readers beyond the basics; all of this with a goal of hearing the voice of God in the text of Scripture. This book will be a help to many!

Andrew M. King, assistant professor of biblical studies,
Midwestern Baptist Theological Seminary & Spurgeon College

Howell's *Ruth: A Guide to Reading Biblical Hebrew* is a helpful companion volume for those studying the Hebrew text of Ruth. Rather than focusing on linguistics or complex syntax (though he neglects neither), Howell most frequently addresses morphology and Masoretic accentuation—the very aspects of text work with which students most struggle as they transition from grammar to biblical analysis. Howell's pedagogical instincts shine through in his down-to-earth explanations and playful descriptions of complicated structures. Students will find the book informative, approachable, and—dare I say—fun.

Michelle Knight, assistant professor of Old Testament and Semitic Languages,
Trinity Evangelical Divinity School

*A Guide
to Reading
Biblical Hebrew*

•

GRBH

RUTH

A Guide to Reading Biblical Hebrew

RUTH

A Guide to Reading Biblical Hebrew

ADAM J. HOWELL

LEXHAM
ACADEMIC

Ruth: A Guide to Reading Biblical Hebrew

Copyright 2022 Adam J. Howell

Lexham Academic, an imprint of Lexham Press
1313 Commercial St., Bellingham, WA 98225
LexhamPress.com

You may use brief quotations from this resource in presentations, articles, and books. For all other uses, please write Lexham Press for permission. Email us at permissions@lexhampress.com.

Unless otherwise noted, Scripture quotations are the author's own translation.

Print ISBN 9781683595571
Digital ISBN 9781683595588
Library of Congress Control Number 2021941973

Lexham Editorial: Derek Brown, Ryan Davis, James Spinti, Doug Mangum
Cover Design: Kristen Cork, Owen Craft
Typesetting: Justin Marr

CONTENTS

Abbreviations ix
Introduction 1

RUTH
1:1–5 13
1:6–15 33
1:16–18 73
1:19–22 85
2:1–3 101
2:4–13 117
2:14–23 157
3:1–5 185
3:6–16 199
3:17–18 235
4:1–6 243
4:7–12 265
4:13–17 285
4:18–22 299

Glossary 301
Accent Tables 310
Bibliography 315

ABBREVIATIONS

BIBLIOGRAPHICAL

BDB	Francis Brown, S. R. Driver, and Charles A. Briggs. *The Brown-Driver-Briggs Hebrew and English Lexicon: With an Appendix Containing the Biblical Aramaic: Coded with the Numbering System from Strong's Exhaustive Concordance of the Bible*. Peabody, MA: Hendrickson, 1996.
BHRG	Christo H. J. van der Merwe, Jacobus Naudé, and Jan Kroeze. *A Biblical Hebrew Reference Grammar*. Electronic ed. Sheffield: Sheffield Academic Press, 1999.
BHQ	Adrian Schenker, Natalio Fernández Marcos, Jan de Waard, Anthony Gelston, Carmel McCarthy, David Marcus, P. B. Dirksen, Y. A. P. Goldman, R. Schäfer, and Magne Sæbø. *Biblia Hebraica Quinta*. Stuttgart: Deutsche Bibelgesellschaft, 2011.
BHS	Rudolf Kittel, Karl Elliger, Wilhelm Rudolph, Rüger Hans Peter, G. E. Weil, and Adrian Schenker. *Biblia Hebraica Stuttgartensia.* Stuttgart: Deutsche Bibelgesellschaft, 1997.
DCH	David J. A. Clines. *Dictionary of Classical Hebrew*. Sheffield: Sheffield Phoenix, 2011.
GBHS	Bill T. Arnold and John H. Choi. *A Guide to Biblical Hebrew Syntax*. 2nd ed. Cambridge: Cambridge University Press, 2018.

GKC	Wilhelm Gesenius. *Gesenius' Hebrew Grammar*. Edited and enlarged by E. Kautzsch. Translated by A. E. Cowley. Mineola, NY: Dover, 2006.
HALOT	Ludwig Kohler, Walter Baumgartner, M. E. J. Richardson, Johann Jakob Stamm, and Benedikt Hartmann. *The Hebrew and Aramaic Lexicon of the Old Testament*. Leiden: Brill, 2001.
IBH	Russell Fuller and Kyoungwon Choi. *Invitation to Biblical Hebrew: A Beginning Grammar*. Grand Rapids: Kregel, 2006.
IBHS	Russell Fuller and Kyoungwon Choi. *Invitation to Biblical Hebrew Syntax: An Intermediate Grammar*. Grand Rapids: Kregel, 2017.
JM	Paul Joüon. *A Grammar of Biblical Hebrew*. 2nd ed. Translated and revised by T. Muraoka. Rome: Biblical Institute Press, 2006.
LHB	*The Lexham Hebrew Bible*. Bellingham, WA: Lexham Press, 2012.
LXX	Septuagint
Mp	Masora Parva
MT	Masoretic Text
NIDOTTE	Willem A. VanGemeren, ed. *New International Dictionary of Old Testament Theology and Exegesis*. Grand Rapids: Zondervan, 2012.
RJW	Ronald J. Williams. *Williams' Hebrew Syntax*. 3rd ed. Revised and expanded by John C. Beckman. Toronto: University of Toronto Press, 2007.
WO	Bruce K. Waltke and Michael Patrick O'Connor. *An Introduction to Biblical Hebrew Syntax*. Winona Lake, IN: Eisenbrauns, 1990.

GRAMMATICAL

1cp	first-person common plural
1cs	first-person common singular
2fp	second-person feminine plural
2fs	second-person feminine singular
2mp	second-person masculine plural
2ms	second-person masculine singular
3cp	third-person common plural
3fp	third-person feminine plural
3fs	third-person feminine singular
3mp	third-person masculine plural
3ms	third-person masculine singular
fp	feminine plural
fs	feminine singular
mp	masculine plural
ms	masculine singular
R1	first root letter of a triconsonantal verbal root
R2	second root letter of a triconsonantal verbal root
R3	third root letter of a triconsonantal verbal root

INTRODUCTION

The book of Ruth is a masterful idyll containing extraordinary biblical-theological themes. During the tumultuous period of the judges, God's providential care joins a faithful Moabite and a valiant Bethlehemite and they become an integral family in the genealogy of King David. As the genealogy explains in Ruth 4:18–22, Ruth and Boaz find themselves in the family line from Perez to David, demonstrating that God brings good out of tumult (Gen 38; Judg 17–21) and that he fulfills his covenant promises to Abraham that "kings will come from you" (Gen 17:6). In Ruth, we find that this is not just any king who comes from this faithful family, but it is in fact David, the precursor of the Lord Jesus Christ (Matt 1:1–17).

Not only does the book of Ruth point forward to David and ultimately to God's faithfulness to bring about the Christ, but it also points backward to torah. Ruth and Boaz demonstrate extraordinary faithfulness to torah and to the righteousness that comes by faith in Yahweh. During the period of the judges, no one would expect this kind of faithfulness in Israel since "everyone did what was right in his own eyes" (Judg 17:6; 21:25). Additionally, no one would expect this kind of faithfulness from a Moabite widow who assumedly should be excluded from the people of God (Deut 23:3–6). And yet Ruth seems to demonstrate more hope in and faithfulness to Yahweh than even Naomi, the native Israelite. Boaz reinforces the importance of covenant faithfulness in his execution of the redemption rights and his protection of the "least of these," a foreign widow, who for all intents and purposes would be considered destitute in ancient culture. Boaz truly is a faithful redeemer, a "man mighty of moral worth" (אִישׁ גִּבּוֹר חַיִל), who loves torah and walks in faithfulness.

Since the book of Ruth fits so neatly within this biblical-theological framework, it is important that students of the Bible know its content in all its intricate literary beauties. The more I read the Hebrew text of Ruth, the more I find myself delighting in the beauty of a narrative that communicates grand truths about the Lord God and his providential workings in the world. And yet I find that these riches are uniquely derived from the Hebrew text. From the beauty of wordplay to the characterization of the primary actresses, the Hebrew text of Ruth provides rich meaning to these few chapters of God's inspired word.

With that in mind, I hope that this guide on the Hebrew text of Ruth will prove valuable for those who love God's word and desire to mine its depths in the original Hebrew. As students of the Bible, we have to admit that our theological conclusions are derived from the grammar of the original Hebrew text. Therefore, the meaning of a text from which we draw theological conclusions is grounded in the reality that words have meaning, phrases have meaning, clauses having meaning, and sentences, paragraphs, and chapters have meaning. The building blocks for narrative art and theological meaning are found in the details of the Hebrew text. This is not to say that those without a knowledge of Hebrew cannot rightly understand God's word. However, vast riches result from the hard work of mining for gold in the original languages.

To that end, I hope and pray that this guide will help students and pastors know and love the book of Ruth, leading them to know and love our God and Father more in Christ Jesus.

AUDIENCE

This guide is for anyone and everyone who wants to dive deeper into syntactical discussions of Biblical Hebrew. The primary goal is to offer an intermediate study of the Hebrew text of Ruth, discussing grammatical features of the Hebrew language for aid in reading Biblical Hebrew. This guide is not intended to provide an exhaustive study of Hebrew grammar, although many footnotes have been provided, pointing readers to the major Hebrew reference grammars. This guide should serve well those who have covered an entire introductory Hebrew grammar. That being said, when this material was in the "testing" phases, I asked students who were only in their second semester of undergraduate Hebrew to read the manuscript. While many of these grammatical concepts were new to them, this guide became the means by which those concepts were introduced. With brief descriptions of the syntax in Ruth, my students were encouraged to read more Biblical Hebrew even while still completing their first-year grammar.

While the primary audience for this guide is Hebrew students, I also pray that pastors who desire to revive their Hebrew studies can benefit from this guide. Perhaps those who have strayed away from Hebrew can use this book as a guide to jump back into the Hebrew text and mine all the riches that it offers. Perhaps for some, this guide can serve as an independent "exegesis course," and so I have included discussions for how various idioms or complex syntactical constructions get ironed out into a smooth English translation and provide exegetical meaning. I pray that these discussions will benefit both those who are learning to translate and those who desire to revive the level of Hebrew they had years ago.

APPROACH AND SYNTACTIC NOMENCLATURE

One of the challenges of an intermediate guide for Hebrew text is the choice of nomenclature when identifying syntactic features. There is indeed no shortage of approaches to Hebrew grammar and syntax, and for that reason I want to highlight the terminology used in this guide to reduce the potential confusion associated with differing approaches to Hebrew grammar. Additionally, by covering this nomenclature here, I can avoid complicated and detailed discussions throughout the guide. I am glad to admit that not everyone will appreciate this nomenclature, but I have tried to simplify these concepts so as to avoid tedious nuances at every point.[1]

1. In this section, I have intentionally kept the discussions minimalistic to provide clarity for the guide. These explanations will by no means address all the intricacies of these (sometimes) heated conversations among linguists.

PERFECT AND IMPERFECT

First, I have chosen to use the terms "perfect" and "imperfect" when referring to the Hebrew verbal system. When either of these conjugations have a *vav*-consecutive, I have used "perfect/imperfect + *vav*-consecutive." I agree there are good reasons to abandon perfect/imperfect terminology, but since these terms continue to be common in many grammars, I felt no reason to jettison them altogether. In places where tense or aspect or both are the primary foci of the discussion, I have used "perfective" and "imperfective," reserving the titles (perfect/imperfect) of the verbal conjugations for parsing.

NOMINAL AND VERBAL CLAUSES

Second, I will be following the nomenclature of Russell Fuller and Kyounwon Choi regarding verbal and nominal clauses.[2] In this guide, I will define nominal clauses as a clause that *begins with* a noun. Accordingly, I will define a verbal clause as a clause that *begins with* a verb. In many grammars, a nominal clause is a clause consisting only of nouns (i.e., a verbless clause). In some instances, what I will call a nominal clause is also verbless, and in those places I have used "verbless" interchangeably to appeal to a wider audience. However, since a nominal clause begins with a noun, it highlights (and perhaps emphasizes) the noun more than the verbal action. According to this definition, nominal clauses may have a main verb, but it follows the subject (subject-verb word order). Since the typical word order in Hebrew narrative is verb-subject, for the text to diverge from that focuses attention on the fronted subject in what I will call nominal clauses.

When discussing nominal clauses, I will use the terms "initiator" and "announcement" to refer to the subject (initiator) and verb (announcement), respectively. In cases when the initiator and announcement are present in a nominal clause, the initiator will come before the predication about it (the announcement). In true verbless clauses, the initiator and announcement word order may vary.[3] But in what I will call nominal clauses, the subject

2. *IBHS* §37–38; cf. §11b–ii.

3. *IBHS* §11dd–ii.

(initiator) precedes the predicate (announcement). This variation in word order is precisely what draws attention to the fronted subject (focus) of the clause.

Alternatively, verbal clauses are the primary clauses of Hebrew narrative, usually structured around the imperfect + *vav*-consecutive. Since verbal clauses begin with the verb, the verbal action is the primary focus. In Hebrew narrative, this focus on the verbal action essentially becomes the temporal or logical succession of the narrative action. Verbal clauses do not provide "emphasis" unless accompanied by various particles. Hence, most of the time, verbal clauses will not require special discussion in the guide apart from accompanying emphatic particles. Verbal clauses will simply move the narrative action forward in temporal ("And then ...") or logical ("And so ...") progression.

Fuller and Choi provide the simple analogy of sports commentary to explain the interplay between nominal and verbal clauses in Hebrew narrative.[4] In most sporting events, the commentators include a play-by-play commentary and a "color commentary." The Hebrew verbal clause is analogous to the play-by-play commentator: "And now the snap, and [then] the hold, and [then] the kick, and [then] the ball is flying through the uprights, and [so] the kick is good." Within this convoluted English, you likely see the *vav*-consecutive pattern in the play-by-play ("... and then ... and so ..."). The play-by-play commentator is analogous to the verbal clause in Hebrew narrative.

On the other hand, nominal clauses are analogous to the color commentator, who, between plays, comments on a specific player who was involved in the play. "Now, about the kicker ... he played college football at East Tennessee State University, and he had a 90 percent accuracy rating during his time there. He studied mathematical engineering, and so it is no surprise that he can visualize the proper angles for a successful kick." The focus now is on the kicker, similar to how nominal clauses focus the attention on the fronted subject in the clause. After the color commentator

4. *IBHS* §38f.

discusses the focal player, the narrative continues: "And now the teams are lined up for the kickoff, and [then] the kicker prepares, and [then] the approach, and [then] the kick, and … , and … , and …" This return to the play-by-play commentary would be the return to verbal clauses in the Hebrew narrative, once again focusing on the flow of narrative action.

Even though this is a simplistic way to describe narrative, this interplay between nominal and verbal clauses adds artistic beauty to Hebrew narrative. As a narrator, the author of Ruth must move the action of the story forward, and so the primary structure of the book centers on the verbal clause. However, at strategic points, the narrator will shift to a nominal clause to draw the reader's focus to the initiator (fronted subject). When the focus is on the initiator, this structure often involves key components of narrative characterization that add to the joy of reading Hebrew narrative in all its beauty.

CONSTRUCT PACKAGES

A third feature of the nomenclature used here is the terminology associated with construct packages (bound nouns). Since we often translate construct packages with the preposition "of," we must pay special attention to the cognitive meaning of prepositions. Prepositions are the most nuanced aspect of any language. While some linguists describe construct packages as a "genitive" relationship, I have tried to avoid that terminology, though it does creep in at times. Instead, I will discuss "construct packages" or "construct chains." However, to clarify the cognitive meaning of the preposition "of" in these construct packages, I have again followed the method of Fuller and Choi.[5]

In Fuller and Choi's discussion of the genitive, they identify two types of construct relationships, proper annexation and improper annexation. Proper annexation essentially combines two nominals to form one unit of meaning. For example, when the two nouns "house" and "David" are constructed together in a genitive relationship, they become one unit of meaning, "house of David." Alternatively, improper annexation is a "false"

5. *IBHS* §12.

annexation logically, even though the two items are joined grammatically. In other words, the syntax involves a word in the construct state, but the two words cannot make one unit of meaning apart from an idiomatic expression. An example of improper annexation is the description of Joseph in Genesis 39:6, וַיְהִ֣י יוֹסֵ֔ף יְפֵה־תֹ֖אַר וִיפֵ֥ה מַרְאֶֽה, "And Joseph was *beautiful of form* and *beautiful of appearance.*" In both of these construct packages, the second noun fails to create one unit of meaning like "house of David" previously. Rather, the second noun specifies the realm that the adjective ("beautiful") modifies; "beautiful [with regard to; in the realm of] form and beautiful [with regard to; in the realm of] appearance." These idioms express something like "handsome and well-dressed," but that must be determined indirectly.

Proper annexation is the most common of these two types of construct packages. While proper annexation forms one unit of meaning, the cognitive relationship between the two nouns must still be defined. Fuller and Choi simplify the cognitive relationships of construct packages using the notion of implied prepositions, either ל, ב, or מִן. However, even then, more meaning must be deduced at the cognitive level. A ב preposition could be translated "in," "at," "with," and so on, depending on the context. Furthermore, if one determines the ב should mean "at," it could be "at the time of" (temporal) or "at the place of" (locative). For example, the construct package "Bethlehem *of* Judah" implies a locative ב preposition "Bethlehem *in* Judah." While this system of implied prepositions provides a simplified set of possibilities for the meaning of a construct package, it still allows one to explore the deeper cognitive nuances of the genitive relationship. Arnold and Choi, *A Guide to Biblical Hebrew Syntax*, and Williams and Beckman, *Williams' Hebrew Syntax*, offer eighteen genitive relationships. Where it proved helpful to include these nuances in construct packages, I've cited these intermediate grammars for readers to follow up.

MASORETIC ACCENT SYSTEM

A fourth feature to discuss in this introduction is the cantillation/accent system. Having been heavily influenced by my professor, I find great value in the Masoretic accent system. While I realize there is much debate about the value of the accent marks, I most often find that even a basic understanding of the accents helps students to identify syntactical units, guiding them as they translate potentially confusing word arrangements. A basic understanding of the disjunctive and conjunctive accents along with their relative strengths can go a long way to help students recognize something as simple as which word is the subject in a sentence. Likewise, the accents often delineate relative clauses, circumstantial clauses, and conditional clauses in ways that are at least helpful for knowing which words constitute the clause. For reference, readers can turn to the accent charts at the back of the book.

Some argue for an exegetical/interpretive value of the accents, and this is perhaps the most hotly debated function of the accent system. I am inclined to see exegetical value in the accent system (as will be seen in this guide), but I also must recognize that the accent system is neither inspired nor authoritative, and so any interpretive conclusions drawn from the accents must be held with extra caution. Alternatively, even if the accent system fails to provide significant exegetical insights, I hope that the reader will at least be able to see the beauty that they add to the flow and emphasis of the narrative of Ruth. We will see that the (un)expected patterns of the accents often suggest that the Masoretes were pointing us to a helpful focus of the text.

UNIQUE FEATURES OF THIS GUIDE

The focus of this guide is the phrase-by-phrase, clause-by-clause discussion of Hebrew syntax. A few features of this guide make it unique.

First, one will notice that the discussions of verbs often include a morphological emphasis on how we arrive at a particular parsing. I have found that students with one year of Hebrew experience still have trouble with parsing verbs, especially the so-called weak verbs. For that reason, I wanted to include content on morphology so that students can continue to reinforce the principles and patterns to parse Hebrew verbs.

Related to parsing morphology, I have intentionally repeated this information throughout the guide. While this may feel redundant at times, I've done this for two reasons. First, if someone picks up the guide to look at a particular verse, I did not want them to miss information that may have been covered earlier in the guide. It is inevitable that I failed to repeat every aspect of morphology, but I have tried to remain consistent with the descriptions and have focused on the primary attributes of the weak verbs that prove to be most cumbersome to students. A second reason for repeating parsing morphology is that I find that student must encounter the same morphological phenomena several times before they begin to anticipate it. I hope that the repetition of this morphological information will lead to students anticipating my explanation of the verbal morphology. When this happens, I hope students realize this guide was not written simply for information but also for independent learning. I pray that students can use this resource and *learn* Hebrew rather than just gain information *about* Hebrew.

A second unique feature of this guide is the *accent phrasing* associated with each verse. As mentioned above, I find syntactical value in the accent system, and so providing a schema for identifying the major clausal structure according to the accents seemed reasonable to include. The accent phrasing is not intended to be the final word on where clauses may break, but it follows the most heavily disjunctive accents and provides the guide for dividing the text into smaller units to evaluate in the guide.

Another feature of the guide is the method for identifying the Masoretic marginal notes (Mp). These notes include helpful information like *ketiv/qere*, number of occurrences of unique spellings, and even times when one should expect to see something in the text but it is not there (*qere vela ketiv*, "read but not written"). These notes, like the accents, are not inspired, but they often bring clarification. At the least, they let us know that what often appears to be an odd construction or difficult spelling in the Hebrew text also appeared to be odd or difficult to the Masoretes. Hence, they marked it.

In this guide the main text of Ruth is from the Lexham Hebrew Bible. Being an electronic text of the Hebrew Bible, it does not always show where Mp notes occur in the *BHS*. Where it is significant for the discussion, I have included the *BHS/BHQ* marginal notes in the guide. I have tried to format the marginal note as closely as possible to the *BHS/BHQ*, but the typesetting did not always accommodate that. Even so, the information is provided to enhance the discussion of the text.

Finally, along with an attempt to simplify the grammatical conversation, I have included footnotes to reference grammars so that students and pastors can continue with more in-depth study of the Hebrew language. In order to avoid inundation with Hebrew grammars, I have most often cited Ronald J. Williams, *Williams' Hebrew Syntax*, 3rd ed., revised and expanded by John C. Beckman (RJW). I have focused on *Williams' Hebrew Syntax* for a few reasons. First, RJW provides a very helpful outline grammar of the titles given to each syntactical concept along with a brief explanation of the concept. Second, RJW categorizes the grammar in helpful ways, focusing first on syntax of nouns, then on syntax of verbs, then on syntax of particles, and finally on syntax of clauses. In a succinct way, RJW addresses all major components of Hebrew syntax. Finally, and most importantly, the third edition includes expansions by John Beckman, in which he footnotes major reference grammars and articles that discuss these syntactical concepts. Even with this emphasis on RJW in citations, I have also cited major reference grammars where their discussion is particularly appropriate or where RJW fails to specify the exact discussion at hand.

ACKNOWLEDGMENTS

With any writing project, I want to be quick to acknowledge that this book required a team of people to help with its completion. The basic material in this guide began as a series of videos on Daily Dose of Hebrew. I am indebted to Rob Plummer and the Daily Dose family for that opportunity to study deeply the book of Ruth and to begin formulating how to communicate the beauty of the Hebrew text of this delightful idyll.

I want to thank Derek Brown and the editing team at Lexham Press for their gracious help along the way. Our first conversations about this book began in November 2018 in Denver, Colorado, and has led to phone calls, emails, and many other discussions about how to make this the best resource it can be. Derek and the team at Lexham have been a guiding light through this process. I particularly want to thank Doug Mangum for his careful eye in reading the technical Hebrew language discussions in this volume. I readily own the responsibility for all that is written here, but it is a better volume due to Doug's gracious help.

Next, I would like to thank all those who read the manuscript or were a part of the classroom discussions that led to the conclusions presented here. To my students, I want to thank my Intermediate Hebrew I classes at Boyce College. Most recently, I would like to thank the January 2020 Hebrew Review class at Southern Seminary and my spring 2020 Hebrew II class at Boyce College, both of whom carefully read the manuscript and provided helpful feedback to shape my thinking about the Hebrew text of Ruth. More specifically, I would like to thank T. J. Betts, Hannah Portwood, Michael Portwood, Jonathan Ahlgren, and Jackson Morse for their detailed look at the manuscript, catching many mistakes and making the content clearer to the reader. I am indebted to this family of people, but I also must claim the responsibly for all errors and inconsistencies. Any mistakes are my own.

Finally, I could not have completed this project without the constant encouragement from my immediate family. Liz, you are an inimitable reminder of God's kindness to me as you manage our household with faithful and joyful commitment, freeing me up to focus on this work. Noah, Tovah, Judah, and Norah, you light up difficult days and give me hope for the future generations.

1 It came about in the days of the judging of the judges that a famine was in the land.
Now a man from Bethlehem of Judah went to sojourn among the fields of Moab, he
and his wife and the two of his sons. 2 Now the name of the man was Elimelech and
the name of his wife was Naomi and the name(s) of the two of his sons were Mahlon
and Chilion, Ephrathites from Bethlehem of Judah, and they came to the fields of Moab,
and they settled there. 3 And Elimelech, the husband of Naomi, died, and she (Naomi)
was left remaining along with the two of her sons. 4 And they took for themselves
Moabite wives; the name of the first was Orpah and the name of the second was Ruth.
And they dwelled there about ten years. 5 And then they died, even the two of them,
Mahlon and Chilion. And the woman was left remaining without the two of her boys
and without her husband.[1]

1. All English translations are my own.

RUTH

1:1–5

1 וַיְהִ֗י בִּימֵי֙ שְׁפֹ֣ט הַשֹּׁפְטִ֔ים וַיְהִ֥י רָעָ֖ב בָּאָ֑רֶץ וַיֵּ֨לֶךְ אִ֜ישׁ מִבֵּ֧ית לֶ֣חֶם יְהוּדָ֗ה לָגוּר֙
בִּשְׂדֵ֣י מוֹאָ֔ב ה֥וּא וְאִשְׁתּ֖וֹ וּשְׁנֵ֥י בָנָֽיו׃ 2 וְשֵׁ֣ם הָאִ֣ישׁ אֱ֠לִימֶ֠לֶךְ וְשֵׁ֨ם אִשְׁתּ֜וֹ נָֽעֳמִ֗י
וְשֵׁ֥ם שְׁנֵֽי־בָנָ֣יו ׀ מַחְל֤וֹן וְכִלְיוֹן֙ אֶפְרָתִ֔ים מִבֵּ֥ית לֶ֖חֶם יְהוּדָ֑ה וַיָּבֹ֥אוּ שְׂדֵי־מוֹאָ֖ב
וַיִּֽהְיוּ־שָֽׁם׃ 3 וַיָּ֥מָת אֱלִימֶ֖לֶךְ אִ֣ישׁ נָעֳמִ֑י וַתִּשָּׁאֵ֥ר הִ֖יא וּשְׁנֵ֥י בָנֶֽיהָ׃ 4 וַיִּשְׂא֣וּ לָהֶ֗ם
נָשִׁים֙ מֹֽאֲבִיּ֔וֹת שֵׁ֤ם הָֽאַחַת֙ עָרְפָּ֔ה וְשֵׁ֥ם הַשֵּׁנִ֖ית ר֑וּת וַיֵּ֥שְׁבוּ שָׁ֖ם כְּעֶ֥שֶׂר שָׁנִֽים׃
5 וַיָּמ֥וּתוּ גַם־שְׁנֵיהֶ֖ם מַחְל֣וֹן וְכִלְי֑וֹן וַתִּשָּׁאֵר֙ הָֽאִשָּׁ֔ה מִשְּׁנֵ֥י יְלָדֶ֖יהָ וּמֵאִישָֽׁהּ׃

RUTH 1:1

וַיְהִ֗י בִּימֵי֙ שְׁפֹ֣ט הַשֹּׁפְטִ֔ים וַיְהִ֥י רָעָ֖ב בָּאָ֑רֶץ וַיֵּ֨לֶךְ אִ֜ישׁ מִבֵּ֧ית לֶ֣חֶם יְהוּדָ֗ה לָגוּר֙
בִּשְׂדֵ֣י מוֹאָ֔ב ה֥וּא וְאִשְׁתּ֖וֹ וּשְׁנֵ֥י בָנָֽיו׃

ACCENT PHRASING

וַיְהִ֗י בִּימֵי֙ שְׁפֹ֣ט הַשֹּׁפְטִ֔ים
וַיְהִ֥י רָעָ֖ב בָּאָ֑רֶץ
וַיֵּ֨לֶךְ אִ֜ישׁ מִבֵּ֧ית לֶ֣חֶם יְהוּדָ֗ה
לָגוּר֙ בִּשְׂדֵ֣י מוֹאָ֔ב
ה֥וּא וְאִשְׁתּ֖וֹ וּשְׁנֵ֥י בָנָֽיו׃

וַיְהִי

The book of Ruth begins with a Qal imperfect 3ms of היה + *vav*-consecutive. In this form, the *vav*-consecutive, which normally points like the definite article (◌ַו), omits the expected *dāgēš forte* in the initial י because י is a SQeNMLeVY ("Y") letter with a vocal *shewa*.[2]

When narrating past events, Hebrew prose often begins with a perfective verbal form followed by the *vav*-consecutive + imperfective. The *vav*-consecutive "flips" the tense of the imperfect, making what used to be an incomplete action verb (or simple future/imperfective) a completed action (simple past/perfective).[3] The actual function of the *vav*-consecutive is far more complex, but essentially the *vav*-consecutive on the imperfect is a past tense (perfective) meaning and becomes the standard verbal form marking Hebrew narrative. It is common to begin a narrative with

2. SQeNMLeVY is a mnemonic device to remember the letters that will potentially lose the *dāgēš forte* when pointed with a vocal *shewa*. This is a very specific morphological scenario, but one that occurs frequently enough to make a "rule" about it. SQeNMLeVY stands for the Hebrew sibilants (שׂ, שׁ, צ, ס), ק, נ, מ, ל, ו, י. Any of these letters with a vocal *shewa* and a *dāgēš forte* may lose the *dāgēš* (GKC §20m).

3. This form is sometimes referred to as a *wayyiqtol* and is assigned a "tense" and "aspect" that is unique to the verbal form rather than one that describes any sort of "flipping" of an original tense/aspect. In this system, the verbal conjugations are usually listed as *qatal*, *yiqtol*, *weqatal*, and *wayyiqtol*. See RJW §178 for discussion and footnotes about the complexity of labeling the Hebrew verbal system.

וַיְהִי and therefore set the story in past tense (e.g., Josh 1:1; Judg 1:1; 1 Sam 1:1). Something similar to "Once upon a time" might be an appropriate nuance if we omit the connotations of this biblical story being a fairy tale.

בִּימֵי֙ שְׁפֹ֣ט הַשֹּׁפְטִ֔ים

בִּימֵי֙ introduces a temporal clause to identify the exact "time" of the narrative. The use of a "time" noun like יְמֵי makes the temporal notion explicit, but also, the ב preposition with the infinitive construct (שְׁפֹ֣ט) is a common way Hebrew expresses temporal clauses.[4] Literally, the prepositional phrase is "in the days of the judging of the judges," but this is smoothed out in translation as "in the days *when* the judges judged."

Morphologically, the ב points with a *ḥîreq* because of the two vocal *shewa*s at the beginning of the word once the ב is added.[5] The ב preposition points "normally" with a vocal *shewa* at the beginning of a word, but Hebrew will not allow two consecutive vocal *shewa*s. In this case, the first *shewa* becomes a *ḥîreq* and then phonetically joins with the *yôd*, leaving the historic long vowel, *ḥîreq-yôd*.

בְּ + יְמֵי־ = בִּיְמֵי־ ⟵ בִּימֵי־

The infinitive construct of שְׁפֹ֣ט can be tricky to parse because it is morphologically identical to the Qal imperative 2ms. The infinitive (שְׁפֹט) is in a construct package with the participle הַשֹּׁפְטִ֔ים communicating an implied ל of possession; "the judging *belonging to* the judges." The definite article on הַשֹּׁפְטִ֔ים makes this entire construct package definite, providing the translation "in *the* days of *the* judging of *the* judges." הַשֹּׁפְטִ֔ים, while a mp participle in form, functions as a noun ("the ones who judge"—i.e., "the judges").[6]

---

4. RJW §504; cf. §241; *GBHS* §4.1.5(b); §5.2.4. The most common way to express a temporal clause is with a ב preposition directly attached to the infinitive construct. Here, the preposition and infinitive are separated by the word יְמֵי. However, the LXX translates this construction with ἐν τῷ κρίνειν, without "in the days" altogether. On the other hand, the Syriac omits the infinitive construct, "in the days of the judges."

5. "Pointing" refers to the addition or adjustments of the vowels and accents associated with a particular word.

6. RJW §217.

וַיְהִ֥י רָעָ֖ב בָּאָ֑רֶץ

וַיְהִ֥י is the Qal imperfect 3ms of היה + *vav*-consecutive, progressing from the general setting, "the days of the judges," to a more specific set of events, "and there came about a famine in the land." The *vav* in this case is translated "that."[7] The wooden translation of this clause would be "a famine existed/came about (וַיְהִ֥י) in the land." היה, however, functions much like an English copulative verb ("to be"), and so a refined English translation would be "a famine was in the land." רָעָב is the grammatical subject.

With רָעָ֖ב as the grammatical subject, the sentence follows the typical verb-subject word order in Hebrew. The verb-subject package can also be identified by the conjunctive *mêrĕkā* (◌֥) on וַיְהִ֥י and the disjunctive *ṭifḥā* (◌֖) on רָעָ֖ב. The accents suggest these words are to be read together as a distinct grammatical unit.

בָּאָ֑רֶץ is a locative prepositional phrase indicating where the famine occurred. "The land" is a reference to Israel/Judah. The ב preposition points in this instance with a ◌ָ because the normal vowel pointing for the definite article will not allow a *dāgēš forte* in the initial א of אֶ֫רֶץ. The *dāgēš forte* is rejected and the *pataḥ* lengthens to *qāmeṣ* by compensation.[8] The ב supplants the ה of the definite article but retains the same vowel pointing to indicate that the definite article is still present, "in *the* land."

בְּ + הַאֶ֫רֶץ ⟵ בַּאֶ֫רֶץ ⟵ בָּאָ֫רֶץ

וַיֵּ֫לֶךְ אִ֫ישׁ

וַיֵּ֫לֶךְ is a Qal imperfect 3ms of הלך + *vav*-consecutive. הלך morphs like a I-ו "weak" verb, where the *vav* flees in the imperfect 3ms.[9] To "compensate" for the loss of the consonant, the preformative vowel lengthens from a *ḥîreq* (◌◌ִי) to a *ṣērê* (◌◌ֵי). The *vav*-consecutive also retracts the accent to

7. RJW §440.

8. *IBH*, 34, for the ב preposition; cf. *IBH*, 31, for compensatory lengthening of the definite article.

9. *IBH*, 239–41.

the preformative י, and so the thematic vowel is left in a closed and unaccented syllable, shortening to a *sĕgōl* (וַיֵּ֫לֶךְ).

The clause וַיֵּ֫לֶךְ אִישׁ continues to exhibit the typical verb-subject word order. אִישׁ is the subject of the sentence and, without the definite article, refers generally to "a man" who will be named later in the narrative.

מִבֵּית לֶחֶם יְהוּדָה

מִבֵּית לֶחֶם communicates the place from where the man originated. The מִן preposition on בֵּית assimilates the נ with a silent *shewa* into the ב, changing the *dāgēš lene* in בֵּית to a *dāgēš forte* in מִבֵּית. The *dāgēš forte* represents the assimilation and doubling of the ב.

(assimilation)

מִן + בֵּית ⟵ מִנְבֵּית ⟵ מִבְבֵית ⟵ מִבֵּית

This concept is similar to the English negation of "illegitimate" versus "inlegitimate." The negative prefix "in-" assimilates to "il-," duplicating the first consonant of the word.[10] The difference between Hebrew assimilation and English assimilation is that Hebrew will not usually allow consecutive consonants, using a *dāgēš forte* instead.

בֵּית לֶחֶם should be understood as a proper place name rather than "the house of bread." The name "Bethlehem" has two conjunctive accents, a *dargā* (◌֧) on בֵּית, joining the two words together as the proper place name, "Bethlehem," and a *mûnaḥ* (◌֣) on לֶחֶם. The strongest of the two conjunctive accents, the *mûnaḥ* (◌֣), annexes both of these words to יְהוּדָה, giving the sense "Bethlehem *of* Judah."

The larger construct package (בֵּית לֶחֶם יְהוּדָה) generates the logical relationship of an implied ב preposition ("Bethlehem *in* Judah").[11] Therefore, יְהוּדָה functions to explain further which Bethlehem the author has in mind. This man went out from Bethlehem of Judah rather than Bethlehem of Zebulun.

---

10. Cf. "i**rr**esponsible," "i**ll**egal," "i**ll**iterate," "i**rr**eversible," and many others. Cf. also partial assimilation in English with labial letters: "impossible," "impure," etc.

11. *IBHS* §12c.

לָג֖וּר בִּשְׂדֵ֣י מוֹאָ֑ב

לָגוּר is the Qal infinitive construct of גור. The Hebrew infinitive may function at times similarly to the English infinitive ("to sojourn"). In Hebrew, this translation is often portrayed by the infinitive construct (גוּר) along with the ל preposition, communicating a common infinitive translation, "*to* sojourn." In this instance, the Hebrew infinitive communicates a purpose clause, indicating why the man from Bethlehem went (הלך).[12]

The ב preposition on שְׂדֵי is morphologically similar to בִּימֵי in the opening line. The ב preposition normally points with a vocal *shewa*, but Hebrew will not allow two consecutive vocal *shewa*s. Therefore, the two *shewa*s "fight" and the first one becomes a short vowel.[13] The mp construct ending on שְׂדֵי translates as "the fields *of*," forming a construct package with מוֹאָב. The logical relationship in this package communicates the implied ב preposition, "the fields *in* Moab." The conjunctive *mûnaḥ* (◌֣) accent on בִּשְׂדֵ֣י confirms the construct package as one unit of meaning (proper annexation). Additionally, the entire construct package is definite because מוֹאָב is a proper noun ("in *the* fields of Moab"), even though בִּשְׂדֵי does not morphologically have the definite article.

ה֥וּא וְאִשְׁתּ֖וֹ וּשְׁנֵ֥י בָנָֽיו׃

This phrase provides further explanatory information about who sojourned to Moab. הוּא is the third-person singular pronoun, reminding the reader that אִישׁ is the primary character in this part of the narrative. Because of the strong disjunctive *zāqēf qāṭôn* (◌֔) on מוֹאָב in the previous clause, הוּא begins a decisively new phrase rather than a continued description of the land ("it") to which the man traveled. This is also confirmed because אֶרֶץ is a feminine word and would not match הוּא if translated "it." Hence, הוּא refers back to the man from Bethlehem. Again, this becomes clear with the next word since the land of Moab would not have a wife, but the accents also help us see syntactical phrases clearly delineated.

---

12. RJW §520

13. For a *shewa* "fight," see *IBH*, 14 n. 5.

וְאִשְׁתּוֹ may appear irregular at first because of the appearance of the ת when suffixes are added. However, the perceived irregularity is akin to suffixes on other feminine nouns in which a ת appears, replacing the ָה of the fs lexical form (אִשָּׁה). Another example would be תּוֹרָה becoming תּוֹרָתוֹ with a 3ms pronominal suffix.

This explanatory phrase further defines who went with the man from Bethlehem: "his wife and his two sons." On אִשְׁתּוֹ, the conjunctive *vav* points regularly, like the inseparable prepositions (בְּ, לְ, כְּ), with a simple vocal *shewa* (ְ). When added to words beginning with a simple vocal *shewa*, the conjunctive *vav* points with a וּ as in וּשְׁנֵי. Morphologically, the simple conjunctive *vav* joins these words ("*and* his wife *and* his two sons"), but the *vav* on וְאִשְׁתּוֹ is better understood as a *vav* of accompaniment, "*along with* his wife and his two sons."[14]

וּשְׁנֵי is the mp construct numeral, "two of." The entire package could communicate two from a larger group, "two sons from many sons." Or, more likely, it communicates two as the entire group. In this case, we translate the possessive pronoun on בָנָיו before the numeral, "*his* two sons." בָנָיו is the noun בֵּן + the third masculine *singular* (3ms) pronominal suffix on a *plural* noun, "his (singular) sons (plural)."

---

14. RJW §436.

RUTH 1:2

וְשֵׁ֣ם הָאִ֣ישׁ אֱלִימֶ֡לֶךְ וְשֵׁם֩ אִשְׁתּ֨וֹ נָעֳמִ֜י וְשֵׁ֥ם שְׁנֵֽי־בָנָ֣יו ׀ מַחְל֤וֹן וְכִלְיוֹן֙ אֶפְרָתִ֔ים
מִבֵּ֥ית לֶ֖חֶם יְהוּדָ֑ה וַיָּבֹ֥אוּ שְׂדֵי־מוֹאָ֖ב וַיִּֽהְיוּ־שָֽׁם׃

ACCENT PHRASING

וְשֵׁ֣ם הָאִ֣ישׁ אֱלִימֶ֡לֶךְ וְשֵׁם֩ אִשְׁתּ֨וֹ נָעֳמִ֜י וְשֵׁ֥ם שְׁנֵֽי־בָנָ֣יו ׀ מַחְל֤וֹן וְכִלְיוֹן֙ אֶפְרָתִ֔ים
מִבֵּ֥ית לֶ֖חֶם יְהוּדָ֑ה
וַיָּבֹ֥אוּ שְׂדֵי־מוֹאָ֖ב
וַיִּֽהְיוּ־שָֽׁם׃

וְשֵׁ֣ם הָאִ֣ישׁ אֱלִימֶ֡לֶךְ וְשֵׁם֩ אִשְׁתּ֨וֹ נָעֳמִ֜י וְשֵׁ֥ם שְׁנֵֽי־בָנָ֣יו ׀ מַחְל֤וֹן וְכִלְיוֹן֙ אֶפְרָתִ֔ים

Ruth 1:2 continues with background information for the setting of the book. In this first set of clauses, the text provides the name of the man who was previously unknown along with the names of his wife and his sons. These clauses are all verbless, each one beginning with וְשֵׁם. In a nominal clause, Hebrew often emphasizes (perhaps just slightly) the noun that begins the clause.[15] Therefore, the focus of these clauses is on the names of the characters, not any forward movement of the narrative action. In each case, וְשֵׁם precedes the generic character (הָאִ֣ישׁ ... אִשְׁתּ֨וֹ ... שְׁנֵֽי־בָנָ֣יו) followed by the specific name(s) of the character(s). Each use of שֵׁם has a conjunctive accent joining it to the following word:[16] "The name *of* the man/his wife/the two of his sons."

In verbless clauses, one must supply the copulative verb ("to be") for good English, and so in each of these clauses we get "The name of the man/his wife/the two of his sons [*was*] Elimelech/Naomi/Maḥlon and Chilion."

15. The tag "nominal clause" will be used in this guide to refer to a clause that begins with a noun and either is verbless (as here) or has the predicate (verb) following the noun. In most cases, the discussions in this guide will follow *IBHS* §38; cf. §11b–ii, considering the initial noun the "initiator" and the predicate the "announcement" even if those terms are not used directly (see the introduction for discussion of nominal clauses and how they are explained in this guide). Here, שֵׁם הָאִישׁ is the initiator, and what is "announced" about him is that his name "[was] Elimelech."

16. The conjunctive accents in order are the *mûnāḥ* (וְשֵׁ֣ם), *telîša qāṭôn* (וְשֵׁם֩), and *mêrĕkā* (וְשֵׁ֥ם).

One must be careful not to make more out of Hebrew names than is necessary, but Elimelech means "my God is king." This name is indeed fitting as the reader of Scripture encounters the book that describes a faithful family during the period of the judges from whom David, the king, would come. As Israel enters the monarchy, the goal is that the godly king will execute justice as God's vice-regent, recognizing that the Lord is king over his people. Even though Elimelech dies very early in the book of Ruth, his name foreshadows a Davidic kingship and a royal ideal in which יהוה rules supremely over his people.

אֶפְרָתִ֔ים is a gentilic noun, meaning the ִי added to the end makes the noun an adjectival national or territorial identifier.[17] In other words, "Ephrathah" (the place) becomes "an Ephrath*ite*" (adjectival identifier; nationality). In the historical and canonical context of Ruth, this designation becomes important. Likewise, the delay of its placement to the end of the clause provides suspense and significance to this family's designation as "Ephrathites." In many English translations, this final word begins a new sentence, "They were Ephrathites ..." (e.g., ESV, NET, CSB). However, the Masoretic accents suggest there is a grammatical break between אֶפְרָתִ֔ים and the following prepositional phrase. The *zāqēf qāṭôn* on אֶפְרָתִ֔ים is the stronger subordinate disjunctive accent in the *atnāḥ* segment of the verse, and its placement could technically be anywhere in the *atnāḥ* segment of the verse. That the *zāqēf qāṭôn* occurs on אֶפְרָתִ֔ים places an ever-so-slight emphasis on the word owing to the "musical" phrasing of the cantillation system.

Theologically, the emphasis on Naomi's family being Ephrathites makes sense as we enter the book of Ruth. Two other occurrences of this word demonstrate its importance here. First Samuel 17:12 says, "David was the son of an Ephrathite (בֶּן־אִישׁ אֶפְרָתִי) of Bethlehem of Judah, named Jesse." This verse ties King David to the lineage of those who are Ephrathites, as does the genealogy in Ruth (4:18–22). Additionally, prior to David's explicit identity as a son of an Ephrathite, 1 Samuel 1:1 indicates that Elkanah

---

17. GKC §86h; JM §88M(g); *IBHS* §31j. Compare the gentilic ending to the modern nationality adjectives "Israeli," "Kuwaiti," and "Saudi." Notice in the plural (אֶפְרָתִים, "Ephrathites"), the gentilic ִי is followed by the ם of ִים but without the repetition of י.

was an Ephrathite (אֶפְרָתִי) who was from the hill country of Ephraim (מֵהַר אֶפְרָיִם). The "hill country of Ephraim" is important at the beginning of the Samuel narratives because of the massive debacle at the end of the book of Judges centering on the "hill country of Ephraim" (Judg 17–21).

In the Hebrew Bible, Ruth is not between Judges and Samuel, and so Samuel introduces Elkanah as a man from the "hill country of Ephraim" to draw the reader's attention to the tragedies at the end of Judges. The question stands as to who will get Israel out of the mess of every man doing what is right in his own eyes (Judg 21:25). The human answer eventually comes with David, the son of an Ephrathite, but it begins with Elkanah, an Ephrathite, who fathered Samuel, the one who anointed David. Without making an argument for which order of the Old Testament books is best, placing Ruth between Judges and Samuel makes it clear that David is in the lineage of the Ephrathites and therefore will be a hopeful correction to the conundrum in Judges even before the Samuel narrative picks up this same word. The biblical-theological trajectory of the Ephrathites provides a reason beyond just the *zāqēf qāṭôn* for seeing some emphasis on אֶפְרָתִים in Ruth 1:2. The fact that the word is delayed to the end of this description of characters in the narrative also emphasizes the importance of these people being Ephrathites. "The name of the man was Elimelech, and the name of his wife was Naomi, and the name[s] of the two of his sons were Mahlon and Chilion—*Ephrathites!*"

מִבֵּית לֶחֶם יְהוּדָה

This prepositional phrase indicates location, telling where this family lived. Notice that within this prepositional phrase לֶחֶם has a strong disjunctive accent (*ṭifḥā* [◌֖]). We should not, however, understand this disjunctive accent to disrupt the construct package of the prepositional phrase, "from Bethlehem *of* Judah." According to patterns of accents, *ṭifḥā* will usually occur on either the first or the second word before the *atnāḥ* (◌֑) or *sillûq* (◌ֽ). In this particular case, the *ṭifḥā* cannot occur between בֵּית and לֶחֶם since that is the proper place name ("Bethlehem"). As in the previous verse, this prepositional phrase communicates a locative relationship between בֵּית לֶחֶם and יְהוּדָה with an implied ב preposition, "from Bethlehem *in* Judah."

וַיָּבֹ֥אוּ שְׂדֵי־מוֹאָ֖ב וַיִּֽהְיוּ־שָֽׁם׃

וַיָּבֹאוּ is a Qal imperfect 3mp of בוא + *vav*-consecutive. The narrative now moves the action forward with the *vav*-consecutive of logical succession, telling the reader what the characters did as a result of leaving Bethlehem: "*and so* they entered ... and then they settled."[18] שְׂדֵי־מוֹאָב is clearly a construct package with the *maqqēf* (־) and only one accent mark (*ṭifḥā* [שְׂדֵי־מוֹאָ֖ב]). The construct package communicates a logical relationship with an implied ב preposition, "the fields *in* Moab."

וַיִּֽהְיוּ is the Qal imperfect 3mp of היה + *vav*-consecutive. וַיִּֽהְיוּ is often translated "they settled" (NET, CSB) or "they remained" (ESV, NASB, NRSV). שָׁם is the locative adverb, and so וַיִּֽהְיוּ־שָֽׁם connotes the notion of settling or remaining. שָׁם reiterates *where* they settled—namely, in "the fields of Moab."[19]

18. For *vav* of logical succession, see *IBHS* §6p.

19. *IBHS* §13v–w.

וַיָּ֤מׇת אֱלִימֶ֙לֶךְ֙ אִ֣ישׁ נׇעֳמִ֔י וַתִּשָּׁאֵ֥ר הִ֖יא וּשְׁנֵ֥י בָנֶֽיהָ׃

ACCENT PHRASING

וַיָּ֤מׇת אֱלִימֶ֙לֶךְ֙ אִ֣ישׁ נׇעֳמִ֔י
וַתִּשָּׁאֵ֥ר הִ֖יא וּשְׁנֵ֥י בָנֶֽיהָ׃

וַיָּ֤מׇת אֱלִימֶ֙לֶךְ֙

In 1:3, the narrative continues with the Qal imperfect 3ms of מות + *vav*-con-
secutive of temporal succession, "*and then* Elimelech died." Morphologically,
מות is a hollow verb and we typically expect a *šûreq* in the second root letter
position. However, with hollow verbs, the *vav*-consecutive retracts the
accent to the preformative of the imperfect, leaving the final syllable with
the o/u vowel class short vowel, *qāmeṣ-ḥāṭûf*.

אֱלִימֶ֙לֶךְ֙ is the grammatical subject, and the accent pattern (*mêrĕkā-ṭifḥā*
[֥...֖]) sets off the verb-subject portion of the clause from the rest of the
sentence. The *vav* of temporal succession carries the action of the narrative forward without specifically indicating the duration of time between
verses 2 and 3.

אִ֣ישׁ נׇעֳמִ֔י

אִ֣ישׁ נׇעֳמִ֔י is a construct package functioning appositionally to further
describe אֱלִימֶ֙לֶךְ֙. Apposition can be explicative or substitution. This example is explicative, providing explanatory information about Elimelech, not
renaming him fundamentally.[20]

As a construct package, אִ֣ישׁ נׇעֳמִ֔י communicates the logical relationship of an implied ל of possession, "the man *belonging to* Naomi," or, "the
husband of Naomi." It may seem odd for the narrator to describe Naomi
in this way, but since Naomi is now the main character in the story, the

---

20. *IBHS* §26; JM §131.

description is set in terms of her place of primacy rather than Elimelech. The focus of the narrative now shifts to Naomi, and even this appositional modifier suggests as much.[21]

וַתִּשָּׁאֵר הִיא וּשְׁנֵי בָנֶיהָ׃

The next phrase provides the logical outcome of Elimelech's death, marked by the *vav* of logical succession on וַתִּשָּׁאֵר, "*and so* Naomi was left along with her two sons." וַתִּשָּׁאֵר is a Niphal imperfect 3fs + *vav*-consecutive of שׁאר. As a Niphal, the translation is passive, "and she *was* left." The verb is singular, and Naomi is the subject marked explicitly with the pronoun הִיא.

הִיא is also a resumptive pronoun that allows the narrator to provide multiple subjects in light of the singular verb וַתִּשָּׁאֵר.[22] The clause could end with the verb, "and she was left," and would still make sense in the context. However, the narrator wants to communicate that Naomi was left "along with her two sons," and so the resumptive pronoun (הִיא) and compound subject supply the larger context, "and she was left, she (Naomi) and the two of her sons." The *vav* on וּשְׁנֵי בָנֶיהָ is a *vav* of accompaniment, "she *along with* her two sons."

21. Kristin Moen Saxegaard, *Character Complexity in the Book of Ruth* (Tübingen: Mohr Siebeck, 2010), 77.

22. John R. Wilch, *Ruth: A Concordia Hebrew Reader* (Saint Louis: Concordia, 2010), 10; JM §146c.2–3.

RUTH 1:4

וַיִּשְׂא֤וּ לָהֶם֙ נָשִׁ֣ים מֹֽאֲבִיּ֔וֹת שֵׁ֤ם הָֽאַחַת֙ עָרְפָּ֔ה וְשֵׁ֥ם הַשֵּׁנִ֖ית ר֑וּת וַיֵּ֥שְׁבוּ שָׁ֖ם כְּעֶ֥שֶׂר שָׁנִֽים׃

ACCENT PHRASING

וַיִּשְׂא֤וּ לָהֶם֙ נָשִׁ֣ים מֹֽאֲבִיּ֔וֹת
שֵׁ֤ם הָֽאַחַת֙ עָרְפָּ֔ה
וְשֵׁ֥ם הַשֵּׁנִ֖ית ר֑וּת
וַיֵּ֥שְׁבוּ שָׁ֖ם כְּעֶ֥שֶׂר שָׁנִֽים׃

וַיִּשְׂא֤וּ לָהֶם֙ נָשִׁ֣ים מֹֽאֲבִיּ֔וֹת

וַיִּשְׂא֤וּ is the Qal imperfect 3mp of נשׂא + *vav*-consecutive. The *vav* indicates temporal succession as the next verb in the narrative action. The verb נשׂא is I-נ, and because the *nun* is a weak letter, we would expect a *dāgēš forte* in the שׂ (וַיִּשְׂאוּ ⟵ וַיִּנְשְׂאוּ). However, with SQeNMLeVY letters,[23] the consonant will often omit a *dāgēš forte* when pointed with a vocal *shewa*. וַיִּשְׂא֤וּ displays a שׂ (sibilant), and in fact the *dāgēš forte* is missing (וַיִּשְׂא֤וּ). Morphologically, one should still understand the *dāgēš forte* to exist since there is no lengthening of the *ḥîreq* preformative vowel to a *ṣērê*. The preformative syllable is still closed and unaccented (וַיִּשְׂא֤וּ), requiring a short vowel. Some may be tempted to read the *shewa* as a silent *shewa* since it is preceded by a short vowel. However, in verbal morphology, the וּ (vocalic ending) reduces the thematic vowel to a vocal *shewa* (וַיִּשְׂא֤וּ). This phenomenon of verbal vowel reduction, along with the SQeNMLeVY rule, reinforces the pronunciation of the verb (*vayyiśĕʾû*).

The implied subjects of the 3mp verb (וַיִּשְׂא֤וּ) are Naomi's sons, and so they are now the focus even without being explicitly mentioned. לָהֶם֙ is a reflexive ל of advantage, "they lifted up *for themselves*" (i.e., for their own advantage). נָשִׁ֣ים is the direct object, and since it is indefinite, it does not

23. See footnote 2.

receive the definite direct object marker (אֶת־). To "lift up" a wife is idiomatic for "taking" a wife or "getting married."[24]

מֹאֲבִיּוֹת is a gentilic adjective modifying נָשִׁים. Hebrew often views adjectives as appositional descriptive nouns.[25] These are translated in English grammar as an attributive adjective ("Moabite women"), but the literal translation is more likely: "They took wives, Moabite ones." Notice that נָשִׁים and מֹאֲבִיּוֹת agree in gender, number, and (in)definiteness. This grammatical agreement is the same for both appositional constructions and attributive adjectives. While translating this construction as an English attributive adjective ("Moabite wives") shows the most sensitivity to the target language, the construction is technically "wives, Moabite ones," reading מֹאֲבִיּוֹת as a gentilic appositional modifier.

שֵׁם הָאַחַת עָרְפָּה וְשֵׁם הַשֵּׁנִית רוּת

שֵׁם begins the second major clause in verse 4 and is an asyndetic clause. Asyndeton is simply a coordinating clause without the conjunction "and" (ו). הָאַחַת and הַשֵּׁנִית are the feminine ordinal numbers for "first" and "second," respectively. In each clause, שֵׁם and the ordinal numeral are in construct phrases, "the name *of* the first"/"the name *of* the second." As is common with construct packages, if the ending noun is definite, then the entire package is definite. The definite article on both הָאַחַת and הַשֵּׁנִית makes the constructs "*the* name of the first" and "*the* name of the second" even though שֵׁם does not have the definite article.

Because these are verbless clauses, one must supply the English copulative verb, "The name of the first [*was*] Orpah and the name of the second [*was*] Ruth." Even though רוּת is mentioned second, her name takes the heaviest disjunctive accent of the verse, the *atnāḥ* (◌֑). We should again be careful not to give too much significance to the accent system for interpretive arguments, but the Masoretes often put the "meaning" of the verse in the *atnāḥ* segment and so the emphasis here *may* in fact be on the introduction of Ruth into the narrative.[26]

---

24. BDB, 671 §3.d; *HALOT*, 726 §17; *DCH* 5:767 §9.
25. See *IBHS* §23a–e for discussion on adjectives as appositional descriptive nouns.
26. *IBHS*, "Hebrew Accents," §9.

וַיֵּ֥שְׁבוּ שָׁ֖ם כְּעֶ֥שֶׂר שָׁנִֽים׃

The *vav*-consecutive continues the action of the narrative with וַיֵּ֥שְׁבוּ, a Qal imperfect 3mp of ישב. The *vav* indicates temporal succession in the narrative but could also imply the logical conclusion of settling down and taking wives in Moab. "And then (or 'And so') they dwelled there, about ten years." "They," the implied subject, refers now to all the characters in the story, not just Naomi's sons.

Morphologically, ישב is a I-ו verb (ושב). In the imperfective conjugation, the original *vav* drops out of the final form and the preformative vowel lengthens by compensation to a *ṣērê* (וַיֵּ֥שְׁבוּ). This means that the י that is still present in the final verbal form is the י of the imperfective 3mp preformative. The original ו of the root (ושב) is gone. The thematic vowel for a Qal imperfect of ישב would have been a *ṣērê*, but because of the vocalic ending (וּ), the thematic vowel reduces to a vocal *shewa* (וַיֵּ֥שְׁבוּ).

שָׁ֖ם looks back to Moab as a retrospective or resumptive pronoun. "And so they dwelled *there* (referring to Moab)."

The כ preposition, when used with a numeral, often means "about, approximately."[27] This produces the notion that they dwelled in Moab "about" ten years. ישב indicates that the stay in Moab was more than just a sojourn as stated in verse 1 (וַיֵּ֨לֶךְ אִ֜ישׁ מִבֵּ֧ית לֶ֣חֶם יְהוּדָ֗ה לָגוּר֙ בִּשְׂדֵ֣י מוֹאָ֔ב). Perhaps the famine lasted longer than expected and it required them to stay in Moab. Or maybe the unforeseen death of family members caused Naomi to stay longer. Regardless of the reason, the use of ישב, coupled with היה in 1:2b and 1:7, suggests that the family's stay in Moab was more than just a sojourn.

27. BDB, 453; *HALOT*, 454; JM §133g.

RUTH 1:5

וַיָּמ֥וּתוּ גַם־שְׁנֵיהֶ֖ם מַחְל֣וֹן וְכִלְי֑וֹן וַתִּשָּׁאֵר֙ הָֽאִשָּׁ֔ה מִשְּׁנֵ֥י יְלָדֶ֖יהָ וּמֵאִישָֽׁהּ׃

ACCENT PHRASING

וַיָּמ֥וּתוּ גַם־שְׁנֵיהֶ֖ם מַחְל֣וֹן וְכִלְי֑וֹן
וַתִּשָּׁאֵר֙ הָֽאִשָּׁ֔ה מִשְּׁנֵ֥י יְלָדֶ֖יהָ וּמֵאִישָֽׁהּ׃

וַיָּמ֥וּתוּ גַם־שְׁנֵיהֶ֖ם מַחְל֣וֹן וְכִלְי֑וֹן

In 1:5, the narrative presents the unexpected death of Naomi's sons. וַיָּמ֥וּתוּ is a Qal imperfect 3mp + *vav*-consecutive of the root מות. The *vav*-consecutive here resumes the narrative in temporal succession. "And *then* ... the two of them died." The subject of the verb is שְׁנֵיהֶ֖ם with גַם־ as the emphatic particle that highlights the shocking nature of the son's deaths.[28] The narrative sequence continues temporally with the *vav*-consecutive (וַיָּמ֥וּתוּ), but גַם־ adds emphasis to the subject, describing that now *even* Naomi's sons have died. With גַם־ following the verb, the narrator seems to want the reader to raise his or her eyebrows in shock that now Naomi has lost both of her sons too. "And then they died ... *even the two of them*."

The names of the sons function together as explicative appositional modifiers[29] since they are the primary nouns that further *explain* שְׁנֵיהֶ֖ם. If one were to ask, "Who are the two of them?" the answer would be מַחְל֣וֹן וְכִלְי֑וֹן.

וַתִּשָּׁאֵר֙ הָֽאִשָּׁ֔ה מִשְּׁנֵ֥י יְלָדֶ֖יהָ וּמֵאִישָֽׁהּ׃

וַתִּשָּׁאֵר֙ is reminiscent of verse 3, a Niphal imperfect 3fs of שאר + *vav*-consecutive of שאר, this time a *vav* of logical succession. The two men died, "*and so* the woman was left without her two sons." The subject of וַתִּשָּׁאֵר֙ is הָֽאִשָּׁ֔ה, referring to Naomi. Even though the subject is not explicitly the proper name "Naomi," the focus remains on her.

---

28. For the emphatic use of גַּם, see RJW §379.
29. *IBHS* §26. Cf. JM §131h.

The מִן prepositions on מִשְּׁנֵי and וּמֵאִישָׁהּ function in a privative sense.[30] In other words, the woman is deprived of "the two of her boys" and "her husband." We would translate this as "And so the woman was left *without* her boys and *without* her husband." Notice the two מִן prepositions morph differently on each word because of their different constructions. The first is what would be considered normal with the assimilated נ into the שׁ (מִנְשְׁנֵי ⟵ מִשְּׁנֵי). The second has lengthened the *ḥîreq* to *ṣērê* as compensatory lengthening because the consonant in which the נ would assimilate is an א, which does not take a *dāgēš forte* (מִאִישָׁהּ ⟵ מֵאִישָׁהּ). The conjunctive *vav* (וּמֵאִישָׁהּ) points as a *šûreq* because it precedes a BuMaPh letter (labial; בּוּמָף).

Notice that the term used for Naomi's "boys" is יְלָדֶיהָ. The narrator may have used this term to reflect Naomi's motherly perspective. However, the term will be used again in Ruth to refer to another "young male child," Obed, in 4:16–17. Since these are the only two uses of יֶלֶד in Ruth, the narrator foreshadows the end of the story when the family heritage will be restored through Boaz and Ruth.[31]

30. GKC §119w; RJW §321.

31. Robert D. Holmstedt, *Ruth: A Handbook on the Hebrew Text* (Waco, TX: Baylor University Press, 2010), 65–66.

6 And then she arose along with her daughters-in-law, and she returned from the fields
of Moab for she had heard in the field of Moab that the Lord had visited his people
to give to them bread. 7 And she went out from the place where she was along with
the two of her daughters-in-law with her. And they went on the road to return to the
land of Judah. 8 And Naomi said to the two of her daughters-in-law, "Go, return, each
one to the house of her mother. May the Lord do with you lovingkindness just as you
have done with the dead and with me. 9 May the Lord give you and may you find
rest, each one in the house of her husband." Then she kissed them, and they lifted up
their voice and they wept. 10 And they said to her, "Surely with you we will return to
your people." 11 Then Naomi said, "Return, my daughters. Why would you go with
me? Are there yet sons in my womb that they would exist for you as husbands? 12
Return, my daughters, go, for I am too old to exist for a husband [as a wife]. If I said,
'There is to me hope, moreover, [if] I existed tonight for a husband [as a wife], and
moreover [if] I should bear sons, 13 would [it be] for their [benefit] that you wait until
they were grown? Would [it be] for their [benefit] that you be restrained, not to exist
for a husband [as a wife]? No, my daughters, for it is exceedingly more bitter to me
than for you that the hand of the Lord has gone out against me." And they lifted up
their voice and they wept again. 14 And Orpah kissed her mother-in-law, but Ruth
clung to her. 15 And she said, "Behold, your sister-in-law has returned to her people
and to her gods. Return after your sister-in-law."

RUTH

1:6–15

[6] וַתָּ֤קָם הִיא֙ וְכַלֹּתֶ֔יהָ וַתָּ֖שָׁב מִשְּׂדֵ֣י מוֹאָ֑ב כִּ֤י שָֽׁמְעָה֙ בִּשְׂדֵ֣ה מוֹאָ֔ב כִּֽי־פָקַ֤ד יְהוָה֙
אֶת־עַמּ֔וֹ לָתֵ֥ת לָהֶ֖ם לָֽחֶם׃ [7] וַתֵּצֵ֗א מִן־הַמָּקוֹם֙ אֲשֶׁ֣ר הָיְתָה־שָׁ֔מָּה וּשְׁתֵּ֥י כַלֹּתֶ֖יהָ
עִמָּ֑הּ וַתֵּלַ֣כְנָה בַדֶּ֔רֶךְ לָשׁ֖וּב אֶל־אֶ֥רֶץ יְהוּדָֽה׃ [8] וַתֹּ֤אמֶר נָעֳמִי֙ לִשְׁתֵּ֣י כַלֹּתֶ֔יהָ לֵ֣כְנָה
שֹּׁ֔בְנָה אִשָּׁ֖ה לְבֵ֣ית אִמָּ֑הּ יַעֲשֶׂה יְהוָ֤ה עִמָּכֶם֙ חֶ֔סֶד כַּאֲשֶׁ֧ר עֲשִׂיתֶ֛ם עִם־הַמֵּתִ֖ים
וְעִמָּדִֽי׃ [9] יִתֵּ֤ן יְהוָה֙ לָכֶ֔ם וּמְצֶ֣אןָ מְנוּחָ֔ה אִשָּׁ֖ה בֵּ֣ית אִישָׁ֑הּ וַתִּשַּׁ֣ק לָהֶ֔ן וַתִּשֶּׂ֥אנָה
קוֹלָ֖ן וַתִּבְכֶּֽינָה׃ [10] וַתֹּאמַ֖רְנָה־לָּ֑הּ כִּי־אִתָּ֥ךְ נָשׁ֖וּב לְעַמֵּֽךְ׃ [11] וַתֹּ֤אמֶר נָעֳמִי֙ שֹׁ֣בְנָה
בְנֹתַ֔י לָ֥מָּה תֵלַ֖כְנָה עִמִּ֑י הַֽעֽוֹד־לִ֤י בָנִים֙ בְּֽמֵעַ֔י וְהָי֥וּ לָכֶ֖ם לַאֲנָשִֽׁים׃ [12] שֹׁ֧בְנָה בְנֹתַ֛י
לֵ֖כְןָ כִּ֥י זָקַ֖נְתִּי מִהְי֣וֹת לְאִ֑ישׁ כִּ֤י אָמַ֙רְתִּי֙ יֶשׁ־לִ֣י תִקְוָ֔ה גַּ֣ם הָיִ֤יתִי הַלַּ֙יְלָה֙ לְאִ֔ישׁ
וְגַ֖ם יָלַ֥דְתִּי בָנִֽים׃ [13] הֲלָהֵ֣ן ׀ תְּשַׂבֵּ֗רְנָה עַ֚ד אֲשֶׁ֣ר יִגְדָּ֔לוּ הֲלָהֵן֙ תֵּֽעָגֵ֔נָה לְבִלְתִּ֖י הֱי֣וֹת
לְאִ֑ישׁ אַ֣ל בְּנֹתַ֗י כִּֽי־מַר־לִ֤י מְאֹד֙ מִכֶּ֔ם כִּֽי־יָצְאָ֥ה בִ֖י יַד־יְהוָֽה׃ [14] וַתִּשֶּׂ֣נָה קוֹלָ֔ן
וַתִּבְכֶּ֖ינָה ע֑וֹד וַתִּשַּׁ֤ק עָרְפָּה֙ לַחֲמוֹתָ֔הּ וְר֖וּת דָּ֥בְקָה בָּֽהּ׃ [15] וַתֹּ֗אמֶר הִנֵּה֙ שָׁ֣בָה
יְבִמְתֵּ֔ךְ אֶל־עַמָּ֖הּ וְאֶל־אֱלֹהֶ֑יהָ שׁ֖וּבִי אַחֲרֵ֥י יְבִמְתֵּֽךְ׃

RUTH 1:6

וַתָּ֤קָם הִיא֙ וְכַלֹּתֶ֔יהָ וַתָּ֖שָׁב מִשְּׂדֵ֣י מוֹאָ֑ב כִּ֤י שָֽׁמְעָה֙ בִּשְׂדֵ֣ה מוֹאָ֔ב כִּֽי־פָקַ֤ד יְהוָה֙ אֶת־עַמּ֔וֹ לָתֵ֥ת לָהֶ֖ם לָֽחֶם׃

ACCENT PHRASING

וַתָּ֤קָם הִיא֙ וְכַלֹּתֶ֔יהָ
וַתָּ֖שָׁב מִשְּׂדֵ֣י מוֹאָ֑ב
כִּ֤י שָֽׁמְעָה֙ בִּשְׂדֵ֣ה מוֹאָ֔ב
כִּֽי־פָקַ֤ד יְהוָה֙ אֶת־עַמּ֔וֹ
לָתֵ֥ת לָהֶ֖ם לָֽחֶם׃

וַתָּ֤קָם הִיא֙ וְכַלֹּתֶ֔יהָ

Ruth 1:6 continues the narrative sequence with the Qal imperfect 3fs of קום + *vav*-consecutive. Similar to I-ו verbs with *vav*-consecutive, hollow verbs with a *vav*-consecutive also retract the accent to the preformative, leaving the final syllable closed and unaccented. This results in a *qāmeṣ-ḥāṭûf* under the ק (וַתָּ֤קָם). The 3fs subject is הִיא֙ referring to Naomi. As before (1:3), Naomi's daughters-in-law are part of the full subject phrase, but they are included using a *vav* of accompaniment, "*along with* (וְ) her daughters-in-law." Since the grammatical subject is הִיא֙, confirmed by the singular verb (וַתָּ֤קָם), notice the accent pattern also separates וְכַלֹּתֶ֔יהָ from הִיא֙ with the disjunctive *paštā* (◌֙). Therefore, a more wooden translation would be "And she arose along with her daughters-in-law."

The morphology of וְכַלֹּתֶ֔יהָ marks it as a plural noun with a singular pronominal suffix (3fs). The root is כַּלָּה, and with a plural suffix, the final ◌ָה of the lexical form drops and the fp וֹת is added before the 3fs pronominal suffix, "her (singular) daughters-in-law (plural)." In this particular case, וֹת is written defectively without the ו vowel marker.[1]

1. For a vowel to be written defectively simply means that it is written without the consonant of the historic long vowel. For example, a ◌ִי would be written "defectively" without

וַתָּ֫שָׁב מִשְּׂדֵ֣י מוֹאָ֑ב

The narrative action continues with Naomi now returning from the fields of Moab. וַתָּ֫שָׁב is the Qal imperfect 3fs of שׁוב + *vav*-consecutive in temporal succession. The action is tied closely to the previous verb: "And she arose ... *and then* she returned." Notice again that the hollow verb with a *vav*-consecutive retracts the accent to the preformative consonant (*ṭifḥā* [֖]; וַתָּ֖שָׁב), leaving the *qāmeṣ-ḥāṭûf* in the final syllable (וַתָּ֫שָׁב). The verb is singular, keeping the emphasis on Naomi even though all the women are understood to have returned.

מִשְּׂדֵ֣י מוֹאָ֑ב is a locative prepositional phrase, indicating from where Naomi returned. The implication is that Naomi is now headed back to her hometown of Bethlehem. That Naomi was the only one of the women from Bethlehem also points to the use of the singular verb (וַתָּ֫שָׁב). Certainly, Orpah and Ruth consider going with her, but it is Naomi who is "returning." In fact, we will find shortly that Orpah does not return with Naomi and Ruth, even though here the narrative assumes that all the women have risen and are returning. In מִשְּׂדֵ֣י, the מִן preposition is attached directly to the mp construct of שָׂדֶה. The logical relationship of this construct package (מִשְּׂדֵ֣י מוֹאָ֑ב) carries an implied בּ preposition, "the fields *in* Moab."

כִּ֤י שָֽׁמְעָה֙ בִּשְׂדֵ֣ה מוֹאָ֔ב

The כִּי clause provides the ground or reason for the previous statement. Why did Naomi arise and return from the fields of Moab? "*Because/for* she heard [some news while] in the field of Moab." שָֽׁמְעָה is a Qal perfect 3fs of שׁמע and is translated as a simple past, "she heard." Since this is the report of an event that happened in the past, we could get the English past perfect, "she had heard." The Hebrew perfective encompasses both English nuances.

בִּשְׂדֵ֣ה מוֹאָ֔ב now employs the singular construct form, "*field* of Moab." We know it is construct because of the reduction of the vowel in the first root letter (שְׂ) and also because of the conjunctive accent, *mûnaḥ* (֣). Morphologically, the בּ preposition is a secondary addition to the singular

---

the *yôd*, simply as a ִ. Or, as in this case, the וֹ is written "defectively" by appearing only with the ֹ and not the ו.

construct form שְׂדֵה.[2] Perhaps Naomi heard this news in a particular field, or this may be another way to talk about the "territory" of Moab.[3]

כִּֽי־פָקַ֤ד יְהוָה֙ אֶת־עַמּ֔וֹ לָתֵ֥ת לָהֶ֖ם לָֽחֶם׃

The second כִּי provides the content previously missing from the ground clause. What did Naomi hear while in Moab? She heard "that (כִּי) the Lord had visited his people." פָּקַד is a Qal perfect 3ms of פקד with יְהוָה֙ as the subject. The verb fundamentally means "to pay attention" but here expresses the *consequence* of God's paying attention—namely, he "visited" Israel with blessing. The Lord did not just lend his attention, but he actually did something about the situation. This conclusion is further supported by the final infinitive construct phrase (לָתֵת לָהֶם לָחֶם) telling exactly what יהוה did in his "visitation."

עַמּוֹ is the direct object, marked with the definite direct object marker (אֶת־). Remember that three things make a word definite: (1) definite article, (2) proper name (place or person), or (3) a pronominal suffix. In this case, the pronominal suffix makes עַמּוֹ definite, because we are no longer talking about just any people, but we are talking specifically and definitely about "*his* people." The definite direct object marker is used to mark direct objects that are already definite. It does not *make* a word definite.

לָתֵת is a Qal infinitive construct of נתן with a ל preposition. The morphology of נתן is very difficult, and for the infinitive construct especially, it is a form worth memorizing. However, it is also worth noting that the morphology is similar to a I-ו verb in which the initial consonant drops and the infinitive construct takes a ת at the end along with a segolate vowel pattern (תֶּ֫נֶת).[4] Since the segolate vowel pattern (◌ֶ◌ֶ◌) originally represented forms with only a single syllable, we can reconstruct the "original" segolate vowels with that single vowel, תִּנְת (compare to סִפְר ⟵ סֵ֫פֶר when

2. The בּ preposition points using the vocal *shewa*, and Hebrew will not allow two consecutive vocal *shewa*s. The first *shewa* becomes the short vowel (◌ִ), and the second one becomes effectively a silent *shewa*. However, because this is a secondary morphological change, the following ד (BeGaD KePhaT letter) does *not* get a *dāgēš lene*. See GKC §10d.

3. Daniel I. Block, *Ruth: A Discourse Analysis of the Hebrew Bible*, Zondervan Exegetical Commentary on the Old Testament (Grand Rapids: Zondervan, 2015), 68; *NIDOTTE* 3:1217–19.

4. All intermediate morphological forms are hypothetical in this reconstruction. This is more of an attempt to connect the difficult morphology of נתן to other phenomena in Hebrew rather than simply memorizing the form.

adding pronominal suffixes to an i-class segolate noun). Now with the III-נ of נתן in a silent *shewa* position (תִּנְתְּ), it also assimilates as a weak letter and the "original" *ḥîreq* lengthens in a close accented syllable (תֵּת). The final ת does not display evidence of the assimilated III-נ because Hebrew does not "double" final consonants.[5]

תֵּת ⟵ תִּנְתְּ ⟵ תֵּ֫נֶת ⟵ נְתֵן

The infinitive + ל can be a purpose clause, indicating God's purpose for visiting his people.[6] He visited his people "to give to them bread." Another option, however, is an epexegetical infinitive explaining "how" God visited his people.[7] In this case, the translation would be "The Lord visited his people *by giving* them bread." לָהֶם is the prepositional phrase indicating the recipient of the Lord's gift, and לָחֶם is the accusative object, or the thing given.

When reading through Ruth, one may quickly notice the alliteration of the ל at the end of 1:6 (לָתֵת לָהֶם לָחֶם). Even nonnative Hebrew speakers may pause as they read through the narrative and the alliteration catches their attention. Indeed, that is the point. The Lord providing bread for his people surely brings to mind his provision in other dire circumstances in their history, particularly during the wilderness journeys. God's provision, especially of bread, reminds the reader of God's covenant faithfulness to his people. In the context of Ruth, the judges period was one of flagrant individual and community decline for the people of God. And yet, just like in the wilderness generation, God provides for his people. In this section of Ruth, God provides bread for his people so that a faithful family would return to the "house of bread" (בֵּית לֶ֫חֶם), meet a worthy relative, and give birth to King David's grandfather. God's provision of bread in 1:6 leads to God's provision of a king from the "house of bread." I do not think it is coincidental, then, that the narrator of Ruth uses alliteration here to draw the reader's attention to God's faithful provision.

5. Cf. עִם and אֵת ("with") that become עִמִּי and אִתִּי, respectively, when adding suffixes. The lexical forms do not receive a *dāgēš forte* since the doubled consonant is the final consonant. However, once suffixes are added, the doubled consonant becomes explicit.

6. RJW §520.

7. RJW §195.

RUTH 1:7

וַתֵּצֵא מִן־הַמָּקוֹם אֲשֶׁר הָיְתָה־שָּׁמָּה וּשְׁתֵּי כַלֹּתֶיהָ עִמָּהּ וַתֵּלַכְנָה בַדֶּרֶךְ לָשׁוּב
אֶל־אֶרֶץ יְהוּדָה׃

ACCENT PHRASING

וַתֵּצֵא מִן־הַמָּקוֹם אֲשֶׁר הָיְתָה־שָּׁמָּה
וּשְׁתֵּי כַלֹּתֶיהָ עִמָּהּ
וַתֵּלַכְנָה בַדֶּרֶךְ
לָשׁוּב אֶל־אֶרֶץ יְהוּדָה׃

וַתֵּצֵא מִן־הַמָּקוֹם אֲשֶׁר הָיְתָה־שָּׁמָּה

וַתֵּצֵא is the Qal imperfect 3fs of יצא + *vav*-consecutive. The *vav* communicates logical succession, "*and so* she went out." Having heard that the Lord ended the famine in Israel, Naomi "set out from the place where she was." וַתֵּצֵא is a I-י verb morphologically. The initial י has dropped and the preformative vowel lengthened to *ṣērê* (וַתֵּצֵא). מִן־הַמָּקוֹם specifies from where Naomi went out, but it is generically "the place." The idea is that Naomi indeed set out from a specific place within Moab, but that place is only clarified by the relative clause, "from the place *where she was there*" (מִן־הַמָּקוֹם אֲשֶׁר הָיְתָה־שָּׁמָּה).

הָיְתָה is a Qal perfect 3fs of היה. The relative clause literally says, "which (אֲשֶׁר) she was to there." It is common in a relative clause to have an adverb (שָׁמָּה) or pronoun at the end of the clause to indicate how to translate אֲשֶׁר.[8] Since אֲשֶׁר can mean "who," "which," "that," "where," and so on, the resumptive adverb at the end of the clause informs us how to translate אֲשֶׁר. In this case, since שָׁמָּה is locative, אֲשֶׁר is best translated "where." "And so she set out from the place *where* she was."

וּשְׁתֵּי כַלֹּתֶיהָ עִמָּהּ

וּשְׁתֵּי is the feminine construct form of the numeral two with the conjunctive *vav* linking the two daughters-in-law with Naomi. The entire clause

8. GKC §138; WO §19.3b.13–15; *GBHS* §5.2.13(b).

is a nominal clause providing circumstantial information with the nuance of addition.[9] Naomi went out from the place where she was, but under the circumstance of her daughters-in-law being with her. The *vav* is not a *vav* of accompaniment as before because the prepositional phrase at the end of the clause makes this a verbless clause on its own terms. "Naomi went out ... *and* the two of her daughters-in-law *were* with her." In this verbless clause, the verb "were" must be supplied.

וַתֵּלַ֫כְנָה בַדֶּ֫רֶךְ

The narrative continues with the *vav* of temporal succession on וַתֵּלַ֫כְנָה, the Qal imperfect 3fp of הלך. הלך morphs in verbal conjugations as if it were a I-ו. In the imperfect forms, the initial ה flees and the preformative vowel lengthens to *ṣērê* (וַתֵּלַ֫כְנָה). As a 3fp, the verbal action now focuses on all the female characters in view: "And then they (the group of women) went ..."

בַדֶּ֫רֶךְ specifies the means of travel. The ב preposition is often called an instrumental ב, indicating means.[10] They went "*by means of* the way." Notice that the ב preposition points like the definite article (בַּ◌) since it has supplanted the article. The translation "by means of *the* way" is indeed correct, and the definiteness of the prepositional phrase is marked morphologically.

לָשׁ֖וּב אֶל־אֶ֥רֶץ יְהוּדָֽה׃

לָשׁ֖וּב is a Qal infinitive construct of שׁוב + a ל preposition. This infinitive introduces a purpose clause, "They went *for the purpose* of returning." We saw the epexegetical use of the infinitive in verse 6, "they went *by returning*." Here, however, the express purpose of their walking (וַתֵּלַ֫כְנָה) was "to return." They would not have begun walking if the goal was not "to return."

אֶל־אֶ֥רֶץ יְהוּדָֽה is a locative prepositional phrase and indicates where they were returning. Notice that the entire three-word package forms

---

9. Holmstedt, *Ruth*, 70; Wilch, *Ruth*, 20; cf. WO §11.2.14b.
10. JM §132c; WO §11.2.5d; *BHRG* §39.6.3(i).

one construct chain. אֶל is conjoined to אֶ֫רֶץ via the *maqqēf* (־), and the conjunctive *mêrĕkā* on אֶ֥רֶץ (֥) identifies a construct form of the segolate noun (אֶ֫רֶץ). The final noun in this construct package is יְהוּדָֽה, a proper place name. Therefore, the entire construct chain is definite, "to *the* land of Judah," even though אֶ֥רֶץ does not morphologically have the definite article.

RUTH 1:8

וַתֹּ֣אמֶר נָעֳמִי֮ לִשְׁתֵּ֣י כַלֹּתֶ֒יהָ֒ לֵ֣כְנָה שֹּׁ֔בְנָה אִשָּׁ֖ה לְבֵ֣ית אִמָּ֑הּ יַעֲשֶׂה יְהוָ֤ה עִמָּכֶם֙ חֶ֔סֶד כַּאֲשֶׁ֧ר עֲשִׂיתֶ֛ם עִם־הַמֵּתִ֖ים וְעִמָּדִֽי׃

ACCENT PHRASING

וַתֹּ֣אמֶר נָעֳמִי֮ לִשְׁתֵּ֣י כַלֹּתֶ֒יהָ֒
לֵ֣כְנָה שֹּׁ֔בְנָה אִשָּׁ֖ה לְבֵ֣ית אִמָּ֑הּ
יַעֲשֶׂה יְהוָ֤ה עִמָּכֶם֙ חֶ֔סֶד
כַּאֲשֶׁ֧ר עֲשִׂיתֶ֛ם עִם־הַמֵּתִ֖ים וְעִמָּדִֽי׃

וַתֹּ֣אמֶר נָעֳמִי֮ לִשְׁתֵּ֣י כַלֹּתֶ֒יהָ֒

Ruth 1:8 begins the direct discourse between Naomi and the two of her daughters-in-law. The subject (נָעֳמִי֮) follows the verb and identifies Naomi as the focus. וַתֹּ֣אמֶר is the Qal imperfect 3fs of אמר + *vav*-consecutive. Remember that several I-א verbs display evidence of the "Canaanite shift," taking a *ḥōlem* in the preformative of the imperfect.[11] The *vav* may be contrastive since all the women in the previous verse were returning, and yet now Naomi instructs them otherwise, "*But* Naomi said ..."[12] The prepositional phrase לִשְׁתֵּ֣י כַלֹּתֶ֒יהָ֒ specifies to whom Naomi was talking, "the two of her daughters-in-law."

לֵ֣כְנָה שֹּׁ֔בְנָה אִשָּׁ֖ה לְבֵ֣ית אִמָּ֑הּ

The next two verbs begin Naomi's direct speech with imperatives, which communicate the strong emotion of Naomi's command. לֵ֣כְנָה is a Qal imperative 2fp of הלך, and שֹּׁ֔בְנָה is a Qal imperative 2fp of שׁוב. Remember that הלך morphs like a I-ו verb, and in the imperative, the initial ה drops. As a 2fp imperative, נָה- is suffixed to both verbs as the distinguishing mark of the imperative 2fp. The fact that these imperatives are followed by a blessing suggests a loving exhortation rather than a bitter command.

11. GKC §68.

12. RJW §432.

Notice the *dāgēš* in the שׁ of שֹּׁבְנָה. שׁ is not a BeGaD KePhaT letter, and therefore this is not a *dāgēš lene*. Additionally, since שׁ begins the word, this also cannot be a *dāgēš forte.* The *dāgēš* in the שׁ is a *dāgēš conjunctivum* (aka דְּחִיק [*dĕḥîq*]), and it functions to combine these two commands closely together grammatically.[13] The *dāgēš* is unnecessary since לֵ֣כְנָה has the conjunctive *mûnaḥ* (֣) conjoining the two words together syntactically. However, the *dāgēš conjunctivum* is added here to emphasize how adamantly Naomi is commanding Orpah and Ruth to leave her.

אִשָּׁה functions as a distributive, "each one."[14] The *zāqēf qāṭôn* (֔) on שֹּׁבְנָה keeps us from reading אִשָּׁה with the imperatives directly. Therefore, אִשָּׁה carries vocative function identifying and addressing each of the women individually and emphatically. Naomi wants *both* women to return to the house of their mothers, *each one* individually.

לְבֵ֣ית אִמָּהּ specifies the place to which Naomi commands her daughters to go. The construct package (בֵּית אִמָּהּ) communicates a genitive relationship with an implied ל of possession, "to the house *belonging to* her mother." The genitive relationship can be expressed by an English possessive, "Go, return, each one [of you] to *her mother's* house."

יַֽעֲשֶׂה יְהוָ֤ה עִמָּכֶם֙ חֶ֔סֶד יַעַשׂ ק

One will notice what may seem to be an odd vowel pointing on יַעֲשׂה in the text of *BHS*[15]. The consonantal text of the MT preserves the final ה (יעשה), but the vowels do not seem to match an identifiable verbal form (יַעֲשׂה). To clarify this odd form, the margin of *BHS* provides the Masoretic notation for the *qere*. The *qere* is what was "to be read." In order to preserve the consonantal text (יעשה) and also account for the marginal reading (יַעַשׂ), *BHS* writes the vowels that should be associated with the marginal

13. GKC §20.c.2(a).

14. RJW §131; JM §142p, 147d; WO §15.6a–b.

15. The Hebrew text throughout this guide is from the *Lexham Hebrew Bible* (LHB). In instances of a *ketiv-qere* or other text-critical and marginal notations that are important, the marginal notes and citations derive from *Biblia Hebraica Stuttgartensia* (*BHS*) or *Biblia Hebraica Quinta* (*BHQ*). Some marginal notes reproduced in this guide have been adapted, such as by adding vowel pointing to the *qere*.

consonants (◌ַ◌ֶ◌) under the original consonants (יַעֲשֶׂה). Scribes rarely argued for change to the consonantal text, but they added aids for reading in the margin. This is referred to as a *ketiv/qere*, what was "written" (*ketiv*) versus what was "read" (*qere*).[16]

In the case of III-ה verbs, the forms of the imperfect 3ms and the jussive are distinct, and so the *qere* indicates that this imperfective form in the consonantal text should be read as a jussive, "*May* the Lord do," rather than "The Lord will do." As it is written, the consonants would produce the Qal imperfect 3ms of עשׂה. The marginal *qere* consonants, combined with the vowel points of the main text of *BHS*, indicate the verb is the Qal jussive 3ms of עשׂה. In the III-ה verbs, the jussive form drops the ה of the root and follows a segolate vowel pattern (יַעַשׂ), hence the marginal consonants יעשׂ to suggest reading this as a jussive.[17]

Prepositions in any language are difficult to navigate. For עִמָּכֶם, it is important to remember that Hebrew does not have an עִם that means "along with," an עִם that indicates location, and so on. Hebrew simply has עִם. Depending on the context, עִם may communicate different linguistic nuances. In this case, it seems odd in English to say, "May the Lord do *with you*." And yet this is the proper way to express the concept in Hebrew. For English accommodation, we would translate, "May the Lord do *for you*," recognizing that Naomi is blessing her daughters-in-law and desiring for God to do something for their advantage.[18]

חֶסֶד specifies what Naomi wishes the Lord would do for her daughters-in-law. This word connotes loyalty and devotion, often used of the Lord's lovingkindness and covenantal faithfulness to his people.[19] With the full clause in view now, we could smooth out the English even further to "May the Lord show (do) lovingkindness to (for) you."

---

16. For a thorough discussion of *ketiv/qere*, see Emanuel Tov, *Textual Criticism of the Hebrew Bible*, 3rd ed. (Minneapolis: Fortress, 2012), 54–59, with associated bibliography and footnotes.

17. Even though this explanation affirms the jussive translation here, a few verses later, in 1:17, Ruth pronounces a self-imposed curse in which the text preserved an imperfective form of עשׂה (יַעֲשֶׂה), but without the marginal *qere*.

18. RJW §331. Cf. *BHRG* §39.20.2; *GBHS* §4.1.17(b).

19. *NIDOTTE* 2:211–18.

כַּאֲשֶׁר עֲשִׂיתֶם עִם־הַמֵּתִים וְעִמָּדִי׃

כַּאֲשֶׁר conjoins the two clauses following the *atnāḥ*, providing a positive comparison to the lovingkindness Naomi wishes for her daughters. She asks the Lord to show her daughters-in-law the same חֶסֶד that they have shown her.

עֲשִׂיתֶם is a Qal perfect 2mp of עשׂה. The perfective verb connotes that the חֶסֶד shown by Ruth and Orpah has already happened as they have continued with Naomi in spite of the death of her husband and sons. Therefore, given the context, the perfective conjugation is best translated as an English perfect, "have done." One may notice that the verbal morphology is a 2mp, and yet the clear subjects of the action are Naomi's daughters-in-law. Robert Chisholm comments that this is the preservation of an archaic dual common ending referring to "the two of them."[20] Robert Holmstedt proposes that the narrator may be preserving a foreign or archaic feel to the narrative.[21] This explanation is especially appealing if we consider the goal of the narrator to preserve and present the characters in the narrative as real people who originated from (Orpah and Ruth) or lived in (Naomi) a foreign country. The narrator was not afraid to include odd Hebrew forms that were very much at home on the lips of a character who had spent many years in Moab.

The first group to whom Ruth and Orpah demonstrated חֶסֶד is הַמֵּתִים. הַמֵּתִים is a Qal participle mp of מות with the definite article (הַ◌). The participle is substantive, functioning as a noun, "the dead ones." מות is a hollow verb that in the participle loses its middle root letter, replacing it with *ṣērê* as the thematic vowel under the מ (הַמֵּתִים). וְעִמָּדִי is an expanded form of the

20. Robert Chisholm, *A Workbook for Intermediate Hebrew: Grammar, Exegesis, and Commentary on Jonah and Ruth* (Grand Rapids: Kregel, 2006), 113; see also Frederic W. Bush, *Ruth, Esther*, Word Biblical Commentary 9 (Dallas: Word, 1996), 75–76.

21. Holmstedt, *Ruth*, 73; see also pages 47–48 for his discussion on the use of language to create narratively engaging characters. This happens in Ruth in 1:8, 9, 11, 13, 19, 22; 4:11. Gesenius says, "*Masculine* suffixes (especially in the plural) are not infrequently used to refer to *feminine* substantives" (GKC §135o). He then includes in §135o other instances in the Hebrew Bible where this phenomenon occurs.

preposition עִם and is sometimes used when עִם takes pronominal suffixes.[22] Here עִם takes the 1cs pronominal suffix, "with me."

If we translate these two עִם prepositions the same way that we did in the previous clause, it represents advantage of the recipient. Previously, Naomi blessed Ruth and Orpah with a future expectation that the Lord would "do lovingkindness *for* (עִם) them." In this final clause of verse 8, the same meaning applies but is rooted in the past חֶ֫סֶד that Ruth and Orpah "have shown/done (עֲשִׂיתֶם)." Therefore, we translate, "just as you have done *for* the dead ones and *for* me."

22. According to Gesenius, this longer form seems to be limited to עִם with the 1cs pronominal suffix (GKC §103c).

RUTH 1:9

יִתֵּ֤ן יְהוָה֙ לָכֶ֔ם וּמְצֶ֣אןָ מְנוּחָ֔ה אִשָּׁ֖ה בֵּ֣ית אִישָׁ֑הּ וַתִּשַּׁ֣ק לָהֶ֔ן וַתִּשֶּׂ֥אנָה קוֹלָ֖ן וַתִּבְכֶּֽינָה׃

ACCENT PHRASING

יִתֵּ֤ן יְהוָה לָכֶ֔ם
וּמְצֶ֣אןָ מְנוּחָה אִשָּׁ֖ה בֵּ֣ית אִישָׁ֑הּ
וַתִּשַּׁ֣ק לָהֶ֔ן
וַתִּשֶּׂ֥אנָה קוֹלָ֖ן
וַתִּבְכֶּֽינָה׃

יִתֵּ֤ן יְהוָה֙ לָכֶ֔ם

Ruth 1:9 continues the blessing that Naomi desires for Orpah and Ruth. יִתֵּן is a Qal imperfect 3ms of נתן in form but functions as a jussive, following the initial jussive, יַעֲשֶׂה (יַעַשׂ in the *qere* marginal note in *BHS*), from verse 8. Morphologically, remember that נ is a weak letter when pointed with a silent *shewa* (the lack of a vowel). In נתן, the initial נ would have had a silent *shewa* in the standard Qal paradigm (יִנְתֵּן) but assimilates in the imperfectives. In the hypothetical form (יִנְתֵּן), the *dāgēš* is a *dāgēš lene* (יִנְתֵּן). After the I-נ assimilates in the final form (יִתֵּן), the *dāgēš* is now a *dāgēš forte*.

יהוה is the subject, and the ל marks the indirect object. Notice the suffix on לָכֶם. It is technically a masculine ending because of the ם, but this is another example of the possible archaic or foreign dual form.[23]

וּמְצֶ֣אןָ מְנוּחָ֔ה אִשָּׁ֖ה בֵּ֣ית אִישָׁ֑הּ

וּמְצֶאןָ is a Qal imperative 2fp of מצא with an energic *vav*.[24] The final vowel is written defectively without the ה (e.g., וּמְצֶאנָה). The *vav* + imperative,

23. Holmstedt, *Ruth*, 75.

24. For the terminology "energic *vav*," see *IBHS* §6. They say that this construction occasionally communicates purpose following another volitive (§6w).

following a jussive in direct speech, may be translated "that."[25] "May the Lord give to you *that* you may find rest." In this construction, וּמְצֶ֫אןָ is translated with a modal nuance rather than a command: "that you *may* find rest." The syntactic relationship to יִתֵּן is difficult since it is uncommon for a *vav* + imperative to follow a jussive.[26]

מְנוּחָה may suggest the security of marriage and the emotional "rest" that a marriage would bring. Or perhaps, even as a locative, מְנוּחָה may imply the "rest" associated with a home—for example, finding a resting *place* at home with a new family.[27]

As in 1:8, אִשָּׁה functions distributively, meaning "each." בֵּית אִישָׁהּ is a construct phrase functioning as an adverbial accusative of place to limit וּמְצֶאןָ מְנוּחָה, particularly to the בֵּית אִישָׁהּ. Since בֵּית אִישָׁהּ is not part of a formal prepositional phrase, it must be functioning adverbially.[28] With the addition of a specific location (בֵּית אִישָׁהּ), it is likely that the מְנוּחָה Naomi hopes Orpah and Ruth can find is the "rest" associated with the house (בֵּית) of a new husband (אִישָׁהּ). As part of the larger blessing of a hypothetical future situation, the בֵּית אִישָׁהּ does not refer to returning to the household of their dead husbands, but to the prospect of finding "rest" in the security of a new home and a new marriage.

25. *IBHS* §6w. This construction may also express purpose (GKC §110i). Holmstedt proposes "anaculathon," a phenomenon common in daily speech, in which an idea is begun with one grammatical construction, interrupted, and then completed with a different construction (*Ruth*, 75). In this case, the interruption reflects the emotion of the situation in which the author preserves Naomi's difficulty developing expected grammatical constructions.

26. JM §177h makes this *vav* equivalent to an object clause or the thing that is to be given by יהוה. GKC §110i lists Ruth 1:9 as an example of a *vav* + imperative expressing a "consequence which is to be expected with certainty, and often a consequence which is intended, or in fact an intention." In either of these explanations, the translation is "May the Lord give *that* you would/may find rest." "That you may find rest" *is* the thing Naomi asks the Lord "to give" to Ruth and Orpah.

27. *NIDOTTE* 3:56–59.

28. Compare this construction to 2:8, in which the ל preposition is explicit on בֵּית.

וַתִּשַּׁ֣ק לָהֶ֔ן וַתִּשֶּׂ֥אנָה קוֹלָ֖ן וַתִּבְכֶּֽינָה׃

The verbal sequence in this *sillûq* segment[29] of the verse moves the narrative action forward quickly but not the narrative time. The verbs build on one another to provide a scene of deep affection and love in light of the request for Orpah and Ruth to leave. However, the narrative time does not move forward to another scene. These consecutive verbs complete the narrative action of the current scene. וַתִּשַּׁ֣ק is a Qal imperfect 3fs of נשק + *vav*-consecutive. Notice the *dāgēš forte* in the שׁ that represents the assimilated נ of נשק (וַתִּשַּׁק ⟵ וַתִּנְשַׁק).

The *vav* could be understood as temporal or logical succession depending on how one reads the internal context of the narrative. As temporal succession, the *vav* simply moves the action forward: "*And then* she kissed them." Logical succession would make sense if one reads Naomi's sentiment for her daughters-in-law to find rest with another husband as a less-than-optimal outcome. Naomi knows that Orpah and Ruth will be better off in the home of another husband, but that thought indeed saddens her, "*and so* she kissed them." In the immediate context, temporal succession seems more likely for this *vav*-consecutive. Naomi's kissing her daughters-in-law seems simply to be the next action in the narrative.

The ל indicating the direct object (לָהֶ֔ן) with נשק is common.[30] Notice here, the narrator uses the "proper" fp pronominal suffix (-הֶ֔ן). This may be because the narrator has once again picked up the narrative rather than presenting Naomi's direct speech where we often see the gender of suffixes interchange.

וַתִּשֶּׂ֥אנָה is another I-נ weak verb, again displaying the assimilation of the I-נ (וַתִּשֶּׂאנָה ⟵ וַתִּנְשֶׂאנָה). The root is נשׂא and it is a Qal imperfect 3fp + *vav*-consecutive. In this clause, the *vav*-consecutive is clearly providing temporal succession, "*And then* they lifted up their voice." קוֹלָ֖ן morphologically is a singular noun ("voice") with a plural pronominal suffix (3fp;

29. "*Sillûq* segment" refers to the portion of the verse demarcated by the *sillûq/sôf pāsûq* (:ֽ◌◌◌) at the end of the verse and the *atnāḥ* (֑◌), wherever it may occur in the verse. Here, the *atnāḥ* is on אִישָׁ֑הּ, and therefore the *sillûq* segment is :וַתִּשַּׁ֣ק לָהֶ֔ן וַתִּשֶּׂ֥אנָה קוֹלָ֖ן וַתִּבְכֶּֽינָה.

30. BDB, 676. *HALOT*, 730–31.

"their"), "their (plural) voice (singular)." קוֹלָן, therefore, is a collective singular. The women lifted up their individual voices as one collective voice. Without reading too much into the grammatical use of a singular noun (קול), it seems to highlight the unity and love between these women as they are determining what to do with their grim future.

The final verb in this sequence (וַתִּבְכֶּינָה) is a Qal imperfect 3fp of בכה + *vav*-consecutive. בכה is a III-ה weak verb, what some grammars explain as a III-י/ו morphologically.[31] Notice the י in the third root letter position of the conjugated form (וַתִּבְכֶּינָה). The י conveys remnants of the original (hypothetical) root בכי. For parsing purposes, one can also still recognize the ת preformative and נָה- sufformative of the imperfect 3fp. If one can recognize the verbal root (בכה/בכי), then identifying preformatives and sufformatives will lead to the correct parsing.

This sequence of verbs begins with Naomi kissing her daughters-in-law and then all three of them raising their unified voice in sadness, crying together as they face the prospect of leaving one another. The *vav* + imperfective forms keep the action in the past tense from the point of view of the narrator but also connect the action closely together to heighten the effect of the sadness of this scene.

31. E.g., *IBH*, 265–74; Karl V. Kutz and Rebekah L. Josberger, *Learning Biblical Hebrew: Reading for Comprehension; An Introductory Grammar* (Bellingham, WA: Lexham Press, 2018), 305–26.

RUTH 1:10

וַתֹּאמַ֫רְנָה־לָּ֑הּ כִּֽי־אִתָּ֥ךְ נָשׁ֖וּב לְעַמֵּֽךְ׃

ACCENT PHRASING

וַתֹּאמַ֫רְנָה־לָּ֑הּ
כִּֽי־אִתָּ֥ךְ נָשׁ֖וּב לְעַמֵּֽךְ׃

וַתֹּאמַ֫רְנָה־לָּ֑הּ

In 1:10, Naomi's daughters contest her strong command to leave. Hence, the *vav* on וַתֹּאמַ֫רְנָה is adversative, meaning "but."[32] The adversative conjunction is often determined only by context. In this case, the subject changes from Naomi to her daughters-in-law, also adding to the adversative conjunction for this context.

וַתֹּאמַ֫רְנָה is a Qal imperfect 3fp of אמר + *vav*-consecutive. Remember that אמר is one of the I-א verbs that gets a *ḥōlem* as the preformative vowel and quiesces the I-א. Even though the preformative vowels change a bit abnormally, the distinguishing ת preformative and נָה- sufformative of the imperfect 3fp are still readily noticeable for parsing purposes.

Notice the *dāgēš* in the ל of לָּהּ. As in 1:8, this *dāgēš* is another *dāgēš conjunctivum*, or *dĕḥîq* (דְּחִיק). The *dĕḥîq* can occur in the first letter of a monosyllabic word, when closely connected to the preceding word.[33] The *maqqēf* (־) clearly connects these two words, but the Masoretes wanted to stress how these two words are compressed together with the *dĕḥîq*.

32. RJW §432; §552.
33. GKC §20.c.2(a).

כִּי־אִתָּ֥ךְ נָשׁ֖וּב לְעַמֵּֽךְ׃

כִּי begins the direct speech from Orpah and Ruth and is asseverative and emphatic, translated as "Surely."[34] The prepositional phrase (אִתָּ֥ךְ) is fronted for emphasis, "Surely *with you* we will return." נָשׁ֖וּב is a Qal imperfect 1cp of שׁוּב. In light of the asseverative כִּי and the intense emotion of the context, the imperfective verb should be read as a statement of certainty, "We *will* return." The imperfective verb expresses intention, not just simple future action.

לְעַמֵּֽךְ ("to your people") is a locative prepositional phrase, indicating *where* Naomi's daughters-in-law intend to return. "Surely we will return with you, *to your people*." Notice that עַם with suffixes receives a *dāgēš forte*, suggesting an original root עמם.

34. See Chisholm, *Workbook for Intermediate Hebrew*, 115; Holmstedt, *Ruth*, 77; *IBHS* §64h; RJW §449.

RUTH 1:11

וַתֹּ֣אמֶר נָעֳמִי֙ שֹׁ֣בְנָה בְנֹתַ֔י לָ֥מָּה תֵלַ֖כְנָה עִמִּ֑י הַ֥עוֹד־לִ֤י בָנִים֙ בְּֽמֵעַ֔י וְהָי֥וּ לָכֶ֖ם לַאֲנָשִֽׁים׃

ACCENT PHRASING

וַתֹּ֣אמֶר נָעֳמִי֙ שֹׁ֣בְנָה בְנֹתַ֔י
לָ֥מָּה תֵלַ֖כְנָה עִמִּ֑י
הַ֥עוֹד־לִ֤י בָנִים֙ בְּֽמֵעַ֔י
וְהָי֥וּ לָכֶ֖ם לַאֲנָשִֽׁים׃

וַתֹּ֣אמֶר נָעֳמִי֙ שֹׁ֣בְנָה בְנֹתַ֔י

Ruth 1:11 continues the narrative action, introducing Naomi's direct speech. וַתֹּ֣אמֶר is the Qal imperfect 3fs of אמר + *vav*-consecutive in temporal succession. נָעֳמִי֙ is the explicit subject. Her direct speech (שֹׁ֣בְנָה בְנֹתַ֔י ...) is distinguished from the main narrative with the disjunctive accent *pašṭā* (◌֙) on נָעֳמִי֙.

Naomi returns again to her plea for her daughters-in-law to return (שֹׁ֣בְנָה) to their own extended families and find husbands (cf. 1:8). שֹׁ֣בְנָה is the Qal imperative 2fp of שׁוב, with בְנֹתַ֔י as the vocative, "Return, my daughters."[35] Notice in this affectionate interchange, Naomi uses the term בְנֹתַ֔י ("my daughters") rather than כַּלּוֹת ("daughters-in-law") as the narrator does in verses 6–8. We must be careful not to read too much into word variation like this, but it appears the narrator is preserving Naomi's actual speech rather than using the technical term כַּלָּה.

לָ֥מָּה תֵלַ֖כְנָה עִמִּ֑י

Naomi's plea continues with the interrogative לָ֥מָּה and introduces the reasons that Naomi charges Orpah and Ruth to abandon her. The interrogative

35. For a study of the Hebrew vocative demonstrating its complexity, see Cynthia L. Miller, "Vocative Syntax in Biblical Hebrew Prose and Poetry: A Preliminary Analysis," *Journal of Semitic Studies* 55 (2010): 347–64.

suggests the modal nuance of the verb תֵּלַכְנָה.[36] תֵּלַכְנָה is a Qal imperfect 2fp of הלך and is translated subjunctively (modal/jussive), "Why *would* you go with me?" Remember that הלך morphs like a I-ו verb and the initial ה drops. As a result, the preformative vowel lengthens to *ṣērê* (תֵּלַכְנָה), phonetic and morphological evidence that a consonant has fled in the imperfective. Even so, the distinguishing preformative and sufformative of the imperfect 2fp (תּ◌◌ְנָה) are readily noticeable for parsing purposes.

The prepositional phrase עִמִּי is a locative modifier indicating *where* Orpah and Ruth would return if in fact they went with Naomi. The *dāgēš forte* in the מ of עִמִּי may reflect evidence of an original triconsonantal root (עמם; cf. עִמָּךְ in 1:10). Something similar may be at play with the preposition אֵת with suffixes (e.g., אִתִּי) as well as with geminate verbs.

הַעוֹד־לִ֤י בָנִים֙ בְּמֵעַ֔י

הַעוֹד־לִי introduces the first in a series of reasons that Naomi gives to persuade Orpah and Ruth to leave. A good way to translate an interrogative sentence is to remove the interrogative and translate the sentence as a declarative statement. Once we remove the interrogative (הֲ◌◌◌), we are left with a verbless clause that needs an English "to be" verb. "[There are] still to me" or "I have." The interrogative ה turns that declarative sentence into an interrogative sentence, but the "to be" verb still must be supplied. Therefore, this interrogative clause translates, "Are there still to me ... ?" or "Do I still have ... ?" בָנִים is the accusative object of this verbless interrogative clause.

The prepositional phrase בְּמֵעַי specifies the "location" of the sons, although the context is clearly hypothetical. We may smooth out Naomi's question as "Are there sons still in my womb?"

וְהָי֥וּ לָכֶ֖ם לַאֲנָשִֽׁים׃

וְהָיוּ functions modally and introduces a hypothetical result clause. וְהָיוּ is the Qal perfect 3cp + *vav*-consecutive of היה. Notice that the *vav*-consecutive

36. Holmstedt, *Ruth*, 78.

on the perfect points like the conjunctive *vav*. This means that one must determine from context whether this is a simple conjunction between two verbs in a compound predicate or whether the clause communicates something else. As part of the hypothetical interrogative, the modal nuance, which is not common in the perfective conjugation, suggests the *vav* is consecutive. The *vav* + perfective often takes on the implied meaning of the preceding verb(s).[37] Since Naomi introduces a hypothetical situation with הַעֽוֹד־לִ֤י בָנִים֙ בְּמֵעַ֔י, this *vav* + perfective follows the hypothetical situation with a modal meaning, "that they *should* exist for you all." As such, וְהָי֥וּ begins a result clause. If Naomi had sons, the hypothetical result would be "*that* they *should* exist as husbands for you."

לָכֶ֖ם again displays the 3mp suffix even though two females are the object (cf. 1:8, 9). The ל is a ל of advantage. The hypothetical situation of Naomi having sons would imply that those sons would be husbands "for" (ל) Orpah and Ruth's benefit.

The final word, לַאֲנָשִֽׁים, functions adverbially to indicate the situation in which these hypothetical sons would exist if they did: "that they should exist *as* husbands." ל commonly introduces this adverbial accusative of situation following היה.[38] As cumbersome as it may seem, if you can add "in the status of" to the translation, then you likely have identified an adverbial accusative of situation: "that they should exist (וְהָי֥וּ) *in the status of* husbands (לַאֲנָשִֽׁים) for you all (לָכֶ֖ם)."

37. WO §32.1.3; JM §§115, 120.

38. *IBHS* §13z, 13ii.

RUTH 1:12

שֹׁ֤בְנָה בְנֹתַי֙ לֵ֔כְןָ כִּ֥י זָקַ֖נְתִּי מִהְי֣וֹת לְאִ֑ישׁ כִּ֤י אָמַ֙רְתִּי֙ יֶשׁ־לִ֣י תִקְוָ֔ה גַּ֣ם הָיִ֤יתִי הַלַּ֙יְלָה֙ לְאִ֔ישׁ וְגַ֖ם יָלַ֥דְתִּי בָנִֽים׃

ACCENT PHRASING

שֹׁ֤בְנָה בְנֹתַי֙ לֵ֔כְןָ
כִּ֥י זָקַ֖נְתִּי מִהְי֣וֹת לְאִ֑ישׁ
כִּ֤י אָמַ֙רְתִּי֙ יֶשׁ־לִ֣י תִקְוָ֔ה
גַּ֣ם הָיִ֤יתִי הַלַּ֙יְלָה֙ לְאִ֔ישׁ
וְגַ֖ם יָלַ֥דְתִּי בָנִֽים׃

שֹׁ֤בְנָה בְנֹתַי֙ לֵ֔כְןָ

Ruth 1:12 continues Naomi's plea that Orpah and Ruth would return to their own people, recalling verses 8 and 11. These commands mirror 1:8, but in reverse order. שֹׁ֤בְנָה is the Qal imperative 2fp of שׁוב. As in verse 11, בְנֹתַי֙ is vocative as Naomi addresses her "daughters." לֵ֔כְןָ emphasizes the command and is the Qal imperative 2fp of הלך. לֵ֔כְןָ is written defectively without the final ה but retains the proper phonetics to identify the imperative 2fp. Remember that הלך morphs like a I-ו, and so the initial ה flees in the imperative and infinitive.

כִּ֥י זָקַ֖נְתִּי מִהְי֣וֹת לְאִ֑ישׁ

כִּ֥י introduces a ground clause, with Naomi continuing to provide reasons to convince her daughters to leave her. זָקַ֖נְתִּי is a Qal perfect 1cs of the stative verb זקן. מִהְי֣וֹת is a Qal infinitive construct of היה with a comparative מִן preposition. A distinguishing mark of III-ה verbs in the infinitive construct is the וֹת- ending as we see here (מִהְי֣וֹת). The clause is literally "for I am old from existing for a man." The מִן preposition gives the main verb the superlative idea of "too."[39] When combined with the infinitive of היה,

39. Williams calls this the "absolute comparative" (RJW §318). Waltke and O'Connor use the term "comparison of capability" (WO §14.4f). The comparison generated by the מִן is that

the clause translates as "I am *too* old *to exist* for a man." The ל on לְאִישׁ is possessive, "*belonging to* a man." In other words, Naomi is too old to marry again and have a husband.

כִּי אָמַ֫רְתִּי יֶשׁ־לִ֣י תִקְוָ֔ה

כִּי, once again, introduces a ground clause, but this time with an implied conditional idea.[40] So we would translate, "For [if] I should say ..." אָמַ֫רְתִּי is a Qal perfect 1cs of אמר and translates modally as the protasis of the implied conditional, "If I *should* say ..."[41]

יֶשׁ־לִ֣י תִקְוָ֔ה introduces Naomi's embedded hypothetical direct speech as part of her exhortation for her daughters to leave. The clause translates literally as "there is to me hope" but means "I have hope." The ל preposition on לִי indicates possession, showing to whom the תִקְוָה hypothetically would belong. The logic here is that even if Naomi should say, "I have hope," that would not be a sufficient reason for Orpah and Ruth to stay with Naomi. Her situation is so dismal at this point that Naomi does not want to provide any false hope for Orpah and Ruth even if it comes out of her own mouth.

גַּ֣ם הָיִ֤יתִי הַלַּ֙יְלָה֙ לְאִ֔ישׁ

The next clause begins with the additive use of גַּם.[42] Very often, גַּם takes on an emphatic role grammatically to intensify what is being said: "*moreover,* [if] I should exist tonight for a man ..." הָיִ֤יתִי is a Qal perfect 1cs of היה, again translated modally in the implied conditional clause (cf. the previous clause). Notice the final ה of the lexical root is replaced by the "original" י in the third root letter position of the conjugated form (הָיִ֤יתִי).

הַלַּ֙יְלָה֙ is the adverbial accusative of time, providing the detail of *when* Naomi would hypothetically be a wife. Naomi intensifies the rhetoric by claiming that even if she got married that very night, she would not have

the subject has more or less ability to accomplish the thing discussed. Cf. GKC §133c.

40. Holmstedt sees this as an implied conditional (*Ruth*, 80). Fuller and Choi list כִּי as introducing a conditional and translated as "if" on its own terms (*IBHS* §77d).

41. For the modal/conditional perfect, see RJW §166; *BHRG* §19.2.1(iii); GKC §106p; WO §30.5.4; JM §167g–i.

42. RJW §378.

a reason for her daughters to stay with her. The definite article on הַלַּ֫יְלָה is demonstrative. Literally, it is "the night," but like הַיּוֹם ("today") it means "this night" or "tonight."

As in the previous כִּי clause, the ל on לְאִישׁ is possessive, communicating the idea that Naomi would *belong to* a man. This construction should not be understood pejoratively. We could state the same idea more positively, and rather than Naomi "belonging to" a man, we could say, "moreover, [if] I should have a husband tonight …"

וְגַ֖ם יָלַ֥דְתִּי בָנִֽים׃

The final clause of verse 12 begins with another additive גַּם, again escalating the intensity. יָלַ֥דְתִּי is the Qal perfect 1cs of ילד. Notice Naomi's rhetorical move from "hope" (תִּקְוָ֔ה) to marriage (הָיִ֤יתִי … לְאִ֔ישׁ) to children (יָלַ֥דְתִּי בָנִֽים). Even if Naomi would have sons in her old age, it would not warrant Orpah and Ruth staying with her. The implied conditional continues in this third modal perfect, "and moreover, [if] I *should* bear (יָלַ֥דְתִּי) sons …" בָנִֽים is the direct object, adding to the intensity of the situation because "sons" are the very thing Naomi and her daughters need. She desperately needs sons who would protect them, provide for them, and perpetuate the family line. Naomi has presented hypothetical situations that all imply negative outcomes. Even if these things were to happen, Naomi implies that Ruth's and Orpah's situations would still be desperate.

Verse 12 adds to the tension of the narrative, not only because Naomi's rhetoric seems impenetrable, but also because Naomi suggests that childbirth in old age cannot remedy her desperate situation. Indeed, Naomi's logic seems reasonable, but even Sarai found childbirth at an old age unreasonable (Gen 16:1–3). Perhaps to a small degree, Naomi is acting like Sarai, whose logic distorts God's covenantal promises of protection and provision, specifically of a son. The intensity of Naomi's tone to her daughters suggests that Naomi may have all but forgotten God's חֶ֫סֶד at this point. She appreciates her daughters' חֶ֫סֶד (1:8), but she finds it difficult to imagine God's covenant faithfulness helping her now.

RUTH 1:13

הֲלָהֵ֣ן ׀ תְּשַׂבֵּ֗רְנָה עַ֚ד אֲשֶׁ֣ר יִגְדָּ֔לוּ הֲלָהֵן֙ תֵּֽעָגֵ֔נָה לְבִלְתִּ֖י הֱי֣וֹת לְאִ֑ישׁ אַ֣ל בְּנֹתַ֗י כִּֽי־מַר־לִ֤י מְאֹד֙ מִכֶּ֔ם כִּֽי־יָצְאָ֥ה בִ֖י יַד־יְהוָֽה׃

ACCENT PHRASING

הֲלָהֵ֣ן ׀ תְּשַׂבֵּ֗רְנָה עַ֚ד אֲשֶׁ֣ר יִגְדָּ֔לוּ
הֲלָהֵן֙ תֵּֽעָגֵ֔נָה לְבִלְתִּ֖י הֱי֣וֹת לְאִ֑ישׁ
אַ֣ל בְּנֹתַ֗י כִּֽי־מַר־לִ֤י מְאֹד֙ מִכֶּ֔ם
כִּֽי־יָצְאָ֥ה בִ֖י יַד־יְהוָֽה׃

הֲלָהֵ֣ן ׀ תְּשַׂבֵּ֗רְנָה עַ֚ד אֲשֶׁ֣ר יִגְדָּ֔לוּ

There is some debate about הֲלָהֵ֣ן in verse 13. הֲלָהֵ֣ן is composed of the interrogative ה + לָהֵן. At first glance, it may seem like the interrogative (הֲ) and the Aramaic "therefore" (לָהֵן; cf. Dan 2:6, 9; 4:24).[43] In light of some possibly poor grammar throughout the book of Ruth, this explanation may seem reasonable.

Another option is that לָהֵן is a ל preposition with a 3fp pronominal suffix (הֵן-, "to you") understanding Naomi to be asking whether her daughters-in-law (3fp) are willing to wait until her hypothetical sons are grown. This explanation would make more sense if the suffix were a 2fp suffix, "Is there to *you all* that you should wait … ?"

The third explanation is that לָהֵן is a Moabite masculine dual referring to Naomi's hypothetical sons.[44] First, the 3mp verb at the end of the clause (יִגְדָּ֔לוּ) refers to these hypothetical sons, and so the context, both in the previous verse and in this clause, refers to these sons. Second, Naomi has spent nearly ten years in Moab, and we have seen remnants of Naomi's bilingual speech before (cf. 1:8–9). Third, on the basis of this interpretation, the ל would indicate advantage: "Is it to their advantage (הֲלָהֵ֣ן) that you all

43. For the Aramaic word "therefore," see BDB, 1099. Cf. *HALOT*, 521.

44. This explanation is supported by the targumim, the LXX, and the Peshitta. See Wilch, *Ruth*, 27.

would wait (תְּשַׂבֵּרְנָה) until they grow up (עַד אֲשֶׁר יִגְדָּלוּ)?" If Naomi were able to have children, and Orpah and Ruth continue to live with Naomi, these hypothetical sons would benefit. And yet this is Naomi's rhetorical question; would they indeed benefit?

This third explanation not only makes sense of the immediate context but also heightens the tension. Even if Naomi had sons, the question of whether Orpah and Ruth should wait until the boys were at the age of marriage inversely compounds Naomi's rhetoric of despair. The question expects a negative answer, and so, "Even if I had sons, it would *not* be to their benefit that you should wait around until they are marriagable." In a backward kind of way, Naomi's reason for Orpah and Ruth to leave in this clause is that their staying would not benefit her hypothetical future sons. Perhaps Orpah and Ruth would be too old to bear children at that point. If so, then Naomi yet again voices a theology like that of Abraham and Sarai, limiting God as to how old one can be and still bear children (Gen 17:17).

תְּשַׂבֵּרְנָה is a Piel imperfect 2fp of שׂבר. This clause provides the apodosis of the implied conditionals from verse 12. *If* Naomi had sons, *then* would they have the benefit of Naomi's daughters waiting until the boys were grown? The root שׂבר occurs normally as a Piel, and so there is no intensive nuance to the daughters' waiting. Piel is simply the base stem for שׂבר.[45] Combined with the idea of the benefit to Naomi's (hypothetical) sons, תְּשַׂבֵּרְנָה presents a hypothetical action warranting a modal (jussive) translation, "that you all *would/should* wait."

The final prepositional phrase (עַד אֲשֶׁר יִגְדָּלוּ) provides the temporal aspect of how long Orpah and Ruth would wait in this hypothetical situation. יִגְדָּלוּ is a Qal imperfect 3mp of גדל. Morphologically, it is a pausal form.[46] Because of the vocalic ending (וּ), one would expect a vocal *shewa* under the ד. However, with the relatively heavy disjunctive accent, *zāqēf qāṭôn* (◌ׄ), the original theme vowel is revealed (◌ַ) and in this case also lengthens (◌ָ).[47]

45. BDB, 960.

46. JM §32.

47. Pausal forms are forms that have a heavy disjunctive accent, usually a *sillûq* or *atnāḥ*. Occasionally, however, the *zāqēf qāṭôn* or other relatively heavy accents can elicit a pausal

With the preposition עַד, the verb is part of a temporal clause, and since the entire speech is projected into the hypothetical future, the verbal idea of "being great" is best rendered as "becoming great." In the context of people, גדל often means "to grow up."[48]

Literally, then, the question goes like this: "Is there to them that you all would wait until [the time] that they grow up?" If we smooth out this clause, we get "Would they get the benefit that you would wait until they grow old enough [to support you]?"

הֲלָהֵ֣ן תֵּעָגֵ֔נָה לְבִלְתִּ֖י הֱי֣וֹת לְאִ֑ישׁ

This clause begins with the same interrogative as the previous clause (הֲלָהֵ֣ן). "Is there to them (the future hypothetical sons) ... ?" Both of these clauses provide the full apodosis to the hypothetical conditionals of verse 12. תֵּעָגֵ֔נָה is a Niphal imperfect 2fp of עגן, meaning "to shut oneself in." Notice that the preformative vowel has lengthened from *ḥîreq* to *ṣērê* since the I-ע rejects the *dāgēš forte* expected in the first root letter of the Niphal (תֵּעָגֵ֔נָה ← תִּעָּגֵ֔נָה).

Parsing this verb is challenging since we would expect a double נ in the 2fp sufformative (תֵּעָגֵ֔נָה ← תֵּעָגֵ֔נְנָה).[49] In addition, we would expect a *pataḥ* thematic vowel in the Niphal imperfect 2fp, whereas here the text presents a *ṣērê*. If we look to other options for the root, no other root exists that would have fewer morphological problems or fits the context. עגן occurs in the Hebrew Bible only here (*hapax legomenon*) and in the Niphal imperfect 2fp carries the reflexive idea of "shutting oneself in" or "withholding oneself." The verb communicates that the daughters would withhold themselves from marrying someone besides Naomi's hypothetical sons. Similar to the last clause, this situation would *not* be to the benefit of Naomi's hypothetical sons. The root עגן exists in Rabbinic Hebrew and in Aramaic with

---

form. Because of the heavy disjunctive accent, pausal forms will either (1) reveal a vowel that has reduced to a vocal *shewa*, (2) lengthen a short vowel to the nonhistoric long vowel in that vowel class, or (3) reveal the reduced vowel *and* lengthen it. In 1:13, יִגְדָּ֑לוּ has both revealed the thematic vowel *and* lengthened it.

48. BDB, 152; *NIDOTTE* 1:824.

49. See *HALOT*, 785–86, for hypothetical form.

the same meaning, particularly in the context of marriage.[50] Therefore, even with the difficulty in parsing, עגן is the best option.

The negation לְבִלְתִּי is often the negation for an infinitive construct, and so the use here is expected.[51] הֱיוֹת is the Qal infinitive construct of היה and can be understood one of two ways. First, the clause could indicate a negative result: "Would you withhold yourself, with the result that you have no husband?" Second, the infinitive clause could be taken epexegetically, indicating means: "Would you withhold yourself *by not existing* to a husband" or "*by not having* a husband?" If we once again interpretively expand the translation of the verse on the basis of these grammatical considerations, it would read, "Would my hypothetical sons benefit from you withholding yourself from marriage?" Naomi has already stated that she is too old to have children, and so her logic demonstrates her hopelessness. She attempts to convince Orpah and Ruth that it would not benefit her hypothetical sons for them to refrain from marriage now because, indeed, there will not be any hypothetical sons. They cannot benefit if they do not exist. Therefore, Orpah and Ruth should move on and marry rather than withholding themselves from becoming wives to other men.

אַל בְּנֹתַי כִּי־מַר־לִי מְאֹד מִכֶּם

The opening אַל is an emphatic exclamation, "No!"[52] בְּנֹתַי is a vocative address, "my daughters!" The exclamation reiterates Naomi's desire for Ruth and Orpah to leave her. Even in the extreme circumstance that Naomi would have sons, her answer to the girls staying is emphatically, "No, my daughters!"

The following כִּי clause is a ground clause providing the reason Naomi so adamantly wants Orpah and Ruth to leave. Naomi views her situation as "more bitter" than Ruth's and Orpah's situations. מַר is the Qal perfect 3ms of מרר. As such, the clause is literally "[it is] bitter to me," with the implied subject ("it") identifying her situation. Another way to read the

50. See BDB, 723; and *HALOT*, 785–86, for discussions. Cf. *NIDOTTE* 3:320–21.

51. RJW §423.

52. RJW §403.

clause is as a verbless clause with מַר as an adjective, "for bitterness [is] to me."[53] In this second option, Naomi actually possesses the bitterness rather than her simply identifying her situation as "bitter." Either interpretation communicates the same nuance of the clause. Naomi's situation is bitter and therefore she possesses bitterness. Naomi's bitterness is intensified by מְאֹד. The מִן preposition is a comparative מִן and provides the sense of "more than." We can smooth out the translation to say, "for it is exceedingly more bitter for me than for you."

There are a couple of ways that one can interpret Naomi's reason for encouraging Orpah and Ruth to leave. Perhaps Naomi is indeed bitter and she is in no condition to be caring for husbandless daughters-in-law. Alternatively, if Naomi only perceives her situation as bitter, perhaps she does not want to drag Orpah and Ruth through the despair she will likely encounter for the remainder of her life. Regardless of whether Naomi's intention toward Orpah and Ruth is positive, Naomi fails to demonstrate faith in Yahweh's covenant faithfulness. Even though she can appeal to Yahweh to deal kindly with Orpah and Ruth (1:9), she will demonstrate a potential henotheistic outlook when she encourages Ruth to go back to her gods in Moab (1:15). In spite of her bitter situation, Naomi should welcome foreigners, especially ones who have joined themselves to a Yahwistic family. One thing Boaz will do later, in contrast to Naomi, is welcome Ruth as a foreigner rather than encouraging her to return to Moab.

כִּֽי־יָצְאָ֥ה בִ֖י יַד־יְהוָֽה׃

This כִּי clause provides a second, almost appositional ground for why Naomi so strongly tells her daughters, "No." Her situation is bitter "*for* the hand of the Lord has gone out against me." The subject (יַד־יְהוָה) is feminine, and יָצְאָה is the Qal perfect 3fs of יצא. Even though יצא is a I-י and a III-א, in the Qal perfect it morphs as a strong verb. בִי is an adversative ב meaning "against me."[54]

53. Holmstedt, *Ruth*, 84.

54. RJW §242.

In light of all the hypothetical marriage and childbearing possibilities Naomi presents, her reasoning for emphatically telling Orpah and Ruth to leave is that her situation is so bitter that she cannot bear to think of projecting that bitterness onto her daughters *and* that the hand of the Lord has caused this bitterness. Naomi may not trust the Lord's covenant faithfulness in light of her situation, but she surely knows his bitter providence.

As the narrator develops Naomi's character, it is interesting to consider how despairing she is and what might lead her to this place. In this case, Naomi will encourage Ruth to return to her gods as if these were legitimate deities (1:15). Naomi has given up hope that the Lord could produce anything good from this situation, and she has stopped trusting that the Lord can bring life and hope out of death and bitterness. Part of the presentation of Naomi's character has to do with whether these two כִּי clauses are appositional or whether they logically follow each other. The clausal relationships may be represented visually like this:

apposition

כִּֽי־מַר־לִ֤י מְאֹד֙ מִכֶּ֔ם "for it is exceedingly more bitter for me than for you"
כִּֽי־יָצְאָ֥ה בִ֖י יַד־יְהוָֽה׃ "for the hand of Yahweh has gone out against me."

or

logical ground clause

כִּֽי־מַר־לִ֤י מְאֹד֙ מִכֶּ֔ם "for it is exceedingly more bitter for me than for you"
כִּֽי־יָצְאָ֥ה בִ֖י יַד־יְהוָֽה׃ "for the hand of Yahweh has gone out against me."

The first option would render the interpretation already presented. Orpah and Ruth should leave "because" Naomi's situation is more bitter than theirs *and* "because" the hand of the Lord has gone out against Naomi. As apposition, the second ground clause restates the first. In other words, the hand of the Lord going out against Naomi *is* the bitterness Naomi is experiencing.

On the other hand, if the ground clauses proceed logically, the flow of thought is that Orpah and Ruth should leave "because" Naomi's situation is exceedingly bitter, and her situation is bitter "because" the hand of the Lord has made it so. If this is the logic, then Naomi is presented as someone who tells her daughter-in-law to return to her own gods precisely because Yahweh has caused her own bitter situation. Rather than trust Yahweh to uphold his covenant faithfulness, Naomi blames Yahweh for her bitterness and then uses that as a logical argument to get Orpah and Ruth to abandon her.

These are the kinds of decisions that must be made with great care, but the importance of learning Hebrew well is that these decisions are made on the basis of the grammar and syntax of the Hebrew Bible. One interpretation presents Naomi as recognizing that Yahweh brings both good and calamity (cf. Isa 45:7). The other presents her as hopeless, finding no reason to welcome foreigners into the people of God. Regardless of where one lands on this interpretive decision, we must realize that Naomi's situation is indeed bitter. As the narrative continues, we will see whether Naomi begins to recognize God's goodness to her or whether she continues as a bitter antagonist.

RUTH 1:14

וַתִּשֶּׂ֥נָה קוֹלָ֖ן וַתִּבְכֶּ֣ינָה ע֑וֹד וַתִּשַּׁ֤ק עָרְפָּה֙ לַחֲמוֹתָ֔הּ וְר֖וּת דָּ֥בְקָה בָּֽהּ׃

ACCENT PHRASING

וַתִּשֶּׂ֥נָה קוֹלָ֖ן
וַתִּבְכֶּ֣ינָה ע֑וֹד
וַתִּשַּׁ֤ק עָרְפָּה֙ לַחֲמוֹתָ֔הּ
וְר֖וּת דָּ֥בְקָה בָּֽהּ׃

וַתִּשֶּׂ֥נָה קוֹלָ֖ן וַתִּבְכֶּ֣ינָה ע֑וֹד ב̇ חס̇ א

Ruth 1:14 repeats the scene from 1:9 of the women weeping together as they face an uncertain future and a turning point in their relationship. וַתִּשֶּׂ֥נָה is a Qal imperfect 3fp of נשׂא + *vav*-consecutive. The *vav*-consecutive, along with the shift to third person verbs, indicates that the narrative has resumed and Naomi's direct speech to her daughters is complete. As a *vav* of temporal succession, the clause would translate, "*And then* they lifted up their voice." קוֹלָ֖ן is the direct object, the thing being lifted up. See 1:9 for קוֹלָ֖ן as a collective singular.

While the verbal action here is the same as 1:9, the verbal form is slightly different and may pose some difficulty. Notice that the III-א is missing from the root נשׂא. The *Dictionary of Classical Hebrew* (*DCH*) is most helpful here, but only to demonstrate that while this is rare for the root נשׂא, it is not unprecedented.[55] In an attempt to discern this rare form, *DCH* lists two forms of the Qal imperfect 2ms of נשׂא that in the Qumran documents appear to be derived from the root תשׂה or אשׂה, respectively, both displaying evidence of a III-ה verbal root. Specifically with a *vav*-consecutive, *DCH* lists a Qal perfect 1cs form morphologically akin to a III-י (וְנָשִׂיתִי) in some Hebrew manuscripts as well as a perfect 3cp form that morphs like a

55. *DCH* 5:758–59. Joüon calls this a *scriptio defectiva*, citing several forms in which a word is simply written without its א (Paul Joüon, *Ruth: A Philological and Exegetical Commentary*, trans. Homer Heater Jr. [Rome: Editrice Pontificio Biblico, 2013], 40; JM §78f).

III-ה verb (וְנָשׂוּ), again dropping the III-א altogether. Ruth 1:15 seems to be the only occurrence of the א dropping in the imperfect. If this verb is morphing like a III-ה verb, in the imperfect 3fp we would expect to see a י replacing the III-ה (וַתִּשֶּׂינָה). However, since that is not the case with this form, the exact reason for the III-א dropping is inconclusive.

The note listed to the left of the Hebrew phrase above is from the Masora Parva (Mp) in the margin of *BHS/BHQ*. The meaning of this nomenclature is that this form occurs twice (בֿ) in the Hebrew Bible lacking (חסֿ) the *aleph* (א).[56] The other occurrence of this particular form is in Jeremiah 9:17, but there it is also marked only as a unique form with no further explanation of the morphology.

וַתִּבְכֶּינָה completes the action of the scene in temporal succession: "they lifted up their voice *and then* they wept again." וַתִּבְכֶּינָה is a Qal imperfect 3fp of בכה + *vav*-consecutive. בכה is another III-ה verb, and notice again that the ה drops, being replaced by the coalesced ֶי thematic vowel of the 3fp. עוֹד is an adverb modifying both verbs, "again." This is now the second time that the women have lifted their voice and wept.

וַתִּשַּׁק עָרְפָּה֙ לַחֲמוֹתָ֔הּ

וַתִּשַּׁק is a Qal imperfect 3fs of נשׁק + *vav*-consecutive. The *vav* continues the narrative in temporal succession, moving the action forward in the story. It is possible at this juncture to see the *vav* as logical succession if one understands Naomi's argument for why the women should leave as effective. In other words, Naomi argues they should leave, "*and so* Orpah kissed her mother-in-law"—the logical outcome of Naomi's argument.[57] Morphologically, notice the *dāgēš forte* in the שׁ, remnants of the assimilated I-נ of the root נשׁק (וַתִּשַּׁק ⟵ וַתִּנְשַׁק).

56. For a detailed analysis of the Mp notes, see Page H. Kelley, Daniel S. Mynatt, and Timothy G. Crawford, *The Masorah of Biblia Hebraica Stuttgartensia: An Introduction and Annotated Glossary* (Grand Rapids: Eerdmans, 1998).

57. The LXX adds καὶ ἐπέστρεψεν εἰς τὸν λαὸν αὐτῆς to complete the inner narrative for Orpah. This addition may lend itself more to understanding the *vav* as logical succession since it is the final outcome in Orpah's story: "and so finally, Orpah kissed her mother-in-law [and returned to her people]."

עָרְפָּה is the subject, and לַחֲמוֹתָהּ is the direct object. ל often marks the direct object after certain verbs.[58] לַחֲמוֹתָהּ is the singular noun חָמוֹת with a ל preposition and a 3fs pronominal suffix (הּ◌ָ). וֹת- in the middle of the word does not mark a fp form but is part of the original noun.[59]

וְר֕וּת דָּ֥בְקָה בָּֽהּ׃

The final clause is a nominal clause (begins with the subject) drawing attention to Ruth by fronting her in the verse (focus-marking).[60] As a nominal clause, רוּת is the initiator and the announcement is דָּבְקָה בָּהּ. The point of this construction is to break the flow of action in the narrative and say something specifically about Ruth with all attention on her rather than the narrative sequence. With the *vav* disjunctive breaking the narrative sequence, it presents a contrast to Orpah's reaction: "*but* Ruth [in contrast to Orpah] clung to her."

דָּבְקָה is a Qal perfect 3fs of דבק.[61] דבק is a strong verb morphologically, but notice the MT does not always preserve the *metheg* (◌ֽ) in the first root letter position as is often found in the Qal paradigm for beginning grammars (קָֽטְלָה [*qāṭĕlāh*]). The context, however, with an explicit third person feminine subject makes it clear that this is a perfect 3fs verb versus any potential confusion with the long form of the Qal imperative (קָטְלָה [*qoṭlāh*]). בָּהּ is the direct object. Just as ל can introduce the direct object, ב may as well, especially with דבק.[62]

58. RJW §273b.
59. BDB, 327.
60. Holmstedt, *Ruth*, 86.
61. For the theological importance of the root דבק, see *NIDOTTE* 1:911–12.
62. RJW §244; BDB, 179–80; *HALOT*, 209; *DCH* 2:386.

RUTH 1:15

וַתֹּ֗אמֶר הִנֵּה֙ שָׁ֣בָה יְבִמְתֵּ֔ךְ אֶל־עַמָּ֖הּ וְאֶל־אֱלֹהֶ֑יהָ שׁ֖וּבִי אַחֲרֵ֥י יְבִמְתֵּֽךְ׃

ACCENT PHRASING

וַתֹּ֗אמֶר הִנֵּה֙ שָׁ֣בָה יְבִמְתֵּ֔ךְ
אֶל־עַמָּ֖הּ וְאֶל־אֱלֹהֶ֑יהָ
שׁ֖וּבִי אַחֲרֵ֥י יְבִמְתֵּֽךְ׃

וַתֹּ֗אמֶר הִנֵּה֙ שָׁ֣בָה יְבִמְתֵּ֔ךְ אֶל־עַמָּ֖הּ וְאֶל־אֱלֹהֶ֑יהָ

וַתֹּ֗אמֶר is a Qal imperfect 3fs of אמר + *vav*-consecutive of temporal succession. The implied subject is "she," and context suggests that Naomi is speaking.

The narrative progresses quickly at this point as Naomi tells Ruth, "Your sister-in-law has returned" (שָׁ֣בָה יְבִמְתֵּ֔ךְ). הִנֵּה֙ adds slight emphasis to what Naomi is saying. Perhaps the "shock" is due to how quickly Orpah decided to leave. In the previous verse Orpah simply kissed Naomi, a probable sign of departure. However, the perfective here (שָׁ֣בָה) suggests that Orpah has already left. הִנֵּה֙ draws the reader's attention to this reality. In translation, הִנֵּה֙ is part of Naomi's direct speech to Ruth, so it may simply be "Look, your sister-in-law has returned." But grammatically, הִנֵּה֙ catches the reader's attention as to the swiftness of Orpah's departure.

שָׁ֣בָה with the accent on the first root letter indicates that this verb is a Qal perfect 3fs rather than the fs participle. In hollow roots, the Qal perfect 3fs and the fs participle look identical without the accented syllable marked. Here the accent is on the R1, clearly marking the perfect 3fs. יְבִמְתֵּ֔ךְ is the subject, and along with the perfective verb we get, "Look, your sister-in-law *has returned*."

יְבִמְתֵּ֔ךְ occurs only here and in Deuteronomy 25:7, 9 in the Hebrew Bible. In Deuteronomy, the word is in the context of instructions for levirate marriage. John Wilch points out that in later Rabbinic Hebrew the word refers to a "widow of a brother who died without children."[63] Victor Hamilton

---

63. Wilch, *Ruth*, 32–33.

comments that the two clear references to levirate marriage (Gen 38:1–11; Deut 25:5–10) identify a custom that was intended "to provide a son for a childless widow who would carry on the name of the deceased brother. This responsibility fell to the יָבָם, a brother of the deceased."[64] In Ruth, the term is the fs, יְבָמָה, and so Orpah is identified with a word that clearly designates her as the female involved in this levirate custom. Given Naomi's choice of words here, it seems that she thinks the only way for Ruth to be sustained is to return to her own family because the levirate custom appears unable to provide for her a son. Naomi is pleading with Ruth to return, but her choice of words to describe Orpah makes Naomi's plea more desperate.

The designation יְבִמְתֵּךְ once again highlights the character development of Naomi. Naomi has suggested relentlessly that these young women return to their Moabite families, arguing on the basis of her old age and inability to have a husband or children for them to marry. By using a word that implies the levirate custom, Naomi may be suggesting that since she cannot have sons to carry out the levirate custom, Ruth should follow her יְבָמָה and seek a future with her own people.

Since Mahlon and Chilion were Israelites, for Orpah and Ruth to return to Moab is turning away from the levirate custom. If they return to Moab and find new husbands, they are simply marrying a new husband for provision, not gaining provision from a sibling of the deceased husband. Naomi's choice of words places Orpah and Ruth in the category of someone who needs provision rather than expecting them to gain provision strictly through the levirate system. In this sense, Naomi uses the vocabulary associated with the levirate system, but she seems to lack the hope that God will provide a levir for Ruth. Ironically, יְבָמָה is never used in relation to Ruth, the very one who *will* find a redeemer among the people of the one true God rather than fleeing to "her people" (אֶל־עַמָּהּ) and "her god" (וְאֶל־אֱלֹהֶיהָ) as Orpah did. Naomi identifies Orpah with a term familiar to the levirate system even though the context implies that Orpah will not be participating in any way in a levirate marriage since she has returned to Moab.

64. *NIDOTTE* 2:385–86. Cf. Block, *Ruth*, 91, n. 57.

Additionally, Naomi fails to see any hope that Yahweh will provide a levir for Ruth among the Ephrathites. She continues to encourage Ruth to leave.

The two prepositional phrases (אֶל־עַמָּהּ וְאֶל־אֱלֹהֶיהָ) in the *atnāḥ* segment communicate to where Orpah has returned. If we take אֱלֹהֶיהָ as a true plural, it could be that Orpah has returned to the polytheism of Moab ("to her gods"). In this respect, it may seem that Naomi is acknowledging the validity of polytheistic religion even if she knows Israel is strictly monotheistic. If we take it as a plural of majesty suggesting only one god, that god was probably Chemosh, the Moabite patron deity. Neither of these options for understanding אֱלֹהֶיהָ puts Naomi in a theologically orthodox framework.

For a more positive interpretation of Naomi's use of אֱלֹהֶיהָ, it may be that she simply uses the generic word for Moabite "gods" and does not imply they have supremacy over Yahweh. In this sense, the narrator continues to provide a caricature of Naomi that is fitting for the context rather than trying to make Naomi fit into a certain theological tradition. The focus of the narrative is Naomi's plea that Ruth would leave her, and at this point only Orpah has returned to her former heritage both ethnically and religiously.

שׁ֖וּבִי אַחֲרֵ֥י יְבִמְתֵּֽךְ׃

The second clause in Naomi's plea to Ruth is introduced with the command שׁ֖וּבִי, a Qal imperative 2fs of שׁוב. Naomi again strongly suggests that Ruth "return after [her] sister-in-law." אַחֲרֵ֥י is locative, meaning that Naomi suggests Ruth go in the same way as Orpah—namely, back to her people. As a locative, אַחֲרֵ֥י implies following, and so we could translate it as an explanatory phrase, "Return *by following after* your sister-in-law." Again, Orpah is called יְבִמְתֵּֽךְ. Naomi makes it clear that Orpah stands as one in need of a redeemer. And yet she has yet to suggest that either daughter search for that person among the people of God. Even if Naomi knows the Mosaic terminology for one who needs a redeemer, she fails to see how Yahweh can fulfill this need for her daughters-in-law. Hence, she commands Ruth to "return after [her] sister-in-law."

*[16] But Ruth said, "Do not urge me to abandon you by returning from after you, for to
where you go, I will go, and in where you lodge, I will lodge. Your people (will be) my
people, and your God (will be) my God. [17] In where you die, I will die, and there I will
be buried. Thus, may the Lord do to me and thus may he add if this death separates
between me and between you." [18] Then she saw that she strengthened herself to go
with her. And so she ceased to speak with her.*

RUTH
1:16–18

¹⁶ וַתֹּאמֶר רוּת֙ אַל־תִּפְגְּעִי־בִ֔י לְעָזְבֵ֖ךְ לָשׁ֣וּב מֵאַחֲרָ֑יִךְ כִּ֠י אֶל־אֲשֶׁ֨ר תֵּלְכִ֜י אֵלֵ֗ךְ וּבַאֲשֶׁ֤ר תָּלִ֙ינִי֙ אָלִ֔ין עַמֵּ֣ךְ עַמִּ֔י וֵאלֹהַ֖יִךְ אֱלֹהָֽי׃ ¹⁷ בַּאֲשֶׁ֤ר תָּמ֙וּתִי֙ אָמ֔וּת וְשָׁ֖ם אֶקָּבֵ֑ר כֹּה֩ יַעֲשֶׂ֨ה יְהוָ֥ה לִי֙ וְכֹ֣ה יֹסִ֔יף כִּ֣י הַמָּ֔וֶת יַפְרִ֖יד בֵּינִ֥י וּבֵינֵֽךְ׃ ¹⁸ וַתֵּ֕רֶא כִּֽי־מִתְאַמֶּ֥צֶת הִ֖יא לָלֶ֣כֶת אִתָּ֑הּ וַתֶּחְדַּ֖ל לְדַבֵּ֥ר אֵלֶֽיהָ׃

RUTH 1:16

וַתֹּ֤אמֶר רוּת֙ אַל־תִּפְגְּעִי־בִ֔י לְעָזְבֵ֖ךְ לָשׁ֣וּב מֵאַחֲרָ֑יִךְ כִּ֠י אֶל־אֲשֶׁ֨ר תֵּלְכִ֜י אֵלֵ֗ךְ
וּבַאֲשֶׁ֤ר תָּלִ֙ינִי֙ אָלִ֔ין עַמֵּ֣ךְ עַמִּ֔י וֵאלֹהַ֖יִךְ אֱלֹהָֽי׃

ACCENT PHRASING

וַתֹּ֤אמֶר רוּת֙
אַל־תִּפְגְּעִי־בִ֔י לְעָזְבֵ֖ךְ לָשׁ֣וּב מֵאַחֲרָ֑יִךְ
כִּ֠י אֶל־אֲשֶׁ֨ר תֵּלְכִ֜י אֵלֵ֗ךְ
וּבַאֲשֶׁ֤ר תָּלִ֙ינִי֙ אָלִ֔ין
עַמֵּ֣ךְ עַמִּ֔י
וֵאלֹהַ֖יִךְ אֱלֹהָֽי׃

וַתֹּ֤אמֶר רוּת֙

The focus in the narrative now shifts to Ruth's answer to Naomi, and so the subject (רוּת) is explicit. וַתֹּ֤אמֶר is a Qal imperfect 3fs of אמר + *vav*-consecutive. The *vav*-consecutive communicates temporal succession, but since the context will entail a negative response from Ruth, we may translate the *vav* adversatively, "*But* Ruth said …"

אַל־תִּפְגְּעִי־בִ֔י לְעָזְבֵ֖ךְ לָשׁ֣וּב מֵאַחֲרָ֑יִךְ

אַל + the jussive functions as a negative command, particularly when referring to a specific situation in which the desire or intention is that something should *not* happen.[1] The verbal form is a Qal jussive 2fs of פגע. אַל identifies the verb as jussive rather than the indicative (imperfect) because לֹא negates the indicative. ב introduces the direct object, as is often the case with פגע: "Do not press *me*" or "Do not urge *me*."[2]

לְעָזְבֵ֖ךְ is the Qal infinitive construct of עזב. Notice that the vowel under the R1 (ע) is a short *qāmeṣ-ḥāṭûf* in a closed and unaccented syllable (לְעָזְבֵ֖ךְ).

1. RJW §186 §402.
2. BDB, 803.

The infinitive complements the verb to complete the action.[3] We translate the infinitive as an English infinitive, "to abandon," answering the question "Do not urge me to do what?": "Do not urge me *to abandon you*."

לָשׁוּב is a second Qal infinitive construct, this time from שׁוב + ל preposition. Some English translations supply a conjunction and this infinitive becomes the second complement to the main clause אַל־תִּפְגְּעִי־בִי: "Do not urge me to abandon you *or* to return from after you."[4] However, it may be better to understand this infinitive as an epexegetical or explanatory infinitive:[5] "Do not urge me to abandon you *by returning* from after you." A third option is to understand לָשׁוּב as an appositional infinitive, "renaming" לְעָזְבֵךְ, which essentially gives it an explanatory function (explicative apposition): "Do not urge me to abandon you—*namely, to return* from after you."

מֵאַחֲרָיִךְ is a locative prepositional phrase indicating the place where Ruth says she should not be urged to go. She tells Naomi not to urge her to return "from *following* after [her]."

כִּי אֶל־אֲשֶׁר תֵּלְכִי אֵלֵךְ

This final series of clauses provide the reasons why Ruth does not want to abandon Naomi. כִּי governs all the clauses remaining in verse 16 and even into the first half of verse 17.

The initial ground clause fronts the prepositional phrase (אֶל־אֲשֶׁר), perhaps emphasizing Ruth's desire to follow Naomi to a particular place. אֲשֶׁר is locative, "*to where* you go." The verbs are both Qal imperfects of הלך. תֵּלְכִי is the 2fs, and אֵלֵךְ is the 1cs. In both verbs, the first root letter (ה) drops and the preformative vowel lengthens from *ḥîreq* to *ṣērê* (תֵּלְכִי; אֵלֵךְ). The 2fs form (תֵּלְכִי) has the *ḥîreq-yôd* sufformative that is typical of the 2fs imperfectives, and thus reduces the thematic vowel to a vocal *shewa* under the ל. The 1cs form (אֵלֵךְ) is identifiable by the א preformative. The two verbs are

3. For the infinitive generally as a verbal complement, see WO §36.2.1d. For the syntactical tag "complementary infinitive" specifically, see WO §36.2.3b ##5–11d.

4. E.g., ESV, NASB, NIV, CSB, NRSV, KJV.

5. RJW §195.

translated as future. The action has not happened yet, but it is also not a request from Ruth. She says that she "will go" to the place where (אֶל־אֲשֶׁר) Naomi goes (תֵּלְכִי).

וּבַאֲשֶׁר תָּלִינִי אָלִין

This clause is parallel in structure to the previous one. It begins with the prepositional phrase as before (וּבַאֲשֶׁר). The ב preposition is locative because one lodges "in" a place.[6]

The verbs now are a Qal imperfect 2fs (תָּלִינִי) and 1cs (אָלִין), respectively, of the root לין. Being a II-י verb, both forms coalesce the middle י into the thematic vowel that now joins the R1 (ל) and R3 (ן). Also notice that in the Qal stem of II-י verbs, the preformative vowel shifts from i-class to a-class. The preformative vowel is no longer *ḥîreq* as in יִקְטֹל; it is *pataḥ*. In both verbal forms, the preformative vowel lengthens to a *qāmeṣ* because the accent falls on the ל after the middle root letter coalesces as the thematic vowel (ִי). This leaves the originally short *pataḥ* in an open pretonic syllable, and thus it lengthens to *qāmeṣ*. As in the previous construction, the verbs are translated as future tense, indicating an action that Ruth is determined to carry out.

עַמֵּךְ עַמִּי וֵאלֹהַיִךְ אֱלֹהָי׃

The final two clauses both lack an explicit main verb. These verbless clauses suggest that both nominatives are considered equal to each other. "Your people = my people." "Your God = my God." In order to translate these clauses into good English, we must supply the "to be" verb in the appropriate tense. In each clause, עַמִּי and אֱלֹהָי are predicate nominatives following the supplied "to be" verb.

As with many times that we supply verbs, the tense may be an interpretive decision. In this case, following the imperfective verbs in the previous clauses, supplying the future tense may communicate that (1) Ruth has not yet aligned herself with Yahweh, but is planning on it if Naomi

---

6. For the use of the ב with לין, see BDB, 533.

will allow her to follow along, or (2) Ruth has already aligned herself with Yahweh and emphatically states that Naomi's people and God will continue to be her people and God. If we supply the present tense, a third option emerges: (3) Ruth may have aligned herself with Yahweh and the Israelites when she married Mahlon, but she is now bringing that allegiance into this discussion as the reason she refuses to leave. "I will not leave" because "your people *are* my people and your God *is* my God." Options 2 or 3 seem to best fit this situation since Ruth is making an argument for why Naomi should allow her to tag along—namely, Ruth has already aligned herself with Yahweh and his people. Ruth will follow Naomi wherever she goes because Ruth already made the commitment to Israel and to Yahweh almost a decade ago.[7]

7. See discussion in Block, *Ruth*, 94–95.

RUTH 1:17

בַּאֲשֶׁ֤ר תָּמ֙וּתִי֙ אָמ֔וּת וְשָׁ֖ם אֶקָּבֵ֑ר כֹּה֩ יַעֲשֶׂ֨ה יְהוָ֥ה לִי֙ וְכֹ֣ה יֹסִ֔יף כִּ֣י הַמָּ֔וֶת יַפְרִ֖יד בֵּינִ֥י וּבֵינֵֽךְ׃

ACCENT PHRASING

בַּאֲשֶׁ֤ר תָּמ֙וּתִי֙ אָמ֔וּת וְשָׁ֖ם אֶקָּבֵ֑ר
כֹּה֩ יַעֲשֶׂ֨ה יְהוָ֥ה לִי֙ וְכֹ֣ה יֹסִ֔יף
כִּ֣י הַמָּ֔וֶת יַפְרִ֖יד בֵּינִ֥י וּבֵינֵֽךְ׃

בַּאֲשֶׁ֤ר תָּמ֙וּתִי֙ אָמ֔וּת

The initial clause of verse 17 continues the structure from verse 16b and is part of the ground clause (כִּ֣י) beginning in verse 16a. Following the parallel introductory prepositional phrase (בַּאֲשֶׁ֤ר; literally "in which" or "where"), the verbs are Qal imperfect 2fs (תָּמ֙וּתִי֙) and 1cs (אָמ֔וּת), respectively, but now from the verbal root מות. Like II-י verbs, the II-ו verb מות coalesces the middle ו as the thematic vowel uniting R1 (מ) and R3 (ת). Like the II-י verbs, the Qal of hollow roots shifts the preformative vowels from i-class to a-class, and because the accent falls on the מ, the preformative vowel lengthens to *qāmeṣ*. Ruth continues to intensify her argument to follow Naomi back to Bethlehem. Not only will Ruth go and lodge with Naomi, having aligned herself with Naomi's people and Yahweh, but she commits to die in the same place as Naomi.

וְשָׁ֖ם אֶקָּבֵ֑ר

וְשָׁ֖ם is in an emphatic position at the beginning of this clause and looks back to the unspecified place where Naomi will die in the previous clause. אֶקָּבֵ֑ר is a Niphal imperfect 1cs of קבר. The Niphal is the passive of the Qal, "I will *be* buried." אֶקָּבֵ֑ר is a strong verb, and so the morphology matches the paradigm for the Niphal imperfect 1cs.

The emphatic וְשָׁ֖ם, along with Ruth's commitment to die where Naomi dies, communicates clearly Ruth's intention to stay with Naomi for life.

For these women to have lost their husbands means that they would likely have a difficult life ahead. In fact, Naomi said as much trying to convince her daughters to abandon her. And yet Ruth refuses to leave Naomi, but rather commits to her as a loyal daughter for the rest of her life.

כֹּה֩ יַעֲשֶׂה יְהוָה לִי֙ וְכֹ֣ה יֹסִ֔יף

The next clause is an oath clause and follows the classic word structure of the oath (or curse). Literally, the clause translates, "Thus (כֹּה֩), may the Lord do to me (יַעֲשֶׂה יְהוָה לִי֙), and thus may he add (וְכֹ֣ה יֹסִ֔יף)." יְהוָה is the subject, and the imperfective verbs translate modally ("*may* he do," "*may* he add"). יַעֲשֶׂה is a Qal imperfect 3ms of עשׂה, while יֹסִ֔יף is a Hiphil imperfect 3ms of יסף. יַעֲשֶׂה demonstrates a *pataḥ* preformative vowel in the Qal because of the I-ע.

The morphology for יֹסִ֔יף is a bit more complicated. The verbal root is יסף, but the י in the written text is the י of the 3ms imperfect preformative. The *ḥōlem* represents the *aw* ⟶ *ô* contraction (וֹ◌ ⟵ ◌ַו), which is the phonological result of the Hiphil preformative (◌ַי) and the original I-ו of יסף (וסף). The contraction usually results in a historic long *ḥōlem-vav*, but here it is written defectively (without the vowel marker [ו]).

יַוְסִיף ⟶ יוֹסִיף ⟶ יֹסִיף

The full curse formula includes an introduction, the curse formula, and the sworn statement (conditional).[8] Here the introduction ("Listen," "As the Lord lives," or "raising of the hand") is implied, but the curse formula (כֹּה֩ יַעֲשֶׂה יְהוָה לִי֙ וְכֹ֣ה יֹסִ֔יף) and the sworn statement (כִּ֣י הַמָּ֔וֶת יַפְרִ֖יד בֵּינִ֥י וּבֵינֵֽךְ) are explicit. The actual consequence within the curse formula (what the Lord will do) is often omitted, suggesting that the consequence of the curse is so severe that it cannot be mentioned.[9] Therefore, the extent of the curse formula only needs to state, "Thus may the Lord do, and thus may he add." What he actually will "do" and "add" remains unstated because of its severity.

---

8. *IBHS* §§65–68.

9. *IBHS* §§65a, 67. Cf. Holmstedt, *Ruth*, 91–92.

כִּ֣י הַמָּ֔וֶת יַפְרִ֖יד בֵּינִ֥י וּבֵינֵֽךְ׃

This final clause in verse 17 is the sworn statement of the oath clause. כִּ֣י can be tricky in this scenario since we tend to think of it as introducing a ground clause. Here, כִּ֣י is an asseverative, "surely" or "indeed," probably with an implied conditional, "Surely (*if* anything but death) separates ..."[10] We may expect to see אִם introducing this conditional aspect of the sworn statement, but there is precedent in the Hebrew Bible to read כִּי as introducing a conditional in an oath clause.[11]

הַמָּ֔וֶת, the subject, is fronted in the clause for emphasis. The shifted word order to place the subject first highlights the focus of the sentence. יַפְרִ֖יד is a Hiphil imperfect 3ms of פרד. Translated in the given word order, we get "Indeed, death will separate between me and between you." The surety of this statement demonstrates Ruth's commitment to follow Naomi back to Bethlehem. Ruth states that nothing but death will separate them because death will be the thing that surely (כִּ֣י) separates them.

In the last two prepositional phrases (בֵּינִ֥י וּבֵינֵֽךְ), it is common to repeat the prepositions, especially with בֵּין.

10. *IBHS* §68.

11. E.g., 1 Sam 14:44; 20:13; 2 Sam 3:9, 35; 1 Kgs 2:23; 19:2. See also BDB, כִּי 1c; GKC §149; JM §165a–b.

RUTH 1:18

וַתֵּ֕רֶא כִּֽי־מִתְאַמֶּ֥צֶת הִ֖יא לָלֶ֣כֶת אִתָּ֑הּ וַתֶּחְדַּ֖ל לְדַבֵּ֥ר אֵלֶֽיהָ׃

ACCENT PHRASING

וַתֵּ֕רֶא כִּֽי־מִתְאַמֶּ֥צֶת הִ֖יא לָלֶ֣כֶת אִתָּ֑הּ
וַתֶּחְדַּ֖ל לְדַבֵּ֥ר אֵלֶֽיהָ׃

וַתֵּ֕רֶא כִּֽי־מִתְאַמֶּ֥צֶת הִ֖יא לָלֶ֣כֶת אִתָּ֑הּ

The subject of the narrative now shifts back to Naomi but is implied in the 3fs verb. וַתֵּ֕רֶא is a Qal imperfect 3fs + *vav*-consecutive of ראה. The *vav*-consecutive is in temporal succession indicating the next action in the narrative, "Now she (Naomi) saw ..." In III-ה *vav*-consecutive forms, the final ה drops (apocopation) and the vowels follow a segolate pattern ("segolization"; cf. סֵ֫פֶר = תֵּ֫רֶא in its vowel pattern).

The כִּי clause clarifies what Naomi "saw." Naomi saw "*that* she (Ruth) was one who was determined." מִתְאַמֶּ֫צֶת is a Hithpael participle fs of אמץ. As a Hithpael, the verb is reflexive, "to strengthen oneself." According to BDB, when followed by a ל + infinitive, אמץ conveys one's determination to a particular purpose.[12] Here Naomi sees that Ruth has determined לָלֶ֫כֶת אִתָּהּ ("to go with her"). That מִתְאַמֶּ֫צֶת is a participle highlights the durative nature of Ruth's action. She was determined and was not going to budge.

לָלֶ֫כֶת is a Qal infinitive construct of הלך and specifies what Ruth was determined to do. She was determined "to go." Morphologically, the I-ה flees, לֵךְ receives a final ת (לֶכְתְּ), and the final vowel pattern mimics a segolate (מֶ֫לֶךְ = לֶ֫כֶת regarding vowel pattern). With the segolization and the accented R1, the ל preposition points with a *qāmeṣ* in an open pretonic syllable (לָלֶ֫כֶת).

אִתָּהּ specifies where Ruth has determined herself to go: "with her (Naomi)."

12. BDB, 55.

וַתֶּחְדַּל לְדַבֵּר אֵלֶיהָ׃

The final clause provides the logical conclusion to Ruth's commitment to follow Naomi. The main verb is the Qal imperfect 3fs of חדל + *vav*-consecutive of logical succession, "*And so* she ceased." Naomi is the implied subject.

Morphologically, the preformative vowel changes to a *sĕgōl* (תֶּ) as a result of the I-guttural (ח). It is common to have a composite *shewa* under the I-guttural (e.g., יַעֲשֶׂה), but ח will often retain the silent *shewa* of the strong form as it does here. However, even when ח retains the silent *shewa*, the preformative vowel still changes to what it would have been if the silent *shewa* adjusted to a composite *shewa*. In the Qal imperfect, the preformative vowel is normally *ḥîreq*, but in the e/i vowel class, a *ḥāṭēf-ḥîreq* or composite *ḥîreq shewa* does not exist. The e/i vowel class has the *ḥāṭēf-sĕgōl* as its composite *shewa*. Had the ח changed to a composite *shewa*, it would have been a *ḥāṭēf-sĕgōl* (תֶּחֱדַל). Even though the ח retains the silent shewa, the preformative vowel still changes to the *sĕgōl*. Morphologically, the form is not תִּחְדַּל, nor is it תֶּחֱדַל. Rather, it is תֶּחְדַּל.[13]

לְדַבֵּר is the Piel infinitive construct of דבר + ל. The infinitive complements the verb, completing the implicit question "What did Naomi cease?": "And so she ceased *to speak*." As a result of Ruth's determination, Naomi stopped trying to convince Ruth to return to her own Moabite people. The final prepositional phrase, אֵלֶיהָ, indicates to whom Naomi ceased to speak.

13. *IBH*, 192, specifically §29.7.

*[19] And then the two of them walked until their coming to Bethlehem, and it came
about as they came to Bethlehem that all the city murmured concerning them, and
they said, "Is this Naomi?" [20] And she said to them, "Do not call me Naomi. Call me
Mara, for the Almighty has caused great bitterness to me. [21] I went away full, but
empty the Lord has caused me to return. Why would you call me Naomi when the
Lord testified against me and caused me calamity?" [22] So Naomi returned, along with
Ruth, the Moabitess, her daughter-in-law with her, the one who returned from the
fields of Moab, and they came to Bethlehem at the beginning of the harvest of barley.*

RUTH

1:19–22

[19] וַתֵּלַ֣כְנָה שְׁתֵּיהֶ֔ם עַד־בֹּאָ֖נָה בֵּ֣ית לָ֑חֶם וַיְהִ֗י כְּבֹאָ֙נָה֙ בֵּ֣ית לֶ֔חֶם וַתֵּהֹ֤ם כָּל־הָעִיר֙
עֲלֵיהֶ֔ן וַתֹּאמַ֖רְנָה הֲזֹ֥את נָעֳמִֽי׃ [20] וַתֹּ֣אמֶר אֲלֵיהֶ֔ן אַל־תִּקְרֶ֥אנָה לִ֖י נָעֳמִ֑י קְרֶ֤אןָ
לִי֙ מָרָ֔א כִּי־הֵמַ֥ר שַׁדַּ֛י לִ֖י מְאֹֽד׃ [21] אֲנִי֙ מְלֵאָ֣ה הָלַ֔כְתִּי וְרֵיקָ֖ם הֱשִׁיבַ֣נִי יְהוָ֑ה לָ֣מָּה
תִקְרֶ֤אנָה לִי֙ נָעֳמִ֔י וַֽיהוָה֙ עָ֣נָה בִ֔י וְשַׁדַּ֖י הֵ֥רַֽע לִֽי׃ [22] וַתָּ֣שָׁב נָעֳמִ֗י וְר֨וּת הַמּוֹאֲבִיָּ֤ה
כַלָּתָהּ֙ עִמָּ֔הּ הַשָּׁ֖בָה מִשְּׂדֵ֣י מוֹאָ֑ב וְהֵ֗מָּה בָּ֚אוּ בֵּ֣ית לֶ֔חֶם בִּתְחִלַּ֖ת קְצִ֥יר שְׂעֹרִֽים׃

RUTH 1:19

וַתֵּלַ֣כְנָה שְׁתֵּיהֶ֔ם עַד־בֹּאָ֖נָה בֵּ֣ית לָ֑חֶם וַיְהִ֗י כְּבֹאָ֙נָה֙ בֵּ֣ית לֶ֔חֶם וַתֵּהֹ֤ם כָּל־הָעִיר֙ עֲלֵיהֶ֔ן וַתֹּאמַ֖רְנָה הֲזֹ֥את נָעֳמִֽי׃

ACCENT PHRASING

וַתֵּלַ֣כְנָה שְׁתֵּיהֶ֔ם
עַד־בֹּאָ֖נָה בֵּ֣ית לָ֑חֶם
וַיְהִ֗י כְּבֹאָ֙נָה֙ בֵּ֣ית לֶ֔חֶם
וַתֵּהֹ֤ם כָּל־הָעִיר֙ עֲלֵיהֶ֔ן
וַתֹּאמַ֖רְנָה הֲזֹ֥את נָעֳמִֽי׃

וַתֵּלַ֣כְנָה שְׁתֵּיהֶ֔ם

The primary narrative continues with וַתֵּלַ֣כְנָה, the Qal imperfect 3fp of הלך + *vav*-consecutive. The *vav* communicates temporal succession, "*And then* they went." שְׁתֵּיהֶ֔ם is the explicit subject. The pronominal suffix on שְׁתֵּיהֶ֔ם looks masculine even though two women are clearly the contextual subjects. This is another example of the possible archaic dual form (cf. 1:8–9). In light of the fp verb (וַתֵּלַ֣כְנָה) and the two women within the context, the subject must be fp.

עַד־בֹּאָ֖נָה בֵּ֣ית לָ֑חֶם

Beginning with עַד, this clause is the temporal marker for how long Naomi and Ruth "went"—namely, "until their coming to Bethlehem." בֹּאָ֖נָה is a Qal infinitive construct of בוא + 3fp pronominal suffix. The normal 3fp suffix (ָן) lacks the final ָה, but it may have been added here for assonance (repetition of vowel sounds; ָה) with וַתֵּלַ֣כְנָה.[1] עַד־בֹּאָ֖נָה is translated literally as "until the coming of them," or "until their coming." The pronominal suffix in this situation serves as the subject in an English sentence and, when

1. Holmstedt, *Ruth*, 94; JM §94h. The only other occurrences of בֹּאָ֖נָה with the final ָה are Jer 8:7 and later in this verse (כְּבֹאָ֙נָה֙). In Jer 8:7, it is preceded by the verb יָֽדְעָה, also creating assonance.

changed to an indicative sentence, generates the temporal clause, "until *they* came."[2]

בֵּית לָחֶם is the adverbial accusative of place specifying *where* they went.[3] In this temporal clause, it specifies how far they went. The adverbial accusative of place is best translated as "*to* Bethlehem" even though the construction contains neither a preposition nor a directive ה.

Notice that when לֶחֶם is in a pausal form, the original a-class vowel is revealed and also lengthens to a *qāmeṣ* (לָחֶם). Remember that pausal forms can (1) reveal a reduced vowel, (2) lengthen a short vowel, or (3) both. In this case, the pausal form reveals the original vowel (לַחֶם) *and* it lengthens it (לָחֶם).

וַיְהִי כְּבֹאָנָה בֵּית לֶחֶם

This clause, although in the middle of a verse, may introduce a new section.[4] וַיְהִי is a Qal imperfect 3ms of היה + *vav*-consecutive in temporal succession, "*And then* it came about." כְּבֹאָנָה is a Qal infinitive construct of בוא with a כ preposition, forming a temporal clause. The infinitive construct, translated as a gerund ("-ing" noun), provides a durative nuance to the temporal clause, especially with the use of the כ preposition: "as they were entering." The entire temporal clause can be translated as "when they were entering," but it is important to maintain the idea that the next action (the city murmuring about them) seems to have happened immediately upon their entry into Bethlehem. "And it came about *as* they were entering Bethlehem ..." בֵּית לֶחֶם is an adverbial accusative of place as in the previous clause.

וַתֵּהֹם כָּל־הָעִיר עֲלֵיהֶן

This clause is the apodosis to the previous clause. וַתֵּהֹם is a Niphal imperfect 3fs of the hollow root הום + *vav*-consecutive. The *vav* is explicative and specifies the "it" previously implied: "*It* came about ... *that* all the city murmured."[5] The lengthened preformative vowel in וַתֵּהֹם is due to the I-guttural

2. RJW §502.
3. Waltke and O'Connor call this a local accusative (WO §10.2.2b).
4. See Holmstedt, *Ruth*, 95.
5. RJW §434.

(ה) rejecting the *dāgēš forte* in the R1 of the Niphal. The thematic vowel is a result of the a-class vowel under the R1 contracting with the middle ו to make וֹ. This is the same *aw* ⟶ *ô* contraction as in I-ו verbs but is now in the middle of the word. In this particular verb, the contracted וֹ is written defectively in the final form (תֵּהֹם ⟵ תֵּהוֹם ⟵ תֵּהַוֹם).[6] Notice that the verb הום almost carries an onomatopoeic feel. It would be like the word "hum" in English. הום implies an uproar of sorts, but here the context does not seem to warrant a ruckus. Rather, the verb may be best understood as a general "hum" among the people as Naomi and Ruth entered through the city gates.[7] That the city was in an "uproar" is correct insofar as we understand the uproar to be one of inner turmoil and curiosity about Naomi's return. The verb does not connote riotous activity in Bethlehem upon Naomi's return.

כָּל־הָעִיר is the subject, and since עִיר is feminine, the verb is 3fs (וַתֵּהֹם). כָּל־הָעִיר is therefore a collective singular. Certainly, there were more people in the city than just one, and yet the sentence requires the singular verb.

The next prepositional phrase (עֲלֵיהֶן) communicates that the people were stirred "on account of them," Naomi and Ruth. Notice now, from the mouth of the narrator, the proper 2fp pronominal suffix is used (◌ֵיהֶן).

וַתֹּאמַ֖רְנָה הֲזֹ֥את נָעֳמִֽי׃

The final clause in verse 19 presents the question asked by the townswomen as they "murmur" about Naomi and Ruth. וַתֹּאמַרְנָה is a Qal imperfect 3fp of אמר + *vav*-consecutive. The *vav* is in temporal succession to show what happened after the city began to stir. With a 3fp verb, the implied subject "they" probably refers to the women of the city who are now asking the question, "Is this Naomi?"

הֲזֹאת נָעֳמִי begins with the interrogative הֲ. Remember that the interrogative points like the inseparable prepositions with a vocal *shewa*, but since ה is a guttural, it takes a composite *shewa* (הֲ) rather than the simple vocal *shewa*. Since Naomi is only one woman, the fs, near demonstrative pronoun (זאת) is used: "Is *this* Naomi?"

---

6. GKC §72v.

7. Cf. *NIDOTTE* 1:1018–20.

RUTH 1:20

וַתֹּ֥אמֶר אֲלֵיהֶ֖ן אַל־תִּקְרֶ֣אנָה לִ֑י נָעֳמִ֖י קְרֶ֣אןָ לִ֔י מָרָ֔א כִּי־הֵמַ֥ר שַׁדַּ֛י לִ֖י מְאֹֽד׃

ACCENT PHRASING

וַתֹּ֥אמֶר אֲלֵיהֶ֖ן
אַל־תִּקְרֶ֣אנָה לִ֑י נָעֳמִ֖י
קְרֶ֣אןָ לִ֔י מָרָ֔א
כִּי־הֵמַ֥ר שַׁדַּ֛י לִ֖י מְאֹֽד׃

וַתֹּ֥אמֶר אֲלֵיהֶ֖ן

Ruth 1:20 continues the narrative with וַתֹּ֥אמֶר, the Qal imperfect 3fs of אמר + *vav*-consecutive. The *vav* may be understood adversatively since the context indicates that Naomi will command the women *not* to call her נָעֳמִ֖י.[8] The adversative *vav* still advances the temporal succession notion of the *vav*-consecutive pattern. "*But* [*then*] she (Naomi) said to them." Naomi is the implied subject, and אֲלֵיהֶ֖ן marks the women as the recipients of what Naomi is going to say. אֲלֵיהֶ֖ן takes the pronominal suffixes of plural nouns (אֲלֵיהֶ֖ן) even though prepositions do not have grammatical number.

אַל־תִּקְרֶ֣אנָה לִ֑י נָעֳמִ֖י

אַל + the jussive is a negative command, "Do not call me Naomi." תִּקְרֶ֣אנָה is a Qal jussive 2fp of קרא. The ל preposition following קרא carries the sense of calling to someone. In that sense, it marks the direct object, "Do not call *me* ..." נָעֳמִ֖י is the accusative, specifying what she is requesting they *not* call her. The name נָעֳמִ֖י comes from the root נעם meaning "pleasant," so Naomi is playing on the meaning of her name, believing it is not an appropriate designation for her state in life.

קְרֶ֣אןָ לִ֔י מָרָ֔א

Next, Naomi tells the women of the city that they should call her מָרָ֔א. In fact, she commands it. קְרֶ֣אןָ is a Qal imperative 2fp of קרא, written

8. RJW §432.

defectively without the final ה.[9] As in the previous clause, the ל introduces the object. מָרָא is from the lexical form מַר and means "bitter."[10] The form is likely derived from the verbal root מרר, but the expected Hebrew form would be מרה (cf. Exod 15:23; 2 Sam 2:26; Ezek 27:30; Job 21:25; Prov 5:4). The א on the end may be an Aramaized form of the word.[11] Another explanation for מָרָא is that it is a diminutive indicating familiarity, fondness, or youthfulness. In English, this may be like adding a "-y" to the name Tom so that we get Tommy.[12] In this line of meaning, it may indicate Naomi's humility, highlighting her lowly position as one who is bitter. It may also refer to her relative youthfulness at the time her bitter life circumstances occurred. The most likely explanation is that it is an alternative spelling.

כִּי־הֵמַר שַׁדַּי לִי מְאֹד׃

The final clause is the reason why Naomi believes she should be called מָרָא. כִּי introduces the ground clause and הֵמַר is a Hiphil perfect 3ms of מרר. With the causative Hiphil, we get "[he] has caused bitterness ... to me." מרר is a geminate verb, and the morphology is similar to hollow verbs. However, rather than losing the middle consonant as in hollow verbs, geminate verbs may drop the doubled consonant and unite the R1 and R2 with the thematic vowel (here an a-class vowel, ַ◌). When the final consonant of the root is dropped, the original *ḥîreq* (ִ◌) preformative vowel lengthens to a *ṣērê* (ֵ◌) in an open pretonic syllable. The perfective of מרר is best understood as an English perfect, "*has caused* bitterness." The narrative has not yet clarified whether Naomi's bitterness has been alleviated even though the Lord has visited his people (1:6) and at least food provision is now available to Naomi and Ruth. The past action with continuing results is the very reason Naomi tells the women of the city to call her מָרָא. We do not know yet whether Naomi's bitterness has come to an end, but because

9. GKC §46f.

10. BDB, 600.

11. GKC §80h; JM §89k.

12. Wilch, *Ruth*, 40–41.

of her past experience, she continues to remember the bitter hand of the Lord that went out against her (1:13).

שַׁדַּי is the subject, and לִי once again introduces the object. מְאֹד adverbially modifies הֵמַר, and so an English translation would be "for the Almighty has caused *exceeding* bitterness to me." According to BDB, שַׁדַּי is an archaic divine name from the time of the patriarchs.[13] As a proper name, we may transliterate as "Shaddai," but in translation it would be rendered "Almighty," although that seems to be based on the LXX translation.[14] The actual meaning of the word is uncertain but may have been associated with mountains in the ancient Near East.

---

13. BDB, 995.
14. *NIDOTTE* 1:401. Targum Ruth preserves שדי in 1:20–21.

RUTH 1:21

אֲנִי֙ מְלֵאָ֣ה הָלַ֔כְתִּי וְרֵיקָ֖ם הֱשִׁיבַ֣נִי יְהוָ֑ה לָ֣מָּה תִקְרֶ֤אנָה לִי֙ נָעֳמִ֔י וַֽיהוָה֙ עָ֣נָה בִ֔י וְשַׁדַּ֖י הֵ֥רַֽע לִֽי׃

ACCENT PHRASING

אֲנִי֙ מְלֵאָ֣ה הָלַ֔כְתִּי
וְרֵיקָ֖ם הֱשִׁיבַ֣נִי יְהוָ֑ה
לָ֣מָּה תִקְרֶ֤אנָה לִי֙ נָעֳמִ֔י
וַֽיהוָה֙ עָ֣נָה בִ֔י
וְשַׁדַּ֖י הֵ֥רַֽע לִֽי׃

אֲנִי֙ מְלֵאָ֣ה הָלַ֔כְתִּי

Ruth 1:21 continues Naomi's conversation with the members of the city using a nominal clause with the subject (אֲנִי֙) fronted for focus. The narrative subject shifted to Naomi when she began to speak to the women of the city in the previous verse, but she now emphasizes how the Lord has dealt with her.

מְלֵאָ֣ה is an adverbial accusative of situation. The substantive adjective ("a full one") communicates "how" Naomi went out, adverbially modifying הָלַ֔כְתִּי. The adverbial accusative of situation translates, "I went out *in the status* of one who was full." הָלַ֔כְתִּי is a Qal perfect 1cs of הלך and is translated as a simple past, the perfective communicating a completed action. In the perfect, הלך morphs as a strong verb.

וְרֵיקָ֖ם הֱשִׁיבַ֣נִי יְהוָ֑ה

The *vav* on וְרֵיקָ֖ם is an adversative *vav*. With the contrast between מְלֵאָה and רֵיקָ֖ם, the *vav* is translated "but." As in the previous clause, the narrator moves the adverbial modifier, רֵיקָ֖ם, to the front for emphasis. "*But empty* the Lord caused me to return." The ◌ָם ending on רֵיקָ֖ם may be a vestige of a old morphological marker for adverbs. It is sometimes added to words making them adverbs, similarly to how English adds "-ly" to create adverbs.[15]

15. GKC §100g; cf. אֻמְנָם in Gen 18:13; אָמְנָה in Gen 20:12, which is preserved as אָמְנָם in the Syriac; יוֹמָם in Exod 13:21–22; etc.

הֱשִׁיבַנִי is a Hiphil perfect 3ms of שׁוב with a 1cs object suffix. Without the pronominal suffix, the form would have a *ṣērê* in the preformative (הֵשִׁיב). However, with a pronominal suffix, the accent shifts down the word to the ב, leaving the preformative of the Hiphil in an open pro-pretonic syllable. As a result, the original *ṣērê* reduces to a vocal *shewa*. Since gutturals do not take simple vocal *shewa*s, it becomes a composite *shewa* of the same vowel class as the original preformative (ֱ). יְהוָה is the subject or, with the causative Hiphil, the agent causing Naomi's return. "Empty the Lord caused me to return."

Whether intentional or not, Ruth 1:21a has two parallel lines that could classify it as poetic.[16] אֲנִי parallels and contrasts with יהוה. מְלֵאָה parallels and contrasts רֵיקָם. And הָלַכְתִּי parallels and contrasts הֱשִׁיבַנִי. There is no reason to believe that Naomi spoke any other words than these, but the narrator certainly retained the poetic nature of Naomi's discussion with the townswomen.

Ironically, Naomi says she went away "full" during a famine, but now that the Lord has visited his people "to give to them food" (1:6; לָתֵת לָהֶם לָחֶם), she says that she has returned "empty." Naomi attributes her empty return to the hand of the Lord and to the Almighty bringing "calamity" on her (וְשַׁדַּי הֵרַע לִי), but she fails to mention his visiting his people to provide for them and to bring her and Ruth back to Bethlehem. Likewise, Naomi fails to mention that Ruth has journeyed with her and so she is not completely empty. While Naomi's circumstance is indeed dire, she fails to recognize God's goodness to her. The question for the reader who may not yet be familiar with the text of Ruth is whether Ruth will turn out to be a blessing. The narrative seems to indicate that Ruth will prove to be a blessing for Naomi, but if one is unfamiliar with this story, Naomi's lack of hope and her dismissal of God's kindness to her through Ruth may cause one to question how Ruth will play into the rest of the story. In a narratively intriguing way, the author uses Naomi's bitterness to elicit suspense about how/if Ruth will bless Naomi. As it turns out, Ruth will provide for Naomi not just food (3:17) but a son (4:14–16).

---

16. See discussion in Block, *Ruth*, 103–4.

לָ֣מָּה תִקְרֶ֤אנָה לִי֙ נָעֳמִ֔י

Naomi now asks a rhetorical question for emphatic effect. She does not intend to get an answer.[17] She expects to make a point to the townswomen that there is no reason for them to call her נָעֳמִ֔י (as noted earlier the name comes from the root נעם meaning "pleasant"). תִקְרֶ֤אנָה is a Qal imperfect 2fp of קרא translated modally, "Why *would/might* you call."[18] ל introduces the object, as has been the case in each of these naming formulas in verse 20 (קרא ... ל [אַל־]). נָעֳמִ֔י is the accusative, identifying specifically the name they should not call her. In light of Naomi's perceived bitter circumstances, her exclamatory rhetorical question proves the point. There is no reason the townswomen should call her Naomi.

וַֽיהוָה֙ עָ֣נָה בִ֔י

The *vav* with וַֽיהוָה֙ provides circumstantial information with a causal nuance. The *vav* is circumstantial because it provides additional information of what Yahweh has done: "*And* the Lord testified against me." However, this statement is logically subordinate to what precedes as a restatement of God's actions against Naomi (cf. 1:20; כִּי־הֵמַ֥ר שַׁדַּ֛י לִ֖י מְאֹֽד) and is the logical ground for her argument that the townswomen would call her מָרָא. The *vav* then is best translated "for": "Why would you call me Naomi, *for* Yahweh has testified against me ... ?"

The subject is יהוה and is fronted for emphasis. With יהוה fronted, the contrast is conspicuous between Naomi (אֲנִי in the first clause of the verse) and the Lord. In spite of her painful emotions, Naomi demonstrates her understanding that the Lord is in control of her situation even though it is dire. עָ֣נָה is a Qal perfect 3ms of ענה. When combined with the ב preposition, עָ֣נָה often takes a judicial feel, "he *testified* against me."[19]

17. JM §161a.

18. For the interrogative לָ֣מָּה, see JM §161h.

19. BDB, 773.

וְשַׁדַּי הֵרַע לִי׃

The *vav* on וְשַׁדַּי joins these last two clauses, giving Naomi's comments an element of parallelism, creating a short poetic lament. הֵרַע is a Hiphil perfect 3ms of רעע. רעע often takes a preposition as the object marker (here a ל) since one would do evil "against" (ב, עַל) or "to" (ל) someone.[20] יהוה is parallel to שַׁדַּי, and so this second clause compounds the Lord's actions against Naomi, identifying them as "evil" or "calamity."

The parallelism of the names יהוה with שַׁדַּי suggests that Naomi is not referring to a generic deity in ancient Near Eastern culture when using שַׁדַּי. Rather, she identifies שַׁדַּי as יהוה. The verbs used here suggest that יהוה executes justice as he "testifies (עָנָה) against" Naomi but that his testimony against her is within the confines of his omnipotent control even over calamity (רַע). In light of Naomi's struggles with bitterness, she seems to understand that both good and calamity come from Yahweh. As for so many who face hardship, it is one thing to know this truth and to say it out loud; it is quite another thing to allow these truths to bring comfort. Naomi seems to understand that her situation is from the Lord, but rather than this truth drawing her to find comfort in Yahweh, it drives her to bitterness and despair. Again, we cannot dismiss Naomi's dire situation. However, as we begin to see Ruth and Boaz keep covenant faithfulness through gleaning stipulations, we must be aware of the contrast between Naomi's bitter reaction at what Yahweh has dealt and Ruth's persistence in clinging to Yahweh.

---

20. BDB, 949.

RUTH 1:22

וַתָּ֣שָׁב נָעֳמִ֗י וְר֨וּת הַמּוֹאֲבִיָּ֤ה כַלָּתָהּ֙ עִמָּ֔הּ הַשָּׁ֖בָה מִשְּׂדֵ֣י מוֹאָ֑ב וְהֵ֗מָּה בָּ֚אוּ בֵּ֣ית לֶ֔חֶם בִּתְחִלַּ֖ת קְצִ֥יר שְׂעֹרִֽים׃

ACCENT PHRASING

וַתָּ֣שָׁב נָעֳמִ֗י
וְר֨וּת הַמּוֹאֲבִיָּ֤ה כַלָּתָהּ֙ עִמָּ֔הּ
הַשָּׁ֖בָה מִשְּׂדֵ֣י מוֹאָ֑ב
וְהֵ֗מָּה בָּ֚אוּ בֵּ֣ית לֶ֔חֶם בִּתְחִלַּ֖ת קְצִ֥יר שְׂעֹרִֽים׃

וַתָּ֣שָׁב נָעֳמִ֗י וְר֨וּת הַמּוֹאֲבִיָּ֤ה כַלָּתָהּ֙ עִמָּ֔הּ

Ruth 1:22 summarizes the first chapter as a fitting conclusion. The *vav* on וַתָּ֣שָׁב may be called a "summarizing *vav*," although a technical name for it is unnecessary. The translation even as a summary statement would be "And so … ," just without the nuance of logical succession.[21] נָעֳמִ֗י is the subject, and the clause breaks here before moving on to Ruth because of the disjunctive *revîa* accent (◌֗). וַתָּ֣שָׁב is a Qal imperfect 3fs of שׁוב + *vav*-consecutive (without consecutive meaning). Notice that in the hollow roots with a *vav*-consecutive, the accent retracts to the preformative. Hence, the ◌ָ symbol under the שׁ is a *qāmeṣ-ḥāṭûf*. The normal thematic vowel of the Qal imperfect of hollow roots would be a long *ḥōlem*, but when the accent retracts, the final syllable is closed and unaccented, resulting in a short vowel, *qāmeṣ-ḥāṭûf*.

The next *vav* on וְר֨וּת is additive, or a *vav* of accompaniment.[22] Naomi returned "*along with* Ruth." As noted, the disjunctive *revîa* (◌֗) accent separates וַתָּ֣שָׁב נָעֳמִ֗י as the main clause before continuing with the full subject phrase. However, since the verb is singular, the formal subject can only be נָעֳמִ֗י with וְר֨וּת as an additive.

21. JM §118i.

22. RJW §436.

The next two words (הַמּוֹאֲבִיָּה כַלָּתָהּ) are appositional, further describing Ruth. Notice that both הַמּוֹאֲבִיָּה and כַלָּתָהּ are fs now that Orpah is gone. הַמּוֹאֲבִיָּה is a gentilic appositional modifier, further explaining something about Ruth, and hence it is explicative apposition. הַמּוֹאֲבִיָּה further specifies Ruth as a "Moabitess."

Following the *vav* of accompaniment, the rest of the subject phrase could be understood as a verbless clause, "Ruth, the Moabitess, her daughter-in-law [*was*] with her." The prepositional phrase עִמָּהּ in this case is a prepositional phrase communicating *where* Ruth is.

Notice the assonance in the last three words (הַמּוֹאֲבִיָּה כַלָּתָהּ עִמָּהּ) drawing attention to the fact that the foreign daughter-in-law Ruth was "with" Naomi. The previous scenes have depicted a small internal battle between Naomi and her daughters-in-law, and yet Ruth has clung to Naomi throughout. As with the alliteration at 1:6 (לָתֵת לָהֶם לָחֶם), which initiated their return to Bethlehem, the narrator now uses assonance to highlight that Ruth is indeed with Naomi. If we press the significance a bit further, the terms that are assonant speak powerfully to the current situation. Naomi is in despair (and rightly so), and yet she has a "daughter-in-law" (כַלָּתָהּ), who is a "Moabitess" (הַמּוֹאֲבִיָּה), who is indeed "with her" (עִמָּהּ). This is an unexpected situation, and one that may not bring additional hope in Naomi's mind. Even so, the audience realizes that Ruth is going to be a key actress in the screenplay who may yet have more up her sleeve to bring about comfort for Naomi.

הַשָּׁבָה מִשְּׂדֵי מוֹאָב

הַשָּׁבָה is an odd verbal form that deserves attention. This verb carries a significant number of challenges morphologically and text critically. As it stands, the verb is a Qal perfect 3fs of שׁוּב with the accent (◌֫) on the שׁ. The alternative parsing would be a Qal participle fs, but in hollow verbs (שׁוּב) we would expect the accent to be on the final syllable in the participle (שָׁבָ֫ה). The placement of the accent makes this verb clearly a Qal perfect 3fs.

The difficulty is that if it is a Qal perfect, this is an occurrence of a Qal perfect with the definite article (הַ◌). Some read the definite article as a relative use of the definite article and the verb therefore functions as a relative clause modifying Ruth: "… *who* returned from the field of Moab."[23] Read this way, the verbal nuance is perfective, which fits the context well. Ruth has indeed "returned" already with Naomi from Moab; she is not in the process of returning (e.g., the durative nuance of a participle).

However, if we recognize that the Masoretes added both the vowel pointing and accent marks to a consonantal original, the intended form could originally have been a participle (השבה) with the context determining the perfective past tense. Read this way, the form is a Qal participle fs with the definite article modifying וְר֣וּת as "the one who return(ed) from the field of Moab." It is possible in this case that the Masoretes accented what is likely a participle in the consonantal text as a Qal perfect (שָׁ֫בָה) to clarify the intended tense of the verb. This apparently odd accentuation brings clarity to the text so that the form communicates that Ruth has already returned from the field of Moab, rather than a mistaken interpretation that Ruth is currently returning from Moab as if she delayed her "clinging" to Naomi.

מִשְּׂדֵ֣י מוֹאָ֑ב is a locative prepositional phrase describing from where Ruth returned. See 1:1, 6 for explanations of the morphology and logical relationship in the construct package מִשְּׂדֵ֣י מוֹאָ֑ב.

וְהֵ֗מָּה בָּ֚אוּ בֵּ֣ית לֶ֔חֶם בִּתְחִלַּ֖ת קְצִ֥יר שְׂעֹרִֽים׃

This final clause of Ruth 1 retells to where Naomi and Ruth came but also adds when they arrived in Bethlehem. With וְהֵ֗מָּה fronted, the clause focuses on Ruth and Naomi together, "they." The form is masculine (הֵמָּה), but like before, this is likely another example of an archaic dual form. The pronoun now sets Naomi and Ruth as coactresses or coagents in the narrative.[24] בָּ֚אוּ is a Qal perfect 3cp of the root בוא. As a perfective verb, it expresses a simple past action, "[they] came." בֵּ֣ית לֶ֔חֶם is an adverbial accusative of place limiting the verbal action ("entering") to a specific location, "they came [*to*] *Bethlehem*."

23. For examples, see GKC §138k; RJW §91. Cf. JM §145e; WO §19.7d.

24. Holmstedt, *Ruth*, 101.

The ב on בִּתְחִלַּת is a temporal ב, "*at* [the time of] the beginning." Notice the final three words are one long construct package. בִּתְחִלַּת is fs construct with the ending ◌ַת. We know that קְצִיר is construct because of the reduction of the vowel under the ק to a vocal *shewa*. The lexical form is קָצִיר. Additionally, the *mêrĕkā* accent (◌֥) on קְצִ֥יר distinguishes it as a construct form. שְׂעֹרִים is an absolute noun since it is the ending noun of this long construct package. The final prepositional phrase, then, is "at the beginning of the harvest of barley." The last two words, קְצִ֥יר שְׂעֹרִֽים, form a construct package with an implied adjectival meaning.[25] A "harvest of barley" is a "barley harvest," in which שְׂעֹרִים describes the type of harvest.

25. *GBHS* §2.2.5

1 Now, to Naomi (there was) a relative of her husband, a man, mighty of (moral) worth,
from the clan of Elimelech, and his name (was) Boaz. 2 Now Ruth, the Moabitess, said
to Naomi, "Let me go now, and let me glean among the sheaves after which I may
find favor in his eyes." And she said to her, "Go, my daughter." 3 And she went, and
she came, and she gleaned in the field after the reapers. And her chance chanced (it
just so happened) a portion of the field (belonging) to Boaz who was from the clan
of Elimelech.

RUTH

2:1–3

1 וּֽלְנָעֳמִ֞י מְיֻדָּ֣ע לְאִישָׁ֗הּ אִ֚ישׁ גִּבּ֣וֹר חַ֔יִל מִמִּשְׁפַּ֖חַת אֱלִימֶ֑לֶךְ וּשְׁמ֖וֹ בֹּֽעַז׃
2 וַתֹּאמֶר֩ ר֨וּת הַמּוֹאֲבִיָּ֜ה אֶֽל־נָעֳמִ֗י אֵֽלְכָה־נָּ֤א הַשָּׂדֶה֙ וַאֲלַקֳטָ֣ה בַשִּׁבֳּלִ֔ים אַחַ֕ר
אֲשֶׁ֥ר אֶמְצָא־חֵ֖ן בְּעֵינָ֑יו וַתֹּ֥אמֶר לָ֖הּ לְכִ֥י בִתִּֽי׃ 3 וַתֵּ֤לֶךְ וַתָּבוֹא֙ וַתְּלַקֵּ֣ט בַּשָּׂדֶ֔ה
אַחֲרֵ֖י הַקֹּצְרִ֑ים וַיִּ֣קֶר מִקְרֶ֔הָ חֶלְקַ֤ת הַשָּׂדֶה֙ לְבֹ֔עַז אֲשֶׁ֖ר מִמִּשְׁפַּ֥חַת אֱלִימֶֽלֶךְ׃

RUTH 2:1

וְלְנָעֳמִ֗י מְיֻדָּ֣ע לְאִישָׁ֔הּ אִ֚ישׁ גִּבּ֣וֹר חַ֔יִל מִמִּשְׁפַּ֖חַת אֱלִימֶ֑לֶךְ וּשְׁמ֖וֹ בֹּֽעַז׃

ACCENT PHRASING

וְלְנָעֳמִ֗י מְיֻדָּ֣ע לְאִישָׁ֔הּ
אִ֚ישׁ גִּבּ֣וֹר חַ֔יִל
מִמִּשְׁפַּ֖חַת אֱלִימֶ֑לֶךְ
וּשְׁמ֖וֹ בֹּֽעַז׃

וְלְנָעֳמִ֗י מְיֻדָּ֣ע לְאִישָׁ֔הּ מוֹדַע ק

The opening *vav* is disjunctive, not consecutive.[1] Therefore, the *vav* introduces circumstantial information that is vital to the narrative but is not part of the primary action. For the prepositional phrase, we get "Now, to Naomi …" The ל preposition is possessive, indicating that this relative (מְיֻדָּע) "belonged to" Naomi.

As it is pointed in the LHB, מְיֻדָּע is a Pual participle of ידע meaning "one who is known." However, the scribes included a *qere* in the margin of the MT with the typical noun form for "relative" (מוֹדַע),[2] indicating that the Pual participle should be understood as a substantive noun. "One who is known" is a "relative" in this case. The LXX translates, Καὶ τῇ Νωεμιν ἀνὴρ γνώριμος τῷ ἀνδρὶ αὐτῆς, "Now to Naomi (was) a man acquainted with her husband." Targum Ruth 2:1 translates with an Ištaphel perfect 3ms (אשתמודע), maintaining the passive/reflective meaning "one who was known/recognized." The Vulgate uses the term *cōnsanguineus* (adjective meaning "of the same blood, kindred") but relates this "kindred" to Elimelech, not Naomi. None of these versions provide solid conclusions

1. WO §39.2.3c. Remember that the *vav*, other than the *vav*-consecutive, points with a *šûreq* (וּ) before a simple vocal *shewa* (*IBH*, 37).

2. This noun also occurs in Prov 7:4 written defectively (מֹדָע).

about how to render the *ketiv/qere* here, but the idea across all versions is certainly that the narrator is introducing someone related to Naomi.[3]

The prepositional phrase לְאִישָׁהּ is possessive. The idea is that Naomi had a relative "of [*belonging to*] her husband." לְאִישָׁהּ indicates the side of the family that this relative belonged to.[4]

אִ֚ישׁ גִּבֹּ֣ור חַ֔יִל

This phrase functions appositionally to the previous clause and further defines the מְיֻדָּע of Naomi. Robin Wakley mentions the difficulty of translating גִּבּוֹר when combined with חָיִל.[5] On the basis of the Masoretic accents here, I would propose "a man, mighty of ability." This translation understands אִ֚ישׁ as the head noun, and then גִּבֹּ֣ור חַ֔יִל as a construct package appositionally modifying אִ֚ישׁ. Adjectives (like גִּבֹּ֣ור) are often understood as descriptive nouns that, when put together with a governing noun, further describe that governing noun.[6] Here גִּבֹּ֣ור חַ֔יִל modifies אִ֚ישׁ. גִּבֹּ֣ור is clearly in construct with חַ֔יִל because of the conjunctive accent *mûnaḥ* (◌֣). The accent on אִ֚ישׁ is a disjunctive *yĕtîv* (◌֚). *Yĕtîv* is distinguished from the conjunctive *mĕhuppaḥ* because the *yĕtîv* is a prepositive, meaning it occurs in front of the accented syllable. אִ֚ישׁ is monosyllabic, and therefore we must deterimine the accent pattern by other means. In the larger verse, the major accent break is at אֱלִימֶ֑לֶךְ with the *atnāḥ*. Within the *atnāḥ* segment, the near subordinate disjunctive accent is the *ṭifḥā* on מִמִּשְׁפַּ֖חַת, and the far subordinate disjunctive accent is the *zāqēf qāṭôn* on חַ֔יִל. In the *zāqēf* segment, the near subordinate is a *pašṭā*, but one will notice we do not have a *pašṭā* in the verse. The word on which we would expect a *pašṭā* is אִ֚ישׁ, but instead we get the *yĕtîv*. Since the *yĕtîv* can replace the *pašṭā*, then we have concluded once again that the ◌֚ accent is indeed a *yĕtîv*, not a *mĕhuppaḥ*.

---

3. Ellis R. Brotzman and Eric J. Tully, *Old Testament Textual Criticism: A Practical Introduction*, 2nd ed. (Grand Rapids: Baker Academic, 2016), 150.

4. For a לְ essentially making a construct package, see GKC §129a–g. Gesenius calls this "Expression of the Genitive by Circumlocution."

5. *NIDOTTE* 1:810–11.

6. *IBHS* §23a–e.

The difference this makes to the understanding of אִישׁ גִּבּוֹר חַיִל may seem tangential, but I believe it is significant.

In light of this discussion of the accents, the phrase in question means "a man, mighty of ability." Read in this way, גִּבּוֹר חַיִל forms a construct package that modifies אִישׁ as a whole. The logical relationship between חַיִל and גִּבּוֹר is best understood as an implied ל of specification.[7] In other words, this man's (Boaz's) גִּבּוֹר ("might") is specifically in the realm of חַיִל ("ability"). He is "mighty of ability." BDB defines חַיִל as "ability, efficiency, *often involving moral worth*."[8] Boaz's "moral worth" is exactly the point, and so "a man, mighty of (moral) worth" is the best translation. This understanding avoids understanding Boaz merely as a wealthy landowner or a strong warrior. He may indeed be those things, but the text does not indicate such. Instead, we will see Boaz's moral valiance displayed in the remainder of the narrative. He is indeed an אִישׁ גִּבּוֹר חַיִל. We will see a similar description of Ruth (חַיִל) later in the book (3:11), indicating that both of the main characters were of worthy character.[9]

מִמִּשְׁפַּחַת אֱלִימֶלֶךְ

This prepositional phrase continues to describe Naomi's relative (מְיֻדָּע). The preposition מִן points normally on מִשְׁפַּחַת with the *ḥîreq* and then the *dāgēš forte* in the following consonant (מִמִּשְׁפַּחַת).

מִמִּשְׁפַּחַת אֱלִימֶלֶךְ is a construct package communicating an implied ל of possession.[10] The two nouns create one unit of meaning. The "clan *of* Elimelech" is one thing. This is the clan "of" Elimelech in the sense of the clan "belonging to" Elimelech, and hence the implied ל of possession.

7. RJW §273a.

8. BDB, 298 (italics added); despite some lexical entries classifying this phrase from 2:1 under a meaning like "warrior," there seems to be no reason to view Boaz as a military figure.

9. For the rich and nuanced meaning of חַיִל, see *NIDOTTE* 2:116–26; Block, *Ruth*, 116; Tamara Cohn Eskenazi and Tikva Simone Frymer-Kensky, *Ruth: The Traditional Hebrew Text with the New JPS Translation*, The JPS Bible Commentary (Philadelphia: Jewish Publication Society, 2011), 28.

10. *IBHS* §12e.

וּשְׁמ֖וֹ בֹּֽעַז׃

In a stroke of literary genius, the name of this relative is delayed in the sentence (cf. the effective literary delay of אֶפְרָתִ֔ים in 1:2). The *atnāḥ* (֑), the major disjunctive accent in the verse, is delayed until אֱלִימֶ֑לֶךְ, raising the suspense of who this man, mighty of (moral) worth, is. After the anticipatory delay, his name is finally revealed in a verbless clause in which we supply the English "to be" verb, "and his name [*was*] Boaz."

Chapter 2 opens by introducing Boaz, but Boaz will not come onto the stage until verses 3 and 4 when Ruth happens onto his field and he begins a dialogue. It is as if the narrator could not wait to introduce Boaz even though his arrival in the narrative would not come for a few more verses. This literary beauty highlights the importance of Boaz in the narrative, especially when combined with all the descriptors from verse 1 telling us how perfectly Boaz fit the necessary characteristic of one who would (could) redeem Ruth and Naomi. He was a family member (מְיֻדָּע) and a man mighty of moral worth (אִ֚ישׁ גִּבּ֣וֹר חַ֔יִל). At this point, Naomi has not considered this man as a redeemer for her bitterness. Soon his status will be known to her (2:19–23), but the audience already knows where this narrative is headed. There is a man in Bethlehem who is able to redeem Ruth and Naomi, and it sounds like his character is such that he will be eager to do so.

RUTH 2:2

וַתֹּאמֶר֩ ר֨וּת הַמּוֹאֲבִיָּ֜ה אֶֽל־נָעֳמִ֗י אֵֽלְכָה־נָּ֤א הַשָּׂדֶה֙ וַאֲלַקֳטָ֣ה בַשִׁבֳּלִ֔ים אַחַ֕ר
אֲשֶׁ֥ר אֶמְצָא־חֵ֖ן בְּעֵינָ֑יו וַתֹּ֥אמֶר לָ֖הּ לְכִ֥י בִתִּֽי׃

ACCENT PHRASING

וַתֹּאמֶר֩ ר֨וּת הַמּוֹאֲבִיָּ֜ה אֶֽל־נָעֳמִ֗י
אֵֽלְכָה־נָּ֤א הַשָּׂדֶה֙
וַאֲלַקֳטָ֣ה בַשִׁבֳּלִ֔ים
אַחַ֕ר אֲשֶׁ֥ר אֶמְצָא־חֵ֖ן בְּעֵינָ֑יו
וַתֹּ֥אמֶר לָ֖הּ לְכִ֥י בִתִּֽי׃

וַתֹּאמֶר֩ ר֨וּת הַמּוֹאֲבִיָּ֜ה אֶֽל־נָעֳמִ֗י

וַתֹּאמֶר֩ is a Qal imperfect 2fs of אמר with a *vav*-consecutive continuing the flow of the narrative. Remember that אמר is a special case R1-א verb and the preformative vowel *ḥîreq* becomes a *ḥōlem* in the imperfect paradigm. The R1-א quiesces, leaving וַתֹּאמֶר֩.

ר֨וּת is the subject, and הַמּוֹאֲבִיָּ֜ה is the gentilic appositional modifier. This is another example of explicative apposition. Hence, the full subject phrase is "Ruth, the Moabitess." See 1:22 for the discussion on apposition.

אֶֽל־נָעֳמִ֗י is the prepositional complement describing to whom Ruth was speaking.

אֵֽלְכָה־נָּ֤א הַשָּׂדֶה֙

אֵֽלְכָה is a Qal cohortative 1cs of הלך. The cohortative derives from the imperfect paradigm. To create the cohortative, one adds ָה to the end of imperfect 1cs and then reduces the thematic vowel (R2) to a vocal *shewa*.[11] With הלך, the R1-ה morphs like an R1-ו and so the ה drops out of the imperfect (cohortative) and the 1cs preformative vowel (ִ) lengthens to a *ṣērê*

11. The reduction of the thematic vowel is due to the addition of the vocalic ending to the cohortative. In verbs with sufformatives that are *only* a vowel (ִי, ָה, וּ), the general tendency is for the R2 thematic vowel to reduce to a vocal *shewa*. See *IBH*, 104–5.

(compensatory lengthening). The cohortative + נָּא often communicates the idea of a request or permission. The *dāgēš conjunctivum* in נָּא is also known as a *dĕḥîq*, a dot used to mark an extremely close connection between two words (cf. 1:8; 1:10).[12]

Daniel Block proposes a construction put forth by Thomas Lambdin that describes the נָא particle as denoting "that the command in question is a logical consequence, either of an immediately preceding statement or of the general situation in which it is uttered."[13] Here the desire "to go" and "to glean" is the logical consequence of the surrounding context. In this sense, the use of נָא makes this cohortative a strong desire for Ruth. Block interprets the cohortative + נָא as "the declaration of an idea that entered her mind (in effect, 'I think I should go ...') or a strong desire, ('I would like to go ...')."[14]

The strength of Block's proposal is that it shows Ruth's eagerness to provide for Naomi, as if she is taking on the mantle of caring for the widow even though she has experienced similar loss herself. The weakness of this interpretation is that this does not seem to be the conventional use of the נָא particle.[15] The hinge point, explained by Waltke and O'Connor, is whether the one requesting permission can perform the action even without the permission of the one asked.[16] In other words, if Ruth is able to go and glean without Naomi's permission, then Block's proposal for this use of נָא is fitting. If, however, Ruth must get Naomi's permission, then נָא is a polite but strong request. The conclusion here must certainly be one of interpretation, but given the respect, submission, and loyalty Ruth has shown to Naomi thus far, it is difficult to imagine Ruth declaring a strong desire and then taking off to accomplish it without Naomi's permission. Perhaps she does not *need* Naomi's permission to actually accomplish the

12. For the *dĕḥîq* particularly with נָא, see GKC §18i.

13. Block, *Ruth*, 117; quote from Thomas O. Lambdin, *Introduction to Biblical Hebrew* (New York: Charles Scribner's Sons, 1971), 170.

14. Block, *Ruth*, 117.

15. *IBHS* §4n; GKC §108c; JM §§105c, 114d.

16. WO §34.7a.

"going" and "gleaning," but it seems that she *wants* it. Therefore, I would argue, this construction conveys a request for permission to go to the field.

הַשָּׂדֶה is an adverbial accusative of place. It limits the verb regarding place. In the translation, we supply the word "to" in order for the adverbial accusative nuance to be explicit. However, in this particular construction, Hebrew does not require the ל preposition or the preposition אֶל־ to communicate what in English is a prepositional phrase. While the verbiage of "accusative" may seem out of place, Hebrew has what is called a directive ה that functions syntactically the same way.[17] The directive ה is an unaccented ◌ָה that indicates direction ("to/toward"). While it cannot be proven, the directive ה may be a remnant of an old morphological system for marking this adverbial (accusative) function.[18] In this instance with הַשָּׂדֶה, either the morphological marker (◌ָה) has dropped out, or because of the prior presence of ◌ֶה, the morphological marker is absent. Either way, הַשָּׂדֶה functions as an adverbial accusative to mark direction, "to the field(s)."

וַאֲלַקֳטָה[19] בַשִּׁבֳּלִים

וַאֲלַקֳטָה is a Piel cohortative 1cs of לקט + conjunctive *vav*. The conjunctive *vav* simply joins this verbal predicate to the preceding one (אֵלְכָה־נָּא), making a compound predicate, "Let me go ... *and* let me glean." The *vav* is conjunctive in this case because the *vav*-consecutive would point like the definite article when attached to the imperfective conjugation (וַ◌ּ). With אֲ in the initial position, the *vav*-consecutive would have pointed as וָאֲלַקֳטָה, with the א rejecting the *dāgēš forte* (וַאֲלַקֳטָה ⟵ וָאֲלַקֳטָה). However, the current vowel pointing demonstrates an original vocal *shewa* (וְ, "normal" for the conjunctive *vav*) that has become a short vowel because of its juxtaposition with another vocal *shewa* (וְאֲלַקֳטָה ⟵ וַאֲלַקֳטָה). In the case of the composite *shewa*s, the vowel produced from this "*shewa* fight" is the corresponding

17. RJW §61–62; *BHRG* §28; JM §93c–d; WO §10.5b.

18. See especially GKC §90a, c for discussions of the ending as an archaic marker of the accusative case.

19. *BHQ* preserves this form with a *dāgēš forte* in the ט, following the Leningrad Codex (וַאֲלַקֳטָּה). The apparatus comments that this form may be in error and provides the form in the Aleppo Codex and M^{Y} (Ms. 1753) without the *dāgēš* in the ט (וַאֲלַקֳטָה).

vowel of the same vowel class. In this case, it is a *pataḥ*. Again, the cohortative gives the nuance of permission (modal; "let me") and the *vav* continues the previous request: "and let me glean."

Another interesting feature of וַאֲלַקֳטָה is the composite *shewa* under the nonguttural ק. Joüon calls this a "nuanced *shewa*" and suggests that it occurs when the word needs a "slightly stronger" vowel sound than a simple vocal *shewa*.[20] The choice of which composite *shewa* to use does not necessarily follow the expected vowel class of the verb. Here the Piel thematic vowel should be a *ṣērê* in the cohortative 1cs, but the e-class composite *shewa* (ֱ) is rarely used as a "nuanced *shewa*." Therefore, one should not make much of the o-class thematic vowel in a Piel (ֳ); it seems to simply be the vowel chosen to give this word a "slightly stronger" vowel sound.

בַשִּׁבֳּלִים is a prepositional phrase complement providing the location where Ruth is requesting to glean—namely, "among the sheaves." The ב preposition is difficult but is best translated spatially as "among."[21] The spatial notion does not necessarily indicate that Ruth desires to glean from the sheaves themselves. Gleaners would likely glean from the edges of the field, not from the choice harvest that had already been bundled into sheaves (Lev 19:9, 10; 23:22). However, one has to imagine that gleaning among the leftovers would at least put someone "among" the sheaves. Notice that the text presents another example of a nonguttural taking a composite *shewa* (ב in שִׁבֳּלִים).

אַחַר אֲשֶׁר אֶמְצָא־חֵן בְּעֵינָיו

This phrase translates literally as "after which I may find favor in his eyes." To make this phrase clear in English, we must move the resumptive pronoun (ָיו) attached to בְּעֵינָיו to the front of the relative clause and say, "after *him* in whose eyes I may find favor."[22] אַחַר is most likely a temporal adverb

20. JM §9b, d. Gesenius (GKC §10g) discusses extensively the use of composite *shewas* under nongutturals.

21. See discussion in Holmstedt, *Ruth*, 107–8, though he argues that a spatial ב seems least likely from the options.

22. JM §145a.

here. The order of harvest was such that the men would reap the harvest, the women would bundle the sheaves, and then the gleaners would gather what was left. This implies that the gleaners are temporally "after."

אֶמְצָא is a Qal imperfect 1cs of מצא. The verbal nuance is modal, providing the idea of expectation, "I *may* find favor in his eyes." It is unlikely at this point that Ruth has a particular person in mind in whose field she seeks to glean. Given her allegiance to Yahweh and her many years with Naomi, Ruth is hopeful that someone in Bethlehem will show favor to their family according to torah. She is a widow and a foreigner, someone who according to torah should certainly be cared for (cf. Deut 24:20; 26:12). At this point, Ruth shows more faith in Yahweh than does Naomi. Ironically, that faith was likely grounded in what Naomi had taught Ruth over the years while in Moab together.

וַתֹּ֥אמֶר לָ֖הּ לְכִ֥י בִתִּֽי׃

וַתֹּאמֶר is a Qal imperfect 3fs of אמר + *vav*-consecutive resuming the narrative to introduce Naomi's reply to Ruth. The *vav* is in temporal succession, communicating that Naomi spoke these words after Ruth completed her request to glean.

לְכִי is a Qal imperative 2fs of הלך. In the imperative of הלך, the ה drops. The imperative is formed from the imperfect paradigm, and in the imperfect, the 2fs would have been תֵּלְכִי. To create the imperative from this form, we remove the preformative just as we would when creating the imperative in other situations. In the 2fs imperative, the sufformative is ִי, and since it is a vocalic ending, the R2 thematic vowel reduces to a vocal *shewa*. Because of the loss of the preformative *and* the I-ה of the root, this reduced thematic vowel is now under the first letter of the form written (לְכִי).

בִתִּי is a vocative address. Combined with the verb, this becomes "Go, my daughter." Naomi's reply is terse and to the point. We have to be careful about overcharacterization based on assumptions, but it may be that Naomi's quick reply without any hesitation is a note of hope. So far Naomi has countered nearly everything that might bring her hope with some sort of bitter reply. Here, however, either she has given in and will just let life play out as Yahweh would have it, or she sees in Ruth a glimmer of hope that might bring a redeemer into their family to provide what they need. Remember that the audience already knows Boaz is in Bethlehem, but the narrative is unclear whether Naomi knows this. Naomi's words, "Go, my daughter," may express endearment and hope. Finally, someone has given Naomi something to hope for even if it is just the prospect of dinner for the evening via gleaning practices.

RUTH 2:3

וַתֵּ֣לֶךְ וַתָּב֗וֹא וַתְּלַקֵּ֤ט בַּשָּׂדֶה֙ אַחֲרֵ֣י הַקֹּצְרִ֑ים וַיִּ֣קֶר מִקְרֶ֔הָ חֶלְקַ֤ת הַשָּׂדֶה֙ לְבֹ֔עַז
אֲשֶׁ֖ר מִמִּשְׁפַּ֥חַת אֱלִימֶֽלֶךְ׃

ACCENT PHRASING

וַתֵּ֣לֶךְ וַתָּב֗וֹא וַתְּלַקֵּ֤ט בַּשָּׂדֶה֙
אַחֲרֵ֣י הַקֹּצְרִ֑ים
וַיִּ֣קֶר מִקְרֶ֔הָ
חֶלְקַ֤ת הַשָּׂדֶה֙ לְבֹ֔עַז
אֲשֶׁ֖ר מִמִּשְׁפַּ֥חַת אֱלִימֶֽלֶךְ׃

וַתֵּ֣לֶךְ וַתָּב֗וֹא וַתְּלַקֵּ֤ט בַּשָּׂדֶה֙

The narrative action now moves forward quickly via this series of *vav*-consecutives. וַתֵּ֣לֶךְ is a Qal imperfect 3fs of הלך + *vav*-consecutive. The first *vav* in this sequence is a *vav* of logical succession, "*And so* she went," as the logical consequence of Naomi telling her to go. The next two *vav*-consecutives (וַתָּב֗וֹא וַתְּלַקֵּ֤ט) are the temporally successive actions in the narrative. וַתָּב֗וֹא is a Qal imperfect 3fs of בוא + *vav*-consecutive, and וַתְּלַקֵּ֤ט is a Piel imperfect 3fs of לקט + *vav*-consecutive. "And [so] she went, and [then] she came, and [then] she gleaned." Notice that, morphologically, וַתָּב֗וֹא has a ◌ָ as the preformative vowel. A general way to distinguish this form as a Qal from a Hiphil (which also takes an a-class preformative vowel) is that the Qal preformative vowel/thematic vowel pattern is usually A/O (תָּ◌וֹא), whereas the Hiphil preformative vowel/thematic vowel pattern is A/I (תָּבִ◌יא).

בַּשָּׂדֶה֙ is a locative prepositional phrase indicating where Ruth gleaned. The prepositional phrase functions as an adverbial accusative of place limiting the verb to a specific location. It is subtle, but notice that בַּשָּׂדֶה֙ has the definite article as part of the vowel pointing of the inseparable preposition (בַּ◌ּ), introducing the possibility that we are talking now about a specific field—namely, the one belonging to Boaz. However, the definite article was also on שָּׂדֶה in 2:2 when Ruth certainly did not know yet the field in which she would end up. The fact that Ruth is in Boaz's field will become explicit after the *atnāḥ* in this same verse. This use of שָׂדֶה is generic in both places, simply indicating that Ruth was in the area of fields where the act of gleaning occurs.

אַחֲרֵי הַקֹּצְרִים

אַחֲרֵי הַקֹּצְרִים translates as "after the ones reaping." אַחֲרֵי functions parallel to the previous verse and is best understood as temporal. Ruth gleaned "after" the reapers and bundlers had completed their work.

הַקֹּצְרִים is technically a Qal participle mp + definite article. The participle communicates a durative aspect suggesting an occupation or regular practice.[23] As a substantive, the participle translates as "those who reap," or "those who are reaping," but participle morphology commonly marks a form so common that it becomes a noun.[24] Consequently, we translate הַקֹּצְרִים simply as "the reapers" rather than explicitly translating the durative aspect of the participle. The participle form has become the noun as an occupation or title.

וַיִּקֶר מִקְרֶהָ

וַיִּקֶר is a Qal imperfect 3ms of קרה + *vav*-consecutive, meaning "to befall," highlighting the idea of chance. מִקְרֶהָ is a cognate noun meaning "by chance" or "by accident." The literal translation is difficult. Perhaps we get "it befell her by chance" or, even more literally, "her chance chanced." In Ecclesiastes 2:15, this word does *not* carry the idea of chance, so the intentional overstatement with the cognate noun here may be the clue that the narrator believes this meeting to be the work of God guiding Ruth.[25]

In the Hebrew and in good English, the idea of chance or happenstance is probably best. "*It just so happened* that she was at the portion of the field that belonged to Boaz." Michael Grisanti comments, "Rather than

---

23. *IBHS* §16a

24. כֹּהֵן and שֹׁפֵט are two other common examples of participle forms becoming nouns—"a priest" and "a judge," respectively.

25. Wilch, *Ruth*, 59.

emphasizing the accidental nature of this event, the expression highlights the lack of human intent."[26] Therefore, this construction produces an element of narrative excitement. The idea of chance along with "lack of human intent" gives the audience a deeper look into the providence of God to care for Naomi and Ruth.

חֶלְקַת הַשָּׂדֶה לְבֹעַז

חֶלְקַת הַשָּׂדֶה is a construct package that creates one unit of meaning. As a construct package, חֶלְקַת הַשָּׂדֶה functions as the accusative of what happened by chance to Ruth—namely, she happened "[upon] the portion of the field." The second noun (הַשָּׂדֶה) limits the first noun (חֶלְקַת) with an implied partitive מִן preposition.[27] The idea is that Ruth happened upon a "portion of" the entire field (i.e., a *part* of it) that belonged to Boaz.

The ל on לְבֹעַז is possessive; the field "belongs to" Boaz. In English, it can be translated simply as "the portion of the field *of* Boaz."

אֲשֶׁר מִמִּשְׁפַּחַת אֱלִימֶלֶךְ׃

This relative clause further describes Boaz. Boaz was "from the clan of Elimelech." The relative clause is a verbless clause, and since the relative pronoun refers to a person, it is best translated "who." After supplying the "to be" verb, the clause translates, "who [*was*] from the clan of Elimelech." מִמִּשְׁפַּחַת אֱלִימֶלֶךְ is another construct package creating one unit of meaning. As before, the second noun (אֱלִימֶלֶךְ) limits the first noun (מִמִּשְׁפַּחַת), but the two are now related by the implied ל of possession, "the clan *of* (belonging to) Elimelech." The narrator continues to underscore Boaz's familial connection to Naomi to highlight the anticipation of Ruth and Boaz meeting (cf. 2:1).

---

26. *NIDOTTE* 3:984.

27. *IBHS* §12d.

4 And behold, Boaz came from Bethlehem and he said to the reapers, "The Lord be with
you." And they said to him, "May the Lord bless you." 5 And Boaz said to his young man,
the one stationed over the reapers, "To whom (is) this young woman?" 6 And the young
man, the one stationed over the reapers, answered and said, "The young woman, she is
a Moabitess who returned with Naomi from the field of Moab. 7 And she said (to us), 'Let
me glean now and let me gather among the sheaves after the reapers.' And she came and
she stood from then, the morning, and until now, her resting in the house only a little."

8 And Boaz said to Ruth, "Have you not heard, my daughter, do not go to glean in
another field, and moreover, do not cross over from this (one). And thus, you shall
cling with my young women. 9 Your eyes shall be on the field that (the young men)
are reaping and you shall go after them. Have I not commanded the young men not to
touch you? And (when) you thirst, you shall go to the vessels and you shall drink from
that which the young men draw up." 10 And she fell upon her face and she bowed down
to the ground, and she said to him, "Why have I found favor in your eyes that you take
notice of me and (yet) I am a foreigner?" 11 And Boaz answered and he said to her, "It
has surely been declared to me all which you did with (for) your mother-in-law after
the death of your husband, that you abandoned your father and your mother and the
land of your relatives and you came to a people whom you did not know previously. 12
May the Lord complete your deed, and may your wages exist (as) full from the Lord,
the God of Israel, under whose wings you came to find refuge. 13 And she said, "I have
found favor in your eyes, for you have comforted me and because you have spoken to
the heart of your maidservant (although) I do not exist as one of your maidservants."

RUTH

2:4–13

4 וְהִנֵּה־בֹ֗עַז בָּ֚א מִבֵּ֣ית לֶ֔חֶם וַיֹּ֥אמֶר לַקּוֹצְרִ֖ים יְהוָ֣ה עִמָּכֶ֑ם וַיֹּ֥אמְרוּ ל֖וֹ
יְבָרֶכְךָ֥ יְהוָֽה׃ 5 וַיֹּ֤אמֶר בֹּ֙עַז֙ לְנַעֲר֔וֹ הַנִּצָּ֖ב עַל־הַקּוֹצְרִ֑ים לְמִ֖י הַנַּעֲרָ֥ה הַזֹּֽאת׃
6 וַיַּ֗עַן הַנַּ֛עַר הַנִּצָּ֥ב עַל־הַקּוֹצְרִ֖ים וַיֹּאמַ֑ר נַעֲרָ֤ה מֽוֹאֲבִיָּה֙ הִ֔יא הַשָּׁ֥בָה עִֽם־
נָעֳמִ֖י מִשְּׂדֵ֥ה מוֹאָֽב׃ 7 וַתֹּ֗אמֶר אֲלַקֳטָה־נָּא֙ וְאָסַפְתִּ֣י בָֽעֳמָרִ֔ים אַחֲרֵ֖י הַקּוֹצְרִ֑ים
וַתָּב֣וֹא וַֽתַּעֲמ֗וֹד מֵאָ֤ז הַבֹּ֙קֶר֙ וְעַד־עַ֔תָּה זֶ֛ה שִׁבְתָּ֥הּ הַבַּ֖יִת מְעָֽט׃

8 וַיֹּאמֶר֩ בֹּ֨עַז אֶל־ר֜וּת הֲל֧וֹא שָׁמַ֣עַתְּ בִּתִּ֗י אַל־תֵּלְכִי֙ לִלְקֹ֙ט בְּשָׂדֶ֣ה אַחֵ֔ר וְגַ֛ם לֹ֥א
תַעֲבוּרִ֖י מִזֶּ֑ה וְכֹ֥ה תִדְבָּקִ֖ין עִם־נַעֲרֹתָֽי׃ 9 עֵינַ֜יִךְ בַּשָּׂדֶ֤ה אֲשֶׁר־יִקְצֹרוּן֙ וְהָלַ֣כְתְּ
אַחֲרֵיהֶ֔ן הֲל֥וֹא צִוִּ֛יתִי אֶת־הַנְּעָרִ֖ים לְבִלְתִּ֣י נָגְעֵ֑ךְ וְצָמִ֗ת וְהָלַכְתְּ֙ אֶל־הַכֵּלִ֔ים וְשָׁתִ֕ית
מֵאֲשֶׁ֥ר יִשְׁאֲב֖וּן הַנְּעָרִֽים׃ 10 וַתִּפֹּל֙ עַל־פָּנֶ֔יהָ וַתִּשְׁתַּ֖חוּ אָ֑רְצָה וַתֹּ֣אמֶר אֵלָ֗יו מַדּוּעַ֩
מָצָ֨אתִי חֵ֤ן בְּעֵינֶ֙יךָ֙ לְהַכִּירֵ֔נִי וְאָנֹכִ֖י נָכְרִיָּֽה׃ 11 וַיַּ֤עַן בֹּ֙עַז֙ וַיֹּ֣אמֶר לָ֔הּ הֻגֵּ֨ד הֻגַּ֜ד לִ֗י כֹּ֤ל
אֲשֶׁר־עָשִׂית֙ אֶת־חֲמוֹתֵ֔ךְ אַחֲרֵ֖י מ֣וֹת אִישֵׁ֑ךְ וַתַּֽעַזְבִ֞י אָבִ֣יךְ וְאִמֵּ֗ךְ וְאֶ֙רֶץ֙ מֽוֹלַדְתֵּ֔ךְ
וַתֵּ֣לְכִ֔י אֶל־עַ֕ם אֲשֶׁ֥ר לֹא־יָדַ֖עַתְּ תְּמ֥וֹל שִׁלְשֽׁוֹם׃ 12 יְשַׁלֵּ֥ם יְהוָ֖ה פָּעֳלֵ֑ךְ וּתְהִ֨י מַשְׂכֻּרְתֵּ֜ךְ
שְׁלֵמָ֗ה מֵעִ֤ם יְהוָה֙ אֱלֹהֵ֣י יִשְׂרָאֵ֔ל אֲשֶׁר־בָּ֖את לַחֲס֥וֹת תַּֽחַת־כְּנָפָֽיו׃ 13 וַתֹּ֡אמֶר
אֶמְצָא־חֵ֨ן בְּעֵינֶ֤יךָ אֲדֹנִי֙ כִּ֣י נִֽחַמְתָּ֔נִי וְכִ֥י דִבַּ֖רְתָּ עַל־לֵ֣ב שִׁפְחָתֶ֑ךָ וְאָנֹכִי֙ לֹ֣א אֶֽהְיֶ֔ה
כְּאַחַ֖ת שִׁפְחֹתֶֽיךָ׃

RUTH 2:4

וְהִנֵּה־בֹ֗עַז בָּ֚א מִבֵּ֣ית לֶ֔חֶם וַיֹּ֥אמֶר לַקּוֹצְרִ֖ים יְהוָ֣ה עִמָּכֶ֑ם וַיֹּ֥אמְרוּ ל֖וֹ יְבָרֶכְךָ֥ יְהוָֽה׃

ACCENT PHRASING

וְהִנֵּה־בֹ֗עַז בָּ֚א מִבֵּ֣ית לֶ֔חֶם
וַיֹּ֥אמֶר לַקּוֹצְרִ֖ים יְהוָ֣ה עִמָּכֶ֑ם
וַיֹּ֥אמְרוּ ל֖וֹ יְבָרֶכְךָ֥ יְהוָֽה׃

וְהִנֵּה־בֹ֗עַז בָּ֚א מִבֵּ֣ית לֶ֔חֶם

וְהִנֵּה introduces an element of surprise. As Ruth was gleaning, "behold, Boaz." The clause is a nominal clause with Boaz as the initiator and בָּ֚א as the announcement. The sentence focuses on Boaz and so the subject precedes the verb for focus. Combined with הִנֵּה, the nominal clause draws the reader's attention to what Boaz did—namely, בָּ֚א. The nominal clause is not exegetically significant, but narratively, the nominal clause rather than a typical *vav*-consecutive introduces a new section with Boaz as the focus.

בָּ֚א is a Qal perfect 3ms of the root בוא. The form could also be a Qal participle of the root בוא, rendering a translation with a durative verbal aspect, "And behold, Boaz *was coming*." The perfective aspect is best since Boaz is already in the presence of the reapers and is speaking to them.

מִבֵּ֣ית לֶ֔חֶם is the prepositional phrase complement that describes from where Boaz came. He was of the clan of Elimelech, who was also "from Bethlehem" of Judah as we learned earlier in the book (1:1–2). Therefore, the narrative confirms that this is the Boaz that the audience wants to see arriving on the scene. Remember that the מִן preposition can "attach" as a separate word (מִן־), or it can point inseparably as it does here. The final ן of מִן, being in a silent *shewa* position, is a "weak" letter and assimilates into the ב of בֵּית לֶחֶם (מִבֵּית לֶחֶם ⟵ מִנְבֵית לֶחֶם).

וַיֹּ֥אמֶר לַקּוֹצְרִ֖ים

וַיֹּ֥אמֶר is a Qal imperfect 3ms of אמר + *vav*-consecutive and carries the narrative forward in temporal succession. Notice that the *vav*-consecutive retracts the accent to the preformative and affects the dissimilation of the thematic vowel in certain I-א verbs.[1]

As we saw in 2:3, לַקּוֹצְרִים is morphologically a Qal participle mp of the root קצר. Therefore, the participle would carry the idea of "ones who are reaping," but that becomes the noun, "the reapers." This phenomenon would be similar in English to a "welder." The noun implies verbal action (welding), but it is a noun in its own right. We would not say "one who was welding" every time we wanted to speak of a welder. Similarly, "ones who are reaping" are simply "reapers."

The ל indicates to whom Boaz was speaking. Notice that the ל preposition has supplanted the definite article (לַ◌ּ) and so we get "to *the* reapers," a specified group in his cohort of workers.

יְהוָה עִמָּכֶם

This clause is a common blessing or greeting. Because it is a verbless clause, a form of the "to be" verb must be supplied, and since the notion is a blessing or request from God, the modal nuance is best: "*May* the Lord be ..."

עִמָּכֶם is the עִם preposition with the 2mp pronominal suffix. Notice that עִם is likely derived from the triconsonantal root עמם. The *dāgēš forte* that appears when pronominal suffixes are added to עִם indicates such (עִמָּ◌ם).

וַיֹּאמְרוּ לוֹ יְבָרֶכְךָ יְהוָה׃

וַיֹּאמְרוּ is a Qal imperfect 3mp of אמר + *vav*-consecutive. וַיֹּאמְרוּ introduces the direct speech of the reapers in an echoing reply to Boaz's greeting (וַיֹּאמֶר ... וַיֹּאמְרוּ). לוֹ modifies the verb, indicating to whom the reapers were speaking. In context, they are speaking to Boaz.

יְבָרֶכְךָ is a Piel jussive 3ms of ברך + 2ms pronominal object suffix. Notice that the *dāgēš forte* one would expect in the R2 (ר) has been rejected and the R1 vowel has lengthened from a *pataḥ* to a *qameṣ*. יהוה is the subject, and as a jussive, the verbal nuance is again modal as in a petitionary greeting, "*May* the Lord bless you."

---

1. *IBH*, 201–3.

RUTH 2:5

וַיֹּ֣אמֶר בֹּ֔עַז לְנַעֲר֔וֹ הַנִּצָּ֖ב עַל־הַקּֽוֹצְרִ֑ים לְמִ֖י הַנַּעֲרָ֥ה הַזֹּֽאת׃

ACCENT PHRASING

וַיֹּ֣אמֶר בֹּ֔עַז לְנַעֲר֔וֹ
הַנִּצָּ֖ב עַל־הַקּֽוֹצְרִ֑ים
לְמִ֖י הַנַּעֲרָ֥ה הַזֹּֽאת׃

וַיֹּ֣אמֶר בֹּ֔עַז לְנַעֲר֔וֹ

וַיֹּאמֶר is the Qal imperfect 3ms of אמר + *vav*-consecutive. בֹּעַז is the subject, and לְנַעֲרוֹ is the indirect object. Notice the morphology of נַעֲרוֹ with the 3ms pronominal suffix. נַעַר is a segolate noun, and so the base historic form is נַעְר with only one "original" vowel. Once the 3ms suffix is added (וֹ), the ע in a silent *shewa* position (נַעְרוֹ) "flips" to a vocal *shewa* in the final form (נַעֲרוֹ).[2] Gutturals often prefer a composite *shewa* even when a silent *shewa* is expected.

הַנִּצָּ֖ב עַל־הַקּֽוֹצְרִ֑ים

הַנִּצָּב is a Niphal participle ms of נצב + definite article (הַ◌). The participle functions as a substantive noun, further modifying נַעַר of the previous clause, and so we get "the one who was stationed." Morphologically, הַנִּצָּב might be confused with a Piel perfect with the *ḥîreq* and *dāgēš* combination that is typical of the Piel perfect (◌◌◌ִ). However, two things rule out the Piel perfect. First, the definite article on the perfective verb is unusual (though see 1:22 and the next verse). Second, the thematic vowel for the Piel perfect 3ms would normally be a *ṣērê*. With the long *qāmeṣ* under the R2 (◌צָּ◌) and the נ preformative, this must be a Niphal participle. The *dāgēš* in the middle צ, then, is the assimilated נ of the root (נצב). The נ that we see in the verb is the Niphal participle preformative (נִ◌◌◌).

2. See JM §96A h–i.

עַל־הַקּוֹצְרִים is a prepositional phrase modifying הַנִּצָּב, and it gives a notion of rank rather than location. It is not that the young man to whom Boaz is speaking is on top of the reapers; rather, he is the one who outranks them. In other words, he is their "overseer." הַקּוֹצְרִים is again the participle form functioning as a substantive noun, "the reapers."

לְמִי הַנַּעֲרָה הַזֹּאת:

This clause begins the direct speech between Boaz and his servant. Boaz asks, "To whom [is] this young woman?" The demonstrative adjective הַזֹּאת functions attributively to הַנַּעֲרָה since it agrees in gender, number, and definiteness and comes after the noun. "The young woman, the this one" is an extremely literal translation, but one that understands adjectives, even demonstrative adjectives, as descriptive nouns. הַנַּעֲרָה הַזֹּאת gets smoothed out into good English as "this young woman."

The ל on לְמִי is possessive. Boaz is asking, "*To whom* does this young woman belong?"

RUTH 2:6

וַיַּעַן הַנַּעַר הַנִּצָּב עַל־הַקּוֹצְרִים וַיֹּאמַר נַעֲרָה מוֹאֲבִיָּה הִיא הַשָּׁבָה עִם־נָעֳמִי מִשְּׂדֵה מוֹאָב׃

ACCENT PHRASING

וַיַּעַן הַנַּעַר הַנִּצָּב עַל־הַקּוֹצְרִים
וַיֹּאמַר
נַעֲרָה מוֹאֲבִיָּה הִיא
הַשָּׁבָה עִם־נָעֳמִי מִשְּׂדֵה מוֹאָב׃

וַיַּעַן הַנַּעַר הַנִּצָּב עַל־הַקּוֹצְרִים

וַיַּעַן is the Qal imperfect 3ms of ענה + *vav*-consecutive. הַנַּעַר הַנִּצָּב עַל־הַקּוֹצְרִים is the subject phrase made up of the noun הַנַּעַר and the appositional modifier הַנִּצָּב עַל־הַקּוֹצְרִים to further describe this particular lad. Here the apposition is best understood as explicative apposition since we may not have known which servant was answering if the narrator had written only הַנַּעַר. The apposition (הַנִּצָּב עַל־הַקּוֹצְרִים) clarifies (explains) which servant answered Boaz.

הַנִּצָּב is a Niphal participle ms of the root נצב. With the definite article, the participle functions as a substantive, "the one who was stationed." Idiomatically, this means "the overseer."

עַל־הַקּוֹצְרִים is a prepositional phrase indicating over whom this young man stands as the leader. He is "over the reapers." הַקּוֹצְרִים is a Qal participle mp of קצר. The form is written *plene* (fully) with the *ḥōlem-vav* as the R1 vowel.

וַיֹּאמַר

וַיֹּאמַר is a Qal imperfect 3ms of אמר + *vav*-consecutive. The construction feels redundant in English, especially following וַיַּעַן, another verb of speech. However, it is common in Hebrew to introduce direct speech with either a *vav*-consecutive of אמר or לֵאמֹר. The lad (הַנַּעַר) answering Boaz is the implied subject of וַיֹּאמַר.

נַעֲרָ֤ה מֽוֹאֲבִיָּה֙ הִ֔יא

The leader of the reapers now labels Ruth a נַעֲרָה, a general term for "young woman" that is here applied to Ruth as a "young widow."[3] Rather than focusing on Ruth's social status, the leader of the reapers identifies Ruth as a young woman.

Subsequently, he identifies her as a מֽוֹאֲבִיָּה. The construction מֽוֹאֲבִיָּה֙ הִ֔יא is a verbless clause with a resumptive pronoun that is redundant in English. "A Moabitess (is) she." Notice that מֽוֹאֲבִיָּה has the gentilic ִי ending indicating a nationality of those from Moab. Likewise, it ends with the feminine ָה indicating a female from Moab, hence "a Moabi*tess*." The identification as a Moabitess is appositional to נַעֲרָה, further explaining (explicative apposition) something about this young woman Ruth.

הַשָּׁ֥בָה עִֽם־נָעֳמִ֖י מִשְּׂדֵ֥ה מוֹאָֽב׃

For the discussion of הַשָּׁבָה, see 1:22. Here it further modifies נַעֲרָ֤ה מֽוֹאֲבִיָּה֙ הִ֔יא to describe Ruth as one "*who returned* with Naomi from the field of Moab."

עִֽם־נָעֳמִי communicates with whom Ruth returned to Bethlehem, "with Naomi." This phrase continues to describe Ruth in Boaz's hearing. Perhaps the leader of the reapers intended to connect Ruth to Naomi, or perhaps the narrator is simply making this connection clear. Either way, Boaz continues to gather information about who Ruth is, with whom she is associated, and where she is from.

מִשְּׂדֵה מוֹאָב tells us from where Ruth left when she returned with Naomi. She returned "from the field of Moab." Again, the singular שָׂדֶה may refer to the territory of Moab rather than a specific field.

With Ruth being identified here as a מֽוֹאֲבִיָּה and as the one who returned מִשְּׂדֵה מוֹאָב, she is doubly identified as a Moabite but never mentioned by name. It would be difficult to say whether the leader of the reapers is speaking pejoratively about Ruth. In light of Boaz's instructions later that they not touch her or abuse her, it may be that Boaz suspects the reapers might harm Ruth since she is "only" a Moabitess. It is also possible that the leader of the reapers did not know Ruth's name since she was a gleaner and it was

3. *NIDOTTE* 3:126.

probably not a high priority for him to know her by name. Regardless of the implied knowledge of the young man overseeing the reapers, the narrator clearly identifies Ruth as a Moabite foreigner who is associated with Naomi, one of Boaz's relatives.

The narrator at this point intends to highlight Ruth's Moabiteness. As one of the major themes of Ruth and one picked up in the New Testament (Matt 1:5), it is no surprise that the narrator wants to keep on the front of our minds that Ruth is a quintessential example of a foreign widow in Israel who should be cared for according to torah. Possibly out of concern that other reapers might mistreat Ruth, Boaz will take calculated steps to protect and provide for this young woman who returned with Naomi from Moab.

RUTH 2:7

וַתֹּ֗אמֶר אֲלַקֳטָה־נָּא֙ וְאָסַפְתִּ֣י בָֽעֳמָרִ֔ים אַחֲרֵ֖י הַקּוֹצְרִ֑ים וַתָּב֣וֹא וַֽתַּעֲמ֗וֹד מֵאָ֤ז הַבֹּ֙קֶר֙ וְעַד־עַ֔תָּה זֶ֛ה שִׁבְתָּ֥הּ הַבַּ֖יִת מְעָֽט׃

ACCENT PHRASING

וַתֹּ֗אמֶר
אֲלַקֳטָה־נָּא֙ וְאָסַפְתִּ֣י בָֽעֳמָרִ֔ים
אַחֲרֵ֖י הַקּוֹצְרִ֑ים
וַתָּב֣וֹא וַֽתַּעֲמ֗וֹד
מֵאָ֤ז הַבֹּ֙קֶר֙ וְעַד־עַ֔תָּה
זֶ֛ה שִׁבְתָּ֥הּ הַבַּ֖יִת מְעָֽט׃

וַתֹּ֗אמֶר

וַתֹּ֗אמֶר introduces Ruth's direct speech that was spoken previously to the head of the reapers, and now he is repeating it to Boaz. וַתֹּ֗אמֶר is a Qal imperfect 3fs of אמר + *vav*-consecutive. Ruth's comments here are embedded several layers deep in the discourse. This clause is still part of the answer provided to Boaz by the leader of the reapers. He has already identified her as a Moabitess, and now he communicates to Boaz what she said when she came to the field.

אֲלַקֳטָה־נָּא֙ וְאָסַפְתִּ֣י בָֽעֳמָרִ֔ים

אֲלַקֳטָה־נָּה is a Piel cohortative 1cs of לקט. The cohortative communicates a request, and Ruth here says, "Let me glean ..." In 2:2, the same construction (cohortative + נָא) communicates that Ruth politely requests to "go" and to "glean" as a sign of respect for Naomi. Similarly, here Ruth respectfully asks the overseer to glean in the field. Ruth does not beg out of desperation; rather, she makes a respectful request grounded in torah.

The verbal form of the Piel cohortative has an odd *ḥāṭēf qāmeṣ-ḥāṭûf* under the ק. We do not expect the *ḥāṭēf shewa* since the ק is not a guttural. The reduction of the theme vowel to a *shewa* in the cohortative is quite normal, but the *ḥāṭēf* vowel is still puzzling. Neither *HALOT* nor BDB writes the *ḥāṭēf qāmeṣ-ḥāṭûf* when it lists the form.[4] *DCH*, however, does mark the *ḥāṭēf qāmeṣ-ḥāṭûf* under the ק.[5] See 2:2 for discussion of the composite *shewa* under a nonguttural.

וְאָסַפְתִּ֣י is a Qal perfect 1cs of אסף + *vav*-consecutive. The *vav*-consecutive on a perfect verb points like the conjunctive *vav*, and so one must discern which is intended. The first indication of a *vav*-consecutive is the shifted accent to the sufformative of וְאָסַפְתִּ֣י. The 1cs form is normally accented on the thematic vowel syllable (◌סַ֫פְ◌), but here it shifts to the sufformative (-תִּ֣י). The second indication that the *vav* is consecutive and not conjunctive is that a past-tense verb would not make sense in this context. "Let me glean now, and I gathered." Since וְאָסַפְתִּ֣י is still part of Ruth's direct speech request, the more likely *vav* here is consecutive. More specifically, the *vav* expresses consequence, "Let me glean now, *that* I may gather."[6] It is the desired outcome of her gleaning.

בָעֳמָרִ֔ים is a prepositional phrase suggesting that Ruth desires to gather up gleanings "into sheaves." This ב is locative, or the place where Ruth intends to organize her gleanings.

Notice the vowel pointing of the inseparable preposition on בָעֳמָרִים. The pointing could be a ב preposition with a definite article where the *dāgēš* that would have occurred in the ע has been rejected and the preceding vowel lengthened by compensation to a *qāmeṣ* (בָּעֳמָרִים ⟵ בַּעֳמָרִים). Alternatively, the noun could be indefinite, and the vowel is a *qāmeṣ-ḥāṭûf* in front of a *ḥāṭēf qāmeṣ-ḥāṭûf* (בָּעֳמָרִים ⟵ בְּעֳמָרִים). If the vowel pointing includes the definite article, then Ruth is asking to glean "among *the* sheaves" (spatial ב), perhaps specifying a particular area of the field where she asks to glean or implying that she asks to glean in a place she is not permitted. If the word is indefinite, then Ruth is asking to glean "into sheaves," a statement of standard practice. The reapers would reap, the bundlers would bundle, and then the gleaners would glean their own gatherings into sheaves for

4. BDB, 544; *HALOT*, 535.
5. *DCH* 4:576.
6. Wilch, *Ruth*, 62.

themselves. Most English translations read this as the definite article and a spatial ב. The better option, however, is to understand Ruth to be asking to gather "into sheaves" whatever she gleans.[7]

אַחֲרֵי הַקּוֹצְרִים

אַחֲרֵי is temporal. Ruth asks to glean after the reapers have moved through the field. הַקּוֹצְרִים is a Qal participle mp of קצר + definite article, again functioning as a substantive to indicate an occupation.

וַתָּבוֹא וַתַּעֲמוֹד

וַתָּבוֹא continues the young man's response to Boaz but now returns to his narrative of the events, not Ruth's direct comments to him. The narrator has not yet returned to the primary story line, but the *vav*-consecutives return to the narrative of the young man's reply. וַתָּבוֹא is a Qal imperfect 3fs of בוא + *vav*-consecutive. The *vav* is likely logical succession, "*And so* she came ..." Upon Ruth's request being answered, the consequence or logical outcome is that she indeed came to the field to glean.

וַתַּעֲמוֹד is a Qal imperfect 3fs of עמד + *vav*-consecutive. The form is written *plene* (fully) with the *ḥōlem-vav* as the thematic vowel. Also notice the change in the preformative vowel as a result of the I-ע. In the Qal, we expect a *ḥîreq* preformative vowel, but because of the I-ע, we get a *pataḥ*. BDB lists this occurrence of עמד as "to be steadfast."[8] The verb communicates vigilance rather than idleness in this case. Ruth "took her stand" in this field, working diligently. Ruth was not just standing around; rather, she was steadfastly devoted to her task.

מֵאָז הַבֹּקֶר וְעַד־עַתָּה

This combination of prepositional phrases adverbially modifies how Ruth stood. מֵאָז begins the prepositional phrases, "from then ... ," but, being a generic "then," must be further defined. הַבֹּקֶר appositionally modifies

---

7. See Bush, *Ruth, Esther*, 117; Daniel I. Block, *Judges, Ruth*, New American Commentary 6 (Nashville: Broadman & Holman, 1999), 656.

8. BDB, 764.

מֵאָז, specifying when "then" was: "from then, (specifically) the morning." The definite article on הַבֹּקֶר functions as a demonstrative, "this morning." וְעַד־עַתָּה completes this combination of prepositional phrases, "and until now," specifying the length of time that Ruth was working in the field. Ruth demonstrated her work ethic, one that apparently drew the attention of the overseer of the reapers.

זֶה שִׁבְתָּהּ הַבַּיִת מְעָט׃

The final clause is quite difficult but translates literally as "this her dwelling [in/at] the house a little [while]." The versions also struggled to make sense of the difficult Hebrew.

LXX	*οὐ κατέπαυσεν ἐν τῷ ἀγρῷ μικρόν*
Vulgate	et ne ad momentum quidem domum reversa est
Targum	פון זעיר דין דיתבא בביתא ציבחר

The LXX and Vulgate translate the clause to indicate she did not stop working for even a little while, emphasizing the idea of Ruth's hard work ethic. The LXX reads, "She did not stop in the field a little," and the Vulgate states, "And, in fact, she did not return home for a moment." Targum Ruth has "It is only for a short time that she sat in the house but a little while," suggesting Ruth took only a short break for the entire workday. Ruth's "dwelling" or "resting" (שִׁבְתָּהּ) was short-lived.[9] Any of these translations gets at the idea that Ruth was hard at work.

שִׁבְתָּהּ is a Qal infinitive construct of ישׁב + 3fs pronominal suffix. In the literal translation, the pronominal suffix functions as a possessive pronoun; this is "the sitting *of* [that belonged to] Ruth." הַבַּיִת is an adverbial accusative of place indicating where her resting/sitting took place: "[at] the house." מְעָט is an adverbial accusative of time suggesting how long Ruth rested: "a little [while]."

9. See the text critical discussion in Brotzman and Tully, *Old Testament Textual Criticism*, 152–54.

While the Hebrew here is difficult, the sense of what is being communicated is clear. Ruth had been working diligently all day. Her diligence was a sign of her knowledge of God's covenant faithfulness to provide for her and Naomi even though the means of this provision was the result of a social system that labeled her as "the least of these." Even in her downcast situation, Ruth trusted God's faithfulness to his people, and she saw this opportunity to glean as his provision for her and Naomi. She was not going to squander this opportunity. As opposed to Naomi, Ruth's bitter situation drove her to work diligently within a covenantal framework that she understood as God's sovereign hand of provision for the sojourner and the widow.

RUTH 2:8

וַיֹּאמֶר֩ בֹּ֨עַז אֶל־ר֜וּת הֲל֧וֹא שָׁמַ֣עַתְּ בִּתִּ֗י אַל־תֵּֽלְכִי֙ לִלְקֹ֨ט בְּשָׂדֶ֣ה אַחֵ֔ר וְגַ֛ם לֹ֥א תַעֲבוּרִ֖י מִזֶּ֑ה וְכֹ֥ה תִדְבָּקִ֖ין עִם־נַעֲרֹתָֽי׃

ACCENT PHRASING

וַיֹּאמֶר֩ בֹּ֨עַז אֶל־ר֜וּת
הֲל֧וֹא שָׁמַ֣עַתְּ בִּתִּ֗י
אַל־תֵּֽלְכִי֙ לִלְקֹ֨ט בְּשָׂדֶ֣ה אַחֵ֔ר
וְגַ֛ם לֹ֥א תַעֲבוּרִ֖י מִזֶּ֑ה
וְכֹ֥ה תִדְבָּקִ֖ין עִם־נַעֲרֹתָֽי׃

וַיֹּאמֶר֩ בֹּ֨עַז אֶל־ר֜וּת

The narrative scene now shifts as Boaz begins to speak to Ruth. As the narrator presents it, the transition to the conversation between Boaz and Ruth is fast and abrupt. Boaz wastes no time (cf. 3:18–4:1). בֹּ֨עַז is the subject, and וַיֹּאמֶר֩ is a Qal imperfect 3ms of אמר + *vav*-consecutive, introducing his direct speech to Ruth (אֶל־ר֜וּת).

הֲל֧וֹא שָׁמַ֣עַתְּ בִּתִּ֗י

Boaz's rhetorical question does not seek an answer, and so even though it is introduced by an interrogative particle, the force becomes an affirmative declaration linked to the following statement that Ruth would not glean in another field.[10] Literally, the text translates as "Is there not that you have heard, my daughter … ?" To make sense of questions in Hebrew with the interrogative ה, it is often best to translate the sentence as a standard sentence and then make that sentence a question. For example, we may say here, "You have not heard, my daughter," as the declarative sentence. Then the interrogative ה triggers us to make that sentence a question, "Have you not heard, my daughter … ?"

10. GKC §150e.

As an implied rhetorical affirmative, it seems as if Boaz has made a previous declaration about where Ruth should glean.

שָׁמַעַתְּ is a Qal perfect 2fs of שׁמע. Notice the III-ע in the perfect takes a segolate vowel pattern beginning with the מ (◌מַעַתְּ). A distinguishing characteristic of III-guttural verbs (mainly III-ח and III-ע) is that the Qal perfect 2fs takes this segolate vowel pattern in the final consonants. Here the ע prefers a-class vowels under and before it, and so the ◌מַעַתְּ pattern arises.

אַל־תֵּלְכִי לִלְקֹט בְּשָׂדֶה אַחֵר

As part of Boaz's conversation with Ruth, he repeats here what it is that Ruth presumably has heard: "Do not go to glean in another field."

תֵּלְכִי is a Qal jussive 2fs of הלך. אַל־ + jussive expresses a negative command that may communicate the nuance of urgency.[11] The narrator here presents Boaz as both desiring for Ruth to stay in this field *and* exercising light authority to suggest to her where she ought to glean.

לִלְקֹט is a Qal infinitive construct of לקט with a ל of purpose. Combined with the negative command, Boaz has encouraged Ruth (commanded her?—אַל־תֵּלְכִי) not to go to any other field with the intention of gleaning there.

בְּשָׂדֶה אַחֵר is the prepositional modifier indicating the specific place that Boaz tells Ruth not to go to glean. The construction is an attributive adjective (אַחֵר) following its noun and agreeing in gender (masculine), number (singular), and (in)definiteness, "in another field."

Boaz has now made it clear through a negative command that Ruth is not to glean in another field. In some sense, he is already staking a claim on her, but in the context of gleaning, he is staking a claim on her to protect her and provide for her. This is not a flippant attraction. Boaz's interest at this point is that Ruth has a safe place in which to glean. Boaz's young worker has explained who Ruth is, and it seems that Boaz is already fulfilling his role as a redeemer even though the total picture of family connections and other redeemers has not yet been fully explained. Later, when

11. WO §34.2.1b. GKC and JM comment that אַל־ + jussive can express negative wish, warning, dissuasion, or negative prayer (GKC §109c; JM §114i). If we were to specifically categorize this construction, it would be a negative wish (request) with a flavor of dissuasion.

Ruth asks Boaz to "spread his wings over her" (3:9), Boaz replies that there is a nearer redeemer. Either this is information he has found out since this meeting in 2:8, or he has known this all along. If Boaz already knows there is a nearer redeemer, but he commits even here to protect Ruth and provide for her, he truly is an אִישׁ גִּבּוֹר חַיִל (2:1).

וְגַם לֹא תַעֲבוּרִי מִזֶּה

וְגַם introduces a strong additive and emphatic command. "And *moreover* (!), do not pass over (or leave) from this (one)."

As opposed to the previous negative wish (אַל־תֵּלְכִי), the construction לֹא תַעֲבוּרִי is a direct prohibition.[12] It is not as if Boaz is being authoritarian, but he intends to make certain that Ruth stays in his field.

תַעֲבוּרִי is a Qal imperfect 2fs of עבר. The *pataḥ* as the preformative vowel may be confusing with parsing this verb as a Qal. In the Qal, we expect to see a *ḥîreq* preformative vowel (*sĕgōl* in the 1cs א), but here we get the *pataḥ*, usually expected for the Hiphil stem (יַ◌◌◌). The *pataḥ* in the Qal is due to the I-guttural (ע) influencing the vowel change. Notice also that the normal silent *shewa* in the Qal paradigm under the first root letter is a composite *shewa* (◌ֲ). This phenomenon occurs regularly with gutturals and a vocal *shewa*, but only in certain circumstances when a silent *shewa* is expected under the guttural. The guttural ח can retain a silent *shewa*; ה and ע will often "flip" it to composite; א will usually quiesce; and ר, the semi-guttural, has no problems with retaining a silent *shewa*. In this case, the I-ע "flips" the silent *shewa* to a *ḥāṭēf pataḥ* and the preformative vowel follows suit. Also notice that the thematic vowel, which we expect to be a ֹ, is a וּ.[13] Both vowels are within the o/u vowel class and do not directly affect the parsing of the verb.

The prepositional phrase מִזֶּה is the מִן preposition on the demonstrative particle זֶה, "from this." With the demonstrative functioning substantivally (as a noun), "one" must be added to the translation, "from this [one],"

12. JM §107o.

13. For discussion on the unexpected וּ as the theme vowel, see GKC §47g and JM §44c, who both argue this form along with Exod 18:26 and Prov 14:3 is "anomalous" or "faulty."

meaning "from this [field]." Boaz specifies the location from which Ruth is not to leave.

וְכֹה תִדְבָּקִין עִם־נַעֲרֹתָי׃

The final clause introduces the intended result of the instructions: "But thus ..." כֹּה refers to a location—namely, the field in which they are speaking.[14] The *vav* is translated adversatively ("but") since Boaz is now giving Ruth positive instructions. The alternative between the negative commands (אַל־תֵּלְכִי ... לֹא תַעֲבוּרִי) and the positive instructions warrants a contrastive conjunction. Since כֹּה refers to the location, we may translate it "But here ..."

תִדְבָּקִין is a Qal imperfect 2fs of דבק with a paragogic *nun*. The only aspect of the verb morphology that may be difficult here is the long *qāmeṣ* under the middle root letter (ב). BDB shows that the root דבק is an a-class verb in the imperfective. The a-class thematic vowel is normally a *pataḥ*, but because of the paragogic *nun*, the accent shifts to the final syllable, leaving the short *pataḥ* in an open pretonic syllable, which requires a long vowel.[15] The verb is translated as a simple future but is a mild command or wish. "But here, *you shall cling* with [to] my young women."

The use of עִם following the root דבק rather than ב indicates proximity. "You shall cling (close) to my young women." Notice that Boaz continues to protect Ruth by mildly commanding her to cling to his young *women*, not the young men (cf. 2:21). While it seems that Boaz has a good hold on his hired workers, he also knows that anything can happen. In light of the information he has been given about who Ruth is, he intends at every angle to protect her.

---

14. See discussion in Holmstedt, *Ruth*, 120–21.

15. Thematic vowels in verbs do not always lengthen in pretonic open syllables. A standard verbal vowel reduction pattern is that the thematic vowel reduces to a vocal *shewa*. However, in a-class thematic vowels, pretonic open syllables usually lengthen; see Kutz and Josberger, *Learning Biblical Hebrew*, 67.

RUTH 2:9

עֵינַ֜יִךְ בַּשָּׂדֶ֤ה אֲשֶׁר־יִקְצֹרוּן֙ וְהָלַ֣כְתְּ אַחֲרֵיהֶ֔ן הֲל֥וֹא צִוִּ֛יתִי אֶת־הַנְּעָרִ֖ים לְבִלְתִּ֣י
נָגְעֵ֑ךְ וְצָמִ֗ת וְהָלַכְתְּ֙ אֶל־הַכֵּלִ֔ים וְשָׁתִ֕ית מֵאֲשֶׁ֥ר יִשְׁאֲב֖וּן הַנְּעָרִֽים׃

ACCENT PHRASING

עֵינַ֜יִךְ בַּשָּׂדֶ֤ה אֲשֶׁר־יִקְצֹרוּן֙ וְהָלַ֣כְתְּ אַחֲרֵיהֶ֔ן
הֲל֥וֹא צִוִּ֛יתִי אֶת־הַנְּעָרִ֖ים לְבִלְתִּ֣י נָגְעֵ֑ךְ
וְצָמִ֗ת וְהָלַכְתְּ֙ אֶל־הַכֵּלִ֔ים
וְשָׁתִ֕ית מֵאֲשֶׁ֥ר יִשְׁאֲב֖וּן הַנְּעָרִֽים׃

עֵינַ֜יִךְ בַּשָּׂדֶ֤ה אֲשֶׁר־יִקְצֹרוּן֙ וְהָלַ֣כְתְּ אַחֲרֵיהֶ֔ן

Ruth 2:9 begins with a nominal clause that is best translated with an implied jussive. "(*Let*) your eyes (be) on the field which they are reaping, and you should go after them." עֵינַ֜יִךְ is the initiator in the nominal clause, and the announcement is the implied jussive, "let them be." Keeping one's eyes on the field is idiomatic for intentional focus. Boaz tells Ruth not to be distracted by other fields but rather to keep her exclusive focus on this one.

בַּשָּׂדֶ֤ה אֲשֶׁר־יִקְצֹרוּן֙ is a prepositional complement. As such, it communicates *where* Ruth is to put her attention. יִקְצֹרוּן֙ is a Qal imperfect 3mp of קצר with the paragogic *nun*. The verb is a strong verb morphologically and is 3mp because the men would be the ones reaping. The women would follow behind them, and hence Ruth, the gleaner, is to "go after them (the women; fp suffix)" (אַחֲרֵיהֶ֔ן).

וְהָלַ֣כְתְּ is the Qal perfect 2fs of הלך + *vav*-consecutive. Remember that the *vav*-consecutive on a perfect points like the conjunctive *vav* (וְ), and therefore one must decide whether this is a compound predicate (two verbal ideas joined together with the simple conjunction "and") or whether this is a consecutive verbal idea.

The consecutive verbal notion is correct in this case since the *vav* + perfective often continues the nuance of the verb that precedes it in sequence. Since Boaz's conversation began with an implied jussive ("[Let]

your eyes [be] on the field"), the *vav* + perfective continues that modal nuance with another mild suggestion, "and you *should* go after them (הֶן-; the young women)."

In *BHQ*, וְהָלַכְתְּ ends in a *ḥîreq* following the Leningrad Codex (וְהָלַכְתִּ). Unfortunately, *BHQ* fails to provide discussion on the form and only marks in the apparatus that הָלַכְתִּ occurs in Leningrad (M^L) and the expected form, הָלַכְתְּ, occurs in the Aleppo Codex (M^A) and in the Cambridge University manuscript Ms. 1753. There are two possible explanations for the form in Leningrad.

First, the final *ḥîreq* may represent a reading tradition that was concerned about confusion of the phonetics between the two words הָלַכְתְּ אַחֲרֵיהֶן. Reading these two words together quickly would result in the phonetics of a 2ms perfective (הָלַכְתָּ). The 2fs verb ending in a silent *shewa* (תְּ-) and then leading into the א phoneme of the next word may have sounded like תָּ of the 2ms perfective. To ensure that this pronunciation mistake would not happen, it is possible that Leningrad preserved a reading tradition that inserted the slight "i" sound between the two words to avoid the confusion.

A second explanation can be deduced from Gesenius.[16] He discusses seven instances where the 2fs independent pronoun (אַתְּ) is preserved with a *ḥîreq-yôd* in the consonantal text (אַתִּי). In *BHS*, these are all *ketiv/qere* situations, and in accordance with its practices, *BHS* preserves all the consonants of the original text (אתי) but supplies the corrected vowels.[17] This generates the form אַתְּי with the *shewa* as well as the final *yôd*. This practice makes the morphological problem seem even worse. In the *BHS* margin, the *qere* indicates the form should be אַתְּ. Gesenius argues the pronoun was "originally אַתִּי as in Syriac, Arabic, and Ethiopic."[18] He then also points to the *ḥîreq-yôd* ending on 2fs perfectives with pronominal suffixes (e.g., קְטַלְתִּינִי 2fs perfect + 1cs suffix). If we look specifically at the 2fs

16. GKC §32h.

17. None of these seven instances occur in books currently available in *BHQ*. Therefore, the evidence must be deduced from *BHS* at least for now.

18. GKC §32h.

perfective verbs in *BHS*, Logos Bible Software reports 217 perfective 2fs forms.[19] Of these 217 verb forms, around seventeen of them have a *yôd* consonant after the final תְּ-.[20] Nearly all of these are in Jeremiah and Ezekiel, but at least it demonstrates there is evidence for reading the final *ḥîreq* in וְהָלַכְתְּ as a 2fs.[21] According to this explanation, the final *ḥîreq* on וְהָלַכְתְּ in *BHQ* may be evidence of an "original" 2fs perfective verb form.

The same verbal form occurs later in the verse with the same modal nuance ("you should go"), again from the mouth of Boaz. However, the second occurrence of the verb in 2:9 does not receive comment in the *BHQ* apparatus because Leningrad, Aleppo, and Ms. 1753 all contain the expected form (הָלַכְתְּ). If we consider the phonological explanation above, the verb later in 2:9 is followed by the -א phoneme, but there is no possibility to confuse הָלַכְתְּ with הָלַכְתָּ as the words are read together (וְהָלַכְתְּ אֶל־הַכֵּלִים). Contextually, a 2ms perfective would make little sense here anyway, but phonetically, the very slight *ḥîreq* sound between הָלַכְתְּ and אַחֲרֵיהֶן makes it certain that the hearer is not confused about whether Boaz is talking to Ruth (2fs) or perhaps one of his workers (2ms).

הֲלוֹא צִוִּיתִי אֶת־הַנְּעָרִים לְבִלְתִּי נָגְעֵךְ

The clause begins with the interrogative (הֲ) introducing a rhetorical question (one that does not require an answer). Literally, the clause translates as "Is it not that I have commanded the young men not to touch you?" צִוִּיתִי is a Piel perfect 1cs of the root צוה. Notice that the III-ה verb demonstrates evidences of an original III-י (צִוִּיתִי). Even though the ה (original י) of the lexical root coalesces as a *ḥîreq-yôd* thematic vowel, this verb is distinctively a Piel perfect with the *ḥîreq/dāgēš* pattern in the R1/R2 (◌ִ◌ּ◌). אֶת־הַנְּעָרִים is the direct object, clearly shown by the definite direct object marker (אֶת־).

19. Morphological search of the *BHS* SESB edition using Logos 9.

20. Jer 2:33; 3:4, 5; 4:19; 6:2; 15:10; 31:21; 46:11; Ezek 16:13, 18, 22, 31, 43, 47, 51; Ruth 2:9; 3:4. None of the examples outside Ruth have been published in *BHQ* as of the writing of this volume, and therefore we cannot yet see how *BHQ* will render these occurrences.

21. To make this situation even more difficult, the seventeen forms from *BHS* used for comparison here actually end with a consonantal י as the vowel marker. The form presented in *BHQ*, derived from Leningrad, does *not* have the י vowel marker but only preserves the *ḥîreq*. In the consonantal text, there would be no way to know that this 2fs form "needed" a subtle "i" sound at the end.

לְבִלְתִּי introduces a negative clause and is used to negate the infinitive construct. Therefore, נָגְעֵךְ is a Qal infinitive construct of נגע + 2fs pronominal suffix (ךְ◌ֵ). Morphologically, notice the *qāmeṣ-ḥāṭûf* under the R1 when the infinitive construct has a pronominal suffix. This rhetorical question provides a sense of safety and comfort for Ruth: "Have I not commanded the young men not to touch you?" In this context, the meaning of נגע likely implies violent behavior.[22] The rhetoric behind Boaz's question suggests that he has already taken steps to ensure Ruth's safety among the young men who may abuse her.

וְצָמִת וְהָלַכְתְּ אֶל־הַכֵּלִים

Boaz now gives Ruth instructions regarding provision while she is gleaning. Earlier in 2:9 he provided safety; now he permits her to drink water. וְצָמִת is a Qal perfect 2fs of the root צמא + *vav*-consecutive. Many understand this construction as a hypothetical future or a temporal protasis, supplying the word "when."[23] "And *when* you thirst ..." צמא is an III-א verb, and when the III-א is in a silent *shewa* position, it will quiesce and, consequently, could be omitted as it is here.[24]

וְהָלַכְתְּ is a Qal perfect 2fs of הלך + *vav*-consecutive and carries an imperatival or permissive nuance as the apodosis of the implied temporal protasis (וְצָמִת).[25] "And [when] you thirst, [then] you shall go (you may go) to the vessels." אֶל־הַכֵּלִים is the prepositional phrase completing the thought of where Ruth is to go to get something to drink, "to the vessels."

וְשָׁתִית מֵאֲשֶׁר יִשְׁאֲבוּן הַנְּעָרִים׃

וְשָׁתִית is a Qal perfect 2fs of the root שתה + *vav*-consecutive, continuing the permission that Boaz gives to Ruth. Boaz tells Ruth to drink from the water that the young men draw up, a move uncommon in the cultural context.[26] Morphologically, שתה is a III-ה verb, and therefore the ה is replaced with

22. *NIDOTTE* 3:23; Block, *Ruth*, 131.
23. Holmstedt, *Ruth*, 123.
24. GKC §74k.
25. Block, *Ruth*, 131, n. 66. Cf. GKC §159e; JM §167a–b; WO §38.2b.
26. Block, *Judges, Ruth*, 660.

a י (וְשָׁתִ֫ית). When preceded by a vowel, as it is here, the final ת of the perfective 2fs does not display the silent *shewa* typical of the Qal paradigm (קָטַלְתְּ), hence the form וְשָׁתִית.

The final preposition with relative pronoun (מֵאֲשֶׁר) is translated "*from what* the young men draw up." This phrase specifies what Ruth should drink when she is thirsty. יִשְׁאֲבוּן is a Qal imperfect 3mp of שׁאב with a paragogic *nun*. הַנְּעָרִים is the subject. Notice the composite *shewa* under the א in the second root letter of שׁאב. Even with the paragogic *nun*, the verbal form morphs as if the ending is a vocalic ending (sufformative is *only* a vowel), resulting in the thematic vowel reduction (יִשְׁאֲבוּן), an expected verbal vowel reduction phenomenon. Since the א is a guttural letter, the vocal *shewa* must be composite (ֲ).

RUTH 2:10

וַתִּפֹּל֙ עַל־פָּנֶ֔יהָ וַתִּשְׁתַּ֖חוּ אָ֑רְצָה וַתֹּ֣אמֶר אֵלָ֗יו מַדּ֨וּעַ מָצָ֤אתִי חֵן֙ בְּעֵינֶ֙יךָ֙
לְהַכִּירֵ֔נִי וְאָנֹכִ֖י[27] נָכְרִיָּֽה׃

ACCENT PHRASING

וַתִּפֹּל֙ עַל־פָּנֶ֔יהָ וַתִּשְׁתַּ֖חוּ אָ֑רְצָה
וַתֹּ֣אמֶר אֵלָ֗יו
מַדּ֨וּעַ מָצָ֤אתִי חֵן֙ בְּעֵינֶ֙יךָ֙ לְהַכִּירֵ֔נִי
וְאָנֹכִ֖י נָכְרִיָּֽה׃

וַתִּפֹּל֙ עַל־פָּנֶ֔יהָ וַתִּשְׁתַּ֖חוּ אָ֑רְצָה

The narrative continues in 2:10 with a *vav*-consecutive of temporal succession, the verbal action describing Ruth's response to Boaz's kindness. וַתִּפֹּל֙ is a Qal imperfect 3fs of נפל. Notice the assimilation of the I-נ of the root into the פ (תִּפֹּל ← תִּנְפֹּל). עַל־פָּנֶ֔יהָ is the prepositional phrase indicating where Ruth fell. The root word for "face" is commonly plural (פָּנִים) by nature. The singular term (פָּנֶה) refers to the front surface of something, like the face of a building. The plural form is used for a person's face.[28] Here, since it refers to Ruth's face, notice the noun takes the 3fs pronominal suffix of *plural* nouns (ֶ◌יהָ) even though in English "a face" is not a plural noun.

וַתִּשְׁתַּ֖חוּ is a Hishtaphel imperfect 3fs of חוה + *vav*-consecutive. The morphology is odd because חוה is triply "weak" (I-guttural, II-ו, III-ה) and is a Hishtaphel. The III-ה is dropped, so we do not see the final ה of the root. The shortened (apocopated) form is common in III-ה verbs with a *vav*-consecutive. Thankfully, this verb is the only one that is a so-called Hishtaphel stem, but it is consistently a Hishtaphel, so the nomenclature has been generally accepted. Since the stem is unique, it does not take a special nuance beyond the past completed action of a typical *vav*-consecutive + imperfective.

27. וְאָֽנֹכִ֖י in Leningrad. See discussion below.

28. *NIDOTTE* 3:637–39.

The narrative simply continues at this point with the successive verbal action, "*and* she bowed."

אָ֫רְצָה is the noun אֶ֫רֶץ with the directive ה. It translates as a locative prepositional phrase although it functions syntactically as an adverbial accusative of place, "*to* the ground." Ruth's posture is not one of worship but one of humble submission as a result of Boaz's demonstration of חֶ֫סֶד.

וַתֹּ֣אמֶר אֵלָ֔יו

וַתֹּ֣אמֶר introduces Ruth's direct speech to Boaz. וַתֹּ֣אמֶר is a Qal imperfect 3fs of אמר + a *vav*-consecutive. אֵלָ֔יו is the prepositional phrase indicating to whom Ruth is talking, "to him." Notice that the preposition אֶל with suffixes takes the suffixes of plural nouns (ָיו). Since prepositions cannot be plural, this is nothing more than a morphological phenomenon, but one to remember for recognizing the object of the preposition אֶל.

מַדּ֨וּעַ מָצָ֨אתִי חֵ֤ן בְּעֵינֶ֙יךָ֙ לְהַכִּירֵ֔נִי

In a posture of submission, Ruth asks why she has found such favor with Boaz. מַדּ֨וּעַ is a long form of the interrogative "Why?" BDB proposes that it potentially derives from מַה־יָּדוּעַ, "What being known?" or "From what motive?"[29] The question is not rhetorical but rather expects a response.[30]

מָצָ֨אתִי is a Qal perfect 1cs of מצא. The use of the perfective verb here suggests that Ruth has already received the חֵן that she sought in 2:2. Notice the lengthened thematic vowel because of the quiescent א (מָצָאתִי ⟵ מָצַאְתִּי). Notice also that when the א quiesces, the ת of the perfective 1cs is now preceded by a vowel sound, and so it does not get a *dāgēš lene*. חֵ֤ן is the indefinite direct object, the thing that was "found." Since it is indefinite, it does not receive the definite direct object marker but still functions as the direct object grammatically. בְּעֵינֶ֙יךָ֙ is a prepositional phrase idiomatically expressing *where* Ruth has found favor. The expression means that Boaz

29. BDB, 396.

30. Ronald T. Hyman, "Questions and Changing Identity in the Book of Ruth," *Union Seminary Quarterly Review* 39, no. 3 (1984): 197.

has demonstrated unconditional favor toward Ruth. It was Boaz's prerogative to demonstrate חֵן, and Ruth understands this.

לְהַכִּירֵנִי is a Hiphil infinitive construct of נכר + ל preposition + a 1cs suffix. The root is נכר, and we again see the assimilation of the I-נ as a *dāgēš forte*, this time in the כ (לְהַכִּירֵנִי ⟵ לְהַנְכִּירֵנִי). The infinitive expresses a result clause, "Why have I found favor in your eyes *with the result that* you noticed me?"[31] The root נכר formally means "to recognize, regard," and in this sense it is "to regard with favor" (cf. Jer 24:5 with לְטוֹבָה).[32] Hence, Boaz's "noticing" of Ruth is not just knowing who she is; the verb connotes treating her favorably just as the first part of the clause highlighted.

וְאָנֹכִ֖י נָכְרִיָּֽה׃

The final וְאָנֹכִי is a nominal clause that is circumstantial, emphasizing Ruth's status as a foreigner. The ו is translated concessively as "although" or "even though," and since this is a verbless clause, we have to supply the English "to be" verb: "even though I [am] a foreigner."

One interesting thing to note here is that *BHQ* includes a *mappîq* in the א (וְאָנֹכִי). Like the *ḥîreq* at the end of הָלַכְתְּ in 2:9, this is a morphological anomaly in which Leningrad disagrees with Aleppo and other manuscripts. The Leningrad Codex includes the *mappîq*, while Aleppo and Ms. 1753 do not have the *mappîq* in the א.[33]

What appears to be another random mark in the Masoretic tradition can be explained on phonological grounds. The *mappîq* is used to mark an original consonant, and in this case the א needs to be represented as original to avoid the phonetic combination of the vocal *shewa* running into the *qāmeṣ* (◌ָא◌ְ), resulting in the potential loss of a consonant. Something

---

31. RJW §198.

32. *HALOT*, 699–700.

33. וְאָנֹכִי M^L | וְאָנֹכִי M^A M^Y is the text-critical citation from *BHQ* apparatus. M^Y is the Cambridge manuscript Ms. 1753. Gesenius (GKC §14d) suggests that in the manuscripts the *mappîq* is used to signify that the א is to be read expressly as a consonant. Gesenius lists four verses (Gen 43:26; Lev 23:17; Ezra 8:18; Job 33:21) that preserve the *mappîq*ed א in the printed editions of his day. Leningrad and hence *BHQ* preserve more, including this one in Ruth.

similar to this phonological situation occurs regularly when the inseparable prepositions supplant the definite article.

בְּהַדָּבָר ⟵ בַּדָּבָר

As the speed of speaking increased with familiarity, these vowel blends were very natural, resulting in the loss of a consonant. However, the Masoretes knew that a silent consonant, א, was in the text, and so, to preserve the text with accuracy, they marked the א with a *mappîq*. While it may not have always been for phonological reasons, manuscript evidence indicates that in some places this practice was carried out far more frequently than we see in Leningrad.[34]

34. See Christian Ginsburg, "The *Dāgēš*hed Alephs in the Karlsruhe MS," in *Verhandlungen des Berliner Orientalisten-Kongresses*, Berlin, i. 1881, cited in GKC §14d.

RUTH 2:11

וַיַּ֤עַן בֹּ֙עַז֙ וַיֹּ֣אמֶר לָ֔הּ הֻגֵּ֨ד הֻגַּ֜ד לִ֗י כֹּ֤ל אֲשֶׁר־עָשִׂית֙ אֶת־חֲמוֹתֵ֔ךְ אַחֲרֵ֖י מ֣וֹת אִישֵׁ֑ךְ
וַתַּעַזְבִ֞י אָבִ֣יךְ[35] וְאִמֵּ֗ךְ וְאֶ֙רֶץ֙ מֽוֹלַדְתֵּ֔ךְ וַתֵּ֣לְכִ֔י אֶל־עַ֕ם אֲשֶׁ֥ר לֹא־יָדַ֖עַתְּ תְּמ֥וֹל
שִׁלְשֽׁוֹם׃

ACCENT PHRASING

וַיַּ֤עַן בֹּ֙עַז֙ וַיֹּ֣אמֶר לָ֔הּ
הֻגֵּ֨ד הֻגַּ֜ד לִ֗י כֹּ֤ל אֲשֶׁר־עָשִׂית֙ אֶת־חֲמוֹתֵ֔ךְ
אַחֲרֵ֖י מ֣וֹת אִישֵׁ֑ךְ
וַתַּעַזְבִ֞י אָבִ֣יךְ וְאִמֵּ֗ךְ וְאֶ֙רֶץ֙ מֽוֹלַדְתֵּ֔ךְ
וַתֵּ֣לְכִ֔י אֶל־עַ֕ם אֲשֶׁ֥ר לֹא־יָדַ֖עַתְּ תְּמ֥וֹל שִׁלְשֽׁוֹם׃

וַיַּ֤עַן בֹּ֙עַז֙ וַיֹּ֣אמֶר לָ֔הּ

וַיַּ֤עַן continues the primary narrative with the standard reply formula (וַיַּ֤עַן ... וַיֹּ֣אמֶר). וַיַּ֤עַן is a Qal imperfect 3ms of ענה + *vav*-consecutive with בֹּ֙עַז֙ as the subject. וַיֹּ֣אמֶר is a Qal imperfect 3ms of אמר + *vav*-consecutive. The formal object phrase, or what was said, comes in the next clause, but the prepositional phrase (לָ֔הּ) indicates to whom Boaz was talking. "Her" (◌ָהּ) is Ruth in context.

Boaz answers why Ruth has found such favor in his eyes, and one should not overlook his answer. Boaz will say in the next clause that he has heard everything that she did for her mother-in-law and how she abandoned her home comforts to align herself with a people she had not previously known. The emphasis on what Boaz has heard (הֻגֵּ֨ד הֻגַּ֜ד) suggests that Boaz knows everything Ruth did and said, including her commitment to Yahweh and his people (1:16; עַמֵּ֣ךְ עַמִּ֔י וֵאלֹהַ֖יִךְ אֱלֹהָֽי). If this is true, then Boaz demonstrates חֵן ("favor"; 2:10) to Ruth because she is a sojourner who should receive this kind of compassion after having joined herself to Yahweh and

35. אָבִ֣יךְ M^L | אָבִ֣יךְ M^A M^Y (text-critical citation from *BHQ* apparatus). See discussion of the "*mappîq*ed א" in the previous verse.

his people (cf. Deut 10:19; 14:21, 29; 24:17, 19–21; 27:19; 28:43; 31:12). Not only that, but Boaz also now knows clearly to whom Ruth is related, and I like to think he is hopeful that this situation will work out as the torah instructs (Deut 25:5–10).

הֻגֵּד הֻגַּד לִי כֹּל אֲשֶׁר־עָשִׂית אֶת־חֲמוֹתֵךְ

הֻגֵּד הֻגַּד is an absolute object construction, also known as a cognate accusative.[36] This construction juxtaposes the infinitive absolute (הֻגֵּד) with a finite verbal form (הֻגַּד) of the same root (נגד here). הֻגֵּד is the Hophal infinitive absolute of נגד. הֻגַּד is a Hophal perfect 3ms of נגד. Notice morphologically that the only difference between these two is the thematic vowel (הֻגֵּד vs. הֻגַּד). Both verbs assimilate the נ of the root and then change the preformative *qāmeṣ-ḥāṭûf* (הָ) of the Hophal to a *qibbûṣ* (הֻ) when followed by a doubled consonant. The passive Hophal translates literally as "Having *been* told, it (3ms) *has been* told to me." The absolute object emphasizes the verb: "It has *indeed* been told to me (לִי)."

כֹּל introduces the explicit subject phrase of the passive Hophal. The "it" that has indeed been told is כֹּל אֲשֶׁר־עָשִׂית אֶת־חֲמוֹתֵךְ. The relative clause (אֲשֶׁר) further modifies כֹּל. עָשִׂית is a Qal perfect 2fs of עשׂה. Since this is a III-ה verb, the final ה of the root is replaced by the ִי and the sufformative is added directly to this coalesced vowel (◌ִית). In this case, the perfective translation is best understood as an English pluperfect, "had done," since this was an action done in the past by Ruth with continuing significance. The initial Hophal perfective (הֻגַּד) helps set all of Boaz's reply in the past tense.

אֶת is the preposition "with," but the context cannot mean that Ruth did something "along with" Naomi. As with all prepositions, the contextual meaning transcends the lexical basics. Here אֶת suggests something akin to a ל of advantage.[37] Boaz knows everything that Ruth did "*for* Naomi."

36. RJW §205.

37. RJW §341.

אַחֲרֵי מוֹת אִישֵׁךְ

The temporal אַחֲרֵי is used to indicate that Ruth demonstrated faithfulness to Naomi even after there was no longer a direct familial connection through marriage to her son Mahlon. Ruth remained faithful to Naomi "after" (temporally) her husband died. At a time when Ruth should be mourning her own losses, she continued to cling to her mother-in-law.

מוֹת אִישֵׁךְ is a definite construct package, "*the* death *of* your husband." One may be inclined to see מות as an infinitive absolute of the verbal root מות, but it would be misplaced grammatically to have an infinitive absolute form functioning in a construct package. If this were an infinitive functioning as a noun, one would expect the infinitive construct (מוּת). Additionally, BDB lists this exact form of the construct noun (from מָוֶת) as מות.[38] The definiteness of this construct package ("*the* death of your husband") comes from the pronominal suffix (ךְ◌ֵ) on אִישׁ. Boaz is not talking about just any husband; he is talking about "*your* husband." Therefore, the entire construct package is definite, "*the* death of your husband." The construct package carries the implied meaning of a ל of possession, "the death *belonging to* your husband"—that is, the death he experienced.

וַתַּעַזְבִי אָבִיךְ וְאִמֵּךְ וְאֶרֶץ מוֹלַדְתֵּךְ

Boaz's reply continues with details of what has been declared to him about Ruth. The *vav* on וַתַּעַזְבִי is explicative, detailing what is meant by כֹּל אֲשֶׁר־עָשִׂית אֶת־חֲמוֹתֵךְ ("all that [Ruth] had done for her mother-in-law").[39] וַתַּעַזְבִי is a Qal imperfect 2fs of עזב, and with the explicative *vav* it translates, "*How* you abandoned."

וַתַּעַזְבִי has three objects in this clause, and none is marked with the definite direct object marker (אֶת) even though all are definite.[40] The final construct package (וְאֶרֶץ מוֹלַדְתֵּךְ), for example, is definite because the final noun of the package has a pronominal suffix making the entire package definite. The land is not just any (indefinite) land but "*the* land of *your*

---

38. BDB, 560.
39. RJW §434.
40. אָבִיךְ וְאִמֵּךְ וְאֶרֶץ מוֹלַדְתֵּךְ are all definite because they have pronominal suffixes.

relatives." Notice finally that the segolate singular construct of אֶ֫רֶץ is identical to the absolute. If this were a construct noun, we would expect to see a conjunctive accent mark. Here, however, the doubled *paštā* accent (◌֙◌֙) is a disjunctive accent that would normally divide these two words syntactically. In the current segment, the accent pattern leaves the doubled *paštā* as the only accent that can occur here, and so the form must be read as a construct form grammatically, not accentually. וְאֶ֙רֶץ֙ is a construct form of אֶ֫רֶץ even with a disjunctive accent.

וַתֵּ֣לְכִ֔י אֶל־עַ֕ם אֲשֶׁ֥ר לֹא־יָדַ֖עַתְּ תְּמ֥וֹל שִׁלְשֽׁוֹם׃

וַתֵּ֣לְכִ֔י is a Qal imperfect 2fs of הלך + *vav*-consecutive in temporal succession with the previous verb. הלך morphs like a I-ו verb, and in the imperfect, the initial consonant (ה) flees and the preformative vowel lengthens (תֵּ) to compensate for the missing consonant. The final ◌ִי and the reduced thematic vowel (◌לְ◌) are the standard distinguishing marks of the imperfect 2fs. The previous *vav*-consecutive (וַתַּֽעַזְבִ֞י) was explicative and translated as "*how* you abandoned." Since וַתֵּ֣לְכִ֔י follows that same verbal nuance, it also further explains Ruth's actions of which Boaz is claiming to be aware. The "temporal" sequence of these verbs is difficult to ascertain since it is embedded several layers deep in the discourse. Boaz is restating something that was told to him as an explanation to answer why Ruth has found favor in his eyes. The "temporal" sequence is that וַתֵּ֣לְכִ֔י is what Ruth did *after* she וַתַּֽעַזְבִ֞י אָבִ֣יךְ וְאִמֵּ֗ךְ וְאֶ֙רֶץ֙ מֽוֹלַדְתֵּ֔ךְ. However, both of these are still explicative *vavs* since they both reside at the discourse level of Boaz explaining why Ruth has found favor in his eyes. אֶל־עַ֕ם is a prepositional modifier telling to whom Ruth went.

אֲשֶׁ֥ר is the relative modifier that describes the עַם to whom Ruth went. לֹא־יָדַ֖עַתְּ is a negated Qal perfect 2fs of ידע. Notice the effect of the III-ע on the pronunciation. Rather than the normal Qal perfect 2fs pointing (קָטַלְתְּ), the guttural will not take a silent *shewa* and the vowel pattern (יָ◌ַ◌ַתְּ) mimics a segolate noun with a guttural in the R2 position (cf. נַ֫עַר). Here the guttural is in the R3 position of the verbal root, but since the verb is accented on the R2, the pronunciation pattern is the same as segolates with R2 gutturals.

Notice that within the relative clause, a *vav*-consecutive imperfect would be inappropriate to communicate past time even though it regularly does so elsewhere in narrative. Therefore, the perfective of ידע accurately communicates the past tense of the story.

תְּמוֹל שִׁלְשׁוֹם is an idiomatic expression meaning "previously." Literally, these two words translate as "previously (תְּמוֹל) of three days ago (שִׁלְשׁוֹם)." This adverbial modifier should not be understood literally as if Ruth had just arrived in Bethlehem three days earlier. Instead, the idiomatic "previously" is best.

RUTH 2:12

יְשַׁלֵּ֥ם יְהוָ֖ה פָּעֳלֵ֑ךְ וּתְהִ֨י מַשְׂכֻּרְתֵּ֜ךְ שְׁלֵמָ֗ה מֵעִ֤ם יְהוָה֙ אֱלֹהֵ֣י יִשְׂרָאֵ֔ל אֲשֶׁר־
בָּ֖את לַחֲס֥וֹת תַּֽחַת־כְּנָפָֽיו׃

ACCENT PHRASING

יְשַׁלֵּ֥ם יְהוָ֖ה פָּעֳלֵ֑ךְ
וּתְהִ֨י מַשְׂכֻּרְתֵּ֜ךְ שְׁלֵמָ֗ה מֵעִ֤ם יְהוָה֙ אֱלֹהֵ֣י יִשְׂרָאֵ֔ל
אֲשֶׁר־בָּ֖את לַחֲס֥וֹת תַּֽחַת־כְּנָפָֽיו׃

יְשַׁלֵּ֥ם יְהוָ֖ה פָּעֳלֵ֑ךְ

Boaz now blesses Ruth with a petition to the Lord. יְהוָ֖ה is the subject, and יְשַׁלֵּ֥ם is a Piel jussive 3ms of שׁלם. This root means "to be complete" and expresses a state of being. In the Piel, it is a causative of that state (factitive), so we get the nuance "to *make* complete."[41] As a jussive, it translates, "May the Lord make complete." פָּעֳלֵ֑ךְ is the object, and with the Piel expressing a causative state, the object becomes the thing to be made complete: "May the Lord make *your work* complete." Morphologically, notice the *qāmeṣ-ḥāṭûf* in the R1 as an o-class segolate noun with a pronominal suffix. With the guttural (ע) in the R2 position, the normal silent *shewa* in segolate nouns with suffixes "flips" to a *ḥāṭēf-shewa* (פָּעֳלֵךְ ⟵ פָּעְלֵךְ). Here it is a *ḥāṭēf qāmeṣ-ḥāṭûf* because פֹּ֫עַל is an o-class segolate (*poʿŏlēk*).

The idea of work being complete is not just completing a task. The idiom expresses the notion of Ruth's work "coming full circle," or being "repaid" for its worth. Most English versions translate יְשַׁלֵּ֥ם as "reward" or "repay," and that is indeed appropriate.[42] The idea is that the Lord would make Ruth's gracious and kind actions toward Naomi "come full circle/be complete" back on Ruth.

41. The name "factitive" derives from the Latin *facere*, "to make." With stative verbs in the Piel, the factitive meaning indicates that the object is "made" or "put" into that state of being. *IBHS* §7d.

42. *NIDOTTE* 4:130.

וּתְהִ֨י מַשְׂכֻּרְתֵּ֜ךְ שְׁלֵמָ֗ה מֵעִ֤ם יְהוָה֙ אֱלֹהֵ֣י יִשְׂרָאֵ֔ל

וּתְהִי continues Boaz's blessing with the Qal jussive 3fs of היה. The *vav* is conjunctive, not consecutive. It simply joins two jussives (יְשַׁלֵּם ... וּתְהִי) rather than expressing existence in past time. The conjunctive *vav* is easily distinguished on the imperfect/jussive forms. Here the וּ is the vowel pointing for the conjunctive *vav*, whereas the *vav*-consecutive on an imperfect/jussive would point like the definite article (וַ◌).

מַשְׂכֻּרְתֵּךְ, "your wages," is the subject and is grammatically feminine, hence the 3fs verb (וּתְהִי). Notice the *qibbûṣ* in a closed, unaccented syllable (◌◌כֻּרְ◌◌). The lexical form is מַשְׂכֹּרֶת with a segolization of the final two syllables (מַשְׂכֹּרֶת). Once the suffix is added, the morphology follows expected segolate patterns. The shift from o-class *ḥōlem* in the lexical form to the *qibbûṣ* should not be alarming as they are both in the o/u vowel class. Hebrew tends to prefer the *qibbûṣ* in the o/u vowel class prior to a doubled consonant.[43] The word מַשְׂכֻּרְתֵּךְ communicates the notion of recompense or reward—that is, something that is due.

היה functions in this clause similarly to the English copulative ("to be") verb. This construction, with שְׁלֵמָה in the predicate, communicates a predicate adjective, "may your wages *be* complete." An alternative way of describing this construction is as an adverbial accusative expressing the status or situation in which the wages should exist—namely, with the status of fullness.[44] "And may your wages exist (היה) *in the status of* full." שְׁלֵמָה is from the same root as the verb יְשַׁלֵּם used previously, but carries the more common meaning of "fullness" or "peace."

The doubled preposition מֵעִם is equivalent to simply saying "from ..." יְהוָה֙ אֱלֹהֵ֣י יִשְׂרָאֵ֔ל is the object of the prepositional phrase, indicating the source of Ruth's fullness if Boaz's blessing is fulfilled. "May your wages exist [as] full from the Lord God of Israel (as the source)."

אֲשֶׁר־בָּ֖את לַחֲס֥וֹת תַּֽחַת־כְּנָפָֽיו׃

The final relative clause further specifies יְהוָה֙ אֱלֹהֵ֣י יִשְׂרָאֵ֔ל. Since it further modifies יְהוָה, it is translated "who" rather than "which." However, for good

43. GKC §9n–o.

44. *IBHS* §13z.

English we must go to the end of the relative clause to pick up the resumptive pronoun (כְּנָפָיו). If we translate the clause woodenly, we get "whom you came to take refuge under his wings." Using the relative "whom" and the pronoun "his" seems redundant in English, and indeed it would be. If we bring the preposition and pronoun to the front of the relative clause, we translate, "*under whose* wings you have come to take refuge." Even with the resumptive pronoun at the end of the clause, we would begin the clause as "under *whose* wings" for good English. The relative pronoun essentially gets absorbed into the prepositional phrase (תַּחַת־כְּנָפָיו).

בָּאת is a Qal perfect 2fs of בוא. In the Qal perfect of בוא (and other hollow roots), the thematic vowel uniting the R1 and R3 is a-class, here a long *qāmeṣ*. The standard paradigm would have a silent *shewa* under the א, but here it quiesces and hence the ת sufformative of the perfect 2fs (◌◌◌ְתְּ) loses its *dāgēš lene* and makes the final silent *shewa* implicit.

בָּאְתְּ ⟵ בָּאתְ ⟵ בָּאת

לַחֲסוֹת is a Qal infinitive construct of חסה, "to seek refuge." For III-ה verbs, the infinitive construct ends with וֹת-, replacing the final ה of the lexical root. The simple vocal *shewa* of the paradigm form (קְטֹל) becomes a composite *shewa* in חסה because of the I-guttural (ח). Finally, the ל preposition points with the corresponding vowel of the *ḥāṭēf shewa*, here a *pataḥ* (cf. לֶאֱכֹל; לַעֲשׂוֹת). לַחֲסוֹת communicates "why" Ruth "has come." Ruth has come to Bethlehem with Naomi "to seek refuge" from a sad and dire situation in Moab. In this sense, the infinitive communicates purpose. Ruth has come to take refuge under the wings of Yahweh, but not hypothetically as if someone "comes to know" something. Rather, Ruth has intentionally identified herself with Yahweh and has therefore found refuge in him.

RUTH 2:13

וַתֹּ֗אמֶר אֶמְצָא־חֵ֨ן בְּעֵינֶ֤יךָ אֲדֹנִי֙ כִּ֣י נִֽחַמְתָּ֔נִי וְכִ֥י דִבַּ֖רְתָּ עַל־לֵ֣ב שִׁפְחָתֶ֑ךָ וְאָנֹכִי֙ לֹ֣א אֶֽהְיֶ֔ה כְּאַחַ֖ת שִׁפְחֹתֶֽיךָ׃

ACCENT PHRASING

וַתֹּ֗אמֶר
אֶמְצָא־חֵ֨ן בְּעֵינֶ֤יךָ אֲדֹנִי֙
כִּ֣י נִֽחַמְתָּ֔נִי וְכִ֥י דִבַּ֖רְתָּ עַל־לֵ֣ב שִׁפְחָתֶ֑ךָ
וְאָנֹכִי֙ לֹ֣א אֶֽהְיֶ֔ה כְּאַחַ֖ת שִׁפְחֹתֶֽיךָ׃

וַתֹּ֗אמֶר

וַתֹּאמֶר is a Qal imperfect 3fs of אמר + *vav*-consecutive of temporal succession. The main narrative now resumes with Ruth's direct speech to Boaz.

אֶמְצָא־חֵ֨ן בְּעֵינֶ֤יךָ אֲדֹנִי֙

אֶמְצָא is a Qal imperfect 1cs of מצא. The verbal conjugation (imperfective) is a bit odd here. We saw this construction earlier in the chapter (2:2, 10), but the contexts there did not render the verbal conjugation confusing. We would expect the imperfective here to mirror verse 2 in which Ruth seeks to find favor in someone's eyes while in the field and to glean after that person, a clearly future reference, warranting the imperfective. However, a basic indicative, "I will find favor in your eyes," does not fit this context.

A better option for rendering אֶמְצָא־חֵן is as a modal imperfective with a slight variation compared to the standard cohortative.[45] As a basic cohortative, the clause would translate, "*May* I find favor in your eyes," but even then we should not see this as a request since Ruth is answering back to Boaz *about* the favor he has already expressed to her. Joüon describes this use of the cohortative form to render an optative mood. The difference

45. Joüon, *Ruth*, 54. Joüon points to his grammar (JM §114bN) to suggest that III-א verbs do not take ָה as the ending for the cohortative.

is that a basic cohortative usually expresses a wish or desire by means of a request, whereas an optative expresses a hopeful desire that a present situation will continue.[46] In this sense, we could translate אֶמְצָא־חֵן as "May I find favor," but with the nuance of Ruth respectfully saying, "I want to always find favor in your eyes." It is a situation that is not yet completed, and hence the imperfective aspect is fitting. Ruth's unconventional syntax sharpens the expression of her desire to continue receiving favor from Boaz. Therefore, אֶמְצָא־חֵן is an optative statement (exclamation), not a petition.[47]

In this verse, חֵן refers to "interhuman activity," especially "beneficent actions that are freely offered or received and contribute to the well-being of another or to the health of an ongoing relationship."[48] As this scene moves forward, Boaz shows favor to Ruth by letting her glean in his field and by gently commanding her not to go to another field (2:8). In 2:14–16, we will see Boaz expand the favor he shows to Ruth, but at this point, Ruth's statement about desiring favor with Boaz is based only on his allowing her to glean. Surely, this was more than a societal kindness from Boaz, but the order in which the narrative presents these ideas suggests that Ruth sees חֵן from Boaz grounded in torah's demand to care for the vulnerable. There is no indication that Boaz informed Ruth of their family relationship, and so Ruth likely does not know this until she returns to Naomi and learns in whose field she gleaned (2:19–20). At this specific point in the narrative, the favor Ruth recognizes from Boaz is the favor of a man who loves and follows torah. She therefore sees *God's* provision for her and Naomi through the kindness of Boaz. The kindnesses that Boaz is about to offer will go above and beyond simply gleaning in a field, and the audience surely anticipates Boaz's contribution to the well-being of Ruth beyond physical sustenance.

---

46. RJW §184a.

47. For more discussion on this challenging construction, see Block, *Ruth*, 134–35; Holmstedt, *Ruth*, 130; Wilch, *Ruth*, 75–76.

48. *NIDOTTE* 2:204.

בְּעֵינֶיךָ is the prepositional phrase that completes the expression אֶמְצָא־חֵן בְּעֵינֶיךָ. אֲדֹנִי is a term of respect, not ownership (from Boaz's perspective) or subservience (from Ruth's perspective) (cf. Gen 24:18; 32:5; 1 Sam 25:24).

כִּי נִחַמְתָּנִי וְכִי דִבַּרְתָּ עַל־לֵב שִׁפְחָתֶךָ

These כִּי clauses express the ground or reason Ruth knows she has found favor and will find favor with Boaz. The reason is that he has already comforted her (נִחַמְתָּנִי) and spoken kindly (דִבַּרְתָּ עַל־לֵב) to her as his maidservant. נִחַמְתָּנִי is a Piel perfect 2ms of נחם + 1cs pronominal object. נחם may be understood as a stative verb, "to be in a state of comfort or sorrow." Therefore, the Piel communicates putting someone into the state of comfort (factitive), which means "to comfort." "For you have comforted me." The perfective aspect of the verb is best understood as an English perfect, "you have comforted me," a past action with ongoing results.

Notice the morphology of the Piel with a guttural in the second root letter position (נִחַמְתָּנִי). The guttural (ח) will not accept the *dāgēš forte* one would expect in the Piel stem. With some gutturals, the preceding vowel will lengthen when a *dāgēš* is rejected.[49] With ח, the preceding vowel will never lengthen in a Piel; hence, the *dāgēš forte* is "implied."[50] The first syllable is still treated as a closed and unaccented syllable taking a short vowel (נִ) even without the *dāgēš forte* in the ח.

וְכִי introduces a second ground clause, providing yet another reason Ruth knows she has found favor with Boaz. She has found favor because he has comforted her and because he has spoken "upon [her] heart." דִבַּרְתָּ is a Piel perfect 2ms of דבר. Notice there is no *dāgēš lene* in the initial ד because the preceding word (וְכִי) ends in a vowel. Hence, the BeGaD KePhaT letter (ד) is not preceded by a silent *shewa*. עַל־לֵב is an idiomatic

49. Cf. בֵּרַךְ where the initial *ḥîreq* of the Piel perfect has lengthened to *ṣere* because the ר rejected the *dāgēš forte* and lengthened the preceding vowel by compensation.

50. *IBH*, 207–8. Since this phenomenon occurs most often with the ה and ח, Kutz and Josberger say that this is "H"onorary doubling (*Learning Biblical Hebrew*, 404). The *dāgēš* is "honorary" in the "H" consonants. It is not visible but should be understood as present since the preceding vowel does not lengthen.

way to say that Boaz has spoken "kindly" or "reassured" Ruth (cf. Gen 34:3; 50:21; Judg 19:3; 2 Sam 19:8; Isa 40:2; Hos 2:16).[51] שִׁפְחָתֶךָ is Ruth's self-designation as Boaz's "maidservant." Here Ruth describes herself with the low status of a laborer.[52]

וְאָנֹכִי לֹא אֶהְיֶה כְּאַחַת שִׁפְחֹתֶיךָ׃

The final clause begins with a disjunctive *vav* to communicate circumstance. Ruth declares that her status was *not* one of the שִׁפְחָה even though she is now being welcomed as such. The disjunctive *vav* in a circumstantial clause translates, "*even though* I do not exist as one of your maidservants."[53]

לֹא אֶהְיֶה is the negated Qal imperfect 1cs of היה. The imperfective is present tense, stating a current status for Ruth. The present tense imperfective is common in direct speech.[54]

כְּאַחַת שִׁפְחֹתֶיךָ is an adverbial accusative with the preposition (כ, "as") explicitly written indicating Ruth's status or situation. "I do not exist *as* (in the status of) one of your maidservants."[55] The numeral אַחַת (fs) does not distinguish morphologically between absolute and construct states. Here the accent is a disjunctive *ṭifḥā*, but the form must be construct ("one *of* your maidservants"). In the accent pattern used here, the *ṭifḥā* must occur one or two words in front of the *sôf-pāsûq/sillûq* (שִׁפְחֹתֶיךָ׃), but it cannot occur on אֶהְיֶה since that is the main verb. Therefore, the *ṭifḥā* must occur on כְּאַחַת even though the word is in construct with שִׁפְחֹתֶיךָ. The disjunctive accent does not dismiss the construct state of כְּאַחַת. It is simply the accent required in this particular pattern. The construct package (כְּאַחַת שִׁפְחֹתֶיךָ)

51. Wilch, *Ruth*, 74.

52. *NIDOTTE* 4:212. Cf. C. Cohen, "Studies in Extrabiblical Hebrew Inscriptions: The Semantic Range and Usage of the Terms אמה and שפחה," *Shnaton* 5–6 (1978/79): xxv–liii; A. Jepsen, "Amah und Schiphchah," *Vetus Testamentum* 8 (1958): 293–97, 425.

53. Fuller and Choi (*IBHS* §74d) list ו as a particle that can introduce a concessive clause, "even though."

54. RJW §167(1).

55. Fuller and Choi (*IBHS* §13z) comment that the adverbial accusative of situation often implies the כ preposition. Here it is simply written explicitly but functions syntactically the same as if כ were not written in other adverbial accusatives of situation.

communicates an implied meaning related to the preposition מִן, "one *from among* your maidservants." Ruth grounds the favor she is receiving from Boaz in the fact that he has treated her as one of his maidservants even though she is not one technically. Boaz does not treat Ruth like a foreign widow; rather, he treats her as a native Israelite servant.

It is worth continuing to note that Boaz's treatment of Ruth is indicative of his character when he is first introduced as an אִישׁ גִּבּוֹר חַיִל (2:1). Boaz is not the typical patriarchal male in society, but rather seems to go out of his way to treat his maidservants with dignity and respect. Ruth relates the kindness he has shown her to the same kindness he shows to his maidservants. She is being treated with dignity and finds comfort in Boaz's provision. Even though Ruth is not one of Boaz's maidservants, her self-designation based on Boaz's favor toward her suggests that Boaz is indeed an אִישׁ גִּבּוֹר חַיִל.

*14 And Boaz said to her, "Draw near here and eat from the bread (food) and dip
your morsel in the vinegar (wine)." And so she sat beside the reapers and he
reached out to her roasted grain and she ate, and she was satisfied, and she had
some left over. 15 And then she arose to glean. And Boaz commanded his young
men, saying, "Moreover between the sheaves she shall glean and you shall not put
her to shame. 16 And moreover, you shall surely draw out for her from the bundles
and you shall abandon (them) so she shall glean, and you shall not rebuke her."*

*17 And so she gleaned in the field until evening. And she beat out that which she had
gleaned, and it was (about) an ephah of barley. 18 And she lifted (it) up and she came
to the city, and her mother-in-law saw that which she had gleaned, and she brought
(it) out and she gave to her that which she had left over from her satisfaction. 19 And
her mother-in-law said to her, "Where did you glean today, and where did you work?
May the one who took notice of (recognized) you be blessed." And she declared to her
mother-in-law with whom she had worked and she said, "The name of the man with
whom I worked today (was) Boaz." 20 And Naomi said to her daughter-in-law, "Blessed
(be) he by the Lord who has not abandoned his lovingkindness with the living or the
dead." And Naomi said to her, "Near to us the man; he is from our redeemers." 21 And
Ruth the Moabitess said, "Moreover he said to me, 'With my young men, you shall
cling until they have completed all of the harvest which is to me.' " 22 And Naomi said
to Ruth, her daughter-in-law, "(It is) good, my daughter, that you go out with his
young women that they [masc.] may not encounter you in another field." 23 And so
she clung to the young women of Boaz to glean until the end of the harvest of barley
and the harvest of wheat. And she dwelled with her mother-in-law.*

RUTH

2:14–23

14 וַיֹּאמֶר֩ לָ֨ה בֹ֜עַז לְעֵ֣ת הָאֹ֗כֶל גֹּ֤שִֽׁי הֲלֹם֙ וְאָכַ֣לְתְּ מִן־הַלֶּ֔חֶם וְטָבַ֥לְתְּ פִּתֵּ֖ךְ בַּחֹ֑מֶץ
וַתֵּ֙שֶׁב֙ מִצַּ֣ד הַקּֽוֹצְרִ֔ים וַיִּצְבָּט־לָ֣הּ קָלִ֔י וַתֹּ֥אכַל וַתִּשְׂבַּ֖ע וַתֹּתַֽר׃ 15 וַתָּ֖קָם לְלַקֵּ֑ט וַיְצַו֩
בֹּ֨עַז אֶת־נְעָרָ֜יו לֵאמֹ֗ר גַּ֣ם בֵּ֧ין הָעֳמָרִ֛ים תְּלַקֵּ֖ט וְלֹ֥א תַכְלִימֽוּהָ׃ 16 וְגַ֛ם שֹׁל־תָּשֹׁ֥לּוּ
לָ֖הּ מִן־הַצְּבָתִ֑ים וַעֲזַבְתֶּ֥ם וְלִקְּטָ֖ה וְלֹ֥א תִגְעֲרוּ־בָֽהּ׃

17 וַתְּלַקֵּ֥ט בַּשָּׂדֶ֖ה עַד־הָעָ֑רֶב וַתַּחְבֹּט֙ אֵ֣ת אֲשֶׁר־לִקֵּ֔טָה וַיְהִ֖י כְּאֵיפָ֥ה שְׂעֹרִֽים׃
18 וַתִּשָּׂא֙ וַתָּב֣וֹא הָעִ֔יר וַתֵּ֥רֶא חֲמוֹתָ֖הּ אֵ֣ת אֲשֶׁר־לִקֵּ֑טָה וַתּוֹצֵא֙ וַתִּתֶּן־לָ֔הּ אֵ֥ת
אֲשֶׁר־הוֹתִ֖רָה מִשָּׂבְעָֽהּ׃ 19 וַתֹּ֩אמֶר֩ לָ֨הּ חֲמוֹתָ֜הּ אֵיפֹ֨ה לִקַּ֤טְתְּ הַיּוֹם֙ וְאָ֣נָה עָשִׂ֔ית
יְהִ֥י מַכִּירֵ֖ךְ בָּר֑וּךְ וַתַּגֵּ֣ד לַחֲמוֹתָ֗הּ אֵ֤ת אֲשֶׁר־עָשְׂתָה֙ עִמּ֔וֹ וַתֹּ֗אמֶר שֵׁ֤ם הָאִישׁ֙ אֲשֶׁ֨ר
עָשִׂ֧יתִי עִמּ֛וֹ הַיּ֖וֹם בֹּֽעַז׃ 20 וַתֹּ֨אמֶר נָעֳמִ֜י לְכַלָּתָ֗הּ בָּר֥וּךְ הוּא֙ לַיהוָ֔ה אֲשֶׁר֙ לֹא־עָזַ֣ב
חַסְדּ֔וֹ אֶת־הַחַיִּ֖ים וְאֶת־הַמֵּתִ֑ים וַתֹּ֧אמֶר לָ֣הּ נָעֳמִ֗י קָר֥וֹב לָ֙נוּ֙ הָאִ֔ישׁ מִֽגֹּאֲלֵ֖נוּ
הֽוּא׃ 21 וַתֹּ֖אמֶר ר֣וּת הַמּוֹאֲבִיָּ֑ה גַּ֣ם ׀ כִּי־אָמַ֣ר אֵלַ֗י עִם־הַנְּעָרִ֤ים אֲשֶׁר־לִי֙ תִּדְבָּקִ֔ין
עַ֣ד אִם־כִּלּ֔וּ אֵ֥ת כָּל־הַקָּצִ֖יר אֲשֶׁר־לִֽי׃ 22 וַתֹּ֥אמֶר נָעֳמִ֖י אֶל־ר֣וּת כַּלָּתָ֑הּ ט֣וֹב
בִּתִּ֗י כִּ֤י תֵֽצְאִי֙ עִם־נַ֣עֲרוֹתָ֔יו וְלֹ֥א יִפְגְּעוּ־בָ֖ךְ בְּשָׂדֶ֥ה אַחֵֽר׃ 23 וַתִּדְבַּ֗ק בְּנַעֲר֥וֹת בֹּ֙עַז֙
לְלַקֵּ֔ט עַד־כְּל֥וֹת קְצִֽיר־הַשְּׂעֹרִ֖ים וּקְצִ֣יר הַחִטִּ֑ים וַתֵּ֖שֶׁב אֶת־חֲמוֹתָֽהּ׃

RUTH 2:14

וַיֹּ֩אמֶר֩ לָ֨ה בֹ֜עַז לְעֵ֣ת הָאֹ֗כֶל גֹּ֤שִֽׁי הֲלֹם֙ וְאָכַ֣לְתְּ מִן־הַלֶּ֔חֶם וְטָבַ֥לְתְּ פִּתֵּ֖ךְ בַּחֹ֑מֶץ
וַתֵּ֙שֶׁב֙ מִצַּ֣ד הַקּוֹצְרִ֔ים וַיִּצְבָּט־לָ֣הּ קָלִ֔י וַתֹּ֥אכַל וַתִּשְׂבַּ֖ע וַתֹּתַֽר׃

ACCENT PHRASING

וַיֹּ֩אמֶר֩ לָ֨ה בֹ֜עַז לְעֵ֣ת הָאֹ֗כֶל
גֹּ֤שִֽׁי הֲלֹם֙ וְאָכַ֣לְתְּ מִן־הַלֶּ֔חֶם וְטָבַ֥לְתְּ פִּתֵּ֖ךְ בַּחֹ֑מֶץ
וַתֵּ֙שֶׁב֙ מִצַּ֣ד הַקּוֹצְרִ֔ים
וַיִּצְבָּט־לָ֣הּ קָלִ֔י
וַתֹּ֥אכַל וַתִּשְׂבַּ֖ע וַתֹּתַֽר׃

וַיֹּ֩אמֶר֩ לָ֨ה בֹ֜עַז לְעֵ֣ת הָאֹ֗כֶל

Ruth 2:14 continues the main narrative, now with Boaz's response to Ruth. וַיֹּ֩אמֶר֩ is the Qal imperfect 3ms of אמר + *vav*-consecutive of temporal succession. בֹ֜עַז is the subject and לָ֨ה is the ל preposition with the 3fs pronominal suffix. The normal *mappîq* of the 3fs suffix (ָהּ) is missing in the ה (cf. Num 32:42; Zech 5:11).[1] The lack of a *mappîq* suggests that the final ה is not to be pronounced. The marginal note in *BHS* reads, ג לא מפק ה ("three [times] without *mappîq* [in the] ה").[2] Why and how the ה would be "unpronounced" here is lost to our modern ears.

לְעֵ֣ת הָאֹ֗כֶל literally translates as "to the time of the food." Being definite, these two words taken together indicate a typical meal of the day, probably a lunch that would have been eaten in the field.[3] ל + עֵת is temporal, "at the time of."

1. The ה without a *mappîq* in Zechariah 5:11 is, however, marked with a *rafe* over the ה. For *rafe*, see JM §12a. For לָהֿ in Zechariah 5:11, Ruth 2:13, and Numbers 32:42, see JM §25a. For *mappîq*, see JM §11a; GKC §14b, e.

2. Kelley, Mynatt, and Crawford, *Masorah of Biblia Hebraica Stuttgartensia*, 144–45.

3. Wilch, *Ruth*, 75.

גֹּֽשִׁי הֲלֹם֙ וְאָכַ֣לְתְּ מִן־הַלֶּ֔חֶם וְטָבַ֥לְתְּ פִּתֵּ֖ךְ בַּחֹ֑מֶץ

גֹּֽשִׁי is a Qal imperative 2fs of the root נגשׁ. In the Qal imperative of I-נ verbs, the initial נ flees (*aphaeresis*),[4] and the *dāgēš* left in the ג is the *dāgēš lene*. The *ḥōlem* associated with the ג is also odd in this form since a *shewa* would be expected because of the vocalic ending of the imperative 2fs (ִי). Gesenius calls this the נָסוֹג אָחוֹר, where the accent on the first word retracts to the penultimate syllable (here the ג) for "rhythmical reasons."[5] Notice the accent *mĕhuppaḥ* (֤) on גֹּֽשִׁי has retracted to the ג, but a vocal *shewa* cannot be accented. Therefore, the vowel must lengthen to the original *ḥōlem*.

הֲלֹם֙ is an adverbial accusative indicating *where* Ruth shall approach, "here." וְאָכַ֣לְתְּ is a Qal perfect 2fs of אכל + *vav*-consecutive. The *vav*-consecutive, following the previous imperative (גֹּֽשִׁי), continues the imperatival force, "Approach here, and *eat*."[6] מִן is partitive, meaning that Ruth may eat from *some of* the bread. Even translated as "some," מִן is not limiting in the sense that Boaz is limiting Ruth to only a portion. מִן communicates "some of" the category of bread, not "some of" the quantity of bread.

וְטָבַ֥לְתְּ is a Qal perfect 2fs of טבל + *vav*-consecutive and continues the imperatival force at the beginning of the clause (גֹּֽשִׁי). פִּתֵּ֖ךְ is the direct object of the verb, "your morsel." פִּתֵּ֖ךְ is the noun derived from the verbal root פתת, "to break up, crumble."[7] The geminate verbal root is the reason for the *dāgēš forte* in פִּתֵּ֖ךְ. When suffixes are added to the noun פַּת, the *dāgēš forte* appears. חֹ֑מֶץ is most often understood as a sort of wine. The ב on בַּחֹ֑מֶץ is locative, the place where Ruth is to dip her morsel. In this verse, Boaz heightens his kindness by offering Ruth the same meal as all the other servants.

וַתֵּ֙שֶׁב֙ מִצַּ֣ד הַקּֽוֹצְרִ֔ים

וַתֵּ֙שֶׁב֙ returns to the formal narrative and provides the logical succession to Boaz's invitation to eat, "And so she sat ..." וַתֵּ֙שֶׁב֙ is a Qal imperfect 3fs of

4. GKC §§66a, 19h.
5. GKC §29e. See also the example given in Gesenius's discussion of the I-נ verbs in §66c.
6. RJW §179.
7. BDB, 837.

ישב + *vav*-consecutive. ישב is a I-י verb in the lexicon but behaves morphologically like a I-ו. In the Qal imperfect, the ו flees and the preformative vowel lengthens (◌◌תֵּ).

מִצַּד is the locative מִן preposition and the noun צַד. מִן is not locative in the sense of moving away from something but should be understood as a spatial relationship. To be "*from* the side of the reapers" is to be in their vicinity, or "beside" them.[8] The accent (◌֣, *mûnāḥ*) on מִצַּ֣ד indicates a construct package with הַקּֽוֹצְרִ֑ים, so Ruth sat "from the side *of* the reapers," or "beside the reapers."

וַיִּצְבָּט־לָ֣הּ קָלִ֔י

וַיִּצְבָּט is a Qal imperfect 3ms of צבט + *vav*-consecutive. The 3ms verb makes Boaz the contextual subject. Morphologically, notice that the thematic vowel is a *qāmeṣ-ḥāṭûf*. With the *maqqēf* (־), the accent shifts from וַיִּצְבָּט and falls on לָ֣הּ, leaving the final syllable of the verb (וַיִּצְבָּט) closed and unaccented, requiring a short vowel. The original *ḥōlem* therefore shortens to a *qāmeṣ-ḥāṭûf*. קָלִ֔י is the direct object, indicating what Boaz offered to Ruth (לָ֣הּ).

וַתֹּ֥אכַל וַתִּשְׂבַּ֖ע וַתֹּתַֽר׃

The narrative now moves forward quickly with three successive verbal actions. וַתֹּאכַל is a Qal imperfect 3fs of אכל + *vav*-consecutive. The *vav* could be understood as temporal succession or logical succession. If temporal succession, Ruth simply eats after having been given the roasted grain. If it is logical succession, then Ruth eats as a consequence of having been given grain: "and *so* she ate." Logical succession is more likely the meaning here.

וַתִּשְׂבַּע is a Qal imperfect 3fs of שׂבע + *vav*-consecutive. Again, the *vav* can be temporal or logical succession. Temporal succession would imply that Ruth was satisfied after having eaten. Logical succession implies that Ruth was satisfied as a result of eating.

---

8. RJW §323a.

Finally, וַתֹּתַ֑ר is a Hiphil imperfect 3fs of יתר + *vav*-consecutive. This *vav* is temporal succession since there is not a clear logical link between "eating," "being satisfied," and "having some left over." Someone could eat to satisfaction and not have some left over. Additionally, the Hiphil stem communicates a causative, suggesting that Ruth intended to have some left over or saved some specifically for Naomi. We will see in 2:18 that Ruth gives Naomi some of this leftover, and we can safely infer that Ruth intentionally saved some for Naomi. Therefore, the *vav* is likely temporal succession. Intentionally leaving some grain left over was the next action in the narrative, not the logical outcome of eating and being satisfied.

Morphologically, the standard Hiphil paradigm would produce the form וַתּוֹתִיר. The preformative vowel becomes *ḥōlem-vav*, which is the result of the aw ⟶ ô contraction (תּוֹ ⟵ תַּוְ) but is written defectively here as a *ḥōlem*. The normal thematic vowel in the Hiphil is *ḥîreq-yôd*. However, the Hiphil *vav*-consecutive is a *ṣērê* form, so rather than a *ḥîreq-yôd* thematic vowel one would expect a *ṣērê*. BDB, *HALOT*, and *DCH* all list this form from 2:14 but fail to comment on the reason for the *pataḥ* thematic vowel.[9] It seems that the Hiphil imperfect 3fs and jussive 2ms form (Gen 49:4) of יתר have a *pataḥ* thematic vowel, whereas all other forms of the Hiphil imperfect or jussive have a *ḥîreq-yôd* or *ṣērê* as expected.

9. BDB, 451; *DCH* 4:344; *HALOT*, 452.

RUTH 2:15

וַתָּ֖קָם לְלַקֵּ֑ט וַיְצַו֩ בֹּ֨עַז אֶת־נְעָרָ֜יו לֵאמֹ֗ר גַּ֣ם בֵּ֧ין הָעֳמָרִ֛ים תְּלַקֵּ֖ט וְלֹ֥א תַכְלִימֽוּהָ׃

ACCENT PHRASING

וַתָּ֖קָם לְלַקֵּ֑ט
וַיְצַו֩ בֹּ֨עַז אֶת־נְעָרָ֜יו לֵאמֹ֗ר
גַּ֣ם בֵּ֧ין הָעֳמָרִ֛ים תְּלַקֵּ֖ט וְלֹ֥א תַכְלִימֽוּהָ׃

וַתָּ֖קָם לְלַקֵּ֑ט

After Ruth's meal with Boaz, the main narrative now continues. וַתָּ֖קָם is the Qal imperfect 3fs of קום + *vav*-consecutive. Notice in the *vav*-consecutive of קום (and other hollow roots) that the accent retracts to the preformative syllable (וַתָּ֖קָם) and so the thematic vowel (normally *ḥōlem-vav*) is a short *qāmeṣ-ḥāṭûf* in a closed unaccented syllable (וַתָּ֖קָם).

לְלַקֵּ֑ט is a Piel infinitive construct of לקט + the ל of purpose. Rather than simply completing the verbal notion of Ruth rising up "to glean," this infinitive indicates the reason she rose up.

וַיְצַו֩ בֹּ֨עַז אֶת־נְעָרָ֜יו לֵאמֹ֗ר

וַיְצַו֩ is the Piel imperfect 3ms of צוה + *vav*-consecutive. צוה is a III-ה verb, and the *vav*-consecutive forms are apocopated forms where the final ה drops. Since the ו is now the final letter of the word, it cannot take the *dāgēš forte* of the Piel. Hebrew generally will not allow doubled final consonants. בֹּ֨עַז is the subject and אֶת־נְעָרָ֜יו is the definite direct object, "his young men." Notice that the suffix is the 3ms suffix for a plural noun (◌ָיו), "his young *men*." לֵאמֹ֗ר introduces Boaz's direct speech but may feel redundant in English and can often be left untranslated.

גַּ֣ם בֵּ֧ין הָעֳמָרִ֛ים תְּלַקֵּ֖ט וְלֹ֥א תַכְלִימֽוּהָ׃

גַּ֣ם begins Boaz's direct speech and is emphatic. גַּ֣ם may introduce some sort of addition to a previous command. In 2:9, we read that Boaz has already commanded the young men not to touch Ruth. Here Boaz includes the additional (positive) command to allow her to glean among the הָעֳמָרִים, hence the use of an additive גַּם. בֵּין is spatial rather than locative, "among" as opposed to "between."[10]

גַּם sometimes emphasizes an entire sentence or clause, but more often it emphasizes the word or phrase immediately following (בֵּין הָעֳמָרִים).[11] The emphasis here is on the fact that Boaz is letting Ruth glean "among the sheaves" of harvested grain rather than just at the edges of the field. The construction may even imply that Ruth does not have to wait until the women have gone through the field to gather the cut grain into sheaves. Rather, she is allowed to glean alongside the female workers, a phase of the harvest in which she would normally be prohibited as a foreigner. Hence, the place where Ruth may glean is emphatic, "*Even* among the sheaves."

תְּלַקֵּט is a Piel jussive 3fs of לקט, translated modally as "she may glean." Unfortunately, there is no morphological indicator for the jussive. In the context, Boaz is commanding his young men to "let" Ruth glean. He is not informing them that "she *will* glean."

וְלֹא תַכְלִימוּהָ is Boaz's negative command to his young men. תַכְלִימוּהָ is a negated Hiphil imperfect 2mp of כלם + 3fs object suffix. Notice that the 3fs suffix attaches directly to the verb. With the historic long vowel sufformative (תַּכְלִימוּ) of the imperfect 2mp, there is no need for a connecting vowel as in the alternative 3fs suffix on verbs (ֶהָ or ֶהָ). In the causative Hiphil, כלם translates as "You shall not *cause* her to be humiliated." The idea is that the young men are not to expose Ruth to shame or reproach by humiliating her in the field. This entails any sort of physical harm but also extends to any verbal reproach. Ruth is allowed to glean among the sheaves without any recourse to snide comments from Boaz's young men.

10. See 2:7 for a similar interpretation of the sheaves. See also Joüon, *Ruth*, 57.

11. BDB, 168–69.

RUTH 2:16

וְגַם שֹׁל־תָּשֹׁלּוּ לָהּ מִן־הַצְּבָתִים וַעֲזַבְתֶּם וְלִקְּטָה וְלֹא תִגְעֲרוּ־בָהּ׃

ACCENT PHRASING

וְגַם שֹׁל־תָּשֹׁלּוּ לָהּ מִן־הַצְּבָתִים
וַעֲזַבְתֶּם וְלִקְּטָה וְלֹא תִגְעֲרוּ־בָהּ׃

וְגַם שֹׁל־תָּשֹׁלּוּ לָהּ מִן־הַצְּבָתִים

וְגַם is now additive *and* emphatic. It adds to Boaz's previous command in 2:15, and it continues the emphatic nature of the present commands to his young men to allow Ruth to glean in the fields.

שֹׁל־תָּשֹׁלּוּ is an absolute object (cognate accusative). שֹׁל is morphologically the Qal infinitive construct of the geminate root שׁלל but functions in 2:16 as an infinitive absolute. In geminate verbs, the infinitive absolute would appear as a strong verb (שָׁלוֹל), but with the *maqqēf* (־) here, the morphology shifts to mimic the infinitive construct.[12] As is standard with the absolute object, the second verbal form (תָּשֹׁלּוּ) is a finite verbal form, the Qal imperfect 2mp of שׁלל. The geminate root is noticeable here with the *dāgēš forte* in the ל (תָּשֹׁלּוּ). Because only one of the two geminate root letters is explicit, the preformative vowel lengthens in a pretonic open syllable (תָּשֹׁלּוּ). As an absolute object, the emphatic statement is "And moreover, *you shall surely pull out* for her from the bundles." לָהּ is a ל of advantage ("for her"). What the young men pull out from the bundles is for Ruth's advantage.

מִן־הַצְּבָתִים is a prepositional complement communicating from where the young men are to pull grain—namely, "from the bundles." מִן is partitive, meaning that the young men are to pull out grain from *some of* the bundles, but not necessarily all of them. הַצְּבָתִים is a *hapax legomenon*. According to *HALOT*, the word is related to cognate verbal roots having to do with

12. JM §123q.

grasping or seizing.[13] Since הַצְּבָתִים is a nominal form, *HALOT* concludes the word is understood as the bundles/sheaves of corn (i.e., grain) composed of the ears that are "grasped in the left hand while being cut with the right."[14] With גַּם and the absolute object (שֹׁל־תָּשֹׁלּוּ), there is no question about what Boaz requires of his young men. Ruth is allowed to glean בֵּין הָעֳמָרִים (2:15), and now the young men are to actively pull out for her מִן־הַצְּבָתִים. Boaz intentionally moves beyond the torah regarding the minimal provision for gleaners (Lev 19:9–10; 23:22; Deut 24:19–21).[15]

וַעֲזַבְתֶּם וְלִקְּטָה וְלֹא תִגְעֲרוּ־בָהּ׃

וַעֲזַבְתֶּם is the Qal perfect 2mp of עזב + *vav*-consecutive. The *vav* + perfective is future tense following the initial imperfect (תָּשֹׁלּוּ). Even as future tense, both verbs are mildly imperative, "you *shall* pull out ... and you *shall* leave alone." Notice that the *vav*-consecutive on the perfective points like the conjunctive *vav*, here taking the *pataḥ* in place of the normal *shewa* because of the *ḥāṭēf-pataḥ* (ֲ) under the ע (וַעֲזַבְתֶּם ⟵ וְעֲזַבְתֶּם).

וְלִקְּטָה is a Piel perfect 3fs of לקט + *vav*-consecutive. The *vav* communicates an implied purpose clause, "so that she may glean." As a standard *vav*-consecutive, it would continue the same verbal nuance as the previous *vav* + perfective, "and she *shall* glean." However, since the level of discourse is Boaz's conversation with his young men rather than direct communication with Ruth, a mild imperative to her does not fit best.

Another element that factors into this discussion is the question of what Boaz instructs the young men to "leave." The object of וַעֲזַבְתֶּם is null (absent or missing). If the object is what the men pull out from the bundles ("it"), then Boaz is saying, "leave [it] that she may glean [it]," reading וְלִקְּטָה as a purpose clause.[16] A second, though less likely, option is to see וַעֲזַבְתֶּם as Boaz's instructions to his young men to "leave [her]" alone and

---

13. *HALOT*, 1000.

14. *HALOT*, 1000. See also *NIDOTTE* 3:741. *NIDOTTE* is more inconclusive about what exactly these "bundles" are. Wilch, *Ruth*, 80.

15. Block, *Ruth*, 137–38.

16. Wilch, *Ruth*, 81; Block, *Ruth*, 138; Joüon, *Ruth*, 59.

not bother Ruth while she gleans. In this case, וְלִקְּטָה functions essentially as a *vav*-consecutive perfect, "and she shall glean," but with the implications that she will glean without worrying about the men being around. The primary value of this second option is that it again reinforces Boaz's commitment to protect Ruth from potential harm while in the field. They are to leave the field altogether, "and then" Ruth shall glean. The difficulty with this reading is that the instructions in the next clause seem unnecessary if Boaz has already told his young men to leave the field outright. How could they rebuke her if they were not there? Therefore, the object of וַעֲזַבְתֶּם is what they pull out from the bundles ("it"), and וְלִקְּטָה is a modal perfect expressing the purpose for why they are to leave what they pull out, "*so that* she may glean [it]."

וְלֹא תִגְעֲרוּ־בָהּ׃ is an emphatic prohibition, now with the use of לֹא + the imperfect.[17] תִגְעֲרוּ is a Qal imperfect 2mp of גער, "to rebuke." בָהּ is the accusative object. With the verb גער, ten of the fourteen occurrences take ב as the direct object marker.[18] As in 2:15, Boaz commands the men not to rebuke Ruth, but now with a different verb (גער). Regardless of how many synonymous terms it takes, Boaz is making certain to protect Ruth while she is in the field gleaning. Naomi will express concern in 2:22 without necessarily knowing all the ways that Boaz has provided for Ruth already. However, the narrator shows the audience clearly that Boaz is indeed an אִישׁ גִּבּוֹר חַיִל who has taken significant steps to protect this disenfranchised woman.

17. *IBHS* §§4i, 42a, c.

18. BDB, 172.

RUTH 2:17

וַתְּלַקֵּ֥ט בַּשָּׂדֶ֖ה עַד־הָעָ֑רֶב וַתַּחְבֹּט֙ אֵ֣ת אֲשֶׁר־לִקֵּ֔טָה וַיְהִ֖י כְּאֵיפָ֥ה שְׂעֹרִֽים׃

ACCENT PHRASING

וַתְּלַקֵּ֥ט בַּשָּׂדֶ֖ה עַד־הָעָ֑רֶב
וַתַּחְבֹּט֙ אֵ֣ת אֲשֶׁר־לִקֵּ֔טָה
וַיְהִ֖י כְּאֵיפָ֥ה שְׂעֹרִֽים׃

וַתְּלַקֵּ֥ט בַּשָּׂדֶ֖ה עַד־הָעָ֑רֶב

The narrative continues now with Ruth's actions, the result of Boaz's instructions to his workers. The *vav* on וַתְּלַקֵּט is a consequential action (logical succession), "And *so* she gleaned." וַתְּלַקֵּט is a Piel imperfect 3fs of לקט, and the following prepositional phrases provide the place and time of Ruth's gleaning. Ruth gleaned בַּשָּׂדֶה (place) and עַד־הָעָרֶב (time). Notice morphologically that the ב preposition supplants the article (בַּ◌), so we get "in *the* field." Also notice the long *qāmeṣ* under the ע in הָעָרֶב since the word is a pausal form with the strong disjunctive accent, *atnāḥ* (◌֑).

וַתַּחְבֹּט֙ אֵ֣ת אֲשֶׁר־לִקֵּ֔טָה

וַתַּחְבֹּט is a Qal imperfect 3fs of חבט + *vav*-consecutive. The *vav* is in temporal succession, "And *then* she beat out." Notice the *pataḥ* as the preformative vowel because of the I-ח. The ח will often retain a simple silent *shewa* in the first root letter position, but even when it does, it will push the preformative vowel to the vowel class that it would have been had the I-guttural changed to a composite *shewa*. In this case, the ח retains the silent *shewa*, but the preformative vowel shifts from the expected *ḥîreq* of the Qal to a *pataḥ* because of the influence of the I-ח.

אֲשֶׁר־לִקֵּטָה is the direct object relative clause marked by the definite direct object marker (אֵת).[19] לִקֵּטָה is the Piel perfect 3fs of לקט and translates as a pluperfect, "she had gleaned," since it refers to an action that

19. JM §125g.

happened prior to וַתַּחְבֹּט. In English, we do not think of a relative pronoun ("which") as a "thing" that could serve syntactically as an object of the verb. Therefore, it is best to supply "that" as the "thing" serving as the object for better English syntax: "And then she beat out *that* which she had gleaned."

וַיְהִי כְּאֵיפָה שְׂעֹרִים׃

The final clause describes how much Ruth gleaned and threshed out, summarizing the narrative rather than moving it forward. וַיְהִי is a Qal imperfect 3ms of היה + *vav*-consecutive. The implied subject is "it," referring to the grain. "It was about an ephah of barley." The כְּ on אֵיפָה is an approximation, similar to 1:4 regarding the number of years Ruth and Naomi were in Moab (כְּעֶשֶׂר שָׁנִים). כְּאֵיפָה is an absolute noun even though the translation seems that it is in the construct state, "an ephah *of* barley." שְׂעֹרִים specifies what the אֵיפָה consists of, modifying it appositionally.[20] שְׂעֹרִים is plural even though it only indicates the content of the אֵיפָה, not a particular number of barley(s). Ruth beat out "about an ephah, (specifically) barley," or "an ephah *of* barley."

20. Holmstedt, *Ruth*, 137; *GBHS* §2.4.4.

RUTH 2:18

וַתִּשָּׂא֙ וַתָּב֣וֹא הָעִ֔יר וַתֵּ֥רֶא חֲמוֹתָ֖הּ אֵ֣ת אֲשֶׁר־לִקֵּ֑טָה וַתּוֹצֵא֙ וַתִּתֶּן־לָ֔הּ אֵ֥ת
אֲשֶׁר־הוֹתִ֖רָה מִשָּׂבְעָֽהּ׃

ACCENT PHRASING

וַתִּשָּׂא֙ וַתָּב֣וֹא הָעִ֔יר
וַתֵּ֥רֶא חֲמוֹתָ֖הּ אֵ֣ת אֲשֶׁר־לִקֵּ֑טָה
וַתּוֹצֵא֙ וַתִּתֶּן־לָ֔הּ אֵ֥ת אֲשֶׁר־הוֹתִ֖רָה מִשָּׂבְעָֽהּ׃

וַתִּשָּׂא֙ וַתָּב֣וֹא הָעִ֔יר

The narrative now continues with Ruth's movement back to the city. וַתִּשָּׂא֙ is a Qal imperfect 3fs of נשׂא + *vav*-consecutive of temporal succession. The I-נ assimilates into the שׂ, and the III-א in the Qal imperfect takes a *pataḥ* thematic vowel that lengthens by compensation when the א quiesces (וַתִּשָּׂא ⟵ וַתִּשַּׂא). It is appropriate to include "it" (the ephah of barley) as an implied direct object, "And then she lifted [*it*] up." וַתִּשָּׂא֙ is active indicative, and with Ruth as the subject, some*thing* was lifted up.

וַתָּב֣וֹא is a Qal imperfect 3fs of בוא + *vav*-consecutive. The *vav* is temporal succession; Ruth lifted up the barley, "and *then* she came." הָעִ֔יר is the adverbial accusative of place, "to the city."[21] This construction is often marked with the directive ה. However, as in this verse, nouns can function as an adverbial accusative of place even without the unaccented ◌ָה.

וַתֵּ֥רֶא חֲמוֹתָ֖הּ אֵ֣ת אֲשֶׁר־לִקֵּ֑טָה

וַתֵּ֥רֶא is a Qal imperfect 3fs of ראה + *vav*-consecutive. With the III-ה verbs, the *vav*-consecutive form shortens (loses the final ה) and then typically displays segolization in the vowel pattern. Here, with the accent retracting to the preformative, the segolization is of the pattern ◌ֵ◌ֶ◌ (תֵּ֫רֶא), like סֵ֫פֶר.

The accents indicate that חֲמוֹתָ֖הּ is the subject. Notice that with the pronominal suffix (◌ָהּ), the vowel under the initial ח reduces to a vocal

21. JM §125n.

shewa—more specifically, a composite *shewa* (ֲ) because the ח is a guttural. With חֲמוֹתָהּ as the subject, the clause translates, "her mother-in-law saw."

The object phrase of וַתֵּרֶא is the relative clause אֵת אֲשֶׁר־לִקֵּטָה. As in 2:17, לִקֵּטָה is a Piel perfect 3fs of לקט and is translated as a pluperfect, "[that] which she *had gleaned*."

וַתּוֹצֵא וַתִּתֶּן־לָ֫הּ אֵת אֲשֶׁר־הוֹתִרָה מִשָּׂבְעָהּ׃

וַתּוֹצֵא is a Hiphil imperfect 3fs of יצא + *vav*-consecutive. In the Hiphil, it is literally "she *caused* to go out." The idea is that she "took out." The implied object, or the thing she "caused to go out," was the provision she brought back from Boaz (both the barley and אֵת אֲשֶׁר־הוֹתִרָה מִשָּׂבְעָהּ).

וַתִּתֶּן is the Qal imperfect 3fs of נתן + *vav*-consecutive. The *vav* is temporal succession. The act of giving to Naomi the leftovers follows temporally after removing it from her sack. The context indicates that the subject is Ruth. The *dāgēš forte* in the middle ת is the assimilated I-נ of נתן. We would normally expect a *ṣērê* as the thematic vowel, but with the *maqqēf* (־), the accent shifts to לָ֫הּ and so the final syllable of וַתִּתֶּן־ is closed and unaccented, requiring a short *sĕgōl* (וַתִּתֶּן־).

אֵת אֲשֶׁר־הוֹתִרָה מִשָּׂבְעָהּ is the definite direct object phrase—namely, what Ruth gave to Naomi. הוֹתִרָה is a Hiphil perfect 3fs of יתר, the thematic vowel written defectively with only a *ḥîreq* (הוֹתִרָה) rather than the normal *ḥîreq-yôd*. The Hiphil causative would be "which she *caused* to be left over," referring to the elements of Boaz's provisions that Ruth intentionally saved to bring to Naomi (cf. 2:14). When she was with Boaz, Ruth took what he extended to her and she ate it and was satisfied and she "saved some" for her mother-in-law. Now Ruth brings that abundance and gives it to Naomi along with the barley.

מִשָּׂבְעָהּ could be a noun meaning "from her abundance" or "from her satiation." However, it could also be an infinitive construct + מִן + a 3fs suffix and would be temporal, "after her satisfaction." The latter implies that Ruth took out food and ate in front of Naomi until she was full and only then gave some to Naomi. The more natural reading is to see מִשָּׂבְעָהּ as a noun referring to what Ruth had left over from the previous meal. "And she (Ruth) gave to her (Naomi) what she (Ruth) had remaining *from her abundance*."

RUTH 2:19

וַתֹּאמֶר֩ לָ֨הּ חֲמוֹתָ֜הּ אֵיפֹ֨ה לִקַּ֤טְתְּ הַיּוֹם֙ וְאָ֣נָה עָשִׂ֔ית יְהִ֥י מַכִּירֵ֖ךְ בָּר֑וּךְ וַתַּגֵּ֣ד לַחֲמוֹתָ֗הּ אֵ֤ת אֲשֶׁר־עָשְׂתָה֙ עִמּ֔וֹ וַתֹּ֗אמֶר שֵׁ֤ם הָאִישׁ֙ אֲשֶׁ֨ר עָשִׂ֧יתִי עִמּ֛וֹ הַיּ֖וֹם בֹּֽעַז׃

ACCENT PHRASING

וַתֹּאמֶר֩ לָ֨הּ חֲמוֹתָ֜הּ
אֵיפֹ֨ה לִקַּ֤טְתְּ הַיּוֹם֙ וְאָ֣נָה עָשִׂ֔ית
יְהִ֥י מַכִּירֵ֖ךְ בָּר֑וּךְ
וַתַּגֵּ֣ד לַחֲמוֹתָ֗הּ אֵ֤ת אֲשֶׁר־עָשְׂתָה֙ עִמּ֔וֹ
וַתֹּ֗אמֶר
שֵׁ֤ם הָאִישׁ֙ אֲשֶׁ֨ר עָשִׂ֧יתִי עִמּ֛וֹ הַיּ֖וֹם בֹּֽעַז׃

וַתֹּאמֶר֩ לָ֨הּ חֲמוֹתָ֜הּ

וַתֹּאמֶר֩ is the Qal imperfect 3fs + *vav*-consecutive of temporal succession. The narrative moves forward with Naomi's reply to Ruth. חֲמוֹתָ֜הּ is the subject. The object phrase, or what Naomi said, comes in the next clause. לָ֨הּ indicates to whom Naomi is talking, and the "her" of the 3fs object pronoun is Ruth.

אֵיפֹ֨ה לִקַּ֤טְתְּ הַיּוֹם֙ וְאָ֣נָה עָשִׂ֔ית

Naomi's question begins with the locative adverb אֵיפֹ֨ה, "where." לִקַּ֤טְתְּ is the Piel perfect 2fs of לקט, indicating completed action, "Where *did you glean* today ... ?" The definite article on הַיּוֹם֙ is the demonstrative article, "this day," but this is the common way of expressing "today."[22]

Naomi's question continues with another locative, וְאָ֣נָה, followed by עָשִׂ֔ית, a Qal perfect 2fs of עשׂה. Naomi asks Ruth, "Where did you *work*?" with עשׂה carrying the meaning of "doing" labor—that is, "working."

יְהִ֥י מַכִּירֵ֖ךְ בָּר֑וּךְ

יְהִ֥י is a Qal jussive 3ms of היה translated modally as "May (he) exist/be." The explicit subject is מַכִּירֵ֖ךְ, a Hiphil participle ms of נכר with a 2fs pronominal

22. BDB, 399.

suffix. Translated substantively as the subject, it is "the one who recognized you." In this verbal form, the I-נ assimilates, hence the *dāgēš forte* in the כ (מַכִּירֵ֫ךְ ⟵ מַנְכִּירֵ֫ךְ).

בָּר֑וּךְ is a Qal ms passive participle of ברך. The passive participle is identified by the וּ between the R2 and R3 of the verbal root. Since participles are verbal adjectives, בָּר֑וּךְ functions as the predicate adjective following היה. Another way to describe this syntax is as an adverbial accusative indicating status or situation.[23] "May the one who took notice of you exist *in the status of* one who is being blessed."

וַתַּגֵּ֣ד לַחֲמוֹתָ֗הּ אֵ֤ת אֲשֶׁר־עָשְׂתָה֙ עִמּ֔וֹ

וַתַּגֵּ֣ד is a Hiphil imperfect 3fs of נגד + *vav*-consecutive of temporal succession. The narrator moves forward now with Ruth as the implied subject. With נגד, the I-נ assimilates in a silent *shewa* position (תַּגֵּד ⟵ תַּנְגֵּד). Also notice that the *vav*-consecutive in the Hiphil is a *ṣērê* form in the thematic vowel.[24]

אֵ֤ת אֲשֶׁר־עָשְׂתָה֙ עִמּ֔וֹ is the accusative object, again a relative clause. The relative clause communicates "what" Ruth declared. עָשְׂתָה֙ is a Qal perfect 3fs of עשה, and since this action happened before וַתַּגֵּ֣ד, it is best translated as a pluperfect, "she had worked."

Interestingly, Naomi asks Ruth "where" she had worked (twice!; אֵיפֹה ... וְאָ֣נָה), but Ruth declares "with *whom* she worked." The resumptive 3ms pronoun on עִמּ֔וֹ brings a person into the relative clause, not just an object, leading us to read the relative אֲשֶׁר as "whom." For good English, we bring the preposition and pronoun to the front of a relative clause and translate, "*with whom* she had worked." Perhaps Ruth was so excited to tell Naomi about Boaz that she skipped Naomi's actual question of where she had worked that day. This can be supported by the following clauses when Ruth finally identifies Boaz by name.

23. For participles as an accusative of situation, see *IBHS* §16l.

24. The Hiphil *ṣere* forms are the **j**ussive, **i**nfinitive absolute, **i**mperative 2ms, and *vav*-consecutive, all getting an "E" as the thematic vowel (J.I.I.V.E; the "jive forms").

וַתֹּ֣אמֶר שֵׁ֤ם הָאִישׁ֙ אֲשֶׁ֨ר עָשִׂ֧יתִי עִמּ֛וֹ הַיּ֖וֹם בֹּֽעַז׃

וַתֹּ֣אמֶר is a Qal imperfect 3fs of אמר + *vav*-consecutive, introducing Ruth's direct speech within the narrative framework. The *revîa* accent (◌֗) separates this introductory verb from the actual direct speech.

Ruth's direct speech is a long verbless clause with an embedded relative clause. The subject of the verbless clause (initiator) is שֵׁ֤ם הָאִישׁ֙ אֲשֶׁ֨ר עָשִׂ֧יתִי עִמּ֛וֹ הַיּ֖וֹם. The goal of Ruth's comment is to identify the man with whom she worked today, and so שֵׁ֤ם הָאִישׁ֙ is the primary subject (initiator). שֵׁ֤ם הָאִישׁ֙, however, is further defined with the relative clause, אֲשֶׁ֨ר עָשִׂ֧יתִי עִמּ֛וֹ. As in the previous relative clause, the preposition and resumptive pronoun (עִמּ֛וֹ) must be brought to the front of the clause for good English, "with whom I worked." עָשִׂ֧יתִי is the Qal perfect 1cs of עשׂה, again with the III-ה shifting to a III-י and coalescing with the thematic vowel. The normal תִי- of the perfective 1cs remains. הַיּ֖וֹם is an adverbial accusative of time indicating when she worked—namely, "today."

This verbless clause has a similar structure to Ruth 2:1, when Boaz is first introduced to the audience by the narrator. In 2:1, the *atnāḥ* (◌֑) falls very late in the verse, and the *ṭifḥā* (◌֖) of the *sillûq* (◌ֽ) segment occurs right after the *atnāḥ*.

וּֽלְנָעֳמִ֞י מְיֻדָּ֣ע לְאִישָׁ֗הּ אִ֚ישׁ גִּבּ֣וֹר חַ֔יִל מִמִּשְׁפַּ֖חַת **אֱלִימֶ֑לֶךְ וּשְׁמ֖וֹ בֹּֽעַז׃**

This construction delays the identity of Boaz until the very end of the sentence, heightening the suspense of his introduction. Now, in 2:19, when Ruth introduces Boaz to Naomi, the accents suggest a similar delay, saving the identity of Boaz until the end.

To complete the large verbless clause, we supply the copulative verb "to be" before revealing Boaz's name: "The name of the man with whom I worked today [*is*] ... Boaz." The ellipsis in the translation is not because information is skipped but to capture the suspense of the accent pattern that waits to reveal Boaz's name. In both 2:1 and 2:19, the *ṭifḥā* (◌֖) sets off Boaz's name from the rest of the verse.

2:1 וּֽלְנָעֳמִ֞י מְיֻדָּ֣ע לְאִישָׁ֗הּ אִ֚ישׁ גִּבּ֣וֹר חַ֔יִל מִמִּשְׁפַּ֖חַת אֱלִימֶ֑לֶךְ **וּשְׁמ֖וֹ בֹּֽעַז׃**

2:19 וַתֹּ֣אמֶר שֵׁ֤ם הָאִישׁ֙ אֲשֶׁ֨ר עָשִׂ֧יתִי עִמּ֛וֹ **הַיּ֖וֹם בֹּֽעַז׃**

While we know this story well enough to know who this man is, the text was constructed beautifully to capture the narrative anticipation that Boaz was the man with whom Ruth worked that day. Even if the audience already knows the content of the story (and we do), to "watch" Naomi experience the same anticipation prior to Boaz's name being revealed is delightful. It is as if you can see the expression on her face as she asks Ruth "where" she had worked but the reply is "with whom" she worked. Why would Ruth shift the topic from location to person unless that person mattered to Naomi and Ruth's situation? Surely Naomi's eyes began to widen and hope filled her countenance as Ruth reveals שֵׁ֤ם הָאִ֨ישׁ. The delay of Boaz's name until the last word of the sentence allows the reader to identify with Naomi as she anticipates the revelation of this man's name.

RUTH 2:20

וַתֹּ֨אמֶר נָעֳמִ֜י לְכַלָּתָ֗הּ בָּר֥וּךְ הוּא֙ לַֽיהוָ֔ה אֲשֶׁר֙ לֹא־עָזַ֣ב חַסְדּ֔וֹ אֶת־הַחַיִּ֖ים וְאֶת־הַמֵּתִ֑ים וַתֹּ֧אמֶר לָ֣הּ נָעֳמִ֗י קָר֥וֹב לָ֙נוּ֙ הָאִ֔ישׁ מִֽגֹּאֲלֵ֖נוּ הֽוּא׃

ACCENT PHRASING

וַתֹּ֨אמֶר נָעֳמִ֜י לְכַלָּתָ֗הּ
בָּר֥וּךְ הוּא֙ לַֽיהוָ֔ה
אֲשֶׁר֙ לֹא־עָזַ֣ב חַסְדּ֔וֹ אֶת־הַחַיִּ֖ים וְאֶת־הַמֵּתִ֑ים
וַתֹּ֧אמֶר לָ֣הּ נָעֳמִ֗י
קָר֥וֹב לָ֙נוּ֙ הָאִ֔ישׁ
מִֽגֹּאֲלֵ֖נוּ הֽוּא׃

וַתֹּ֨אמֶר נָעֳמִ֜י לְכַלָּתָ֗הּ

וַתֹּאמֶר is a Qal imperfect 3fs of אמר + *vav*-consecutive, continuing the narrative of discourses between Ruth and Naomi. נָעֳמִי is now the explicit subject, and לְכַלָּתָהּ is the one to whom Naomi is talking—namely, Ruth ("her daughter-in-law").

A minor morphological feature to note here is that when feminine words ending in the lexicon with ָה take pronominal suffixes, the final ה is seemingly replaced by a "feminine ת." Here, because the noun is singular ("daughter-in-law"), the ת points with a *qāmeṣ*, ָתָהּ. Had the noun been plural ("daughters-in-law"), the ת would have pointed as ות (cf. כַּלֹּתֶיהָ, three times in 1:6–8, all written defectively without the ו).

בָּר֥וּךְ הוּא֙ לַֽיהוָ֔ה

בָּרוּךְ is a Qal passive participle ms of ברך. הוּא is the subject. In this blessing formula, Naomi is blessing Boaz for his lovingkindness shown to them. Because this is a passive participle, the English passive "be" should be included: "May he *be* blessed." The ל on יהוָה indicates the agent or source of the blessing, so the clause translates as "Blessed be he *by* the Lord," or "May he be blessed *by* the Lord."[25]

אֲשֶׁר לֹא־עָזַב חַסְדּוֹ אֶת־הַחַיִּים וְאֶת־הַמֵּתִים

אֲשֶׁר could modify יהוה or הוּא. In the nearest grammatical context, it seems to further modify הוּא, describing how Boaz behaved. With יהוה in a prepositional phrase, it seems more natural for the subject הוּא to be the antecedent for the relative clause. But even if we narrow down the antecedent to הוּא, the syntax could be understood two ways.

First, the resumptive pronoun on חַסְדּוֹ would literally translate as "who he did not abandon his lovingkindness." However, when combined with אֲשֶׁר, we get "whose lovingkindness did not abandon." In this case, חַסְדּוֹ is the subject of לֹא־עָזַב, the negated Qal perfect 3ms of עזב. Additionally, if translated this way, אֶת־ on אֶת־הַחַיִּים and וְאֶת־הַמֵּתִים marks the direct objects, or the nouns who received the benefit of Boaz's lovingkindness not being abandoned. The question then is how Boaz has extended lovingkindness to the dead husbands (הַמֵּתִים).

A second way to understand the relative clause with הוּא as the antecedent is with חַסְדּוֹ as the object of לֹא־עָזַב: "who did not abandon his lovingkindness." In this case, אֶת־ on אֶת־הַחַיִּים and וְאֶת־הַמֵּתִים is the preposition "with": "who did not abandon his lovingkindness *with* the living or *with* the dead." Either of these two options with הוּא as the antecedent suggests that Boaz did not forsake his lovingkindness toward Ruth (אֶת־הַחַיִּים) and her family (וְאֶת־הַמֵּתִים).

However, another option is grammatically possible (probable?), and that is to see יהוה as the antecedent of the relative pronoun.[26] In this case, the one whose lovingkindness has not failed is Yahweh. Boaz has not yet technically shown חֶסֶד to Ruth's dead husband, except in the fact of extending חֶסֶד to Ruth by providing grain for her. Boaz will formally demonstrate lovingkindness to Mahlon when he marries Ruth and redeems her along with Naomi's plot of land. So the one who has shown lovingkindness to both the living and the dead at this point in the narrative is Yahweh. If the prepositional phrase earlier in the verse (לַיהוָה) is taken as a ל of source, then Naomi

25. RJW §280; JM §132f.

26. Wilch, *Ruth*, 91; Holmstedt, *Ruth*, 141–42; Joüon, *Ruth*, 60.

now ties the blessing to Yahweh who extends his lovingkindness to all of his covenant people. Indeed, "his steadfast love (חֶסֶד) endures forever" (Ps 136).

וַתֹּאמֶר לָהּ נָעֳמִי

נָעֳמִי now informs Ruth that Boaz is a near relative. וַתֹּאמֶר is a Qal imperfect 3fs of אמר + *vav*-consecutive and is in temporal succession. וַתֹּאמֶר introduces Naomi's direct speech.

קָרוֹב לָנוּ הָאִישׁ

קָרוֹב, an adjective, is fronted for emphasis. A literal translation produces "Near to us the man." הָאִישׁ is the subject and קָרוֹב is a predicate adjective, and so we must supply the "to be" verb in this verbless clause, "The man [*is*] near to us." This is the first occurrence of קָרוֹב in Ruth, but it will occur again in 3:12 when Boaz explains there is a redeemer "nearer than" him (יֵשׁ גֹּאֵל קָרוֹב מִמֶּנִּי). The emphasis now is that the מְיֻדָּע from 2:1 is also קָרוֹב, and hence able to redeem Ruth and Naomi. The emphasis will perhaps cause a gasp when we get to 3:12 and find that there is a redeemer nearer than Boaz. What seems to be relief in the narrative at 2:20 will momentarily be upended in 3:12 until Boaz confronts the nearer redeemer in chapter 4, thus securing Ruth's (and Naomi's) redemption for himself.

מִגֹּאֲלֵנוּ הוּא׃

מִגֹּאֲלֵנוּ is a Qal participle mp construct of גאל + 1cp objective pronoun and a partitive מִן preposition.[27] The plural construct of the participle is slightly veiled because it is written defectively without the י of the normal construct ending (◌ֵי). מִגֹּאֲלֵנוּ is an explicative appositional modifier to קָרוֹב, further modifying who he is. The plural participle is significant here. Naomi now identifies Boaz as "one from our kinsmen redeemers." The contextual implication is that Boaz is one among several kinsmen redeemers. However, even though Naomi may be aware of several potential redeemers within the family, she recognizes the hand of Yahweh in singling out this man who has already shown חֶסֶד to Ruth in extraordinary ways.

---

27. For partitive מִן, see RJW §324; *GBHS* §4.1.13(f).

RUTH 2:21

וַתֹּ֖אמֶר ר֣וּת הַמּוֹאֲבִיָּ֑ה גַּ֣ם ׀ כִּֽי־אָמַ֣ר אֵלַ֗י עִם־הַנְּעָרִ֤ים אֲשֶׁר־לִי֙ תִּדְבָּקִ֔ין עַ֣ד אִם־כִּלּ֔וּ אֵ֥ת כָּל־הַקָּצִ֖יר אֲשֶׁר־לִֽי׃

ACCENT PHRASING

וַתֹּ֖אמֶר ר֣וּת הַמּוֹאֲבִיָּ֑ה
גַּ֣ם ׀ כִּֽי־אָמַ֣ר אֵלַ֗י
עִם־הַנְּעָרִ֤ים אֲשֶׁר־לִי֙ תִּדְבָּקִ֔ין
עַ֣ד אִם־כִּלּ֔וּ אֵ֥ת כָּל־הַקָּצִ֖יר אֲשֶׁר־לִֽי׃

וַתֹּ֖אמֶר ר֣וּת הַמּוֹאֲבִיָּ֑ה

וַתֹּ֖אמֶר is the Qal imperfect 3fs of אמר + *vav*-consecutive of temporal succession, carrying the narrative sequence forward in this dialogue between Ruth and Naomi. ר֣וּת is the explicit subject of the 3fs verb, and הַמּוֹאֲבִיָּ֑ה modifies ר֣וּת appositionally, recalling the fact that Ruth is a foreigner. The narrator does not want this detail to fall from the front of the reader's mind. Boaz has shown lovingkindness to the quintessential "least of these" and has provided a hopeful outcome for Ruth.

In the narrative, it is easy enough to see a kind man faithfully obeying the law toward a foreign widow, allowing her to glean in his field. However, in the larger context of the narrative and redemptive history, this is *the* display of lovingkindness that brings us to David (4:18–22) and eventually to Christ (Matt 1:5). It is indeed significant to keep in mind that Ruth could have been scorned because of ethnic elitism. And yet Yahweh, through Boaz, demonstrated his exceeding kindness to his people.

גַּ֣ם׀ כִּֽי־אָמַ֣ר אֵלַ֗י

גַּ֣ם here + the כִּי clause is a bit cumbersome. גַּ֣ם has a light disjunctive accent, the *lĕgarmēh* (׀ ֣), and so, rather than reading these two words together, it is best to see them as lightly disconnected although related. In other words, כִּי is asseverative, "indeed" or "surely," and גַּ֣ם is an emphatic particle, so we get "Moreover (גַּ֣ם ׀), indeed (כִּי) he said to me …" A smoother rendition of this clause would be "He *even* said to me …"

אָמַר is the Qal perfect 3ms of אמר, and אֵלַי is the prepositional phrase indicating to whom Boaz was speaking when he said these things to Ruth. "Me" is Ruth in this context.

עִם־הַנְּעָרִים אֲשֶׁר־לִי תִּדְבָּקִין

עִם begins what Boaz said to Ruth as it is relayed from Ruth now to Naomi. Here Ruth begins the quote with the prepositional phrase (עִם־הַנְּעָרִים), likely for emphasis. The הַנְּעָרִים with whom Ruth is to cling are the ones אֲשֶׁר־לִי, "who [belong] to me (Boaz)," a possessive relative clause. הַנְּעָרִים is a mp but more likely refers generically to all the workers in the field rather than just the young men. Boaz explicitly told Ruth to cling to his young women (2:8; וְכֹה תִדְבָּקִין עִם־נַעֲרֹתָי׃). There is no reason to believe that Ruth is being untruthful, but perhaps Naomi will clarify things when she seems to redundantly encourage Ruth to go out with Boaz's young women in the next verse (טוֹב בִּתִּי כִּי תֵצְאִי עִם־נַעֲרוֹתָיו).

תִּדְבָּקִין is a Qal imperfect 2fs of דבק with a paragogic *nun*. תִּדְבָּקִין is a strong verb morphologically and translates with a slight imperative or suggestive nuance, "you *shall* cling."

עַד אִם־כִּלּוּ אֵת כָּל־הַקָּצִיר אֲשֶׁר־לִי׃

עַד אִם is temporal, "whenever." The idea is a hypothetical situation that has not yet occurred, hence אִם ("until if").[28] The hypothetical "if" places the tense of the verb in the hypothetical future. כִּלּוּ is a Piel perfect 3cp of כלה. In the hypothetical future, the perfective, completed action would translate as an English future perfect, "will have completed." When combined with the previous clause, Boaz instructed Ruth to cling to his workers "until whenever *they will have completed* all the harvest belonging to me." Ruth's primary aim is to communicate to Naomi Boaz's provision, not necessarily his protection. She does not intentionally dismiss Boaz's protection, but her goal is to tell Naomi about his provision. She is to stay with his workers until they have completed אֵת כָּל־הַקָּצִיר אֲשֶׁר־לִי. כָּל־הַקָּצִיר is the definite direct object, and hence the definite direct object marker (אֵת). As before, the relative אֲשֶׁר־לִי is possessive, "which [belongs] to me."

28. WO §38.7a; JM §166p.

RUTH 2:22

וַתֹּ֥אמֶר נָעֳמִ֖י אֶל־ר֣וּת כַּלָּתָ֑הּ ט֣וֹב בִּתִּ֗י כִּ֤י תֵֽצְאִי֙ עִם־נַ֣עֲרוֹתָ֔יו וְלֹ֥א יִפְגְּעוּ־בָ֖ךְ בְּשָׂדֶ֥ה אַחֵֽר׃

ACCENT PHRASING

וַתֹּ֥אמֶר נָעֳמִ֖י אֶל־ר֣וּת כַּלָּתָ֑הּ
ט֣וֹב בִּתִּ֗י כִּ֤י תֵֽצְאִי֙ עִם־נַ֣עֲרוֹתָ֔יו
וְלֹ֥א יִפְגְּעוּ־בָ֖ךְ בְּשָׂדֶ֥ה אַחֵֽר׃

וַתֹּ֥אמֶר נָעֳמִ֖י אֶל־ר֣וּת כַּלָּתָ֑הּ

וַתֹּ֥אמֶר is the Qal imperfect 3fs of אמר + *vav*-consecutive, continuing the primary narrative in temporal succession. נָעֳמִ֖י is the explicit subject shifting the direct speech back to her. אֶל־ר֣וּת explicitly identifies to whom Naomi is talking even though the dialogue between the two women seems obvious enough.

Ruth is identified appositionally as כַּלָּתָ֑הּ. In the previous verse, Ruth was identified as הַמּוֹאֲבִיָּ֑ה. Now she is tied in as family (כַּלָּתָ֑הּ), forming an *inclusio* with the beginning of 2:20 (וַתֹּ֨אמֶר נָעֳמִ֜י לְכַלָּתָ֗הּ). In spite of Ruth being הַמּוֹאֲבִיָּ֑ה, she is indeed family, highlighted by this *inclusio*. Not only that, but Boaz is one מִֽגֹּאֲלֵ֖נוּ (2:20; "from *our* redeemers"), also tying Ruth closely as family. In light of Ruth's commitment to Naomi (1:16–17), she is ethnically הַמּוֹאֲבִיָּ֑ה but functionally כַּלָּתָ֑הּ.

ט֣וֹב בִּתִּ֗י כִּ֤י תֵֽצְאִי֙ עִם־נַ֣עֲרוֹתָ֔יו

ט֣וֹב בִּתִּ֗י is a verbless clause with an indirect subject. The clause requires an English "to be" verb: "*It is* good, my daughter." בִּתִּ֗י is vocative, and ט֣וֹב is a predicate adjective once we supply "it is." While the subject of the verbless clause is initially implied ("it"), the subject becomes explicit beginning with כִּ֤י. The "it" of "It is good" is "*that* (כִּ֤י) you would go out with his young women."[29] In contrast to the possibility of Ruth following after the young men in the field, ט֣וֹב is best understood as a comparative, "It is better."

29. RJW §451a.

תֵּצְאִי is a Qal jussive 2fs of יצא, translated modally as "that you *would* go out." יצא is a I-ו, and so in the imperfect conjugation, the initial ו drops and the preformative vowel lengthens from *ḥîreq* to *ṣērê* (תִ◌◌ִי ⟵ תֵ◌◌ִי). Naomi directs Ruth back to harvesting עִם־נַעֲרוֹתָיו rather than with Boaz's young men. What may have been vague in the previous verse when Ruth talked about all workers (עִם־הַנְּעָרִים), Naomi now clarifies that Ruth should stay with the young women. From the mouth of Naomi, the narrator now recalls Boaz's previous instructions to cling to his young women (2:8). With Ruth's focus on provision in 2:21, and Naomi's words leading the reader to recall Boaz's protection, the narrator efficiently keeps the focus on Boaz as the אִישׁ גִּבּוֹר חַיִל par excellence.

וְלֹא יִפְגְּעוּ־בָךְ בְּשָׂדֶה אַחֵר׃

יִפְגְּעוּ is the negated Qal imperfect 3mp of פגע, recalling 2:9 but with a different, assonant verbal root (נגע rather than פגע). The *vav* (וְלֹא) may carry the idea of purpose, "*so that* they might not meet you in another field." פגע can carry a negative connotation of abuse, and that is likely the nuance here.[30] Ruth is to go out with Boaz's young women *so that* she will not end up in another field and potentially be harmed. Notice the verb is mp. Naomi shifts the subject to the men in the fields who present a very real threat to Ruth. ב introduces the object after פגע.[31]

בְּשָׂדֶה אַחֵר is the prepositional phrase indicating *where* Ruth may find trouble if she does not go out with Boaz's young women. אַחֵר modifies שָׂדֶה attributively, "in another field."

30. *HALOT*, 910, 2.a.

31. BDB, 803.

RUTH 2:23

וַתִּדְבַּ֞ק בְּנַעֲר֥וֹת בֹּ֙עַז֙ לְלַקֵּ֔ט עַד־כְּל֥וֹת קְצִֽיר־הַשְּׂעֹרִ֖ים וּקְצִ֣יר הַחִטִּ֑ים וַתֵּ֖שֶׁב אֶת־חֲמוֹתָֽהּ׃

ACCENT PHRASING

וַתִּדְבַּ֞ק בְּנַעֲר֥וֹת בֹּ֙עַז֙ לְלַקֵּ֔ט
עַד־כְּל֥וֹת קְצִֽיר־הַשְּׂעֹרִ֖ים וּקְצִ֣יר הַחִטִּ֑ים
וַתֵּ֖שֶׁב אֶת־חֲמוֹתָֽהּ׃

וַתִּדְבַּ֞ק בְּנַעֲר֥וֹת בֹּ֙עַז֙ לְלַקֵּ֔ט

Ruth 2:23 now summarizes the immediate context. וַתִּדְבַּ֞ק is a Qal imperfect 3fs of דבק + *vav*-consecutive of logical succession, "And *so* she clung." בְּנַעֲר֥וֹת בֹּ֙עַז֙ prepositionally tells to whom Ruth clung. ב communicates accompaniment in this case.[32] The prepositional phrase is a construct package indicated by the fp construct morphology on נַעֲר֥וֹת and the conjunctive accent (*mêrĕkā*, ֥). The construct package communicates an implied ל of possession; "the young women *of* Boaz" are the "young women *belonging to* Boaz."

לְלַקֵּ֔ט is a Piel infinitive construct of לקט + ל and is either purpose or circumstantial. As purpose, it would be that Ruth clung to the young women "*in order to* glean." As circumstantial, "Ruth clung to the women *while gleaning*." Either translation communicates the summarizing idea well.

עַד־כְּל֥וֹת קְצִֽיר־הַשְּׂעֹרִ֖ים וּקְצִ֣יר הַחִטִּ֑ים

עַד־כְּל֥וֹת recalls 2:21 (עַ֚ד אִם־כִּלּ֔וּ אֵ֥ת כָּל־הַקָּצִ֖יר). Ruth 2:21 used the finite verb כלה rather than the infinitive construct as here. כְּל֥וֹת is the Qal infinitive construct of כלה functioning as a noun, "the end of."

Regarding the harvest(s), 2:21 had the phrase כָּל־הַקָּצִ֖יר. Now הַקָּצִ֖יר is expanded specifically to קְצִֽיר־הַשְּׂעֹרִ֖ים and קְצִ֣יר הַחִטִּ֑ים. These two construct

32. RJW §248.

packages communicate an implied ל of specification, "the harvest *with respect to* barley/wheat."[33] In summary fashion, we discover that Ruth stayed and gleaned through the entire harvest season, not just on the one occasion narrated in this chapter.

וַתֵּ֖שֶׁב אֶת־חֲמוֹתָֽהּ׃

The final clause does not intend to move the narrative forward but simply provides a summary of where Ruth lived during the harvest. וַתֵּ֖שֶׁב is a Qal imperfect 3fs of ישׁב + *vav*-consecutive. ישׁב is a I-ו verb, and in the imperfect the initial ו drops, indicated by the lengthening of the preformative vowel (וַתֵּ֖שֶׁב). Also note, as before, that the *vav*-consecutive retracts the accent to the preformative, which leaves the thematic vowel in a closed and unaccented syllable and thus the short thematic vowel *sĕgōl* (וַתֵּ֖שֶׁב). אֶת־חֲמוֹתָהּ is the prepositional phrase indicating with whom Ruth dwelled while she gleaned: "with her mother-in-law."

33. JM §273a.

1 Then Naomi, her mother-in-law, said to her, "My daughter, is it not that I should seek
for your rest which is good for you? 2 And now, is not Boaz our relative with whose
young women you were? Behold, he is winnowing (at) the threshing floor of barley
tonight. 3 Now wash (yourself) and anoint (yourself) and put your clothing upon you
and go down to the threshing floor. Do not be known to the man until his finishing to
eat and to drink. 4 And it shall come about when he lies down that you will know the
place where he lies down there and you shall enter and you shall uncover (the place
of) his feet and you shall lie down and he will declare to you (that) which you shall
do." 5 And she said to her, "All which you have said [to me] I will do."

RUTH

3:1–5

1 וַתֹּ֥אמֶר לָ֖הּ נָעֳמִ֣י חֲמוֹתָ֑הּ בִּתִּ֗י הֲלֹ֧א אֲבַקֶּשׁ־לָ֛ךְ מָנ֖וֹחַ אֲשֶׁ֥ר יִֽיטַב־לָֽךְ׃ 2 וְעַתָּ֗ה
הֲלֹ֥א בֹ֙עַז֙ מֹֽדַעְתָּ֔נוּ אֲשֶׁ֥ר הָיִ֖ית אֶת־נַעֲרוֹתָ֑יו הִנֵּה־ה֗וּא זֹרֶ֛ה אֶת־גֹּ֥רֶן הַשְּׂעֹרִ֖ים
הַלָּֽיְלָה׃ 3 וְרָחַ֣צְתְּ ׀ וָסַ֗כְתְּ וְשַׂ֧מְתְּ שִׂמְלֹתֵ֛ךְ עָלַ֖יִךְ וְיָרַ֣דְתִּי הַגֹּ֑רֶן אַל־תִּוָּדְעִ֣י לָאִ֔ישׁ
עַ֥ד כַּלֹּת֖וֹ לֶאֱכֹ֥ל וְלִשְׁתּֽוֹת׃ 4 וִיהִ֣י בְשָׁכְב֗וֹ וְיָדַ֙עַתְּ֙ אֶת־הַמָּק֙וֹם֙ אֲשֶׁ֣ר יִשְׁכַּב־שָׁ֔ם
וּבָ֛את וְגִלִּ֥ית מַרְגְּלֹתָ֖יו וְשָׁכָ֑בְתִּי וְהוּא֙ יַגִּ֣יד לָ֔ךְ אֵ֖ת אֲשֶׁ֥ר תַּעֲשִֽׂין׃ 5 וַתֹּ֖אמֶר אֵלֶ֑יהָ
כֹּ֛ל אֲשֶׁר־תֹּאמְרִ֥י ° אֶֽעֱשֶֽׂה׃

RUTH 3:1

וַתֹּ֥אמֶר לָ֖הּ נָעֳמִ֣י חֲמוֹתָ֑הּ בִּתִּ֗י הֲלֹ֧א אֲבַקֶּשׁ־לָ֛ךְ מָנ֖וֹחַ אֲשֶׁ֥ר יִֽיטַב־לָֽךְ׃

ACCENT PHRASING

וַתֹּ֥אמֶר לָ֖הּ נָעֳמִ֣י חֲמוֹתָ֑הּ
בִּתִּ֗י הֲלֹ֧א אֲבַקֶּשׁ־לָ֛ךְ מָנ֖וֹחַ אֲשֶׁ֥ר יִֽיטַב־לָֽךְ׃

וַתֹּ֥אמֶר לָ֖הּ נָעֳמִ֣י חֲמוֹתָ֑הּ

וַתֹּ֥אמֶר is a Qal imperfect 3fs of אמר + *vav*-consecutive in temporal succession. The narrative continues now with a conversation between Naomi and Ruth leading to the encounter with Boaz at the threshing floor. נָעֳמִ֣י חֲמוֹתָ֑הּ is the full subject phrase, with חֲמוֹתָ֑הּ modifying נָעֳמִ֣י appositionally. In apposition, the nouns agree in gender, number, and definiteness and the second noun renames the first. Here חֲמוֹתָ֑הּ renames נָעֳמִ֣י. This is an example of explicative apposition, further "explaining" who נָעֳמִ֣י is, "Naomi, her mother-in-law."

Notice that חָמוֹת looks fp (◌וֹת), but חָמוֹת is simply the lexical form, so the noun is singular. It would not make sense in the context for Ruth to have multiple mothers-in-law, but also the pronominal suffix (◌ָהּ) is the suffix on a singular noun.

בִּתִּ֗י הֲלֹ֧א אֲבַקֶּשׁ־לָ֛ךְ מָנ֖וֹחַ אֲשֶׁ֥ר יִֽיטַב־לָֽךְ׃

בִּתִּ֗י is a vocative address and begins the direct speech. הֲלֹ֧א is literally "is there not," but here it begins a rhetorical question functioning as a strong statement. It would be comparable in English to saying, "Did I not seek for you ... ?" In either Hebrew or English, the person speaking is not asking a formal question, but the strong assertion takes the form of a question.

אֲבַקֶּשׁ is the Piel imperfect 1cs of בקשׁ, and the ל on לָ֛ךְ is a ל of advantage. Something was sought "for" Ruth's advantage. Notice on אֲבַקֶּשׁ the initial vocal *shewa* of the Piel imperfect is a composite *shewa* (◌ֲ) because the imperfect 1cs preformative is a guttural (א). Also notice the thematic vowel is shortened to a *sĕgōl* from a *ṣērê* because of the *maqqēf* (־) shifting the accent of the entire constituent to לָ֑ךְ. This leaves the final syllable of אֲבַקֶּשׁ in a closed and unaccented syllable requiring a short vowel (אֲבַקֶּשׁ־).

מָנ֖וֹחַ is the accusative direct object, or the thing being sought. The final relative clause (אֲשֶׁ֥ר יִֽיטַב־לָֽךְ) further modifies the notion of Naomi seeking rest for Ruth and most likely expresses purposes. Naomi seeks מָנוֹחַ for Ruth "so that" it would be well for Ruth. יִיטַב is a Qal imperfect 3ms of יטב. יטב is an original I-י verb,[1] and hence the initial י remains but coalesces with the preformative vowel to form a ִי (יִיטַב). As before, the ל on לָךְ is a ל of advantage. Naomi assures Ruth that she will seek rest for her so that life may be good *for* her.

1. As opposed to a verb like ישׁב that is a I-י in the lexicon but morphs as an original I-ו.

RUTH 3:2

וְעַתָּ֗ה הֲלֹ֥א בֹ֙עַז֙ מֹֽדַעְתָּ֔נוּ אֲשֶׁ֥ר הָיִ֖ית אֶת־נַעֲרוֹתָ֑יו הִנֵּה־ה֗וּא זֹרֶ֛ה אֶת־גֹּ֥רֶן
הַשְּׂעֹרִ֖ים הַלָּֽיְלָה׃

ACCENT PHRASING

וְעַתָּ֗ה הֲלֹ֥א בֹ֙עַז֙ מֹֽדַעְתָּ֔נוּ
אֲשֶׁ֥ר הָיִ֖ית אֶת־נַעֲרוֹתָ֑יו
הִנֵּה־ה֗וּא זֹרֶ֛ה אֶת־גֹּ֥רֶן הַשְּׂעֹרִ֖ים הַלָּֽיְלָה׃

וְעַתָּ֗ה הֲלֹ֥א בֹ֙עַז֙ מֹֽדַעְתָּ֔נוּ

וְעַתָּה demands the reader's attention as Naomi provides the logical conclusion of her desire to give Ruth "rest." Naomi points out that Boaz is a relative using a negative rhetorical question (הֲלֹא בֹעַז) as a strong assertion just as in the previous verse.[2] מֹדַעְתָּנוּ appositionally modifies בֹעַז and is a *hapax legomenon*, but its constituent parts are familiar. The word is related to מֹידַע (in *BHS*) in 2:1 when Boaz is named as their "relative." The lexical form appears as a participle (מֹדַעַת) built from the verbal root ידע.[3] In מֹדַעְתָּנוּ, the segolization of vowels begins at ־דַעַת, and hence that is the part of the word that is important for morphological changes. מֹ- is unaffected by the morphological changes of adding the pronominal suffix. The segolization in מֹדַעַת displays short *pataḥs* rather than *sĕgōls* because of the guttural letter (ע) in the "middle" of the segolate pattern (◌ַדַעַת, cf. נַעַר). With the addition of the 1cp pronominal suffix (◌ֵנוּ), the form follows a standard segolate pattern with suffixes (מֹדַעְתָּנוּ, cf. מַלְכֵּנוּ, "our king"). So, even though this form occurs only once in the Hebrew Bible, the elements used to construct the word are familiar, "our (◌ֵנוּ) kindred (מֹדַעַת)."

אֲשֶׁ֥ר הָיִ֖ית אֶת־נַעֲרוֹתָ֑יו

אֲשֶׁר modifies מֹדַעְתָּנוּ, referring to Boaz. הָיִית is a Qal perfect 2fs of היה suggesting completed action. אֶת־ is the preposition "with," not the direct

---

2. Wilch, *Ruth*, 103.

3. BDB, 396.

object marker. The resumptive pronoun on נַעֲרוֹתָיו should be moved to the front of the relative clause for good English. A wooden translation would be "who you were with *his* young women." After moving the resumptive pronoun to the front of the relative clause, we would get "*with whose* young women you were," referring to when Ruth gleaned with Boaz's young women as both Boaz and Naomi instructed her. That young *women* (plural) are in view here is clear from the fp וֹת- added to נַעַר before the suffix (נַעֲרוֹתָיו).

הִנֵּה־הוּא זֹרֶה אֶת־גֹּרֶן הַשְּׂעֹרִים הַלָּיְלָה׃

הִנֵּה carries an element of surprise, especially when coupled with the pronoun הוּא and the *revîa* accent (◌֗).[4] The focus now shifts quickly to Boaz and what he is doing. זֹרֶה is a Qal ms participle of זרה, "to winnow or to thresh." The participle communicates a durative aspect, so it may be that Boaz is in the act of winnowing. Alternatively, it may communicate that his habitual work at night was to winnow. It is unlikely that Naomi has a detailed knowledge of what Boaz does at night since she only recently learned that it was his field in which Ruth gleaned. It is more likely that Naomi is simply aware of the normal practices of a man who owns a field that has been freshly harvested that day.[5]

אֶת־גֹּרֶן הַשְּׂעֹרִים is formally the accusative object phrase, but Boaz is not actually winnowing the אֶת־גֹּרֶן itself. Rather, he is winnowing "at" the threshing floor. The accusative אֶת־ marks an adverbial accusative of place in this instance. אֶת־גֹּרֶן is in construct with הַשְּׂעֹרִים, "the threshing floor *of* barley." The implied preposition in this construct package is a לְ of specification, indicating that this is the threshing floor "for" barley, or the one "in relation to" barley. Notice that the definite article is on הַשְּׂעֹרִים and so the entire construct package is definite, "*the* threshing floor of barley." הַלָּיְלָה is the adverbial accusative of time with the demonstrative article, "this night," or "tonight."

---

4. *GBHS* §4.5.
5. Block, *Ruth*, 168–69.

RUTH 3:3

וְרָחַצְתְּ ׀ וָסַכְתְּ וְשַׂמְתְּ שִׂמְלָתֵךְ עָלַיִךְ וְיָרַדְתִּי הַגֹּרֶן אַל־תִּוָּדְעִי לָאִישׁ עַד כַּלֹּתוֹ
לֶאֱכֹל וְלִשְׁתּוֹת׃

ACCENT PHRASING

וְרָחַצְתְּ ׀ וָסַכְתְּ וְשַׂמְתְּ שִׂמְלָתֵךְ עָלַיִךְ וְיָרַדְתִּי הַגֹּרֶן
אַל־תִּוָּדְעִי לָאִישׁ
עַד כַּלֹּתוֹ לֶאֱכֹל וְלִשְׁתּוֹת׃

שִׂמְלֹתַיִךְ
ק
וְיָרָדְתְּ
ק

וְרָחַצְתְּ ׀ וָסַכְתְּ וְשַׂמְתְּ שִׂמְלָתֵךְ עָלַיִךְ וְיָרַדְתִּי הַגֹּרֶן

Ruth 3:3 begins Naomi's formal instructions to Ruth via a series of *vav* + perfectives with an imperatival force. The *vav* + perfective can translate as a future tense if the context allows, or it can be "you shall/should" as a strong suggestion.[6] As a strong suggestion, the intended outcome is not optional. Naomi fully expects Ruth to go, hence the perfective aspect of the verbs. The translation requires future "time" ("you *shall* wash"), but the meaning is such a strong suggestion that it is as if it has already happened (i.e., perfective; completed action aspect).

וְרָחַצְתְּ ׀ is a Qal perfect 2fs of רחץ + *vav*-consecutive. וָסַכְתְּ is a Qal perfect 2fs of סוך + *vav*-consecutive. סוך is a hollow root (II-ו), and so the middle ו drops in the perfect conjugation, leaving a short *pataḥ*. The distinguishing mark of the perfective 2fs (תְּ◌ְ) is still readily visible for parsing purposes. The *lĕgarmēh* (◌ָ׀) and *revîa* (◌֗) accent pattern separates וְרָחַצְתְּ ׀ and וָסַכְתְּ off from וְשַׂמְתְּ שִׂמְלָתֵךְ עָלַיִךְ. In other words, Ruth is to "wash," then "anoint," and only then "place" her cloak on herself. The accents are unnecessary to communicate this logical progression of human behavior, but they also support an accurate grammatical reading of this series of *vav* + perfectives.

6. For discussion of the *vav* + perfective, see RJW §179 and associated footnotes.

וְשַׂמְתְּ is a Qal perfect 2fs of שׂים + *vav*-consecutive. שׂים is another hollow root, hence the loss of the middle י of the lexical root, which is replaced by a *pataḥ* in the perfective conjugation just as with וְסַכְתְּ. שִׂמְלָתֵךְ is the accusative direct object, the thing being "placed." Notice above that this form has a *qere* reading in the margin of *BHS*. The *qere* (שִׂמְלֹתַיִךְ) suggests merely that the 2fs suffix is on a plural noun and Ruth's "clothing" at this point is more than just a cloak (cf. הַמִּטְפַּחַת in 3:15).[7] עָלַיִךְ is a prepositional phrase telling where Ruth is to place her outer garment. Since this is *Ruth's* outer garment being placed "on *Ruth*," the English reflexive pronoun is best, "on *yourself*."

וְיָרַדְתִּי is a Qal perfect 2fs of ירד + *vav*-consecutive and also has a *qere* form above. The *ketiv*, or what was written, looks like a 1cs verbal form (וְיָרַדְתִּי). However, it would make little sense for Naomi to now say that she would go down to the threshing floor. "You wash up and anoint yourself, and *I* will go down ..." The *qere* specifies that the verbal form should be a 2fs like the previous verbs in this verse. Once again, the author preserves an archaic verbal form from the mouth of Naomi. This one is likely an archaic 2fs form from West Semitic dialects.[8] We will see this form again in the next verse. As with the previous perfects, this one is also modal, "you *should* go down." הַגֹּרֶן is an adverbial accusative of place, so we supply the directional preposition, "*to* the threshing floor."

אַל־תִּוָּדְעִי לָאִישׁ

אַל־תִּוָּדְעִי is the negated Niphal jussive 2fs of ידע. ידע is a I-ו "weak" verb, but with the characteristic *dāgēš forte* of the Niphal in the initial ו, the consonant remains. The other distinguishing elements of the jussive 2fs paradigm are

7. *HALOT* lists Ruth 3:15 in the definitions for both an "outer garment, cloak, mantle" and "garments, clothing" on the basis of the *qere*. The singular and plural both fit the context, but most commentators and English translations understand שִׂמְלָתֵךְ as a singular noun referring to an outer garment.

8. John Huehnergard, "Semitic Languages," in *Civilizations of the Ancient Near East*, ed. J. M. Sasson (New York: Charles Scribner's Sons, 1995), 2130; Holmstedt, *Ruth*, 152–53.

noticeable (תִּ◌◌◌ִי) for parsing purposes. The thematic vowel is obscured with a vocal *shewa* (תִּוָּדְעִי) because of the vocalic ending (◌ִי).

As a Niphal, the verb is the passive/reflexive of the Qal, and so instead of "to know," we get "to *be* known." As a negated jussive, we would translate, "*Let* you not *be* known." In better English, we would say, "Do not let yourself be known." לָאִישׁ indicates to whom Ruth is not to make herself known, referring to Boaz. Naomi is telling Ruth that she is to stealthily make her way to the threshing floor.

עַד כַּלֹּתוֹ לֶאֱכֹל וְלִשְׁתּוֹת׃

עַד begins the temporal clause and כַּלֹּתוֹ completes it. כַּלֹּתוֹ is a Piel infinitive construct of כלה + 3ms pronominal suffix. If understood as a true verbal noun, כַּלֹּתוֹ is "the finishing of (belonging to) him," or "his finishing." This would describe an infinitive functioning as a noun in construct with a pronominal suffix. The implied preposition in this construct would be a ל of possession. This is a nuanced way to read the infinitive construct here. However, Hebrew regularly expresses the subject and verb of a temporal clause using this construction, especially with temporal particles like עַד.[9] Reading this as a standard temporal clause, we get "until he is finished."

לֶאֱכֹל and וְלִשְׁתּוֹת are both Qal infinitive constructs of אכל and שׁתה, respectively. Notice that לֶאֱכֹל is a I-א and thus gets a *ḥāṭēf-sĕgōl* in the infinitive construct because of the I-guttural. This vowel change also causes the ל preposition to take a *sĕgōl* as its vowel mirroring the *ḥāṭēf* of the I-א. וְלִשְׁתּוֹת is a III-ה verb and in the infinitive construct follows the III-ה paradigm, ending with וֹת-. These infinitives complement the main verb (כַּלֹּתוֹ) and translate as English gerunds ("-ing" nouns). The entire clause is "until he is finished *eating* and *drinking*."

9. RJW §§311, 502

RUTH 3:4

וִיהִ֣י בְשָׁכְב֗וֹ וְיָדַ֙עַתְּ֙ אֶת־הַמָּקוֹם֙ אֲשֶׁ֣ר יִשְׁכַּב־שָׁ֔ם וּבָ֛את וְגִלִּ֥ית מַרְגְּלֹתָ֖יו
וְשָׁכָ֑בְתְּי וְהוּא֙ יַגִּ֣יד לָ֔ךְ אֵ֖ת אֲשֶׁ֥ר תַּעֲשִֽׂין׃

ACCENT PHRASING

וִיהִ֣י בְשָׁכְב֗וֹ
וְיָדַ֙עַתְּ֙ אֶת־הַמָּקוֹם֙ אֲשֶׁ֣ר יִשְׁכַּב־שָׁ֔ם
וּבָ֛את וְגִלִּ֥ית מַרְגְּלֹתָ֖יו וְשָׁכָ֑בְתְּי
וְהוּא֙ יַגִּ֣יד לָ֔ךְ אֵ֖ת אֲשֶׁ֥ר תַּעֲשִֽׂין׃

וִיהִ֣י בְשָׁכְב֗וֹ

וִיהִ֣י is a Qal jussive 3ms of היה + conjunctive *vav*. Notice the form is וִיהִי rather than וַיְּהִי. The jussive form would be יְהִי, and when the conjunctive *vav* is added (וְ), the vowel pattern shifts to וִיהִי (וִיהִי ⟵ וְיְהִי). This vowel pointing is the phonetic recipe for the Hebrew contraction וִי ⟵ וְיְ. The preformative י now with a silent *shewa* (וְיְ◌◌) produces the same phonetic value as the coalesced form (וִי◌◌). Naomi continues to give Ruth instructions for a future situation, and so the modal jussive is fitting: "May it be," or "Let it be." As a jussive, וִיהִ֣י carries an imperatival force, "and it *shall* come about."

בְשָׁכְב֗וֹ is a Qal infinitive construct of שׁכב with a 3ms suffix and a ב preposition. A literal translation is "at [the time of] the lying down of him." But like עַד כַּלֹּתוֹ in the previous verse, the infinitive construct + pronominal suffix + temporal particle (ב) produces a temporal clause, "*when* he lies down."[10] This initial clause introduces what Ruth should do at a certain point in the night. The details will become apparent in the following clause.

וְיָדַ֙עַתְּ֙ אֶת־הַמָּקוֹם֙ אֲשֶׁ֣ר יִשְׁכַּב־שָׁ֔ם

וְיָדַ֙עַתְּ֙ is explanatory and continues Naomi's instructions to Ruth. "Let it come about when he lies down *that* you will know the place." וְיָדַ֙עַתְּ֙ is a Qal perfect

10. *GBHS* §3.4.1(b.1).

2fs of ידע + *vav*-consecutive. Notice that וְיָדַ֫עַתְּ is a III-ע and therefore shifts the expected silent *shewa* under the R3 in the perfect 2fs (קָטַלְתְּ) to a *pataḥ* (וְיָדַעַתְּ) to vocalize the silent letter. אֶת־הַמָּקוֹם is the definite direct object.

אֲשֶׁר introduces a relative clause further defining הַמָּקוֹם. The entire relative clause feels a bit redundant in English but is well-written Hebrew. הַמָּקוֹם is further specified as "where he lies down there." יִשְׁכַּב is a Qal imperfect 3ms of שׁכב, and שָׁם is a resumptive adverb that can be left untranslated in good English. Even though שָׁם is left untranslated at the end of the relative clause, it informs the translation of אֲשֶׁר as a place ("where") rather than "who" or "which."

וּבָ֣את וְגִלִּ֧ית מַרְגְּלֹתָ֛יו וְשָׁכָ֖בְתִּי וְשָׁכָֽבְתְּ ק

The next verb sequence communicates what Ruth is to do when she finds Boaz. Naomi communicates her plan using *vav* + perfectives with an imperatival nuance similar to what we saw in 3:3. וּבָ֣את is a Qal perfect 2fs of בוא + *vav*-consecutive. Following וְיָדַ֫עַתְּ, and with Ruth's knowledge of where Boaz is, she is to "come" to where he is. The *vav*- consecutive on the perfect follows the meaning of the previous *vav* + perfects, "and you *shall* come."

וְגִלִּ֧ית is a Piel perfect 2fs of גלה + *vav*-consecutive. Notice the evidences of the III-ה root (גלה) with the י in וְגִלִּ֧ית. Since the III-י coalesces with the thematic vowel (ִי), the *shewa* under the perfective 2fs sufformative is implicit.

מַרְגְּלֹתָ֛יו is a word that gets much attention in Ruth. The lexical form is רֶ֫גֶל, referring most basically to "feet." It is true that רֶ֫גֶל has been interpreted euphemistically to refer to sexual organs.[11] However, even if it does refer to genitals, the passages in which it does so do not imply sexual promiscuity. The word merely identifies the sexual organs in those contexts. In this particular use of רֶ֫גֶל, the prefixed מ as well as the "plural of local extension"[12] (וֹת-) indicates *the place* of the feet rather than the feet as objects. While it may be difficult to distinguish between the place of the feet and the feet

11. See *NIDOTTE* 3:1048, #6–7, for biblical examples that are euphemistic.
12. See GKC §124a–b for the "plural of local extension."

themselves, it appears that the narrator is merely referring to a location, "the place of his feet."[13]

וְשָׁכָ֫בְתְּי recalls the archaic perfective 2fs (cf. וְיָרַדְתִּי in 3:3). The *qere* (וְשָׁכָבְתְּ in the note above) confirms the 2fs of שׁכב. The *vav*-consecutive here follows the consecutive pattern in this series of clauses with an imperatival force, "and you *shall* lie down."

וְהוּא֙ יַגִּ֣יד לָ֔ךְ אֵ֖ת אֲשֶׁ֥ר תַּעֲשִֽׂין׃

וְהוּא introduces a nominal clause with a disjunctive *vav*, shifting the focus in the narrative from Ruth to Boaz. Rather than carry the narrative action forward, the narrator now gives information about what Boaz will do, highlighting his role in the conversation at the threshing floor: "and *he*."

יַגִּ֣יד is a Hiphil imperfect 3ms of נגד. Notice the assimilated נ from the root into the R2-ג (יַגִּיד ⟵ יַנְגִּיד). The *ḥîreq-yôd* thematic vowel rules out that this is a Piel imperative or infinitive, both of which display a *pataḥ* in the R1 and *dāgēš forte* in the R2 (cf. ◌ַ◌ֵּ◌ֵ). This verbal form must be a Hiphil imperfect with an assimilated נ.

לָ֔ךְ is the indirect object, and אֵ֖ת marks the accusative relative clause as the direct object phrase. What is Boaz going to declare? He will declare אֵ֖ת אֲשֶׁ֥ר תַּעֲשִֽׂין. תַּעֲשִׂין is a Qal imperfect 2fs of עשׂה with a paragogic *nun* and translates with a modal nuance of obligation, "what you *should* do."[14] עשׂה is a bit tricky morphologically since it is both a I-ע and a III-ה verb. First, the I-ע "flips" an expected silent *shewa* in the standard Qal paradigm to a composite vocal *shewa* (תַּעֲשִׂין ⟵ תַּעְשִׂין). This phonetic change also shifts the preformative vowel in the Qal to a *pataḥ*. Second, the III-ה is recognizable by the י now in the R3 position of the final form (תַּעֲשִׂין). In her plan for Ruth to initiate this nighttime encounter, Naomi also leaves room for Boaz to take the lead in the redemption process. He will tell Ruth what she should do.

13. Block, *Ruth*, 171–72.

14. JM §113m.

RUTH 3:5

וַתֹּ֥אמֶר אֵלֶ֑יהָ כֹּ֛ל אֲשֶׁר־תֹּאמְרִ֥י ׄ אֶֽעֱשֶֽׂה׃

ACCENT PHRASING

וַתֹּ֥אמֶר אֵלֶ֑יהָ
כֹּ֛ל אֲשֶׁר־תֹּאמְרִ֥י ׄ אֶֽעֱשֶֽׂה׃

וַתֹּ֥אמֶר אֵלֶ֑יהָ

וַתֹּ֥אמֶר shifts the contextual subject back to Ruth even though the subject is not explicit. וַתֹּ֥אמֶר is a Qal imperfect 3fs of אמר + *vav*-consecutive in temporal succession. אֵלֶ֑יהָ refers to Naomi, who receives this reply from Ruth.

כֹּ֛ל אֲשֶׁר־תֹּאמְרִ֥י ׄ אֶֽעֱשֶֽׂה׃ אלי חד מן י̇ קר̇ ולא כת̇

כֹּ֛ל begins Ruth's direct speech as the accusative object, fronted for emphasis. אֲשֶׁר־תֹּאמְרִ֥י further defines כל as that "which you say." תֹּאמְרִ֥י is a Qal imperfect 2fs of אמר. Ruth is recalling not just anything generically (כל) but specifically the things that Naomi has said (אֲשֶׁר־תֹּאמְרִ֥י) in this immediate context.

Toward the end of this clause, we have an odd *ketiv*/*qere*. The note above first provides the *ketiv* (אלי) and then says, "One (חד) from (מן) the ten [occurrences] (י̇) is read (קר̇) but not (ולא) written (כת̇)."[15] The *ketiv*, or what was "written," is actually missing, indicated in the LHB by the superscripted symbol כ̇ and in *BHS* by writing the vowels without consonants.[16] This is called the "*qere vela ketiv*" (קר̇ ולא כת̇), or "read but not written." The *qere* is אֵלַ֖י to complete a full sentence structure, but the prepositional phrase is technically unnecessary. Some argue this could be an occurrence

---

15. Brotzman and Tully, *Old Testament Textual Criticism*, 161–62; Tov, *Textual Criticism of the Hebrew Bible*, 222–24.

16. If you are using the LHB in Logos, you can click on the "aleph/omega" icon ᴬΩ and select "Inline Interlinear." This will also allow you to choose the "Kethiv Reading," the "Qere Reading," and the "Kethiv-Qere Hybrid Form," allowing you to see the variant forms. The full Mp (Masorah Parva) notation is not available, but to see the variant forms is helpful.

of parablepsis; that is, the scribe began the א of אֵלַי, looked up, and then continued with the א of אֶעֱשֶׂה, leaving out אֵלַי altogether.[17] Rather than alter the consonantal text, the scribes simply clarified the syntax in the marginal notes.

אֶעֱשֶׂה is a Qal imperfect 1cs of עשׂה. This imperfective is translated as a simple future as an affirmation. Ruth says that she will certainly do all that Naomi has said: "all which you say, I *will* do."

17. Holmstedt, *Ruth*, 157.

6 And so she went down to the threshing floor and she did according to all that her
mother-in-law commanded her. 7 And Boaz ate and drank, and his heart was merry
(good). And so he came to lie down at the edge of the heap [of grain]. And she entered
with secrecy and she uncovered (the place of) his feet and she laid down. 8 And
it came about in the half of the night that the man was startled and so he rolled
himself over and, behold, a woman [was] lying at (the place of) his feet. 9 And he
said, "Who are you?" And she said, "I am Ruth, your maidservant, and now you
shall spread your wing over your maidservant for a redeemer you [are]." 10 And he
said, "May you be blessed by the Lord, my daughter. You have caused your latter
lovingkindness to be better than the first, to not go after the available young men,
whether poor or rich." 11 And now, my daughter, do not fear. All which you say, I will
do for you, for all of the gate of my people know that you [are] a woman of valor. 12
And now, truly indeed, even surely, a redeemer [am] I, but also there is a redeemer
nearer than I. 13 Lodge [here] tonight and it will come about in the morning, if he
will redeem you, [then] good, let him redeem, but if he does not delight to redeem
you, then I myself will redeem you as the Lord lives. Lie down until the morning.

14 And so she laid down at (the place of) his feet until the morning. And then she
arose before a man could recognize his friend. And he said, "Do not let it be known
that the woman came to the threshing floor." 15 And he said, "Give your shawl that is
upon you and hold it [out]." And so she held it [out] and he measured six [measures]
of barley and he put [it] upon her. Then he came to the city. 16 And then she came to
her mother-in-law and she said, "Who are you my daughter?" And she declared to
her all that the man had done for her.

RUTH
3:6–16

⁶ וַתֵּ֖רֶד הַגֹּ֑רֶן וַתַּ֕עַשׂ כְּכֹ֥ל אֲשֶׁר־צִוַּ֖תָּה חֲמוֹתָֽהּ: ⁷ וַיֹּ֨אכַל בֹּ֤עַז וַיֵּשְׁתְּ֙ וַיִּיטַ֣ב לִבּ֔וֹ

וַיָּבֹ֕א לִשְׁכַּ֖ב בִּקְצֵ֣ה הָעֲרֵמָ֑ה וַתָּבֹ֣א בַלָּ֔ט וַתְּגַ֥ל מַרְגְּלֹתָ֖יו וַתִּשְׁכָּֽב: ⁸ וַיְהִי֙ בַּחֲצִ֣י

הַלַּ֔יְלָה וַיֶּחֱרַ֥ד הָאִ֖ישׁ וַיִּלָּפֵ֑ת וְהִנֵּ֣ה אִשָּׁ֔ה שֹׁכֶ֖בֶת מַרְגְּלֹתָֽיו: ⁹ וַיֹּ֖אמֶר מִי־אָ֑תְּ

וַתֹּ֗אמֶר אָֽנֹכִי֙ ר֣וּת אֲמָתֶ֔ךָ וּפָרַשְׂתָּ֤ כְנָפֶ֙ךָ֙ עַל־אֲמָ֣תְךָ֔ כִּ֥י גֹאֵ֖ל אָֽתָּה: ¹⁰ וַיֹּ֗אמֶר

בְּרוּכָ֨ה אַ֤תְּ לַֽיהוָה֙ בִּתִּ֔י הֵיטַ֛בְתְּ חַסְדֵּ֥ךְ הָאַחֲר֖וֹן מִן־הָרִאשׁ֑וֹן לְבִלְתִּי־לֶ֙כֶת֙ אַחֲרֵ֣י

הַבַּחוּרִ֔ים אִם־דַּ֖ל וְאִם־עָשִֽׁיר: ¹¹ וְעַתָּ֗ה בִּתִּי֙ אַל־תִּ֣ירְאִ֔י כֹּ֥ל אֲשֶׁר־תֹּאמְרִ֖י

אֶֽעֱשֶׂה־לָּ֑ךְ כִּ֤י יוֹדֵ֙עַ֙ כָּל־שַׁ֣עַר עַמִּ֔י כִּ֛י אֵ֥שֶׁת חַ֖יִל אָֽתְּ: ¹² וְעַתָּה֙ כִּ֣י אָמְנָ֔ם כִּ֥י אִ֖ם

גֹּאֵ֣ל אָנֹ֑כִי וְגַ֛ם יֵ֥שׁ גֹּאֵ֖ל קָר֥וֹב מִמֶּֽנִּי: ¹³ לִ֣ינִי ׀ הַלַּ֗יְלָה וְהָיָ֤ה בַבֹּ֙קֶר֙ אִם־יִגְאָלֵ֥ךְ טוֹב֙

יִגְאָ֔ל וְאִם־לֹ֨א יַחְפֹּ֜ץ לְגָֽאֳלֵ֗ךְ וּגְאַלְתִּ֤יךְ אָנֹ֙כִי֙ חַי־יְהוָ֔ה שִׁכְבִ֖י עַד־הַבֹּֽקֶר:

¹⁴ וַתִּשְׁכַּ֤ב מַרְגְּלוֹתָו֙ עַד־הַבֹּ֔קֶר וַתָּ֕קָם בְּטֶ֛רֶם יַכִּ֥יר אִ֖ישׁ אֶת־רֵעֵ֑הוּ וַיֹּ֙אמֶר֙ אַל־

יִוָּדַ֔ע כִּי־בָ֥אָה הָאִשָּׁ֖ה הַגֹּֽרֶן: ¹⁵ וַיֹּ֙אמֶר֙ הָ֤בִי הַמִּטְפַּ֙חַת֙ אֲשֶׁר־עָלַ֖יִךְ וְאֶֽחֳזִי־בָ֑הּ

וַתֹּ֣אחֶז בָּ֗הּ וַיָּ֤מָד שֵׁשׁ־שְׂעֹרִים֙ וַיָּ֣שֶׁת עָלֶ֔יהָ וַיָּבֹ֖א הָעִֽיר: ¹⁶ וַתָּבוֹא֙ אֶל־חֲמוֹתָ֔הּ

וַתֹּ֖אמֶר מִי־אַ֣תְּ בִּתִּ֑י וַתַּ֙גֶּד־לָ֔הּ אֵ֛ת כָּל־אֲשֶׁר־עָֽשָׂה־לָ֖הּ הָאִֽישׁ:

RUTH 3:6

וַתֵּ֖רֶד הַגֹּ֑רֶן וַתַּ֕עַשׂ כְּכֹ֥ל אֲשֶׁר־צִוַּ֖תָּה חֲמוֹתָֽהּ׃

ACCENT PHRASING

וַתֵּ֖רֶד הַגֹּ֑רֶן
וַתַּ֕עַשׂ כְּכֹ֥ל אֲשֶׁר־צִוַּ֖תָּה חֲמוֹתָֽהּ׃

וַתֵּ֖רֶד הַגֹּ֑רֶן

וַתֵּ֖רֶד is a Qal imperfect 3fs of ירד + *vav*-consecutive, resuming the primary narrative. The *vav*-consecutive communicates logical succession as the outcome of Ruth's affirming she will do what Naomi said: "And *so* she went down." הַגֹּ֑רֶן is the adverbial accusative of place indicating to where Ruth went down.

וַתַּ֕עַשׂ כְּכֹ֥ל אֲשֶׁר־צִוַּ֖תָּה חֲמוֹתָֽהּ׃

וַתַּ֕עַשׂ is the Qal imperfect 3fs of עשׂה + *vav*-consecutive, continuing the action of the narrative in temporal succession. Being a III-ה verb, עשׂה has an apocopated ("shortened") *vav*-consecutive form (תַּ֕עַשׂ). The accent retracts to the preformative (תַּ), and the apocopated form follows a segolate vowel pattern (תַּ֕עַשׂ, cf. נַ֫עַר).

The כ preposition on כְּכֹ֥ל communicates manner, indicating *how* Ruth did ("according to"), but in English it comes across more as *what* she did.[1] As a true comparative כ, it would be comparing what Ruth did (כֹ֥ל אֲשֶׁר־צִוַּ֖תָּה חֲמוֹתָֽהּ) with any other hypothetical action she could have done.[2] כְּכֹ֥ל communicates that she did *completely* what Naomi told her.

אֲשֶׁר־צִוַּ֖תָּה is the relative clause that further defines כְּכֹ֥ל. The question may stand: What is the "all" that Ruth did? The answer is "all *that her mother-in-law commanded her*." צִוַּ֖תָּה is a Piel perfect 3fs of צוה + 3fs object pronoun. Contextually, the Piel perfect (צִוַּ֖תָּה) could be translated as an English

1. Holmstedt, *Ruth*, 157.
2. RJW §256.

pluperfect, "had commanded," since Ruth is now doing what had been previously commanded.

The morphology of צִוַּתָּה needs explanation. The components of the word would initially be הָ + צִוַּת. However, the ה of the suffix assimilates into the ת, resulting in the *dāgēš forte* in the ת and shifting the *qāmeṣ* under the ת. The final ה in the form we see in the text, then, is actually not part of the 3fs pronoun, but rather the *mater lectionis* (vowel marker).

final form	*mater lectionis* + assimilated form	suffix attached directly	3fs suffix + 3fs verb
צִוַּתָּה	⟵ ה + צִוַּתָּ	⟵ צִוַּתְהָ	⟵ הָ + צִוַּת

It is relatively common for a ה to assimilate in scenarios when the pronunciation effectively drops the ה anyway. For example, to say צִוַּתְהָ quickly sounds exactly like צִוַּתָּה. In a consonantal text, there would be no difference (צותה). The details of these vowel markings suggest that the Masoretes worked to meticulously preserve the pronunciation of the text *in addition to* the correct morphology. If the consonantal text is the same either way, the addition of the *dāgēš forte* in the final ת is how the Masoretes preserved the ה of the הָ suffix while also pointing the word such that the pronunciation reflects what was actually said in the traditional readings.

RUTH 3:7

וַיֹּ֨אכַל בֹּ֤עַז וַיֵּ֙שְׁתְּ֙ וַיִּיטַ֣ב לִבּ֔וֹ וַיָּבֹ֕א לִשְׁכַּ֖ב בִּקְצֵ֣ה הָעֲרֵמָ֑ה וַתָּבֹ֣א בַלָּ֔ט וַתְּגַ֥ל
מַרְגְּלֹתָ֖יו וַתִּשְׁכָּֽב׃

ACCENT PHRASING

וַיֹּ֨אכַל בֹּ֤עַז וַיֵּ֙שְׁתְּ֙ וַיִּיטַ֣ב לִבּ֔וֹ
וַיָּבֹ֕א לִשְׁכַּ֖ב בִּקְצֵ֣ה הָעֲרֵמָ֑ה
וַתָּבֹ֣א בַלָּ֔ט
וַתְּגַ֥ל מַרְגְּלֹתָ֖יו
וַתִּשְׁכָּֽב׃

וַיֹּ֨אכַל בֹּ֤עַז וַיֵּ֙שְׁתְּ֙ וַיִּיטַ֣ב לִבּ֔וֹ

Ruth 3:7 moves the narrative focus back to Boaz with the 3ms verbs. Additionally, בֹּ֤עַז is the explicit subject of וַיֹּ֨אכַל and the implied subject of the following 3ms verbs (וַיֵּ֙שְׁתְּ֙ וַיִּיטַ֣ב ... וַיָּבֹ֕א). וַיֹּ֨אכַל is a Qal imperfect 3ms of אכל + *vav*-consecutive. The *vav* is temporal succession with בֹּ֤עַז now as the focus, but at a slightly later time narratively.

וַיֵּ֙שְׁתְּ֙ is a Qal imperfect 3ms of שתה + *vav*-consecutive. שתה is a III-ה verb and therefore exhibits the apocopated form in the *vav*-consecutive. The accent mark here is a *pašṭā* (◌֙) and is a postpositive, meaning that it occurs at the end of the word. With two silent *shewa*s at the end of וַיֵּ֙שְׁתְּ֙, the *pašṭā* actually marks the entire final syllable (ו | יֵּ֙שְׁתְּ֙) as the accented syllable even though it is at the end of the word. Hebrew will not formally accent a silent *shewa*, but since the *pašṭā* is a postpositive accent, it occurs over the consonant with a silent *shewa* in this example.

The narrative action in these first two verbs is contemporaneous rather than purely successive. Even as a *vav*-consecutive, it functions more like a conjunctive *vav* communicating a compound predicate with two things Boaz was doing ("he ate *and* he drank"). The *pašṭā* (◌֙) provides a grammatical break and also indicates that וַיֹּ֨אכַל and וַיֵּ֙שְׁתְּ֙ are syntactically related—"Now Boaz ate and drank"—prior to the description of "it [being] well for his heart" (וַיִּיטַ֣ב לִבּ֔וֹ).

וַיִּיטַב is the Qal imperfect 3ms of יטב + *vav*-consecutive. The subject of the verb is לִבּוֹ, and the idiom (וַיִּיטַב לִבּוֹ) means that he was "of good spirits." This *vav* again is contemporaneous with "eating" and "drinking." Even as a contemporaneous action, the *vav*-consecutive communicates resultant action (logical succession), "and *subsequently*, his heart was happy." Indeed, it may have taken some time for any dinner wine to make Boaz "of good spirits," but the narrative does not communicate that Boaz is intending to be drunk; rather, he is jolly and satisfied with his evening meal as he prepares to turn in for the night.

וַיָּבֹא לִשְׁכַּב בִּקְצֵה הָעֲרֵמָה

וַיָּבֹא is a Qal imperfect 3ms of בוא + *vav*-consecutive. The *vav* is in temporal succession, moving the story forward with Boaz's action. בוא is a hollow root but in the imperfective maintains the phonetics of a strong verb (◌ָ◌◌ֹ). In many cases, it is written fully (*plene*), displaying the original ו of the root (cf. יָבוֹא in Gen 32:9, 12, etc.). In this case the *ḥōlem-vav* of the thematic vowel is written defectively. לִשְׁכַּב is the Qal infinitive construct of שכב + a ל preposition, expressing purpose: Boaz "went *in order to* lie down."

Finally, בִּקְצֵה הָעֲרֵמָה is locative, and the construct chain literally means "at the end *of* the heap." הָעֲרֵמָה was likely a heap of grain, and the קָצֶה of a round heap would practically be "beside" the heap, or around its "border/ perimeter." קָצֶה is formally an "edge or extremity," but a round heap does not technically have an "edge" as in a quadrilateral. So to be "at the edge of the heap" would be "beside" it. The implication is that Boaz laid down beside the heap of grain, a sure sign he is at the threshing floor and Naomi's plan is working out perfectly.

וַתָּבֹא בַלָּט

וַתָּבֹא is a Qal imperfect 3fs of בוא + *vav*-consecutive of temporal succession. Notice the same morphology as in the 3ms previously (וַיָּבֹא), but now with the ת preformative for the imperfect 3fs. Ruth is now the implied subject.

בַלָּט is a combination of the ב preposition and the word לָט, meaning "secret." Notice the pointing of the definite article with the ב preposition (בַ◌). Literally, the phrase is "in *the* secret." Since this is a ב of circumstance or manner, we simply have an adverbial notion of *how* Ruth is to approach Boaz, “secretly” or “stealthily.”[3]

וַתְּגַל מַרְגְּלֹתָיו

וַתְּגַל is the Piel imperfect 3fs of גלה + *vav*-consecutive. With the III-ה verb גלה, we lose the final ה of the root (apocopated form in the *vav*-consecutive), and therefore we do not get the distinctive Piel *dāgēš forte* in the original second root letter, the ל. However, we can still recognize the Piel vowel pattern on the preformative and first root letter (תְּ◌ַ◌◌). The *vav* is in temporal succession, presenting Ruth’s next action in the narrative: “then she uncovered.” מַרְגְּלֹתָיו is once again locative, indicating the place she uncovered: “the place of his feet.”

וַתִּשְׁכָּב׃

וַתִּשְׁכָּב is a Qal imperfect 3fs of שׁכב + *vav*-consecutive and is in temporal sequence with the other verbs. Notice morphologically the *dāgēš* in the כ is a *dāgēš lene* because it is a BeGaD KePhaT letter preceded by the silent *shewa* under the שׁ. Also notice how the a-class thematic vowel, normally a *pataḥ*, lengthened because the *sillûq* (◌ֽ) and *sôf pāsûq* (:) indicate that וַתִּשְׁכָּב׃ is a pausal form.

The verbal progression here and in 3:4 are identical. In verse 4, Naomi tells Ruth to “come” (בוא), “uncover” (גלה), and “lie down” (שׁכב). Now that Ruth is carrying out what her mother-in-law told her, she “comes” (בוא), “uncovers” (גלה), and “lies down” (שׁכב). Indeed, Ruth has completed what she affirmed to Naomi in 3:5, כֹּל אֲשֶׁר־תֹּאמְרִי אֶעֱשֶׂה.

3. RJW §252 calls this a “ב of state or condition,” “also called a beth of the norm or a beth of manner.” WO 11.2.5d uses the syntactical tag, ב of “circumstance,” and notes that this is to be translated as an adverb.

RUTH 3:8

וַיְהִי֙ בַּחֲצִ֣י הַלַּ֔יְלָה וַיֶּחֱרַ֥ד הָאִ֖ישׁ וַיִּלָּפֵ֑ת וְהִנֵּ֣ה אִשָּׁ֔ה שֹׁכֶ֖בֶת מַרְגְּלֹתָֽיו׃

ACCENT PHRASING

וַיְהִי֙ בַּחֲצִ֣י הַלַּ֔יְלָה
וַיֶּחֱרַ֥ד הָאִ֖ישׁ וַיִּלָּפֵ֑ת
וְהִנֵּ֣ה אִשָּׁ֔ה שֹׁכֶ֖בֶת מַרְגְּלֹתָֽיו׃

וַיְהִי֙ בַּחֲצִ֣י הַלַּ֔יְלָה

וַיְהִי֙ is the Qal imperfect 3ms of היה + *vav*-consecutive, introducing the next action of the narrative with an indistinct subject. The "it" that "came about" is generic. The details of "it" will become clear later in the verse.

בַּחֲצִ֣י הַלַּ֔יְלָה is a temporal prepositional phrase communicating *when* this scene occurred: "in the half of the night." Rather than specifying a time of the night (exact midnight), this idiom is used to indicate sometime within the night, but certainly while it was still "in the middle of the night" even as the English idiom would communicate. בַּחֲצִ֣י הַלַּ֔יְלָה is a construct package with a meaning that implies a ב preposition. "In the middle *of* the night" means "in the middle *within* the night."

וַיֶּחֱרַ֥ד הָאִ֖ישׁ וַיִּלָּפֵ֑ת

וַיֶּחֱרַ֥ד is a *hapax legomenon*; it occurs only here in the Hebrew Bible. The word is from the root חרד, likely related to the Assyrian *ḫarâdu*, meaning "to tremble," or perhaps the Ugaritic *ḥrd*.[4] The verb is the Qal imperfect 3ms + *vav*-consecutive, and so the past tense, "he trembled," is appropriate. Following the temporal introduction, the *vav* is translated as "that": "It came about in the middle of the night *that* the man trembled/was startled." הָאִ֖ישׁ is the explicit grammatical subject. The meaning of Boaz "trembling" could range anywhere from his being startled that someone was now

4. Cf. BDB, 353; *HALOT*, 350.

beside him in the night to him shivering from the cold now that his feet were uncovered. Regardless of the exact reason, we know that he awoke and that whatever awakened him was sufficiently disturbing to make him "turn [over]" (וַיִּלָּפֵת) to see what it was.[5]

וַיִּלָּפֵת is the Niphal imperfect 3ms of לפת + a *vav*-consecutive. The verb means "to turn or grasp" and likely implies turning while also grasping (cf. Judg 16:29).[6] The idea is that, having been startled, Boaz turned his attention to what was going on at the place of his feet. "Turning" with the implication of "grasping" communicates how someone would discover what was going on, not aggression. Boaz likely would be turning *and* groping around to figure out who is there and why they are there.

וְהִנֵּה אִשָּׁה שֹׁכֶבֶת מַרְגְּלֹתָיו׃

וְהִנֵּה signals surprise, both to the reader and in the mind of Boaz. The *zāqēf qāṭôn* (◌ֹ) separates וְהִנֵּה אִשָּׁה from the rest of the clause with a mild syntactical break. It is possible for a subject (אִשָּׁה) and verb (שֹׁכֶבֶת) to be separated by a disjunctive accent.[7] While there is no exegetical significance to the accent pattern here, grammatically it causes the audience to read "And behold a woman!" before considering what she was doing. A mild syntactical break, but a syntactical break nonetheless. Notice that אִשָּׁה is indefinite to convey that Boaz does not yet know who this is. She is only "a woman" at this point.

שֹׁכֶבֶת is a Qal participle fs ("t-form") of שכב. Understanding it as a substantive adjective with durative aspect in a verbless clause, we supply the "to be" verb and get "a woman *was* one who was lying down." This gets smoothed out as "a woman was lying down." מַרְגְּלֹתָיו is the adverbial accusative of place, modifying the verb as to *where* she was lying down.

5. Block, *Ruth*, 179 n. 47.

6. See Wilch, *Ruth*, 118, for discussion.

7. A search in Accordance Bible Software for a grammatical subject with a *zāqēf qāṭôn* followed by a participle only one word away yields 127 hits in 78 verses of the Hebrew Bible. After a quick perusal of these occurrences, some of the verses (about 23) do not fit the intended search criteria. The outliers in the search appear to be in verses where the grammatical subject with the *zāqēf qāṭôn* is itself a participle. Even so, one can confidently argue that this construction with *zāqēf qāṭôn*, a heavy disjunctive accent, separating a subject from its participial predicate occurs with some regularity (about 100 times).

RUTH 3:9

וַיֹּ֖אמֶר מִי־אָ֑תְּ וַתֹּ֗אמֶר אָנֹכִי֙ ר֣וּת אֲמָתֶ֔ךָ וּפָרַשְׂתָּ֤ כְנָפֶ֙ךָ֙ עַל־אֲמָ֣תְךָ֔ כִּ֥י גֹאֵ֖ל
אָֽתָּה׃

ACCENT PHRASING

וַיֹּ֖אמֶר מִי־אָ֑תְּ
וַתֹּ֗אמֶר אָנֹכִי֙ ר֣וּת אֲמָתֶ֔ךָ
וּפָרַשְׂתָּ֤ כְנָפֶ֙ךָ֙ עַל־אֲמָ֣תְךָ֔
כִּ֥י גֹאֵ֖ל אָֽתָּה׃

וַיֹּ֖אמֶר מִי־אָ֑תְּ

וַיֹּ֖אמֶר is a Qal imperfect 3ms of אמר + *vav*-consecutive. The narrative continues now with Boaz's direct speech to Ruth at the threshing floor. מִי־אָ֑תְּ is a verbless interrogative clause, and we supply the copulative verb to get "Who [*are*] you?"

Notice the *atnāḥ* (◌֑) at this point, very early in the verse. While the *atnāḥ* often marks the middle of a verse or the place where a natural syntactical break would occur, the *atnāḥ* may also mark a break in the sentence where the Masoretes intended the "meaning" or emphasis of the verse to be noticed.[8] Here the *atnāḥ* falls on Boaz's question of who Ruth is. Boaz has already met Ruth and spoken with her, knowing everything that she did for her mother-in-law Naomi (2:11). Perhaps here he questions her identity because it is dark and he cannot see her well (cf. 3:14 when he sends her away while it is still dark), or perhaps he recognizes her but is curious about her motives. In this second sense, he is questioning her character. "Who are you? You are not acting like who I thought you were." Commentaries will discuss the meaning of Boaz's question, but the syntax here certainly draws our attention.[9] The exegetical significance of Boaz's question is not found in the *atnāḥ* itself, and so we must be careful not to

8. *IBHS*, "Hebrew Accents," §9.

9. E.g., Eskenazi and Frymer-Kensky, *Ruth*, 58.

put too much theological weight on the accent system. And yet it is also available to help us, especially in places like this where we do not expect the *atnāḥ* so early in the verse. The accentuation in 3:9 certainly puts some emphasis on Boaz's question about this woman lying at his feet.

וַתֹּ֗אמֶר אָנֹכִי֙ ר֣וּת אֲמָתֶ֔ךָ

The subject now shifts to Ruth with the Qal imperfect 3fs of אמר + *vav*-consecutive of temporal succession. Ruth reveals her identity with a verbless clause. אָנֹכִי֙ is the subject (initiator), we supply the copulative verb "am," and then ר֣וּת אֲמָתֶ֔ךָ is the predicate nominative (announcement). אֲמָתֶ֔ךָ is an explicative appositional modifier for Ruth, specifying who she is: "Ruth, *your maidservant*."

The significance of Ruth's self-identity is that it surely recalls the previous conversation between Ruth and Boaz (2:8–13). There Boaz calls Ruth בִּתִּי (2:8; "my daughter"), and by her self-identification she is a נָכְרִיָּה (2:10; "foreigner") and שִׁפְחָתֶךָ (2:13; "your maidservant"). So Ruth is identified as foreign and yet a "daughter" and as a servant, but not an אָמָה as here. The operative distinction lexically is the difference between שִׁפְחָה and אָמָה. Richard Schultz presents a helpful chart based on lexical research that highlights the distinction between the two terms for a maidservant, and the context of Ruth seems fitting as to why she would use one term over the other (see table 1).[10]

TABLE 1. TWO TERMS FOR A MAIDSERVANT

Category	*ʾāmâ*	*šipḥâ*
relationship	serving master	serving mistress
marital status	married, eligible to marry	unmarried or virgin
social status	higher	lower
genre	in legal texts	in narrative texts
emphasis	as female	as property and laborer

We can apply these distinctions to the context of Ruth. Ruth previously identified herself as an unmarried, lower-status laborer (שִׁפְחָתֶךָ) because

10. Table reproduced from *NIDOTTE* 1:419.

her goal in Boaz's field was to glean barley. Now Ruth identifies herself as a higher-status servant with an emphasis on her femininity and eligibility to marry (אֲמָתֶךָ). Her goal now is marriage and redemption, and that is seen even in how she identifies herself to Boaz.[11] Describing herself as a servant, Ruth continues to express her dependence on Boaz. Shultz concludes, "The use of this self-designation indicates the woman's utter dependence on the addressee's favor to grant her request."[12]

וּפָרַשְׂתָּ כְנָפֶךָ עַל־אֲמָתְךָ ל̇ חס למערב

וּפָרַשְׂתָּ is a Qal perfect 2ms of פרשׂ + *vav*-consecutive, communicating Ruth's request with a mild imperatival nuance. Ruth describes what Boaz *should* do for her but in a humble and respectful manner.[13] כְנָפֶךָ is the direct object and is definite (because of the pronominal suffix) even though it is not marked by אֶת־.

עַל־אֲמָתְךָ is technically a locative prepositional phrase indicating *where* Boaz is to spread his wing, but the idiom makes a physical location irrelevant. Ruth repeats her self-designation as an אָמָה, emphasizing her eligibility to marry, as a reply to Boaz's initial question of who she is.

Notice that כְנָפֶךָ could be singular if taken as a pausal form where the disjunctive *paštā* (◌ּ◌; doubled to mark the accented syllable [◌פֶּ◌◌]) revealed the reduced vowel (◌ֶךָ ⟵ ◌ְךָ). Or it could be plural if the suffix is taken as a plural noun written defectively without the י (◌ֶךָ ⟵ ◌ֶיךָ).[14] To spread one's wing (singular) over another is metaphorical for marriage.[15] If כְנָפֶךָ is plural, it *could* refer merely to protection. While there is some debate among the Western (Israel/Syria) and Eastern (Babylonia) Masoretes about the correct pointing, it is best understood as a singular, "Spread your wing over your servant," as an invitation for marriage.[16]

---

11. Cf. Robert L. Hubbard, *The Book of Ruth*, New International Commentary on the Old Testament (Grand Rapids: Eerdmans, 1988), 211.

12. *NIDOTTE* 1:420.

13. Joüon, *Ruth*, 69; JM §119w.

14. Brotzman and Tully, *Old Testament Textual Criticism*, 164–65.

15. Block, *Ruth*, 180; Joüon, *Ruth*, 69–70.

16. See discussion in Wilch, *Ruth*, 119–21. The marginal note in *BHS* means "Once (ל̇) defectively (חס) [by the] Westerners (למערב)" [i.e., the Masoretes from Syria/Israel]. That

כִּ֥י גֹאֵ֖ל אָֽתָּה׃

The final כִּי clause is the ground for why Ruth believes Boaz should marry her: "*For* (כִּי) you (אָתָּה) [are] a kinsman redeemer (גֹּאֵל)." The clause is a verbless clause even though גֹּאֵל is morphologically a Qal participle. It is simply the noun "redeemer." In Hebrew word order, אָתָּה is the predicate nominative ("a redeemer [are] you"), but in good English, the pronoun would be the first word in the sentence, "*You* are a redeemer." Perhaps the Hebrew word order emphasizes Boaz as a גֹּאֵל. In naming Boaz as a גֹּאֵל, Ruth implicitly asks him to marry her since that seems to be part of the role of a גֹּאֵל. In addition, this term also implies a benefit to Naomi since Boaz would be redeeming Naomi's field as part of the kinsman-redeemer role (cf. 4:3).

In a beautiful twist of character identification, the verse begins with Boaz questioning who Ruth is (מִי־אָתְּ) but ends with Ruth identifying who Boaz is (גֹּאֵל אָתָּה). It seems that everyone is aware of their respective roles in these relationships. No single character needs to be informed of what was expected in torah. But using strokes of literary beauty, the author keeps the reader's attention in wondering whether each character will actually fulfill his or her role with integrity and humility.

---

the note specifies a pointing from the Westerners suggests that there was not agreement on whether the form is a defectively written plural noun or a pausal form singular noun.

RUTH 3:10

וַיֹּ֗אמֶר בְּרוּכָ֨ה אַ֤תְּ לַֽיהוָה֙ בִּתִּ֔י הֵיטַ֛בְתְּ חַסְדֵּ֥ךְ הָאַחֲר֖וֹן מִן־הָרִאשׁ֑וֹן לְבִלְתִּי־לֶ֗כֶת אַחֲרֵי֙ הַבַּ֣חוּרִ֔ים אִם־דַּ֖ל וְאִם־עָשִֽׁיר׃

ACCENT PHRASING

וַיֹּ֗אמֶר
בְּרוּכָ֨ה אַ֤תְּ לַֽיהוָה֙ בִּתִּ֔י
הֵיטַ֛בְתְּ חַסְדֵּ֥ךְ הָאַחֲר֖וֹן מִן־הָרִאשׁ֑וֹן
לְבִלְתִּי־לֶ֗כֶת אַחֲרֵי֙ הַבַּ֣חוּרִ֔ים אִם־דַּ֖ל וְאִם־עָשִֽׁיר׃

וַיֹּ֗אמֶר

וַיֹּ֗אמֶר is a Qal imperfect 3ms of אמר + *vav*-consecutive, moving the narrative forward now with Boaz pronouncing a blessing on Ruth. The *vav* is temporal succession.

בְּרוּכָ֨ה אַ֤תְּ לַֽיהוָה֙ בִּתִּ֔י

Boaz's blessing on Ruth begins with the Qal passive participle fs of ברך. The passive participles reduce the vowel in the R1 position when adding sufformatives (בְּרוּכָה) as opposed to the active participles, which retain the historic long i often written defectively (קוֹטְלָה ;קֹטְלָה). אַ֤תְּ is the subject, and with the jussive nuance of a blessing/request, we translate, "*May* you be blessed." The ל on לַֽיהוָה֙ indicates source.[17] The blessing Boaz intends will come from the Lord. בִּתִּ֔י is a vocative address and should be understood not as pejorative but as endearing. By addressing her as בִּתִּ֔י, Boaz communicates clearly that she is under his care.[18]

הֵיטַ֛בְתְּ חַסְדֵּ֥ךְ הָאַחֲר֖וֹן מִן־הָרִאשׁ֑וֹן

This clause is a bit cumbersome. הֵיטַ֛בְתְּ is the Hiphil perfect 2fs of יטב, translated literally as "You have caused good." In the Hiphil perfect, the

17. JM §132f; *GBHS* §4.1.10(l) lists it as a ל of "agent."

18. Block says, "He expresses his respect for and sense of obligation to Ruth" (*Judges, Ruth*, 692).

typical preformative vowel would be a *ḥîreq* (הִ◌◌◌). Notice here that the I-י verb (יטב) coalesces the I-י as the preformative vowel, resulting in a *ṣērê-yôd* (הֵיטַ֫בְתְּ).

חַסְדֵּךְ is the direct object, and הָאַחֲרוֹן מִן־הָרִאשׁוֹן are temporal modifiers, "the afterward/last" and "the beginning/first," respectively. מִן is comparative, and that becomes the crux of how to translate this clause.[19] With the accents, חַסְדֵּךְ הָאַחֲרוֹן are conjoined and become "your last lovingkindness."

הֵיטַבְתְּ	*ṭifḥā mêrĕkā* חַסְדֵּךְ הָאַחֲרוֹן	מִן־הָרִאשׁוֹן

As the direct object, this is what Ruth "caused to be good" (הֵיטַבְתְּ). The מִן preposition compares this "last lovingkindness" to "the first one" (הָרִאשׁוֹן). If we rearrange the words for good English and make the verb a comparative, we get "Your last lovingkindness *is better than* the first." The implication is that the הָרִאשׁוֹן was also a lovingkindness. The comparison, then, is between this appearance at the threshing floor and the familial lovingkindness she showed to Naomi in abandoning her own family and heritage for Naomi's sake (cf. 2:11). Boaz concludes that this appearance at the threshing floor so that Ruth can secure provision *for Naomi* through a redeemer is better than just simply joining with her for companionship. While Ruth's visit to the threshing floor is part of what is meant by her demonstration of חֶסֶד, in the next clause Boaz will also interpret this lovingkindness as Ruth not pursuing other men.

לְבִלְתִּי־לֶכֶת אַחֲרֵי הַבַּחוּרִים אִם־דַּל וְאִם־עָשִׁיר׃

The final clause explains what Ruth did to deserve Boaz's praise in the first half of the verse. This "last" lovingkindness to arrive at the threshing floor is better than Ruth just joining herself to Naomi, but why? Boaz will say that it is "better" because Ruth has pursued a family redeemer, not just any eligible bachelor.

19. RJW §317.

לְבִלְתִּי־לֶ֫כֶת is the negated Qal infinitive construct of הלך. בִּלְתִּי is the typical negation for infinitives and often occurs with the ל preposition as well (לְבִלְתִּי).[20] לְבִלְתִּי־לֶ֫כֶת is epexegetical, explaining *how* Ruth displayed חֶ֫סֶד. In English, epexegetical or explanatory infinitives are translated with "by" and a gerund ("-ing" noun), "by not going."[21]

אַחֲרֵי is a locative, not temporal. "Going *after*" is related to courtship and eligibility, not temporal movement. While marital eligibility is not technically a "locative" (following behind the suitor), the preposition clearly fails to communicate someone following temporally.

הַבַּחוּרִ֔ים are choice young men who are eligible for marriage, not just your run-of-the-mill guys. John Walton points out that these young men are "the most robust and energetic—the hope represented in the next generation."[22] As such, הַבַּחוּרִ֔ים could suggest that Boaz is older, also implied by his calling Ruth בִּתִּ֔י earlier. He commends her for not going after an eligible young man closer to her age. It could also point to Ruth's faithfulness to torah to pursue a גֹּאֵל in the family rather than just any eligible man even if that גֹּאֵל is older. Boaz is impressed with Ruth's covenant faithfulness, not simply her outward appearance.

Both occurrences of אִם mean "whether" and communicate an either-or idea.[23] אִם־דַּ֖ל וְאִם־עָשִֽׁיר is a merism. It expresses polar ends to represent the whole subset.[24] In 3:10, Boaz praises Ruth for following Naomi's advice and pursuing a covenantal kinsman redeemer rather than just any other eligible man. This חֶ֫סֶד is indeed better than merely accompanying Naomi back to Bethlehem.

---

20. RJW §423.

21. Waltke and O'Connor call this a gerundive or explanatory infinitive (WO §36.2.3e). See also RJW §195; JM §124o.

22. *NIDOTTE* 1:634–35.

23. RJW §455.

24. Holmstedt, *Ruth*, 163.

RUTH 3:11

וְעַתָּ֗ה בִּתִּי֙ אַל־תִּ֣ירְאִ֔י כֹּ֥ל אֲשֶׁר־תֹּאמְרִ֖י אֶֽעֱשֶׂה־לָּ֑ךְ כִּ֤י יוֹדֵ֙עַ֙ כָּל־שַׁ֣עַר עַמִּ֔י כִּ֛י אֵ֥שֶׁת חַ֖יִל אָֽתְּ׃

ACCENT PHRASING

וְעַתָּ֗ה בִּתִּי֙ אַל־תִּ֣ירְאִ֔י
כֹּ֥ל אֲשֶׁר־תֹּאמְרִ֖י אֶֽעֱשֶׂה־לָּ֑ךְ
כִּ֤י יוֹדֵ֙עַ֙ כָּל־שַׁ֣עַר עַמִּ֔י
כִּ֛י אֵ֥שֶׁת חַ֖יִל אָֽתְּ׃

וְעַתָּ֗ה בִּתִּי֙ אַל־תִּ֣ירְאִ֔י

Ruth 3:11 opens with the temporal adverb וְעַתָּה, drawing a *logical* conclusion.[25] Boaz again uses the vocative בִּתִּי֙ to address Ruth, the one whom he has now committed to protect and provide for.

אַל־תִּ֣ירְאִ֔י is the negated Qal jussive 2fs of ירא. אַל, as the negation, identifies the jussive. Even so, the force of this construction is an imperative/prohibition, "Do not fear." Notice the I-י of the root ירא coalesces as the preformative vowel (תִּ֣ירְאִ֔י), and yet all the elements of the verbal root are still present (תיראי). The preformative/sufformative (תִּ◌◌◌ִי) combination of the jussive 2fs remains readily noticeable from the Qal paradigm.

כֹּ֥ל אֲשֶׁר־תֹּאמְרִ֖י אֶֽעֱשֶׂה־לָּ֑ךְ

כֹּל marks the beginning of the accusative object phrase for the main verb (אֶֽעֱשֶׂה), but it is fronted for emphasis. אֲשֶׁר־תֹּאמְרִ֖י is the relative clause that specifies כֹּל. תֹּאמְרִי is the Qal imperfect 2fs of the אמר and, as an imperfective, expresses incomplete action. Boaz is not necessarily saying that he will do whatever Ruth says in any future situation, but he will indeed carry out what she is currently asking (3:9; וּפָרַשְׂתָּ֤ כְנָפֶ֙ךָ֙ עַל־אֲמָ֣תְךָ֔). In the context, Boaz is committing to marry Ruth and therefore also to act as a גֹּאֵל for both Ruth and Naomi.

25. WO §39.3.4f.

אֶעֱשֶׂה is the main verb and is a Qal imperfect 1cs of עשׂה. Since עשׂה is a I-guttural, the guttural letter (here an ע) takes a composite *shewa*. Since it is a 1cs with the א preformative, the composite *shewa* matches the vowel class of the preformative (◌ֶ◌ֱ). עשׂה is also a III-ה weak verb, but in this case that only entails the thematic vowel becoming a *sěgōl* (◌ֶה). The final ה of the lexical form remains as a vowel marker.

The final prepositional phrase (לָּ֑ךְ) is the ל of advantage with the 2fs pronominal suffix. Boaz says, "All that you say, I will do *for* you."[26] The dot in the ל is another example of a *děḥîq*, which, along with the *maqqēf* (־), closely connects אֶֽעֱשֶׂה־לָּ֑ךְ.

כִּ֤י יוֹדֵ֙עַ֙ כָּל־שַׁ֣עַר עַמִּ֔י

כִּ֤י provides a ground clause for *why* Boaz will do all that Ruth has said. יוֹדֵ֙עַ֙ is a Qal participle ms of ידע. III-guttural, nonfinite verbs (i.e., infinitives and participles) retain the thematic vowel of the introductory Qal paradigm and then supply the phonetic glide with the furtive *pataḥ* to attain the long *ā* sound preferred by gutturals.[27]

כָּל־שַׁ֣עַר עַמִּ֔י is the subject phrase. כָּל־שַׁ֣עַר is the formal subject, and עַמִּ֔י is the construct modifier, specifying which gate Boaz is referring to. The idiom "gate of my people" does not refer to a specific gate in the city but is a reference to all of the townspeople.[28] "All of the gate of my people" implies a plurality of people, and yet because כָּל־שַׁ֣עַר is grammatically singular, the verbal יוֹדֵ֙עַ֙ is also singular.

Translating the participle (יוֹדֵ֙עַ֙) provides some unique nuances to the verse. The participle is a verbal adjective, technically describing כָּל־שַׁ֣עַר עַמִּ֔י. This is who they are and what they do. Applying the durative nuance of the participle to the verse, we get the idea that the townspeople know and have known what Boaz is getting ready to say about Ruth (כִּ֛י אֵ֥שֶׁת חַ֖יִל אָֽתְּ). As we will see, the town that formerly "murmured" (הום in 1:19) when

26. RJW §271a; GKC §119s; JM §133d.

27. *IBH*, 216.

28. L. Daniel Hawk, *Ruth*, Apollos Old Testament Commentary 7B (Downers Grove, IL: InterVarsity Press, 2015), 110.

Naomi and Ruth returned will celebrate the marriage of Boaz and Ruth as well as the birth of a son (4:13–17). Even though the townspeople have taken a backstage position in the narrative, Boaz indicates that regardless of Naomi's disposition, the townspeople know that Ruth is an אֵ֫שֶׁת חַיִל. They did not just know a fact or two about Ruth; rather, their status was one of "knowing" about Ruth's character.

כִּ֛י אֵ֥שֶׁת חַ֖יִל אָֽתְּ׃

The second כִּי clause *explains* what the townspeople know.[29] They know "*that*" אֵ֥שֶׁת חַ֖יִל אָֽתְּ ("a woman of [moral] worth you are"). The idea of Ruth being a woman of worth, or a worthy woman, matches the description of Boaz in 2:1, where he is an אִ֫ישׁ גִּבּ֣וֹר חַ֔יִל. As discussed before, one reason we know that nothing promiscuous happened at the threshing floor is that both Boaz and Ruth are described as having strong moral character.

The Hebrew phrase אֵ֫שֶׁת חַ֫יִל occurs only three times in the Hebrew Bible (Prov 12:4; 31:10; Ruth 3:11). In Proverbs, the phrase refers to the woman who "is the crown of her husband" (12:4) and who "is far more precious than jewels" (31:10). In the Hebrew Bible, Ruth follows Proverbs, so it is possible that Ruth, via the order of the Hebrew canon, is portrayed as the quintessential "excellent wife."

To translate this last clause, we must supply the English copulative verb "are." אָֽתְּ is the subject and אֵ֥שֶׁת חַ֖יִל the predicate nominative, fronted here for focus: "a worthy woman you [*are*]." אֵ֥שֶׁת חַ֖יִל is a construct package that communicates an attribute, much like an attributive adjective.[30] Hence, אֵ֥שֶׁת חַ֖יִל is "a woman of [moral] worth," or "a worthy woman."

29. RJW §451a.

30. *GBHS* §2.2.5.

RUTH 3:12

וְעַתָּה֙ כִּ֣י אָמְנָ֔ם כִּ֥י אִם גֹאֵ֖ל אָנֹ֑כִי וְגַ֛ם יֵ֥שׁ גֹּאֵ֖ל קָר֥וֹב מִמֶּֽנִּי׃

ACCENT PHRASING

וְעַתָּה֙ כִּ֣י אָמְנָ֔ם
כִּ֥י אִם גֹאֵ֖ל אָנֹ֑כִי
וְגַ֛ם יֵ֥שׁ גֹּאֵ֖ל קָר֥וֹב מִמֶּֽנִּי׃

וְעַתָּה֙ כִּ֣י אָמְנָ֔ם כִּ֥י אִ֗ם גֹאֵ֖ל אָנֹ֑כִי אם חד מן ח̇ כת̇ ולא קר̇ / אם כת̇ ולא ק̇

Ruth 3:12 opens with the adverbial עַתָּה to focus the audience's attention on the information about to be shared. וְעַתָּה that introduced 3:11 certainly drew the audience's attention to what was being said, but it was information that positively moved the narrative in the expected direction. This וְעַתָּה֙ introduces vital information to the story, but it is adversative to the movement of the narrative toward Ruth and Boaz's marriage.

The first כִּ֣י is an asseverative, "indeed," that introduces the nature of the information; it is factual information.[31] אָמְנָ֔ם is an adverb translated "truly," and notice the adverbial ending ָם on the root אמן.[32]

כִּי אִם proves to be a bit more difficult but is the *ketiv* ("what was written") in the consonantal text. Notice the two *qere* notes above. The first (אם חד מן ח̇ כת̇ ולא קר̇) is the Masora Parva (Mp) note from *BHS*, and the second (אם כת̇ ולא ק̇) is the Mp note from *BHQ*. The *BHS* note explains that this verse is one of eight examples where the *ketiv* is written but *not* read (*ketiv vela qere*). The Mp from *BHQ* reads, "אִם is written but not read."[33] While this may be an example of dittography,[34] אִם may occur following כִּי as what

31. RJW §449.

32. WO §39.3.4; JM §164.

33. Israel Yeivin, *Introduction to the Tiberian Masorah*, trans. E. J. Revell, Masoretic Studies 5 (Missoula, MT: Scholars Press, 1980), §102.

34. Dittography would argue that the scribe began writing כי אמ of כי אמנם but then looked away for a moment and, when he returned to the manuscript, inadvertently began writing

Williams calls a "pleonastic אִם."[35] Williams says this use of אִם is primarily for stylistic reasons after certain particles but is left untranslated and is unnecessary. כִּי אִם is best understood as an emphatic assurance in an oath clause and, when coupled with the previous asseverative כִּי, puts significant emphasis on this true statement from Boaz.

גֹאֵל is a Qal participle ms functioning as a substantive (predicate nominative). אָנֹכִי is the subject, and we must supply the English "to be" verb to get "A redeemer I [*am*]."

וְגַ֛ם יֵ֥שׁ גֹּאֵ֖ל קָר֥וֹב מִמֶּֽנִּי׃

וְגַם is additive, providing additional information for the narrative and signaling important information, not just random details. In this sense, גַּם is a strong additive. The *vav* is adversative, providing the contrasting reality of Boaz as Ruth's גֹּאֵל. If we understand the adversative as a concessive, we get "However, there is ..." and this is a better translation since Boaz is bringing up a situation that contrasts his own role as a redeemer.[36] "Indeed, I am a redeemer; *however* (וְ), there is *even* (גַּם) a redeemer nearer than I."

יֵשׁ is the particle of existence, "there is/are." קָרוֹב מִמֶּנִּי is literally "near from me," but the מִן preposition is comparative, "there is a redeemer near*er than* I."[37] Notice that the מִן preposition with pronominal suffixes reduplicates and assimilates the *nuns* in silent *shewa* positions.

מִנְמִנְנִי ← מִמֶּנִּי

כי אם again before moving on to גאל. For a discussion of dittography generally, see Brotzman and Tully, *Old Testament Textual Criticism*, 123. For כי אם functioning together grammatically without the need to emend the text, see Brotzman and Tully, *Old Testament Textual Criticism*, 166–67; Holmstedt, *Ruth*, 165–67.

35. For the "pleonastic" אִם, see RJW §457; for כִּי אִם forming a strong asseverative, see JM §164c.

36. RJW §382.

37. RJW §317.

RUTH 3:13

לִ֣ינִי ׀ הַלַּ֗יְלָה וְהָיָ֤ה בַבֹּ֙קֶר֙ אִם־יִגְאָלֵ֥ךְ טוֹב֙ יִגְאָ֔ל וְאִם־לֹ֨א יַחְפֹּ֧ץ לְגָֽאֳלֵ֛ךְ
וּגְאַלְתִּ֥יךְ אָנֹ֖כִי חַי־יְהוָ֑ה שִׁכְבִ֖י עַד־הַבֹּֽקֶר׃

ACCENT PHRASING

לִ֣ינִי ׀ הַלַּ֗יְלָה
וְהָיָ֤ה בַבֹּ֙קֶר֙
אִם־יִגְאָלֵ֥ךְ טוֹב֙ יִגְאָ֔ל
וְאִם־לֹ֨א יַחְפֹּ֧ץ לְגָֽאֳלֵ֛ךְ וּגְאַלְתִּ֥יךְ אָנֹ֖כִי חַי־יְהוָ֑ה
שִׁכְבִ֖י עַד־הַבֹּֽקֶר׃

לִ֣ינִי ׀ הַלַּ֗יְלָה

לִ֣ינִי is a Qal imperative 2fs of לין. הַ on הַלַּ֗יְלָה is demonstrative, "this night," or idiomatically "tonight." Notice that לין is a II-י verb that coalesces the II-י with the thematic vowel (ִי). With hollow roots, the perfect and participle drop the middle ו or י in the Qal, but all other conjugations coalesce the ו or י with the thematic vowel.[38] In this case we do not have a preformative letter to indicate the imperfect, but we also do not have the "dropping" of the II-י to point us toward the perfect. Knowing that the imperative is formed by removing the preformative of the imperfect, we can discern this parsing as the imperative. It has all the vowels expected from a II-י imperfect 2fs, just no preformative. The ִי at the end distinguishes the imperative 2fs from the 2ms.

While grammatically לִ֣ינִי is a command, Boaz invites Ruth to stay at the threshing floor for the night, not as a means of promiscuity, but rather to protect her. Later in the verse, he commits to redeem her the next day, and in 3:14 we will see that Boaz sends her away while it is still dark. Boaz initially protects her from danger by telling her to spend the night (לִ֣ינִי). Later he will protect her from ridicule as a result of everyone knowing she spent the night at the threshing floor.

38. Kutz and Josberger, *Learning Biblical Hebrew*, 343–51.

וְהָיָה בַבֹּקֶר

וְהָיָה is a Qal perfect 3ms of היה + *vav*-consecutive. With the *vav*, it translates as future tense, introducing a temporally future event, "and it *shall* come about." בַבֹּקֶר is the prepositional phrase that specifies the time of this future event.

אִם־יִגְאָלֵךְ טוֹב יִגְאָל

אִם introduces the protasis of the first conditional clause, "*If* he will redeem you."[39] יִגְאָלֵךְ is a Qal imperfect 3ms of גאל + 2fs pronominal suffix. In English, we can supply "then" to introduce the apodosis before טוֹב. If we turn it into a complete sentence, we get "If he will redeem you, [then *it is*] good." However, the terse nature of the apodosis energizes the discussion: "If he will redeem you, good." יִגְאָל is a Qal imperfect 3ms of גאל in form but jussive in meaning. Context must drive this conclusion, but since Boaz is allowing for the nearer redeemer to redeem if he so desires, the modal meaning fits for a hypothetical future action, "*let* him redeem."

וְאִם־לֹא יַחְפֹּץ לְגָאֳלֵךְ וּגְאַלְתִּיךְ אָנֹכִי חַי־יְהוָה

אִם now introduces a second conditional sentence, the inverse of the previous one. The *vav* is contrastive since this is the opposite situation of the previous conditional clause: "*But* if he does not desire to redeem." יַחְפֹּץ is a Qal imperfect 3ms of חפץ, and לְגָאֳלֵךְ is a Qal infinitive construct of גאל + 2fs suffix complementing the previous verb (יַחְפֹּץ). The apodosis of this second conditional clause is introduced by וּגְאַלְתִּיךְ. If the nearer redeemer will not redeem Ruth, "then" (ו) Boaz will redeem Ruth.

וּגְאַלְתִּיךְ is the Qal perfect 1cs of גאל + 2fs object suffix + *vav*-consecutive. The repetition of the subject pronoun (אָנֹכִי) provides emphasis, "I *myself* will redeem you." Finally, Boaz is so committed to redeeming Ruth that he interjects an oath clause, חַי־יְהוָה. Literally the phrase reads, "the life of the Lord," with the construct package identifying the one against whom the oath rests, "*by* the life of the Lord." This package therefore communicates

---

39. RJW §453.

either an implied instrumental ב or an implied מִן of source.[40] What Boaz communicates is an oath exclamation,[41] but the oath implies the surety of his actions based on and motivated by the "life of the Lord." Hence, the "life of the Lord" is either the "instrument" of Boaz's commitment or the "source" of his commitment (or both). In English translation, the phrase often translates as a simple oath exclamation, "As the Lord lives." The surety of Yahweh's existence grounds the surety that Boaz will redeem Ruth if the nearer redeemer refuses.

שִׁכְבִ֖י עַד־הַבֹּֽקֶר׃

The final clause reiterates Boaz's initial command (לִ֣ינִי) at the beginning of the verse, but with a different verb. שִׁכְבִ֖י is the Qal imperative 2fs of שׁכב. עַד־הַבֹּֽקֶר is the temporal prepositional phrase describing until *when* Ruth is to lie down: "until the morning."

40. For instrumental ב, see RJW §243; cf. RJW §320a for a מִן of means. For מִן of source, see RJW §322. For an explanation of the logical concepts presented here, but using "genitive" terminology, see *GBHS* §2.2.9 and RJW §45b on "genitive of means." Remember that the options for implied prepositions in construct packages are מִן, ב, ל. However, these prepositions have a wide range of logical meaning, hence the difficulty of specifically classifying every construct package. Here the difference between an instrumental ב and a מִן of source/means is extremely minimal.

41. Holmstedt, *Ruth*, 169.

RUTH 3:14

וַתִּשְׁכַּ֤ב מַרְגְּלֹתָו֙ עַד־הַבֹּ֔קֶר וַתָּ֕קָם בִּטְר֛וֹם יַכִּ֥יר אִ֖ישׁ אֶת־רֵעֵ֑הוּ וַיֹּ֨אמֶר֙ אַל־יִוָּדַ֔ע כִּי־בָ֥אָה הָאִשָּׁ֖ה הַגֹּֽרֶן׃

ACCENT PHRASING

וַתִּשְׁכַּ֤ב מַרְגְּלֹתָו֙ עַד־הַבֹּ֔קֶר
וַתָּ֕קָם בִּטְר֛וֹם יַכִּ֥יר אִ֖ישׁ אֶת־רֵעֵ֑הוּ
וַיֹּ֨אמֶר֙
אַל־יִוָּדַ֔ע כִּי־בָ֥אָה הָאִשָּׁ֖ה הַגֹּֽרֶן׃

וַתִּשְׁכַּ֤ב מַרְגְּלֹתָו֙ עַד־הַבֹּ֔קֶר (ק מרגלותיו)

וַתִּשְׁכַּ֤ב is a Qal imperfect 3fs of שׁכב + *vav*-consecutive of logical succession, "And *so* she lay down." מַרְגְּלֹתָו֙ is an adverbial accusative of place, specifying the location of where Ruth laid down: "[at] the place of his feet." The *ketiv* looks singular (מַרְגְּלֹתָו֙), and so the marginal *qere* (מרגלותיו) specifies the plural "feet" rather than "foot." עַד־הַבֹּ֔קֶר provides the temporal notion of how long she stayed—namely, "until the morning."

וַתָּ֕קָם בִּטְר֛וֹם יַכִּ֥יר אִ֖ישׁ אֶת־רֵעֵ֑הוּ (ק בטרם; יתיר ו)

וַתָּ֕קָם is a Qal imperfect 3fs of קום + the *vav* of temporal succession: "And *then* she arose." In hollow roots, the imperfective would be תָּקוּם, but with the *vav*-consecutive, the accent retracts to the preformative (וַתָּ֕קָם). This forces the final syllable to be closed and unaccented, resulting in the short *qāmeṣ-ḥāṭûf* (וַתָּ֕קָם). Even though the written vowel is short, the phonetics of the Qal imperfect (o-class thematic vowel) is still present.

בִּטְר֛וֹם literally translates as "in the before(ness)." The *ḥōlem-vav* in the *ketiv* (בִּטְר֛וֹם) is unnecessary, so the *qere* (בטרם) provides a marginal variant that is more akin to what one would expect. The marginal note also comments on the superfluous *vav* (יתיר ו).[42] With either morphology, the meaning is simply "before."

---

42. For discussion of both of these *ketiv/qere* situations, see Brotzman and Tully, *Old Testament Textual Criticism*, 167–68.

בְּטְרֹ֫ום יַכִּ֥יר אִ֖ישׁ אֶת־רֵעֵ֑הוּ is idiomatic for "very early in the morning." The clause literally reads, "before a man [could] recognize his friend." אִישׁ is the subject, and יַכִּיר is the Hiphil imperfect 3ms of נכר. Translate יַכִּיר as a modal jussive, we get the nuance of ability: "before a man *could* recognize his friend."[43] Morphologically, נכר is a I-נ verb and the initial נ has assimilated into the middle כ. However, the a-class preformative vowel and the standard *ḥîreq-yôd* thematic vowel of the Hiphil both remain for parsing purposes.

אֶת־רֵעֵהוּ is the direct object and marked as such with the definite direct object marker (אֶת־). רֵעֵהוּ is definite because of the pronominal suffix. We are talking about not just any friend but specifically "*his* friend."

The hypothetical situation in which a man could not see his friend indicates that Ruth left very early in the morning while it was still dark. Just as Boaz protected Ruth from nighttime dangers by having her lodge at the threshing floor until the morning, he now protects her from ridicule for being seen after spending the night at a morally compromising location. Both Boaz's and Ruth's consciences are clear, but Boaz still protects Ruth from the potential shame of being labeled as a promiscuous foreigner.

וַיֹּ֫אמֶר

וַיֹּ֫אמֶר introduces direct speech from Boaz, "And so he said ..." וַיֹּ֫אמֶר is a Qal imperfect 3ms of אמר + *vav*-consecutive of logical succession. The next logical action after Ruth's arising (וַתָּ֫קָם) was for Boaz to give her instructions regarding her departure: "And *so* he said ..."

אַל־יִוָּדַ֕ע כִּי־בָ֥אָה הָאִשָּׁ֖ה הַגֹּֽרֶן׃

אַל־יִוָּדַ֕ע is the negated Niphal imperfect 3ms of ידע. ידע is an original I-ו. The *dāgēš forte* in the R1 of the Niphal stem cements the first root letter, and therefore we see that the first root letter is a *vav* even though the lexical form is ידע. The verb is jussive because of the negation אַל־, and the clause is a mild prohibition, "Do not let it be known." The Niphal stem communicates the passive voice of the translation, "Do not let it *be* known."

43. WO §31.4c; GKC §107c.

כִּי introduces the complement to what should not be known (a "normalizing כִּי").[44] "Do not let it be known *that* the woman came to the threshing floor." הָאִשָּׁה is the subject and בָּאָה is a Qal perfect 3fs of בוא. The perfective highlights the completed action that Ruth has already been to the threshing floor and is getting ready to leave: "that the woman *came*." Rather than being remotely pejorative, הָאִשָּׁה is a general title that heightens the narrative secrecy of Ruth's visit to the threshing floor by leaving her unnamed in the clause.[45] הַגֹּרֶן is the adverbial accusative of place. Even without the directive ה, we supply the preposition "to" to indicate where she came, "*to* the threshing floor."

It should be emphasized that Boaz is not trying to hide a promiscuous encounter. Rather, he protects Ruth's reputation by sending her back to Naomi before anyone would accuse her of promiscuous behavior.

44. RJW §451a.

45. Edward F. Campbell Jr., *Ruth: A New Translation with Introduction, Notes, and Commentary*, Anchor Bible 7 (Garden City, NY: Doubleday, 1975), 130; Wilch, *Ruth*, 128.

RUTH 3:15

וַיֹּאמֶר הָבִי הַמִּטְפַּחַת אֲשֶׁר־עָלַיִךְ וְאֶחֳזִי־בָהּ וַתֹּאחֶז בָּהּ וַיָּמָד שֵׁשׁ־שְׂעֹרִים
וַיָּשֶׁת עָלֶיהָ וַיָּבֹא הָעִיר׃

ACCENT PHRASING

וַיֹּאמֶר
הָבִי הַמִּטְפַּחַת אֲשֶׁר־עָלַיִךְ וְאֶחֳזִי־בָהּ
וַתֹּאחֶז בָּהּ
וַיָּמָד שֵׁשׁ־שְׂעֹרִים
וַיָּשֶׁת עָלֶיהָ
וַיָּבֹא הָעִיר׃

וַיֹּאמֶר

וַיֹּאמֶר is the Qal imperfect 3ms of אמר + *vav*-consecutive in logical succession, "And *so* he said." Ruth 3:15 introduces the consequent actions of Boaz to give Ruth grain for Naomi. Boaz is sending Ruth home, but he sends her with barley in her outer shawl.

הָבִי הַמִּטְפַּחַת אֲשֶׁר־עָלַיִךְ וְאֶחֳזִי־בָהּ

הָבִי is the Qal imperative 2fs of יהב. Note the fully written vowel ָ where we would expect a composite shewa for the imperative (הֲבִי).[46] Literally, the verb means "to give," but in the sense of "give me your hand," meaning "extend out" or "bring." הַמִּטְפַּחַת is the accusative direct object. Boaz tells Ruth to bring her shawl or to extend it out. אֲשֶׁר־עָלַיִךְ specifies הַמִּטְפַּחַת—namely, the one "which [is] upon you." This is likely a garment that would

46. Gesenius (GKC §69o) points out that the vowel lengthens here as an analogy to the plural form that accents the final syllable (הָבוּ), leaving the ה in a pretonic open syllable (cf. Deut 32:3). However, on the basis of the standard Qal paradigm for I-ו verbs like יהב, one expects a *shewa* under the ה (הֲבִי) also with an accented final syllable (הֲבִ֫י). Here and in Judges 6:22, however, the ה is accented (*telîšā gādôl*, ◌֠) *and* the vowel is lengthened (הָ֠בִי). So the form here is anomalous but not unattested. While not all the elements of "hiatus" are present here, Ruth 3:15 may portray a similar result. Hiatus is a specific situation in which the accent of a word shifts for rhythmic purposes similar to a pausal form (Gen 29:21; JM §33).

be an overcoat or a type of shawl that could be used to carry goods.[47] In this case, Ruth will carry six measures of barley.

Boaz continues his instruction in the next clause with וְאֶֽחֳזִי, the Qal imperative 2fs of אחז + conjunctive *vav*. When this is combined with הָֽבִי, Boaz's complete instructions are "Bring … and hold." Notice that the *ḥāṭēf qāmeṣ-ḥāṭûf* under the ח retains the vowel class (o-class) but also is a reduced vowel because of the vocalic ending (◌ִי). The *sĕgōl* under the א is also a bit tricky. We would expect a *shewa* in the imperative, but with the *ḥāṭēf qāmeṣ-ḥāṭûf* under the ח, Hebrew will not allow two vocal *shewa*s consecutively. It is likely that the *metheg* (◌ֽ) under the א indicates that an abnormal vowel change has occurred.[48] That the expected *shewa* under the א changes to a *sĕgōl* is a bit odd. Usually we would expect the initial *shewa* to produce the short vowel of the following *ḥāṭēf shewa* (expected form may be אָחֳזִי with a *qāmeṣ-ḥāṭûf* under the א). However, it appears the א retains its desired e-class vowel, *sĕgōl*.

final form		R_2 reduction due to vocalic ending		hypothetical form before changes
אֶֽחֳזִי	⟵	אֱחֳזִי	⟵	אֱחֹזִי

בָּהּ marks the accusative object, and the 3fs suffix has הַמִּטְפַּחַת as its antecedent, also fs.

וַתֹּאחֶז בָּהּ

וַתֹּאחֶז is the Qal imperfect 3fs of אחז + *vav*-consecutive, describing that Ruth did as Boaz requested. The *vav* is therefore logical succession, "and *so* she held it [out]." Morphologically, notice that אחז is a I-א verb that morphs like אמר with a *ḥōlem* as the preformative vowel in the Qal imperfect.[49] As

47. *NIDOTTE* 2:928.

48. Gesenius points out that the *metheg* is used primarily to mark the secondary stress of a word so that the vowel is noticed and therefore pronounced (GKC §16c–i; cf. JM §14, particularly §14c.3 for this usage of the *metheg*). In this case, the *metheg* marks the secondary stress for sure, but it does so because the expected pronunciation mark would be a *shewa*. Therefore, the primary reason for including the *metheg* is due to the vowel change from a *shewa* to a *sĕgôl*, marking the vowel as needing to be pronounced with a secondary stress in the word.

49. The other I-א verbs that morph in this manner are אמר, אכל, אבד, אפה, אבה. See *IBH*, 200–203, for explanations of the morphology and thematic vowel dissimilation.

in the previous clause, אחז takes the ב preposition to mark the direct object, and the 3fs suffix (הּ; "it") refers to the fs הַמִּטְפַּחַת.

וַיָּמָד שֵׁשׁ־שְׂעֹרִים

The narrative now shifts back to Boaz as the implied subject of the 3ms verb. וַיָּמָד is a Qal imperfect 3ms of מדד + *vav*-consecutive. Having held out her הַמִּטְפַּחַת, the next logical step is for Boaz "to measure" out barley to put in it, and hence this *vav* is one of logical succession. מדד is a geminate verb, and in the forms with no sufformative, the geminated consonant often drops or is left "hanging" until something is added to the word (cf. the 3mp form with *dāgēš forte* in the ד in Exod 16:18, וַיָּמֹדּוּ).[50] Notice that geminate roots will retract the accent in a *vav*-consecutive form similar to hollow verbs. This leaves the final syllable closed and unaccented, requiring a short vowel, *qāmeṣ-ḥāṭûf*.

שֵׁשׁ־שְׂעֹרִים is the direct object and literally translates as "six barleys." The plural of שְׂעֹרִים implies six "measures" of barley, not just six pieces of barley. The actual amount of barley is left unspecified, and so the likely unit of a "measure" here was whatever vessel Boaz used to scoop the barley (i.e., cupped hands, a shovel, or a small container lying around).[51]

וַיָּשֶׁת עָלֶיהָ

Having filled Ruth's shawl with barley, Boaz next puts the shawl "upon her" so that she can easily carry it back to Naomi. וַיָּשֶׁת is a Qal imperfect 3ms of שׁית, and the direct object is omitted. The direct object is unnecessary and is often left out when it is only a pronoun and it is obvious what receives the action of the verb. Here the shawl filled with barley is clearly implied, and so we have to supply the pronoun "it": "Then he placed [*it*] upon her." עָלֶיהָ is the locative prepositional phrase indicating *where* he placed the filled shawl.

---

50. The Qal imperfect of geminate roots may sometimes "transpose" the gemination, meaning that rather than the R2 doubling, the R1 will double, theoretically producing the form וַיִּמֹּד (*IBH*, 280–81). However, this transposition cannot be predicted and does not occur in the Hebrew Bible with the root מדד.

51. Block, *Judges, Ruth*, 697–98.

וַיָּבֹא הָעִיר׃

The next clause is in temporal sequence and explains that *Boaz* "came to the city." וַיָּבֹא is the Qal imperfect 3ms of בוא + *vav*-consecutive. הָעִיר is an adverbial accusative of place, and so we supply the preposition "to" even without the directional ה, "*to* the city." After discussing plans with Ruth and sending her away with plenty of provision, Boaz now goes to the city to complete the task of redeeming Ruth along with Naomi's field.

It may seem odd that the narrator would tell us that Boaz went to the city when he had just prepared Ruth for a journey back to Naomi. In fact, about forty manuscripts, the Syriac, and Latin have the 3fs verbal form, "And *she* came to the city."[52] However, the next verse is where we learn that Ruth also (and obviously) went back to Naomi, and so this short phrase in verse 15b highlights Boaz's commitment to take care of this issue immediately.

The text-critical discussion in *BHQ* points out that the LXX specifies the subject of the next 3fs verb in 3:16 (*καὶ* Ρουθ *εἰσῆλθεν*) whereas the subject ("Ruth") in 3:16 is implied in the MT. In the narrator's conclusion to the threshing floor encounter, the 3ms verb in 3:15 has the same subject as the previous 3ms forms in chapter 3—namely, Boaz. Boaz gives Ruth instructions, he provides for her needs, he sends her away early to protect her reputation, and then *he* immediately returns to the city to find the nearer redeemer and initiate a conversation with him regarding Ruth and Naomi's redemption.

---

52. See *BHQ* apparatus: וַיָּבֹא G T | *καὶ εἰσῆλθεν* Ῥούθ G^{Mss} (V) (S) (harm-synt, cf KR). Also see the discussion in the text-critical apparatus of *BHQ*, 55.

RUTH 3:16

וַתָּבוֹא אֶל־חֲמוֹתָהּ וַתֹּאמֶר מִי־אַתְּ בִּתִּי וַתַּגֶּד־לָהּ אֵת כָּל־אֲשֶׁר עָשָׂה־לָהּ הָאִישׁ׃

ACCENT PHRASING

וַתָּבוֹא אֶל־חֲמוֹתָהּ
וַתֹּאמֶר
מִי־אַתְּ בִּתִּי
וַתַּגֶּד־לָהּ אֵת כָּל־אֲשֶׁר עָשָׂה־לָהּ הָאִישׁ׃

וַתָּבוֹא אֶל־חֲמוֹתָהּ

The subject now shifts back to Ruth as she returns to Naomi. וַתָּבוֹא is a Qal imperfect 3fs of בוא + *vav*-consecutive in temporal succession. Notice that in the Qal imperfect of the hollow root בוא, the preformative vowel shifts to a-class (usually *pataḥ*) and is a long *qāmeṣ* because it is in an open pretonic syllable (וַתָּבוֹא). Remember the *paštā* accent (◌ּ) is a postpositive accent occurring at the end of the word but also accenting the final syllable (וַתָּבוֹא).

אֶל־חֲמוֹתָהּ is a locative prepositional phrase indicating where Ruth came—namely, "to her mother-in-law." With the addition of the 3fs pronominal suffix (◌ָהּ), the original full vowel under the ח of חָמוֹת reduces to a vocal *shewa*, but under a guttural ח it must be a *ḥāṭēf-shewa* (◌ֲ). The pronominal suffix is technically in construct with חָמוֹת communicating an implied ל of possession, "the mother-in-law *of* (belonging to) her" or, in smoother English, "her mother-in-law."

וַתֹּאמֶר מִי־אַתְּ בִּתִּי

וַתֹּאמֶר is the Qal imperfect 3fs of אמר + *vav*-consecutive and introduces Naomi's question to Ruth. Naomi is the implied subject. The accent pattern in this segment separates the verb introducing the direct speech (וַתֹּאמֶר) from the direct speech itself (מִי־אַתְּ בִּתִּי).

◌◌֖◌ | ◌◌־◌֥◌ ◌◌֑◌

The *ṭifḥā* on וַתֹּ֖אמֶר must occur one or two constituents before the *atnāḥ*. With מִי־אַתְּ joined by a *maqqēf* (־), מִי־אַ֥תְּ serves as one constituent, and so the disjunctive *ṭifḥā* (◌֖) is indeed on the second constituent before the *atnāḥ* and is used to separate the narrative introduction of the direct speech (וַתֹּ֖אמֶר) from Naomi's actual question (מִי־אַ֥תְּ בִּתִּ֑י).[53]

Naomi says, מִי־אַ֥תְּ בִּתִּ֑י. The verbless clause begins with the interrogative particle (מִי) and is reminiscent of Boaz's question to Ruth at the threshing floor (3:9). As is common with verbless clauses, we must supply the English "to be" verb to get "Who [*are*] you ... ?"

Some commentators take this to be a question of condition and translate מִי as "*How* are you?"[54] Others take it as a question of classification, "Are you now the Ruth who is classified as the one betrothed to Boaz?"[55] The question of classification is best in the given context. Naomi is not overly concerned with Ruth's condition. Rather, she wants to know if the plan worked. Did Ruth accomplish what Naomi intended with her instructions from earlier in the chapter? Boaz is a near relative who is able to redeem them. Did he continue to show Ruth favor? "Are you the Ruth who is now under the wing of Boaz's protection and provision?"

The question of classification parallels the question from Boaz when Ruth appeared at the threshing floor (3:9; וַיֹּ֖אמֶר מִי־אָ֑תְּ). There we argued that Boaz's question was emphasized syntactically by the accent pattern, and here we have a very similar accent pattern only with the addition of the vocative, בִּתִּ֑י. Clearly, these two questions are intended to be read together. Since it is now morning, Naomi certainly knows Ruth's identity. Naomi wants to know about Ruth's classification just as Boaz inquired about Ruth's classification at the threshing floor.

53. Cf. 3:9, וַיֹּ֖אמֶר מִי־אָ֑תְּ.

54. Wilch, *Ruth*, 131. Cf. Amos 7:2; WO §18.2q; Block, *Judges, Ruth*, 699.

55. Holmstedt, *Ruth*, 173. See also WO §18.2d; Jack M. Sasson, *Ruth: A New Translation with a Philological Commentary and a Formalist-Folkorist Interpretation* (Baltimore: Johns Hopkins University Press, 1979), 100–101; Hubbard, *Book of Ruth*, 224, n. 5; Bush, *Ruth, Esther*, 184–85.

Through this use of parallel questions, the narrator takes the reader on a journey of suspense. Is Ruth truly an אֵשֶׁת חַיִל (3:11) as she puts herself into a morally compromised situation at the threshing floor? Then, if Naomi's plan actually did intend promiscuity, did Ruth actually carry out that plan? The ambiguity of Naomi's intent versus what Ruth actually carried out is now brought to the focus of the narrative through these interrogatives. While we have argued that the designation of Ruth and Boaz as people of upright moral character (חַיִל) precludes any promiscuity at the threshing floor, the ambiguity of Naomi's plan still remains. Without negatively caricaturing Naomi extensively, it is almost as if you can see Naomi asking this question slyly, wondering if, through a premature promiscuous encounter, Ruth is already "betrothed" to Boaz. We will see in 3:18 that Naomi tells Ruth only to stay put until Boaz completes "the matter" (כִּי לֹא יִשְׁקֹט הָאִישׁ כִּי־אִם־כִּלָּה הַדָּבָר הַיּוֹם). Naomi does not congratulate Ruth, nor does she celebrate the continuation of a desired plan. Ruth's answer to Naomi about "all which the man did for her" (כָּל־אֲשֶׁר עָשָׂה־לָהּ הָאִישׁ) is also telling. Her answer centers on Boaz's provision of grain for the both of them. Admittedly, I am reading between the lines, but it seems that the answer to Naomi's question about Ruth's classification is less than satisfactory. And yet Naomi's reply, "The man will not rest until the matter is completed today," is surely Naomi's expression of relief and hope that Ruth and Boaz have and will carry out this plan according to torah, exhibiting the חַיִל that is characteristic of both of them.

What began in 3:9 as a question of Ruth's moral fortitude continues now from the mouth of Naomi. Even so, the question now is more indicative of Naomi's ill motive that gets corrected by Ruth sharing "all which the man did for her." Naomi gets her answer to the question, "Who are you?" Her only response at this point is to rest in the surety that this אִישׁ גִּבּוֹר חַיִל who provided for her daughter, an אֵשֶׁת חַיִל, will indeed finish this matter "today."

וַתַּגֶּד־לָהּ אֵת כָּל־אֲשֶׁר עָשָׂה־לָהּ הָאִישׁ:

וַתַּגֵּד continues the narrative sequence and is the Hiphil imperfect 3fs of נגד + *vav*-consecutive. Ruth is once again the implied subject, and the prepositional phrase (לָ֔הּ) refers to Naomi. אֵ֛ת marks the accusative object clause (כָּל־אֲשֶׁ֥ר עָֽשָׂה־לָ֖הּ הָאִֽישׁ). כָּל is formally the head of the direct object but is further specified by the relative clause (אֲשֶׁ֥ר עָֽשָׂה־לָ֖הּ הָאִֽישׁ).

Within the relative clause, עָֽשָׂה is the Qal perfect 3ms of עשׂה and is best translated as an English pluperfect, "had done." הָאִֽישׁ is the explicit subject referring to Boaz, and לָ֖הּ suggests advantage, "*for* her." The things Boaz did and committed to do are "for" Ruth's benefit. That Ruth declares to Naomi what Boaz has done helps answer the question of "who she is" earlier in the verse. Naomi wants to know if the plan worked and Ruth is indeed now under Boaz's care. Therefore, Ruth answers by telling Naomi everything that Boaz did for her. While the full conversation is veiled, surely Ruth's answer includes Boaz's commitment to do everything that Ruth proposed (2:11; כֹּ֛ל אֲשֶׁר־תֹּאמְרִ֖י אֶֽעֱשֶׂה־לָּ֑ךְ)—namely, "to spread his wing over her" in marriage.

17 *And she said, "These six (measures of) barley he gave to me for he said [to me], 'Do*
not go empty to your mother-in-law.' " 18 *And she said, "Sit, my daughter, until you*
know how the matter will fall, for the man will not be quiet except he complete the
matter today."

RUTH

3:17–18

17 וַתֹּ֕אמֶר שֵׁשׁ־הַשְּׂעֹרִ֥ים הָאֵ֖לֶּה נָ֣תַן לִ֑י כִּ֚י אָמַ֣ר כֹ אַל־תָּב֥וֹאִי רֵיקָ֖ם אֶל־חֲמוֹתֵֽךְ׃
18 וַתֹּ֗אמֶר שְׁבִ֣י בִתִּ֔י עַ֚ד אֲשֶׁ֣ר תֵּֽדְעִ֔ין אֵ֖יךְ יִפֹּ֣ל דָּבָ֑ר כִּ֣י לֹ֤א יִשְׁקֹט֙ הָאִ֔ישׁ כִּֽי־אִם־
כִּלָּ֥ה הַדָּבָ֖ר הַיּֽוֹם׃

RUTH 3:17

וַתֹּ֕אמֶר שֵׁשׁ־הַשְּׂעֹרִ֥ים הָאֵ֖לֶּה נָ֣תַן לִ֑י כִּ֚י אָמַ֣ר כ אַל־תָּב֥וֹאִי רֵיקָ֖ם אֶל־חֲמוֹתֵֽךְ׃

ACCENT PHRASING

וַתֹּ֕אמֶר
שֵׁשׁ־הַשְּׂעֹרִ֥ים הָאֵ֖לֶּה נָ֣תַן לִ֑י
כ
כִּ֚י אָמַ֣ר
אַל־תָּב֥וֹאִי רֵיקָ֖ם אֶל־חֲמוֹתֵֽךְ׃

וַתֹּ֕אמֶר

וַתֹּ֕אמֶר is the Qal imperfect 3fs of אמר + *vav*-consecutive and introduces Ruth's explanation of what Boaz had done for her.

שֵׁשׁ־הַשְּׂעֹרִ֥ים הָאֵ֖לֶּה נָ֣תַן לִ֑י

שֵׁשׁ־הַשְּׂעֹרִ֥ים הָאֵ֖לֶּה is the accusative object, potentially fronted for emphasis. The accent pattern packages שֵׁשׁ־הַשְּׂעֹרִ֥ים הָאֵ֖לֶּה together, as does the syntax. The construct package (שֵׁשׁ־הַשְּׂעֹרִ֥ים) is definite since the final noun (הַשְּׂעֹרִ֥ים) in the package is definite. In order for the demonstrative adjective (הָאֵ֖לֶּה) to modify the construct package, it must agree in gender, number, and definiteness. The gender of the near plural demonstrative (הָאֵ֖לֶּה) is unspecified, and so the agreement of number (plural) and definiteness indicates that the text translates as "six barleys, the these ones," or "*these* six [measures of] barley."

נָ֣תַן is the Qal perfect 3ms of נתן. As a perfective (past tense, completed action), the verb describes Boaz's actions that have already happened. לִ֑י marks the indirect object.

כִּ֚י אָמַ֣ר כ אלי ק ולא כת

כִּ֚י introduces Boaz's motivation or reason to provide for Ruth: "*for* he said [to me]..." Notice in the marginal note that this is another occurrence of the *qere vela ketiv* (ק ולא כת), "read but not written" (cf. 3:5). In the MT, the vowels are written without consonants, and the marginal notes (marked in LHB with the symbol כ֒) provide the consonants אלי to suggest the reading of a word that is not written.[1] Like before, the prepositional phrase provides specificity, but it is not entirely necessary for the syntax to be understandable.

אַל־תָּבֹ֥ואִי רֵיקָ֖ם אֶל־חֲמוֹתֵֽךְ׃

אַל־תָּבֹ֥ואִי is the negated Qal jussive 2fs of בוא forming a prohibitional statement. אַל indicates that our verbal element is a jussive rather than imperfective even though the morphological forms are identical. The negative command is not a strict prohibition but expresses Boaz's desire and intention for Ruth, "you *should* not go away." רֵיקָ֖ם is adverbial, indicating the manner in which Boaz did *not* want Ruth to leave—namely, he did not want her to leave "empty." אֶל־חֲמוֹתֵֽךְ indicates to whom Boaz sent Ruth.

That Boaz sent Ruth "to her mother-in-law" with the barley suggests that he may have had in mind provision for Naomi as well. We will soon find out in chapter 4 that the redemption was initially of the field belonging to Naomi and that Ruth was somewhat of a secondary addition to this formal land redemption. Hence, Naomi is the matriarch to be redeemed. Boaz knows this and seeks to provide even for Naomi with the provision he sends back with Ruth (cf. Ruth's provision for Naomi in 2:18).

---

1. The marginal note above is from the Mp in *BHQ*. The *BHQ* apparatus reads, ֱ ֵ | > M^{ket} V (hapl?) | אֱלַ֫י M^{qere} G (S) T (explic?). In the Vulgate (V), the prepositional phrase is absent as in the MT, perhaps evidence of haplography. In the LXX, Syriac, and Targum, the preposition is written.

RUTH 3:18

וַתֹּ֫אמֶר֮ שְׁבִ֣י בִתִּ֔י עַ֚ד אֲשֶׁ֣ר תֵּֽדְעִ֔ין אֵ֖יךְ יִפֹּ֣ל דָּבָ֑ר כִּ֣י לֹ֤א יִשְׁקֹט֙ הָאִ֔ישׁ כִּֽי־אִם־כִּלָּ֥ה הַדָּבָ֖ר הַיּֽוֹם׃

ACCENT PHRASING

וַתֹּ֫אמֶר֮
שְׁבִ֣י בִתִּ֔י עַ֚ד אֲשֶׁ֣ר תֵּֽדְעִ֔ין אֵ֖יךְ יִפֹּ֣ל דָּבָ֑ר
כִּ֣י לֹ֤א יִשְׁקֹט֙ הָאִ֔ישׁ
כִּֽי־אִם־כִּלָּ֥ה הַדָּבָ֖ר הַיּֽוֹם׃

וַתֹּ֫אמֶר֮

וַתֹּ֫אמֶר֮ is the Qal imperfect 3fs of אמר + *vav*-consecutive in temporal succession, introducing direct speech. The subject now shifts to Naomi.

שְׁבִ֣י בִתִּ֔י עַ֚ד אֲשֶׁ֣ר תֵּֽדְעִ֔ין אֵ֖יךְ יִפֹּ֣ל דָּבָ֑ר

שְׁבִ֣י is the Qal imperative 2fs of ישׁב. Naomi is not commanding Ruth to sit in a particular seat; rather, she encourages her to stay put until they find out the result of Boaz's efforts to redeem them. The clause may imply a locative adverb "sit [*here*]," but that is unnecessary to communicate the same point. שְׁבִ֣י is terser and more effective than [שָׁם] שְׁבִ֣י. The idea is that Ruth ought to stick around to learn the outcome of Boaz's efforts. בִתִּ֔י is vocative, referring to Ruth as Naomi's daughter.

עַ֚ד introduces the temporal element of the verse, and the relative pronoun + an imperfective verb (אֲשֶׁ֣ר תֵּֽדְעִ֔ין) is typical to indicate future time.[2] תֵּֽדְעִ֔ין is a Qal imperfect 2fs of ידע + paragogic *nun*. Notice that ידע is a I-ו verb and in the imperfective the initial ו flees, lengthening the preformative (תֵּֽדְעִ֔ין). Literally, the translation is "until which you shall know," but that is smoothed out as simply "until you know."

2. RJW §§311, 502.

אֵיךְ יִפֹּל דָּבָר identifies what Naomi wants Ruth to wait to know. יִפֹּל is the Qal imperfect 3ms of נפל. נפל does not suggest a literal fall, but rather how the matter with Boaz will turn out. נפל is a I-נ verb, and as expected, the I-נ assimilates into the following consonant (יִפֹּל). The other morphological elements of the Qal imperfect (י preformative and ֹ thematic vowel) are still readily visible for parsing purposes. דָּבָר is the subject and is indefinite because the outcome of the situation remains unknown. The "matter" is certainly known and definite, but the outcome remains to be known.[3]

כִּי לֹא יִשְׁקֹט הָאִישׁ

כִּי introduces the reason Naomi gave the command for Ruth to remain. הָאִישׁ is the subject, referring to Boaz. יִשְׁקֹט is the negated Qal imperfect 3ms of שקט, meaning "to be quiet." As this is a negated future verb, we get "For the man *will not be quiet*." It is unlikely that Boaz was constantly talking about this situation, as if he needed to "be quiet" verbally. Rather, the idea is that the man will not be "still" or "idle" until he completes the task of redemption, either himself or through the nearer גֹּאֵל.

כִּי־אִם־כִּלָּה הַדָּבָר הַיּוֹם׃

כִּי־אִם, when taken together, can mean "except that," "but rather," or "unless."[4] This construction sets up an exception clause that indicates a condition that must be met in order for the previous statement to come true. In other words, Boaz will be idle or still only *if* this statement comes true—namely, he completes the matter of the redemption.

כִּלָּה is the Piel perfect 3ms of כלה, "to complete, accomplish, or bring to pass." כלה is a stative verb, expressing the state of being complete or finished, and so in the Piel it is factitive, Boaz "making" the accusative object complete. Boaz is the implied subject and הַדָּבָר is the accusative object, or

---

3. See discussion about definiteness, indefinability, and specificity in Holmstedt, *Ruth*, 176–77.

4. Cf. Wilch, *Ruth*, 133 (exception clause, "unless"); Holmstedt, *Ruth*, 177 (strong adversative, "but rather"). For exceptive clauses, see GKC §163c; WO §38.6b; JM §173b. For the adversative argued by Holmstedt, see GKC §163a; WO §39.3.5d; JM §172c.

the thing that Boaz will "make" complete. הַיּוֹם is a temporal adverb indicating *when* the verbal action will take place. Remember that the article on יוֹם is demonstrative, meaning "this day" or "today." This statement, combined with Boaz's journey to the city (3:15), informs the audience that Boaz will indeed take care of this matter. Boaz is quick to get to the city to accomplish the redemption, and Naomi is confident that Boaz will not rest until he has completed the matter.

1 Now Boaz went up to the gate and he sat down there, and behold, the redeemer [was]
passing by, [the one] whom Boaz spoke [about]. And he (Boaz) said, "Turn aside, sit
here Peloni Almoni." And so he turned aside and he sat down. 2 And he (Boaz) took ten
men from the elders of the city, and he said, "Sit here." And so they sat. 3 And he said
to the redeemer, "A portion of the field which (is/belongs) to our brother, to Elimelech,
Naomi, [who] returned from the fields of Moab, is selling. 4 And I said to myself, I will
uncover your ear (I will declare to you), saying, 'Acquire [it] before those sitting and
before the elders of my people. If you will redeem, [then] redeem, but if he will not
redeem, then declare [it] to me, for I know that there is none except you and me after
you.' " And he (Peloni Almoni) said, "I will [indeed] redeem." 5 And then Boaz said, "On
the day that you acquire the field from the hand of Naomi, Ruth, the Moabitess, the
wife of the dead [one] you shall acquire, [in order] to cause to stand (perpetuate) the
name of the dead [one] concerning his inheritance." 6 And so the redeemer said, "I am
not able to redeem for myself, lest I corrupt my inheritance. You redeem for yourself
with my redemption [right], for I am not able to redeem."

RUTH

4:1–6

1 וּבֹ֨עַז עָלָ֣ה הַשַּׁעַר֮ וַיֵּ֣שֶׁב שָׁם֒ וְהִנֵּ֨ה הַגֹּאֵ֤ל עֹבֵר֙ אֲשֶׁ֣ר דִּבֶּר־בֹּ֔עַז וַיֹּ֛אמֶר ס֥וּרָה
שְׁבָה־פֹּ֖ה פְּלֹנִ֣י אַלְמֹנִ֑י וַיָּ֖סַר וַיֵּשֵֽׁב׃ 2 וַיִּקַּ֞ח עֲשָׂרָ֧ה אֲנָשִׁ֛ים מִזִּקְנֵ֥י הָעִ֖יר וַיֹּ֣אמֶר
שְׁבוּ־פֹ֑ה וַיֵּשֵֽׁבוּ׃ 3 וַיֹּ֨אמֶר֙ לַגֹּאֵ֔ל חֶלְקַת֙ הַשָּׂדֶ֔ה אֲשֶׁ֥ר לְאָחִ֖ינוּ לֶאֱלִימֶ֑לֶךְ מָכְרָ֣ה
נָעֳמִ֔י הַשָּׁ֖בָה מִשְּׂדֵ֥ה מוֹאָֽב׃ 4 וַאֲנִ֨י אָמַ֜רְתִּי אֶגְלֶ֧ה אָזְנְךָ֣ לֵאמֹ֗ר קְ֠נֵה נֶ֥גֶד הַיֹּשְׁבִים֮
וְנֶ֣גֶד זִקְנֵ֣י עַמִּי֒ אִם־תִּגְאַל֙ גְּאָ֔ל וְאִם־לֹ֨א יִגְאַ֜ל הַגִּ֣ידָה לִּ֗י וְאֵ֣דַע כִּ֣י אֵ֤ין זוּלָֽתְךָ֙
לִגְא֔וֹל וְאָנֹכִ֖י אַחֲרֶ֑יךָ וַיֹּ֖אמֶר אָנֹכִ֥י אֶגְאָֽל׃ 5 וַיֹּ֣אמֶר בֹּ֔עַז בְּיוֹם־קְנוֹתְךָ֥ הַשָּׂדֶ֖ה מִיַּ֣ד
נָעֳמִ֑י וּ֠מֵאֵת ר֨וּת הַמּוֹאֲבִיָּ֤ה אֵֽשֶׁת־הַמֵּת֙ קָנִ֔יתִי לְהָקִ֥ים שֵׁם־הַמֵּ֖ת עַל־נַחֲלָתֽוֹ׃
6 וַיֹּ֣אמֶר הַגֹּאֵ֗ל לֹ֤א אוּכַל֙ לִגְאוֹל־לִ֔י פֶּן־אַשְׁחִ֖ית אֶת־נַחֲלָתִ֑י גְּאַל־לְךָ֤ אַתָּה֙ אֶת־
גְּאֻלָּתִ֔י כִּ֥י לֹא־אוּכַ֖ל לִגְאֹֽל׃

RUTH 4:1

וּבֹ֙עַז עָלָ֣ה הַשַּׁעַר֮ וַיֵּ֣שֶׁב שָׁם֒ וְהִנֵּ֨ה הַגֹּאֵ֤ל עֹבֵר֙ אֲשֶׁ֣ר דִּבֶּר־בֹּ֔עַז וַיֹּ֥אמֶר ס֛וּרָה שְׁבָה־פֹּ֖ה פְּלֹנִ֣י אַלְמֹנִ֑י וַיָּ֖סַר וַיֵּשֵֽׁב׃

ACCENT PHRASING

וּבֹ֙עַז עָלָ֣ה הַשַּׁעַר֮
וַיֵּ֣שֶׁב שָׁם֒
וְהִנֵּ֨ה הַגֹּאֵ֤ל עֹבֵר֙ אֲשֶׁ֣ר דִּבֶּר־בֹּ֔עַז
וַיֹּ֥אמֶר ס֛וּרָה שְׁבָה־פֹּ֖ה פְּלֹנִ֣י אַלְמֹנִ֑י
וַיָּ֖סַר וַיֵּשֵֽׁב׃

וּבֹ֙עַז עָלָ֣ה הַשַּׁעַר֮

Ruth 4:1 opens with a nominal clause informing the audience about Boaz. He is now the focus both by implication of the 3ms verb (עָלָ֣ה) *and* by syntactical arrangement (topic fronting).[1] The *vav* on וּבֹ֙עַז may be translated, "Now, as for Boaz … ," in a circumstantial clause. עָלָ֣ה[2] is a Qal perfect 3ms of עלה, and הַשַּׁעַר֮ is the adverbial accusative of place.[3]

וּבֹ֙עַז fronted in the nominal clause clarifies the context between chapters 3 and 4. In 3:15, we know that Boaz came to the city (וַיָּבֹ֖א הָעִֽיר), but the chapter ends by shifting to a conversation between Naomi and Ruth (3:17–18). Chapter 4 now takes us to the scene with Boaz as the primary actor and therefore opens with a topic-fronted clause to bring Boaz back to the forefront of the audience's mind.

וַיֵּ֣שֶׁב שָׁם֒

וַיֵּ֣שֶׁב is a Qal imperfect 3ms of ישׁב + *vav* in temporal sequence. Notice the lengthened preformative vowel (וַיֵּ֣שֶׁב) due to the I-ו of ישׁב fleeing. The י that is present in the text is the י of the 3ms preformative, *not* the י of the

1. For topic fronting, see Holmstedt, *Ruth*, 180. See also RJW §573a.
2. See Wilch, *Ruth*, 140, for the circumstantial explanation.
3. JM §126h.

root. שָׁם is the locative adverb, indicating *where* Boaz sat. If we compare this scene to Deuteronomy 25:7, the text presents the idea of going to a city gate for a court-like business meeting.[4] Boaz went to the city gate intending to accomplish family business.

וְהִנֵּה הַגֹּאֵל עֹבֵר אֲשֶׁר דִּבֶּר־בֹּעַז

וְהִנֵּה introduces an element of surprise when the nearer redeemer arrives on the scene. הַגֹּאֵל introduces another nominal clause, now shifting attention (topic) to the nearer redeemer. הַגֹּאֵל is the initiator (subject) of the nominal clause, and עֹבֵר is the announcement (predicate). עֹבֵר is the Qal participle ms of עבר, and while it is grammatically a substantive adjective ("one who passes by"), it can be understood as the main verbal action in nominal clauses.[5] In this sense, it communicates the durative aspect of the verb while maintaining the contextual tense of the verbal action: "the redeemer *was passing by*." Since the subject is fronted in a nominal clause, a different verbal form is necessary than a standard *vav*-consecutive + imperfective.

The relative clause beginning with אֲשֶׁר further describes הַגֹּאֵל. דִּבֶּר is a Piel perfect 3ms of דבר with בֹּעַז as the subject. The clarification is that this redeemer is precisely the one Boaz needed to see. The relative clause and the perfective verb (דִּבֶּר) suggest this is a redeemer about whom Boaz spoke in an earlier conversation, not a redeemer *with whom* Boaz has spoken. Therefore, given the context, it is appropriate to provide the preposition "about" before the relative pronoun, "the redeemer ... *about whom* Boaz had spoken."

וַיֹּאמֶר סוּרָה שְׁבָה־פֹּה פְּלֹנִי אַלְמֹנִי

Boaz now initiates a conversation with פְּלֹנִי אַלְמֹנִי.[6] וַיֹּאמֶר is a Qal imperfect 3ms of אמר + *vav*-consecutive, introducing Boaz's direct speech.

4. Wilch, *Ruth*, 140.

5. *IBHS* §16c, §16i; GKC §141b.2(b).

6. פְּלֹנִי אַלְמֹנִי is intentionally vague in Ruth, and so it will be used as the proper name for this nearer redeemer even though it more likely is just a reference to "so-and-so." See the

סֽוּרָה is a Qal imperative 2ms of סור (the long form imperative; i.e., it ends with the ָה; cf. קָטְלָה of the base Qal paradigm). שְׁבָה is also a long form Qal imperative 2ms, this time of ישׁב. Some call these emphatic imperatives.[7] However, they do not necessarily communicate intensity of command but may provide a narrative emphasis to draw the reader's attention to the action.[8] Boaz did not emphatically grab פְּלֹנִ֣י אַלְמֹנִ֑י and sit him down somewhere. Instead, the emphatic imperatives focus the audience on Boaz's determination to accomplish his business with the nearer redeemer on this same day (cf. 3:18).

פֹּה is the explicit locative adverb but is unnecessary grammatically. One might imagine that, with such terse imperatives, Boaz was likely pointing to where he wanted the nearer redeemer to sit, and so the explicit adverb provides a bit of urgency to the scene: "Turn aside! Sit down *here*!"

פְּלֹנִי אַלְמֹנִי literally means "a certain someone."[9] We might translate it idiomatically as "so-and-so," referring to a specific person but one whose name is either forgotten or irrelevant. Basically, Boaz has named the redeemer without naming the redeemer. Since he is not a main character in the narrative, the author omits his given name. Ellen F. Davis and Mary Adams Parker propose a modern equivalent, "Joe Schmoe," that reflects the intent of the name given to the nearer redeemer.[10]

וַיָּ֖סַר וַיֵּשֵֽׁב׃

The final clause in 4:1 provides the result of Boaz's instructions. וַיָּ֖סַר and וַיֵּשֵׁב are both Qal imperfect 3ms verbs + *vav*-consecutives of סור and ישׁב, respectively. The first *vav* is logical succession, "*And so* he turned aside," while the second is temporal succession, "*and then* he sat down." סור is a hollow root and often has a u-class thematic vowel. Here, possibly due to the ר (semi-guttural) in the third root letter, the vowel shifts to a-class

thorough discussion in Block, *Ruth*, 205–6.

7. *IBHS* §5e.

8. GKC §48i.

9. For פְּלֹנִי, see BDB, 811–12. For אַלְמֹנִי, see BDB, 48.

10. Ellen F. Davis and Mary Adams Parker, *Who Are You, My Daughter? Reading Ruth through Image and Text* (Louisville: Westminster John Knox, 2003), 97.

in the *vav*-consecutive.[11] When the accent retracts in the *vav*-consecutive form, the a-class vowel must be a *pataḥ* because it is in a closed and unaccented syllable (וַיָּ֫סַר).

For ישׁב, the י that we see is again the י of the 3ms preformative, not the י of the root. Earlier in the verse, we saw the same verbal form, but the *vav*-consecutive retracted the accent to the preformative, resulting in a *sěgōl* thematic vowel (וַיֵּ֫שֶׁב). Here, because the verb occurs at the end of the verse with the disjunctive *sillûq* (ֽ), the final syllable is accented and retains the original *ṣērê* as the thematic vowel (וַיֵּשֵֽׁב).

The fast pace of the narrative action, along with the echoing effect of what Boaz commanded (ס֥וּרָה שְׁבָה־פֹּ֖ה) and what פְּלֹנִ֣י אַלְמֹנִ֑י did (וַיָּ֖סַר וַיֵּשֵֽׁב), adds to the realization in the narrative that Boaz is set on finishing this task the same day just as Naomi anticipated (3:18). Boaz said, “Turn and sit,” and so פְּלֹנִ֣י אַלְמֹנִ֑י indeed “turned and sat.” It may be difficult to imagine a random person being commanded to sit somewhere at the city gate without any explanation. However, that misses the point of the narrative. The focus is now on Boaz’s efforts to redeem Ruth as quickly and efficiently as possible. Additionally, since Boaz knew of this nearer redeemer and since redeemers were in the family line, Boaz and פְּלֹנִ֣י אַלְמֹנִ֑י likely knew each other. It still may have been odd for Boaz to just snag him up and tell him to sit, but perhaps פְּלֹנִ֣י אַלְמֹנִ֑י sensed the importance of his attendance at this meeting and was willing to turn aside from whatever task brought him to pass by the city gate. Regardless of the interpretation of the passage, the text indicates that פְּלֹנִ֣י אַלְמֹנִ֑י did not ask questions but rather did as he was told.

11. GKC §72t.

RUTH 4:2

וַיִּקַּ֞ח עֲשָׂרָ֧ה אֲנָשִׁ֛ים מִזִּקְנֵ֥י הָעִ֖יר וַיֹּ֣אמֶר שְׁבוּ־פֹ֑ה וַיֵּשֵֽׁבוּ׃

ACCENT PHRASING

וַיִּקַּ֞ח עֲשָׂרָ֧ה אֲנָשִׁ֛ים מִזִּקְנֵ֥י הָעִ֖יר
וַיֹּ֣אמֶר שְׁבוּ־פֹ֑ה
וַיֵּשֵֽׁבוּ׃

וַיִּקַּ֞ח עֲשָׂרָ֧ה אֲנָשִׁ֛ים מִזִּקְנֵ֥י הָעִ֖יר

וַיִּקַּ֞ח is a Qal imperfect 3ms of לקח. Remember that לקח morphs similarly to a I-נ verb and assimilates the initial ל in a silent *shewa* position. Therefore, the *dāgēš forte* in the ק is the assimilated ל.

וַיִּלְקַח ⟵ וַיִּקַּח

עֲשָׂרָ֧ה אֲנָשִׁ֛ים is the direct object—namely, whom Boaz "took." Formally, since עֲשָׂרָ֧ה is an absolute noun, it is the direct object, "he took *ten*." The question is naturally, ten what? אֲנָשִׁ֛ים modifies עֲשָׂרָ֧ה regarding kind, "ten, with respect to men," or "ten men."[12] Notice that the masculine form of the numeral (עֲשָׂרָ֧ה) is used to match the mp אֲנָשִׁ֛ים.

The מִן preposition on מִזִּקְנֵ֥י is a partitive מִן meaning that Boaz took *some* of the elders of the city rather than having all the elders come to this judicial meeting.[13] Notice the plural construct ending on מִזִּקְנֵ֥י indicating that it forms a construct package with הָעִ֖יר. The construct package implies a מִן preposition communicating the origin of these elders, "elders *of* (from) the city."

וַיֹּ֣אמֶר שְׁבוּ־פֹ֑ה

וַיֹּ֣אמֶר introduces Boaz's direct speech similarly to 4:1 and is a Qal imperfect 3ms of אמר + *vav*-consecutive of temporal succession. שְׁבוּ־פֹ֑ה echoes Boaz's

12. See the discussion of numerals in *IBHS* §29e, where numerals two through ten often take a plural numerable. See also *IBHS* §13kk, on the numerable as an accusative of specification.

13. RJW §324.

instructions to פְּלֹנִי אַלְמֹנִי and is a Qal imperative 2mp of ישׁב. As an original I-ו verb, ישׁב drops the first root letter in the imperative. The ו sufformative distinguishes the mp imperative from the ms imperative.

With this 2mp imperative, Boaz now commands the plural "elders" to "sit here." As before, פֹּה is the locative adverb emphasizing that all the necessary members of the town are now present ("here") to accomplish this transaction. The implication, of course, is that פֹּה in verses 1 and 2 is the same location.

וַיֵּשֵׁבוּ׃

וַיֵּשֵׁבוּ introduces another result clause, echoing both the syntax and the verbiage of 4:1. Previously פְּלֹנִי אַלְמֹנִי "sat," and now הַזְּקֵנֵי הָעִיר "sit." וַיֵּשֵׁבוּ is a Qal imperfect 3mp of ישׁב + *vav*-consecutive. As we have seen before with ישׁב, the י in the consonantal text is the preformative of the imperfective, not the י of the root. Additionally, the strong disjunctive *sillûq* (ֽ◌) causes the thematic vowel on the final syllable to retain the *ṣērê* even in a *vav*-consecutive form (cf. 4:1). The *vav*-consecutive could indicate temporal or logical succession, and perhaps aspects of both are present. The elders of the city "sat" as the next narrative action temporally, but they also "sat" as the logical result of Boaz's command. John Wilch calls this an "adjunctive *vav*" with the sense of "too" or "also": "and they, *too*, sat down."[14]

14. Wilch, *Ruth*, 142.

RUTH 4:3

וַיֹּ֨אמֶר֙ לַגֹּאֵ֔ל חֶלְקַת֙ הַשָּׂדֶ֔ה אֲשֶׁ֥ר לְאָחִ֖ינוּ לֶאֱלִימֶ֑לֶךְ מָֽכְרָ֣ה נָעֳמִ֔י הַשָּׁ֖בָה
מִשְּׂדֵ֥ה מוֹאָֽב׃

ACCENT PHRASING

וַיֹּ֨אמֶר֙ לַגֹּאֵ֔ל
חֶלְקַת֙ הַשָּׂדֶ֔ה אֲשֶׁ֥ר לְאָחִ֖ינוּ לֶאֱלִימֶ֑לֶךְ
מָֽכְרָ֣ה נָעֳמִ֔י הַשָּׁ֖בָה מִשְּׂדֵ֥ה מוֹאָֽב׃

וַיֹּ֨אמֶר֙ לַגֹּאֵ֔ל

The narrative now shifts to the conversation between Boaz and the nearer redeemer. וַיֹּ֨אמֶר֙ introduces Boaz's direct speech and is a Qal imperfect 3ms of אמר + *vav*-consecutive. לַגֹּאֵ֔ל indicates the recipient of Boaz's instructions. Remember that גֹּאֵל is technically a participle form (◌ֹ◌ֵ◌) functioning as a substantive noun, "a redeemer." לַגֹּאֵ֔ל is definite because of the ל preposition supplanting the vowel pointing of the definite article (הַ◌ ⟵ לַ◌), and so a specific redeemer is in mind, "*the* redeemer" or, in context, פְּלֹנִי אַלְמֹנִי.

חֶלְקַת֙ הַשָּׂדֶ֔ה אֲשֶׁ֥ר לְאָחִ֖ינוּ לֶאֱלִימֶ֑לֶךְ

The accent phrasing in 4:3 may seem a bit odd since this segment does not have an explicit verb and is therefore not formally a clause. However, the accentual/syntactical break focuses attention on the חֶלְקַת֙ הַשָּׂדֶ֔ה. The *atnāḥ* (◌֑) often marks the "meaning" of the verse, or the place where the scribes wanted the reader to focus his or her attention. In 4:3, the *atnāḥ* separates the direct object phrase (חֶלְקַת֙ הַשָּׂדֶ֔ה אֲשֶׁ֥ר לְאָחִ֖ינוּ לֶאֱלִימֶ֑לֶךְ) from the main verb (מָֽכְרָ֣ה), a break that is complex syntactically. When the *atnāḥ* separates the main verb from its object phrase, a stronger syntactical break occurs than when the verb and object are more closely associated. However, notice in the *atnāḥ* segment that there are two *zāqēf qāṭôn*s (◌֔).

וַיֹּ֨אמֶר֙ לַגֹּאֵ֔ל חֶלְקַת֙ הַשָּׂדֶ֔ה אֲשֶׁ֥ר לְאָחִ֖ינוּ לֶאֱלִימֶ֑לֶךְ

In this situation, the first *zāqēf qāṭôn* (לְגָאֵ֔ל) is stronger in terms of the relative "weight" of syntactical disjunction in the verse. This break marks the introduction of the direct speech from the direct speech itself, a clear syntactical break. Beginning with חֶלְקַת, one would expect the next syntactical break to keep the direct object with the main verb (מָכְרָ֥ה), and yet the *atnāḥ* divides these two. Even within the *atnāḥ* segment, the second *zāqēf qāṭôn* (הַשָּׂדֶ֔ה), also a major disjunction, focuses attention on חֶלְקַת הַשָּׂדֶה. Our conclusion regarding this accent pattern, then, is that the Masoretes wanted to draw the reader's attention to the portion of the field belonging to Elimelech more than they wanted to maintain rigid syntactical links with verb and object.

The natural question is why the Masoretes would want to do this. In the context of the book, Boaz is set on redeeming Ruth and yet the nearer redeemer remains an obstacle. At this point in the narrative, we do not know how the nearer redeemer will react, but we know there is focus on the portion of the field, *not* a focus on Ruth ... yet! The focus on the portion of the field may be to highlight that this is indeed a portion belonging to Elimelech, their brother. This point emphasizes that this is a familial agreement, Boaz is part of the family, and he is doing what needs to be done to accomplish Ruth's and Naomi's redemption. Boaz is not just infatuated with Ruth and therefore going through the motions. Instead, he is faithfully fulfilling the requirements of torah.

An additional explanation for the emphasis on the field is that Boaz intentionally sets up the nearer redeemer to focus on the field so that when Boaz suddenly adds Ruth to the agreement (4:5), the initial positive reply to redeem just the field shifts. Boaz presents an agreement that the nearer redeemer would be favorable to (the portion of the field), but then adds Ruth's redemption. The argument cannot be made that the accents always function for exegetical value, and yet here we see a focus on the portion of the field to the exclusion of Ruth's redemption, precisely the effect Boaz intends.

אֲשֶׁר introduces the relative clause that modifies חֶלְקַת הַשָּׂדֶה. The ל prepositions on לְאָחִינוּ and לֶאֱלִימֶלֶךְ are possessive. This field "*belonged to* our brother." לֶאֱלִימֶלֶךְ is appositional, specifying who אָחִינוּ is.

מָכְרָה נָעֳמִי הַשָּׁבָה מִשְּׂדֵה מוֹאָב׃

Following the *atnāḥ*, we now get the main verb. מָכְרָה is a Qal perfect 3fs of מכר. The perfective aspect in this case communicates a completed action in the sense that the *decision* to sell the field is a past, completed action. However, the portion of the field is still in the process of being sold. The perfective aspect is fitting even though the verb translates as a present progressive, "Naomi *is selling*."[15]

נָעֳמִי is the subject and is modified by הַשָּׁבָה. Given the accent, הַשָּׁבָה is morphologically a Qal perfect 3fs of שׁוב with a prefixed relative ה (see discussion of this form in 1:22 and 2:6). מִשְּׂדֵה מוֹאָב is the prepositional phrase indicating from where Naomi returned. While the construct package is definite because the final noun is a proper noun ("*the* field of Moab"), we should not understand Boaz to be referring to a specific field in Moab from which Naomi returned. Rather, Naomi returned from the "territory" of Moab.

15. Waltke and O'Connor call this an "instantaneous perfective" (WO §30.5.1d); cf. RJW §164.

RUTH 4:4

וַאֲנִ֨י אָמַ֜רְתִּי אֶגְלֶ֧ה אָזְנְךָ֣ לֵאמֹ֗ר קְ֠נֵה נֶ֣גֶד הַיֹּשְׁבִ֞ים וְנֶ֣גֶד זִקְנֵ֣י עַמִּ֗י אִם־תִּגְאַל֙
גְּאָ֔ל וְאִם־לֹ֨א יִגְאַ֜ל הַגִּ֣ידָה לִּ֗י וְאֵדַע֙ כִּ֣י אֵ֤ין זוּלָֽתְךָ֙ לִגְא֔וֹל וְאָנֹכִ֖י אַחֲרֶ֑יךָ
וַיֹּ֖אמֶר אָנֹכִ֥י אֶגְאָֽל׃

ACCENT PHRASING

וַאֲנִ֨י אָמַ֜רְתִּי
אֶגְלֶ֧ה אָזְנְךָ֣ לֵאמֹ֗ר
קְ֠נֵה נֶ֣גֶד הַיֹּשְׁבִ֞ים וְנֶ֣גֶד זִקְנֵ֣י עַמִּ֗י
אִם־תִּגְאַל֙ גְּאָ֔ל
וְאִם־לֹ֨א יִגְאַ֜ל הַגִּ֣ידָה לִּ֗י
וְאֵדַע֙ כִּ֣י אֵ֤ין זוּלָֽתְךָ֙ לִגְא֔וֹל
וְאָנֹכִ֖י אַחֲרֶ֑יךָ
וַיֹּ֖אמֶר אָנֹכִ֥י אֶגְאָֽל׃

וַאֲנִ֨י אָמַ֜רְתִּי

וַאֲנִ֨י אָמַ֜רְתִּי introduces Boaz's request to the nearer redeemer. וַאֲנִ֨י puts the focus on Boaz as the fronted subject. וַאֲנִ֨י אָמַ֜רְתִּי is another nominal clause with the pronoun וַאֲנִ֨י as the initiator (subject) and אָמַ֜רְתִּי as the announcement (predicate). Again, the emphasis in this clause structure is on the subject וַאֲנִ֨י. אָמַ֜רְתִּי is a Qal perfect 1cs of אמר. Boaz tells everyone that he has considered what to say. The pronoun (וַאֲנִ֨י) along with a 1cs verb suggests a reflexive verbal action, "I said to myself," or "I (internally) considered."[16]

אֶגְלֶ֧ה אָזְנְךָ֣ לֵאמֹ֗ר

אֶגְלֶ֧ה is a Qal imperfect 1cs of גלה. The imperfective in this case expresses intention, "I *should* uncover your ear." Boaz is telling everyone what he considered to himself—namely, that he *should* go and declare to the nearer redeemer the situation.

16. Campbell, *Ruth*, 144; Bush, *Ruth, Esther*, 204–5.

אָזְנְךָ is the direct object, and the idiomatic expression אֶגְלֶה אָזְנְךָ ("to uncover your ear") means "to declare" something. Boaz diplomatically suggests to the nearer redeemer that this is not a decision made on a whim, but that he has previously considered it. He may have considered it only for a short time on the road from the threshing floor to the city gate, but indeed he considered what to say. Boaz's suggestion of internal deliberation adds to the interpretation that he formulated the proposal so as to favor the result he wanted (see 4:3 and the focus on חֶלְקַת הַשָּׂדֶה אֲשֶׁר לְאָחִינוּ לֶאֱלִימֶלֶךְ).

לֵאמֹר is morphologically a Qal infinitive construct of אמר + ל preposition but is used commonly as an infinitive of means, here telling how Boaz "uncovered" the ear of the nearer redeemer, "*by* saying" or just "saying." In most English translations, לֵאמֹר feels redundant and can often be left out.

קְנֵה נֶגֶד הַיֹּשְׁבִים֙ וְנֶ֣גֶד זִקְנֵ֣י עַמִּ֔י

קְנֵה is the Qal imperative 2ms of קנה and is best translated as "acquire" rather than "purchase" since this setting is a legal petition rather than a business transaction. Admittedly, the verb מָכְרָה was used earlier (4:3, "selling"), but even there the context does not require a monetary transaction. The LXX translates קְנֵה with Κτῆσαι ("get, gain") and translates מָכְרָה in 4:3 with δέδοται ("give, offer"). In Hebrew, both verbs (מכר and קנה) typically imply a business transaction, but the LXX captures the notion of "give/get" in both clauses, which is the idea in this familial redemption.

Both occurrences of נֶגֶד are locative in this clause, and combined together they include all the parties present. הַיֹּשְׁבִים֙ is a Qal participle mp of ישב + הַ◌, functioning as a substantive noun, "the sitters" or "the ones sitting." This group could be the townspeople who have gathered, or it could be a more generic description of זִקְנֵ֣י עַמִּ֔י. In the latter case, the *vav* on וְנֶ֣גֶד זִקְנֵ֣י עַמִּ֔י is epexegetical, further explaining who the הַיֹּשְׁבִים֙ are, "the ones sitting (הַיֹּשְׁבִים) [here]—*namely* (וְ), the elders of my people (זִקְנֵי עַמִּי)."[17] If, however, the *vav* is conjoining two groups of people, then the nearer redeemer is to acquire the field in the presence of both the townspeople

17. RJW §434.

(הַיֹּשְׁבִים) *and* (וְ) the elders (זִקְנֵי עַמִּי).[18] We will see in 4:9–11 that the "witnesses" to this transaction were both the elders *and* (וְ) all the people at the gate, and so that is likely how we should understand this construction as well.

אִם־תִּגְאַל גְּאָל

אִם introduces the first of two conditional clauses. This first conditional clause consists of two verbal forms of the root גאל. תִּגְאַל is the Qal imperfect 2ms and is the protasis of the conditional, "if you will redeem." The apodosis is גְּאָל, the Qal imperative 2ms. The entire conditional clause is "If you will redeem, redeem." To translate a formal apodosis in English, we add "then" to the imperative: "If you will redeem, [*then*] redeem." In both cases, the implied object of redemption is the portion of the field: "If you will redeem [*it*], then redeem [*it*]."

וְאִם־לֹא יִגְאַל הַגִּידָה לִּי

וְאִם introduces the second conditional clause and presents the opposite of the first. Therefore, the conjunctive *vav* is translated adversatively, "*but* if he will not redeem." יִגְאַל is the negated Qal imperfect 3ms of גאל. לֹא + the indicative often expresses a stern prohibition, but in a conditional clause, the imperfective aspect is fitting ("will not redeem"). The conditional clause introduces a hypothetical situation that has yet to happen, and so the incomplete verbal aspect fits.

Notice that the verbal form is a 3ms (יִגְאַל) in contrast to the 2ms (תִּגְאַל) of the previous conditional clause.[19] Even though many manuscripts and most versions have the 2ms form, the 3ms actually makes some sense. There are a couple of options for understanding the 3ms verbal

18. RJW §430a.

19. The *BHQ* apparatus says, יִגְאַל | ἀγχιστεύεις G (V) S (T) (assim?, cf KR). KR refers to the manuscript evidence listed in the editions of Kennicott and de Rossi. The LXX clearly translates the verb as a second person. The question of assimilation (assim?) in the apparatus suggests that the versions have "assimilated" יִגְאַל to a second person form (תִּגְאַל) to match the surrounding context. This conclusion, however, cannot be confirmed and does not address the MT directly, only the versions. There is little evidence that this is a scribal error. It does not seem to be an explainable "accident," and for a scribe to change the 2ms to a 3ms intentionally would be unlikely (see Brotzman and Tully, *Old Testament Textual Criticism*, 174).

form. First, it is possible Boaz directed the first conditional toward the redeemer and the second toward the elders of the city: "If you (פְּלֹנִי אַלְמֹנִי) will redeem ... [Boaz turning and speaking to the elders], but if *he* (פְּלֹנִי אַלְמֹנִי) will not redeem ..."[20] This interpretation understands Boaz to be turning to the elders to convey his desired role in the redemption, making sure everyone present understood his intentions.

Another possibility is that Boaz's use of the third person verb refers to a generic redeemer who may still be out there and of whom he is unaware. "If *he* (any redeemer) will not redeem ..." This second interpretation highlights Boaz's desire to redeem the field (and ultimately Ruth) over any other redeemers who may exist. In this situation, Boaz could be speaking directly to the nearer redeemer or to the entire crowd. We will learn in the next clause that פְּלֹנִי אַלְמֹנִי is the first redeemer, and Boaz is after him. Therefore, using a 3ms verbs to refer to any generic redeemer who might be out there, Boaz makes it clear that he is going to redeem the field (and Ruth) so that no one has to go ask other hypothetical redeemers. In light of the vast manuscript evidence and the evidence from the versions, most scholars read a 2ms here. Even so, there are ways to understand the MT as it stands.

הַגִּ֣ידָה is the Hiphil imperative 2ms of נגד, functioning as the apodosis of the conditional clause. נגד is a I-נ verb, and as we would expect, the I-נ assimilates into the ג. The 2ms imperative argues for reading יִגְאַ֗ל as a 2ms form since it seems that Boaz now returns his attention to the nearer redeemer to ask whether he intends to redeem the portion of the field. However, the 2ms imperative could also refer to the witnesses present as a collective singular. In this case, Boaz would be telling everyone around to declare to him if there is any other redeemer who will redeem. This understanding of the 2ms imperative supports reading the previous verb as a 3ms in this conditional clause. Boaz initially talks to the nearer redeemer (2ms), commanding him to redeem if he will. Next, he looks to the crowd to say, "If any other redeemer (3ms) is around who might redeem (including פְּלֹנִי אַלְמֹנִי), then you (2ms; crowd as a collective singular) declare it to me (לִּ֗י)."

20. Sasson, *Ruth*, 118.

וְאֵדְעָ֞ כִּ֣י אֵ֤ין זוּלָֽתְךָ֙ לִגְא֔וֹל וְאָנֹכִ֖י אַחֲרֶ֑יךָ ואדעה ק

וְאֵדַע is a Qal imperfect 1cs of ידע, but the *qere* clarifies that it should be read as a cohortative. As expected with I-ו verbs, the original ו (אֶוְדַע) flees in the imperfect and the preformative vowel lengthens (אֵדַע). The *vav* is conjunctive (וְ), not consecutive (וָ before an א) and communicates purpose, "*so that* I may know."[21] כִּי introduces the content of what Boaz wants to know.[22] אֵין is the negative particle of existence, "that there is none." זוּלָתְךָ is the prepositional phrase, "except you." לִגְאוֹל is a Qal infinitive construct + ל and completes the content of what Boaz wants to know, "that there is none except you *to redeem*."

וְאָנֹכִי אַחֲרֶיךָ clarifies that Boaz is the next in line to redeem the field and provides the reason why Boaz is pursuing this information from the nearer redeemer. Since Boaz is אַחֲרֶיךָ, then he needs to know the nearer redeemer's intentions so that he can redeem the field if the nearer redeemer says no. In this sense, the preposition אַחַר is an irreal locative. In a hypothetical family tree, Boaz would be "after" the nearer redeemer, but in the case of redemption rights, he is not literally following behind the nearer redeemer in location.

וַיֹּ֖אמֶר אָנֹכִ֥י אֶגְאָֽל׃

The final clause is the redeemer's answer, set off after the *atnāḥ* (֑). וַיֹּאמֶר is the Qal imperfect 3ms of אמר + *vav*-consecutive, moving the narrative action forward. אָנֹכִי is the explicit subject for emphasis. אֶגְאָל is the Qal imperfect 1cs of גאל. With the pronoun explicit and fronted, the construction is emphatic. However, it does not generate an emphatic interpretation. We should not interpret that the nearer redeemer stoically and profoundly said, "I myself will redeem with all the rights and privileges appertaining thereto." Rather, the narrator builds suspense with the emphatic אָנֹכִי as it seems that Boaz's plan to redeem Ruth is not working out.

---

21. RJW §§181a, 187, 518.

22. RJW §451a.

RUTH 4:5

וַיֹּ֣אמֶר בֹּ֔עַז בְּיוֹם־קְנוֹתְךָ֥ הַשָּׂדֶ֖ה מִיַּ֣ד נָעֳמִ֑י וּ֠מֵאֵת ר֣וּת הַמּוֹאֲבִיָּ֤ה אֵֽשֶׁת־הַמֵּת֙
קָנִ֔יתִי לְהָקִ֥ים שֵׁם־הַמֵּ֖ת עַל־נַחֲלָתֽוֹ׃

ACCENT PHRASING

וַיֹּ֣אמֶר בֹּ֔עַז
בְּיוֹם־קְנוֹתְךָ֥ הַשָּׂדֶ֖ה מִיַּ֣ד נָעֳמִ֑י
וּ֠מֵאֵת ר֣וּת הַמּוֹאֲבִיָּ֤ה אֵֽשֶׁת־הַמֵּת֙ קָנִ֔יתִי
לְהָקִ֥ים שֵׁם־הַמֵּ֖ת עַל־נַחֲלָתֽוֹ׃

וַיֹּ֣אמֶר בֹּ֔עַז

וַיֹּ֣אמֶר is a Qal imperfect 3ms + *vav*-consecutive in temporal succession. בֹּ֔עַז is the explicit subject, shifting the narrative back to his continued effort to redeem Ruth.

בְּיוֹם־קְנוֹתְךָ֥ הַשָּׂדֶ֖ה מִיַּ֣ד נָעֳמִ֑י

בְּיוֹם introduces a temporal clause with ב + infinitive construct (separated by יוֹם). קְנוֹתְךָ֥ is the Qal infinitive construct of קנה + 2ms suffix. Literally, we get "On the day of your acquiring," with "acquiring" functioning as a gerund ("-ing" noun). The suffix (ְךָ) added to the end of the infinitive is the subject of the temporal clause and therefore is smoothed out as "When *you* acquire."[23]

הַשָּׂדֶ֖ה is the direct object. One way to recognize that this infinitive construct (קְנוֹתְךָ֥) creates a finite temporal clause is that it takes a direct object. Given the accents, בְּיוֹם־קְנוֹתְךָ֥ הַשָּׂדֶ֖ה is all one package consisting of two constituents (בְּיוֹם־קְנוֹתְךָ֥ + הַשָּׂדֶ֖ה). Quite often you can make guesses about how the accents are "bracketing" constituents together for translation purposes. Here you can see how the *mêrĕkā* (֥) and *ṭifḥā* (֖) "bracket" these two

23. The suffix creates what is effectively a subjective genitive, although that terminology is out of place in Hebrew studies. The "acquiring *of* you" is the "acquiring" that "you" have done or will do. Hence, "when you acquire" is entirely correct syntactically.

constituents together (◌ִ◌◌ ◌ְ◌◌־◌◌◌). The full temporal clause, then, is "On the day of your acquiring of the field," with הַשָּׂדֶה as the ending noun of the construct package.[24]

מִיַּד נָעֳמִי is the prepositional phrase communicating from whom the nearer redeemer will acquire the field. Notice that the focus in this opening line of Boaz's direct speech is still on the field and Naomi. Notice also the *atnāḥ* on this segment of the verse. As we have seen before, the *atnāḥ* may mark the "meaning" of the verse, or the part of the verse where the scribes wanted the reader's attention to land. Here the attention lands on the suspense generated by a temporal clause with no resolution ... yet. "On the day that you purchase the field from the hand of Naomi ..." We still have a field. We still have Naomi. But *what* will happen on the day that פְּלֹנִי אַלְמֹנִי acquires this field from her?

קָנִיתָה
וּ֠מֵאֵת ר֨וּת הַמּוֹאֲבִיָּ֤ה אֵֽשֶׁת־הַמֵּת֙ קָנִ֔יתִי ק

וּמֵאֵת introduces the direct object of the next clause, fronted for emphasis. וּמֵאֵת is most likely a combination of the emphatic מִן preposition and the direct object marker (אֶת), "*even* Ruth the Moabitess."[25] רוּת is the formal direct object, but she is further specified with appositional nouns, הַמּוֹאֲבִיָּה and אֵשֶׁת־הַמֵּת. These terms explain why she is part of this land transaction. Ruth is both a foreigner *and* a widow. הַמֵּת is a Qal participle ms + הַ◌ functioning as a noun, "the dead (one)." We do not know from this construction who "the dead (one)" is, but it is irrelevant to Boaz's point. Ruth is a widow and that is sufficient information for now. We will discover shortly that Ruth was married to Mahlon (4:10), but the point now is that she is widowed.

קָנִיתִי is a little tricky. In the written text (*ketiv*), the verbal form is a Qal perfect 1cs of קנה. However, this would suggest that *Boaz* will acquire Ruth on the day that the nearer redeemer acquires the field. This presumes that the land redeemer and the levir are not the same person, and indeed

24. Williams calls this an objective genitive because the field is the "object" acquired (RJW §38).

25. RJW §325.

this could be the case. However, the *qere* helps clarify the intended meaning, I believe. The *qere* is the Qal perfect *2ms* of קנה, suggesting that Boaz is still talking to the nearer redeemer and now including Ruth as part of the redemption. Following the *qere* is the more common option, but both verbal forms are syntactically and theologically possible.[26]

לְהָקִים שֵׁם־הַמֵּת עַל־נַחֲלָתוֹ׃

The final clause provides the reason that Boaz includes Ruth in the redemption package. לְהָקִים is the Hiphil infinitive construct of קום with a ל preposition, "to *cause* to stand." Notice that in the Hiphil of hollow roots, the thematic vowel coalesces as a *ḥîreq-yôd* (לְהָקִים). Because the thematic vowel coalesces, the preformative ה is now left in an open pretonic syllable resulting in the lengthening of the a-class vowel to a *qāmeṣ* (לְהָקִים). שֵׁם־הַמֵּת is the accusative object, and the idiom ("to cause the name of the dead to stand") communicates the perpetuation of the family name. Therefore, Boaz says that when the nearer redeemer acquires the field from Naomi, he (the redeemer) also acquires Ruth with the explicit purpose to perpetuate the name of Mahlon. עַל־ in עַל־נַחֲלָתוֹ is specification, translated as "*concerning* his inheritance."[27] The acquisition of Ruth is so that the name of the dead will be established in Bethlehem, specifically regarding his inheritance. The situation is not that Mahlon would simply have an inheritance to claim, but that he would also have descendants to inherit it. Hence, the land (inheritance) and Ruth (descendants) are included in the redemption.

26. See Brotzman and Tully, *Old Testament Textual Criticism*, 176–78, for discussion on this text-critical issue. See the discussion in Eskenazi and Frymer-Kensky, *Ruth*, 76–77, for various interpretations.

27. RJW §289; *BHRG* §39.19.4(i).

RUTH 4:6

וַיֹּ֣אמֶר הַגֹּאֵ֗ל לֹ֤א אוּכַל֙ לִגְאוֹל־לִ֔י פֶּן־אַשְׁחִ֖ית אֶת־נַחֲלָתִ֑י גְּאַל־לְךָ֤ אַתָּה֙ אֶת־גְּאֻלָּתִ֔י כִּ֥י לֹא־אוּכַ֖ל לִגְאֹֽל׃

ACCENT PHRASING

וַיֹּ֣אמֶר הַגֹּאֵ֗ל
לֹ֤א אוּכַל֙ לִגְאוֹל־לִ֔י
פֶּן־אַשְׁחִ֖ית אֶת־נַחֲלָתִ֑י
גְּאַל־לְךָ֤ אַתָּה֙ אֶת־גְּאֻלָּתִ֔י
כִּ֥י לֹא־אוּכַ֖ל לִגְאֹֽל׃

וַיֹּ֣אמֶר הַגֹּאֵ֗ל

The narrative dialogue continues in 4:6 with וַיֹּ֣אמֶר, the Qal imperfect 3ms of אמר + *vav*-consecutive. הַגֹּאֵ֗ל is the subject, introducing his reply to Boaz's insistence that he redeem Ruth in addition to the field of Naomi.

לֹ֤א אוּכַל֙ לִגְאוֹל־לִ֔י (ק לִגְאָל)

אוּכַל֙ is the negated Qal imperfect 1cs of יכל, "I am not able." יכל is a bit irregular in relation to the expected I-ו "weaknesses." Notice the א, indicative of the 1cs preformative, and also notice the וּ as the preformative vowel. This preformative vowel is irregular in the Qal imperfect of יכל, but even so, יכל is "regularly irregular" and one can expect this same vowel adjustment when יכל occurs.[28]

לִגְאוֹל is the Qal infinitive construct of גאל + ל preposition, completing the verbal idea of the redeemer's (in)ability. "I am not able to redeem." The difference between the *ketiv* and *qere* here is the *plene* spelling of the long וֹ in the *ketiv* versus the short *qāmeṣ- ḥāṭûf* in the *qere*. Since the infinitive is

28. *IBH*, 243; Gary D. Pratico and Miles V. Van Pelt, *Basics of Biblical Hebrew*, 3rd ed. (Grand Rapids: Zondervan, 2019), 177. According to a search in the LHB, all 193 occurrences of יכל are in the Qal, and the primary (if not only) "weakness" of the verb is preserving the I-י as a וּ in the imperfect (133 occurrences in the imperfect).

joined to לִּי via the *maqqēf* (־), the final syllable of לִגְאוֹל is technically closed and unaccented, expecting a short vowel (hence *qāmeṣ-ḥāṭûf* in the *qere*). However, historic long vowels regularly break the expected vowel rules, and so the fully written ו in the consonantal text is also explainable. Neither spelling changes the meaning or emphasis of the infinitive.

The ל on לִּי is a ל of advantage by name but resulting in a *lack* of advantage when combined with the negated verb (לֹא אוּכַל): "I am not able to redeem *for me* (*myself*)." Had the redeemer been able to redeem, it would have been "for" his advantage. לִּי is best understood as a reflexive since the subject is also a 1cs: "I am unable to redeem *for myself*."[29]

פֶּן־אַשְׁחִית אֶת־נַחֲלָתִי

פֶּן introduces the negative result clause.[30] If the redeemer does redeem Ruth, the negative result would be that he would corrupt his own inheritance. More succinctly, we would say, "*lest* I corrupt." אַשְׁחִית is a Hiphil imperfect 1cs of שׁחת. שׁחת is a II-guttural "weak" verb, but the vowel pointing of שׁחת is normal in this case. The typical problems with II-guttural verbs are related to the *dāgēš forte* of the intensive stems or the vocal *shewa*s when a thematic vowel reduces. Since the Hiphil does not have a doubled R2 and since the thematic vowel is often a historic long ִי, neither of these II-guttural "weaknesses" come into play. אַשְׁחִית is essentially a "strong" verbal form.

אֶת־נַחֲלָתִי is the definite direct object. נַחֲלָה is definite because of the 1cs pronominal suffix. He is talking about a specific inheritance—namely, "my inheritance"—not just any generic (indefinite) inheritance. Notice the inclusion of ָת (feminine ת) before the pronominal suffix (ִי) when the noun is feminine (נַחֲלָה).[31]

גְּאַל־לְךָ אַתָּה אֶת־גְּאֻלָּתִי

The nearer redeemer continues his direct speech to Boaz. גְּאַל־לְךָ is the Qal imperative 2ms of גאל, annexed via the *maqqēf* (־) to the preposition לְךָ,

29. GKC §119s; JM §133.

30. RJW §461.

31. The addition of ָת is actually the addition of ַת. The short *pataḥ* lengthens to *qameṣ* in an open pretonic syllable.

communicating advantage. The 2ms suffix (ךָ◌) is reflexive even though it comes before the subject, אַתָּה. Literally, the clause translates, "Redeem for yourself, you." All the implied and explicit second person pronouns ("[You] redeem for yourself, *you* [do it]!") emphasize that the nearer redeemer wants nothing to do with the transaction now.

אֶת־גְּאֻלָּתִי is a prepositional phrase indicating the means by which Boaz will redeem Ruth, "with my redemption." This is the nearer redeemer's way of saying that his *right* of redemption can be transferred to the next in line. The nearer redeemer will not first redeem the land and Ruth and only then hand them over to Boaz. Rather, the nearer redeemer tells Boaz that because he is unable to redeem, Boaz should take his "right of redemption" and acquire Ruth himself. This understanding of the transfer of redemption rights also supports the conclusion that the land and Ruth are a package redemption. The nearer redeemer cannot say, "I will redeem the land, but you redeem Ruth." Rather, his transfer of the entire redemption right indicates that he is now even willing to give up the land since he is unable (unwilling?) to redeem Ruth also.

כִּי לֹא־אוּכַל לִגְאֹל׃

כִּי introduces the ground clause, repeating what the nearer redeemer said earlier in the verse. This forms an *inclusio* in the verse, perhaps highlighting his unwillingness to redeem Ruth with only the excuse "I am not able to redeem." It would be interesting to know the actual reason he would give if pressed on the issue, but grammatically all we know at this point is that he is "unable to redeem."

As before, אוּכַל is the negated Qal imperfect 1cs of יכל, and לִגְאֹל is the Qal infinitive construct of גאל with a ל preposition. Notice that לִגְאֹל now stands alone rather than being constructed with another word via a *maqqēf* (see discussion of the *ketiv/qere* earlier in the verse). Therefore, the vowel is the expected *ḥōlem* in an accented syllable (לִ◌ְ◌ֹ◌).

7 Now this [was] the custom in Israel concerning the redemption and concerning
the exchange to establish any matter. A man would draw off his sandal and give [it]
to his friend. This [was] the testimony in Israel. 8 And so the redeemer said to Boaz,
"Acquire for yourself." And then he drew off his sandal. 9 Then Boaz said to the elders
and all the people, "Witnesses you [are] today, for I have acquired all which [belongs]
to Elimelech and all which [belongs] to Chilion and Mahlon from the hand of Naomi.
10 And moreover, Ruth, the Moabitess, the wife of Mahlon, I have acquired for myself
as a wife [in order] to perpetuate the name of the dead [one] concerning his inheritance,
[so] that the name of the dead might not be cut off from his brothers or from the
gate of his place. Witnesses you [are] today." 11 And then all the people who [were]
at the gate and the elders said, "Witnesses. May the Lord give the woman, the one
entering to your house like Rachel and like Leah, who, the two of them, built [up] the
house of Israel, and [may he] do valiantly in Ephratha, and may the name be called
in Bethlehem. 12 And may your house exist as the house of Perez who bore Judah to
Tamar, from the offspring which the Lord will give to you from this young woman."

RUTH

4:7–12

7 וְזֹ֨את לְפָנִ֜ים בְּיִשְׂרָאֵ֗ל עַל־הַגְּאוּלָּ֤ה וְעַל־הַתְּמוּרָה֙ לְקַיֵּ֣ם כָּל־דָּבָ֔ר שָׁלַ֥ף אִ֛ישׁ
נַעֲל֖וֹ וְנָתַ֣ן לְרֵעֵ֑הוּ וְזֹ֥את הַתְּעוּדָ֖ה בְּיִשְׂרָאֵֽל׃ 8 וַיֹּ֧אמֶר הַגֹּאֵ֛ל לְבֹ֖עַז קְנֵה־לָ֑ךְ וַיִּשְׁלֹ֖ף
נַעֲלֽוֹ׃ 9 וַיֹּ֨אמֶר בֹּ֜עַז לַזְּקֵנִ֗ים וְכָל־הָעָ֔ם עֵדִ֤ים אַתֶּם֙ הַיּ֔וֹם כִּ֤י קָנִ֙יתִי֙ אֶת־כָּל־אֲשֶׁ֣ר
לֶֽאֱלִימֶ֔לֶךְ וְאֵ֛ת כָּל־אֲשֶׁ֥ר לְכִלְי֖וֹן וּמַחְל֑וֹן מִיַּ֖ד נָעֳמִֽי׃ 10 וְגַ֣ם אֶת־ר֣וּת הַמֹּאֲבִיָּה֩
אֵ֨שֶׁת מַחְל֜וֹן קָנִ֧יתִי לִ֣י לְאִשָּׁ֗ה לְהָקִ֤ים שֵׁם־הַמֵּת֙ עַל־נַ֣חֲלָת֔וֹ וְלֹֽא־יִכָּרֵ֧ת שֵׁם־הַמֵּ֛ת
מֵעִ֥ם אֶחָ֖יו וּמִשַּׁ֣עַר מְקוֹמ֑וֹ עֵדִ֥ים אַתֶּ֖ם הַיּֽוֹם׃ 11 וַיֹּ֨אמְר֜וּ כָּל־הָעָ֧ם אֲשֶׁר־בַּשַּׁ֛עַר
וְהַזְּקֵנִ֖ים עֵדִ֑ים יִתֵּן֩ יְהוָ֨ה אֶת־הָאִשָּׁ֜ה הַבָּאָ֣ה אֶל־בֵּיתֶ֗ךָ כְּרָחֵ֤ל ׀ וּכְלֵאָה֙ אֲשֶׁ֨ר
בָּנ֤וּ שְׁתֵּיהֶם֙ אֶת־בֵּ֣ית יִשְׂרָאֵ֔ל וַעֲשֵׂה־חַ֣יִל בְּאֶפְרָ֔תָה וּקְרָא־שֵׁ֖ם בְּבֵ֥ית לָֽחֶם׃
12 וִיהִ֤י בֵֽיתְךָ֙ כְּבֵ֣ית פֶּ֔רֶץ אֲשֶׁר־יָלְדָ֥ה תָמָ֖ר לִֽיהוּדָ֑ה מִן־הַזֶּ֗רַע אֲשֶׁ֨ר יִתֵּ֤ן יְהוָה֙ לְךָ֔
מִן־הַנַּעֲרָ֖ה הַזֹּֽאת׃

RUTH 4:7

וְזֹאת֩ לְפָנִ֨ים בְּיִשְׂרָאֵ֜ל עַל־הַגְּאוּלָּ֣ה וְעַל־הַתְּמוּרָ֗ה לְקַיֵּם֙ כָּל־דָּבָ֔ר שָׁלַ֥ף אִ֛ישׁ
נַעֲל֖וֹ וְנָתַ֣ן לְרֵעֵ֑הוּ וְזֹ֥את הַתְּעוּדָ֖ה בְּיִשְׂרָאֵֽל׃

ACCENT PHRASING

וְזֹאת֩ לְפָנִ֨ים בְּיִשְׂרָאֵ֜ל עַל־הַגְּאוּלָּ֣ה וְעַל־הַתְּמוּרָ֗ה לְקַיֵּם֙ כָּל־דָּבָ֔ר
שָׁלַ֥ף אִ֛ישׁ נַעֲל֖וֹ
וְנָתַ֣ן לְרֵעֵ֑הוּ
וְזֹ֥את הַתְּעוּדָ֖ה בְּיִשְׂרָאֵֽל׃

וְזֹאת֩ לְפָנִ֨ים בְּיִשְׂרָאֵ֜ל עַל־הַגְּאוּלָּ֣ה וְעַל־הַתְּמוּרָ֗ה לְקַיֵּם֙ כָּל־דָּבָ֔ר

Ruth 4:7 provides an aside for the audience about the customs in Israel at this time. The *vav* on וְזֹאת֩ is disjunctive (but not adversative) in the narrative, "*Now* this …" וְזֹאת֩ is the subject of a verbless clause and לְפָנִ֨ים is the predicate nominative. We have to supply the English "to be" verb to get "Now this [*was*] the custom."

Literally, לְפָנִ֨ים is a temporal adverb but functions here as a noun. This is difficult to translate into English, but something like "before(ness)" would work. However, even that does not work to accommodate the target language. If we use the rest of the clause to help iron out לְפָנִ֨ים, we get the prepositional phrase בְּיִשְׂרָאֵ֜ל, indicating that זאת is something that happened "in Israel" (locative). And we also have the prepositional phrases עַל־הַגְּאוּלָּ֣ה וְעַל־הַתְּמוּרָ֗ה, indicating that זאת is something that was "concerning the redemption and the exchange." So זאת is something with "before(-ness) in Israel concerning the redemption and the exchange." We will discover further that זאת is an *action* by the participants in the redemption (שָׁלַ֥ף אִ֛ישׁ נַעֲל֖וֹ וְנָתַ֣ן לְרֵעֵ֑הוּ), and so a regular practice that has happened "previously in Israel concerning the redemption" is a "custom." "Now this was the *custom* in Israel concerning the redemption and the exchange." The עַל prepositions are both examples of specification, identifying what this matter is about, "concerning."[1]

1. RJW §289.

לְקַיֵּם כָּל־דָּבָר now completes the previous verbless clause by indicating the purpose of the "custom" (לְפָנִים). לְקַיֵּם is the Piel infinitive construct of קום + ל of purpose. Even though we do not yet know the actions associated with the "custom," the purpose of it is to "confirm any matter." כָּל־דָּבָר is the object, or the thing "confirmed." As a Piel, לְקַיֵּם carries a factitive meaning (to cause a state, or to "make" that state), "to make arise" or "to make stand." To "make something to stand" is to "confirm" it. In this aside in the story, the narrator explains to the audience a standard action taken in Israel as the customary way to confirm a matter.

שָׁלַף אִישׁ נַעֲלוֹ

שָׁלַף is a Qal perfect 3ms of שלף. אִישׁ is the subject, and the verb should be translated as a modal perfective, "*would* draw off." The perfective communicates frequentative or habitual action in the past tense, hence making it a custom.[2] The context must determine this use of the perfective. The morphology directs us only to the Qal perfect 3ms. נַעֲלוֹ is the direct object. Technically, the direct object is definite because it has the pronominal suffix and refers specifically to the man's sandal, not just any sandal. However, sometimes the definite direct object marker (אֶת־) is omitted in places where we might expect it.

וְנָתַן לְרֵעֵהוּ

וְנָתַן is another Qal perfect 3ms with a modal nuance, "he *would* give." The direct object is an implied "it," referring to the sandal, and לְרֵעֵהוּ is the indirect object prepositional phrase "he would give [*it*]." Notice that לְרֵעֵהוּ takes an alternative 3ms pronominal suffix (ֵהוּ versus ָיו) for nouns. רֵעַ occurs around 115 times in the Hebrew Bible with this variation of the 3ms pronominal suffix on a singular verb (only once as רֵעוֹ in Jer 6:21).[3] Here רֵעַ

---

2. Holmstedt, *Ruth*, 196. He cites Gen 29:3; 1 Sam 1:3; 9:9 as examples and refers the reader to John A. Cook, "The Biblical Hebrew Verbal System: A Grammaticalization Approach" (PhD diss., University of Wisconsin, 2002), 230–31.

3. BDB, 945. See also GKC §84a.i for his discussion of the development of this suffix specifically with רֵעַ.

is more generic than a "friend," or even a mere acquaintance.[4] The word merely means another person. In the case of the custom, a man would give his sandal to the other participant in the transaction regardless of whether they knew each other well.

וְזֹאת הַתְּעוּדָה בְּיִשְׂרָאֵל׃

The final verbless clause reiterates the beginning of the verse, closing off this aside for the audience. וְזֹאת is again the subject and we must supply the English "to be" verb to get a full clause, "Now this [*was*] ..." Previously, the "custom" was expressed using the temporal adverb (לְפָנִים) as a noun ("beforeness"). Here, הַתְּעוּדָה takes the place of לְפָנִים as the predicate nominative, making it more explicit as to what זאת is—namely, an "attestation/ testimony" or a "legally binding symbolic act."[5] בְּיִשְׂרָאֵל is again the locative prepositional phrase identifying the realm in which this witness took place, "in Israel."

4. BDB lists Ruth 4:7 as an occurrence of רֵעַ referring to a "fellow-citizen ... with whom one stands in reciprocal relations" (BDB, 946). In this sense, the רֵעַ may only be a transaction partner.

5. *NIDOTTE* 3:339.

RUTH 4:8

וַיֹּ֧אמֶר הַגֹּאֵ֛ל לְבֹ֖עַז קְנֵה־לָ֑ךְ וַיִּשְׁלֹ֖ף נַעֲלֽוֹ׃

ACCENT PHRASING

וַיֹּ֧אמֶר הַגֹּאֵ֛ל לְבֹ֖עַז
קְנֵה־לָ֑ךְ
וַיִּשְׁלֹ֖ף נַעֲלֽוֹ׃

וַיֹּ֧אמֶר הַגֹּאֵ֛ל לְבֹ֖עַז

The primary narrative now resumes with the redeemer confirming—in fact, commanding—that Boaz should acquire Ruth and the land for himself. וַיֹּ֧אמֶר is a Qal imperfect 3ms of אמר + *vav*-consecutive of logical succession. Following the present discussions and the mention of the custom in Israel, we now get the nearer redeemer's conclusion, or the logical outcome of the previous dialogue: "And *so* the redeemer said ..." הַגֹּאֵ֛ל is a Qal participle ms in form but functions as a substantive noun. הַגֹּאֵ֛ל is the explicit subject of the verbal clause (וַיֹּ֧אמֶר הַגֹּאֵ֛ל). לְבֹ֖עַז marks Boaz as the addressee.

קְנֵה־לָ֑ךְ

The redeemer's direct speech begins with קְנֵה, the Qal imperative 2ms of קנה. This morphology of a III-ה Qal imperative is expected with the vocal *shewa* in the R1 (קְ) and ◌ֵה- ending the verb. As before, the ל on לָ֑ךְ communicates advantage, and the 2ms suffix is reflexive, "Acquire *for yourself*."[6]

וַיִּשְׁלֹ֖ף נַעֲלֽוֹ׃

This final clause describes what the redeemer did, thus fulfilling the custom of confirming a redemption in Israel. וַיִּשְׁלֹ֖ף is the Qal imperfect 3ms of שׁלף + *vav*-consecutive of temporal succession. It may feel like this *vav* would communicate logical succession ("and so he drew off"), and indeed it may.

---

6. RJW §272.

However, the consecutive here is sequential to the previous consecutive, in which we already had logically successive action ("And *so* he said ... and *then* he drew off").

נַעֲלוֹ is the direct object with the 3ms pronominal suffix. Notice the vowel pointing on נַעֲלוֹ. Remember, נַ֫עַל is a segolate noun with *pataḥ*s because of the guttural (ע). With something like מֶ֫לֶךְ, we would expect to see a silent *shewa* in the R2 position when adding a pronominal suffix (מַלְכּוֹ). However, remember that gutturals, such as those in נַ֫עַל, do not allow a simple silent *shewa*. Thus, they "flip" what would normally be a silent *shewa* to a composite vocal *shewa*, the *ḥāṭēf-pataḥ* (ֲ) in this case. This is a classic vowel pattern for segolate-style nouns with an R2 guttural letter and a pronominal suffix.[7]

7. GKC §93c.

RUTH 4:9

וַיֹּאמֶר֩ בֹּ֨עַז לַזְּקֵנִ֜ים וְכָל־הָעָ֗ם עֵדִ֤ים אַתֶּם֙ הַיּ֔וֹם כִּ֤י קָנִ֙יתִי֙ אֶת־כָּל־אֲשֶׁ֣ר
לֶאֱלִימֶ֔לֶךְ וְאֵ֛ת כָּל־אֲשֶׁ֥ר לְכִלְי֖וֹן וּמַחְל֑וֹן מִיַּ֖ד נָעֳמִֽי׃

ACCENT PHRASING

וַיֹּאמֶר֩ בֹּ֨עַז לַזְּקֵנִ֜ים וְכָל־הָעָ֗ם
עֵדִ֤ים אַתֶּם֙ הַיּ֔וֹם
כִּ֤י קָנִ֙יתִי֙ אֶת־כָּל־אֲשֶׁ֣ר לֶאֱלִימֶ֔לֶךְ
וְאֵ֛ת כָּל־אֲשֶׁ֥ר לְכִלְי֖וֹן וּמַחְל֑וֹן
מִיַּ֖ד נָעֳמִֽי׃

וַיֹּאמֶר֩ בֹּ֨עַז לַזְּקֵנִ֜ים וְכָל־הָעָ֗ם

The narrative continues with Boaz's response and confirmation to acquire the field and Ruth. וַיֹּאמֶר֩ is a Qal imperfect 3ms of אמר + *vav*-consecutive. בֹּ֨עַז is the explicit subject, making certain there is no narrative ambiguity as to who is redeeming everything that belonged to Elimelech and his sons. Boaz directs his statement לַזְּקֵנִ֜ים וְכָל־הָעָ֗ם. The ל could be locative, indicating the direction in which he spoke, "*toward* the elders."[8] Or, even as a locative, the ל could simply mark the addressee(s) of Boaz's upcoming statement, "*to* the elders."

Hebrew often repeats prepositions even when two entities are in play. Here one would not be surprised to see the ל preposition repeated on וְכָל־הָעָ֗ם if it were in true prepositional succession. Since the preposition is not repeated, however, the ו is best understood as a *vav* of accompaniment, "Boaz spoke to the elders *along with* all the people." The accent pattern also supports this reading with the *gereš* (◌֜), a mildly disjunctive accent, on לַזְּקֵנִ֜ים right before the heavier disjunctive *revîa* (◌֗). In this sense, the primary dialogue is between the elders and Boaz, but certainly the people sitting around are also witnesses to this transaction. As Boaz gathered the

8. RJW §267.

people necessary for this transaction, he gathered פְּלֹנִי אַלְמֹנִי and ten of the elders of the city (4:1–2). The elders were the primary audience, but this transaction would have surely garnered attention from the townspeople in a small town like Bethlehem.

עֵדִים אַתֶּם הַיּוֹם

עֵדִים אַתֶּם is a verbless clause with the predicate nominative (עֵדִים) fronted for focus. As is common with verbless clauses, we supply the English "to be" verb according to the proper tense of the context. Here Boaz is currently speaking to the people: "Witnesses you (all) [*are*] today."

כִּי קָנִיתִי אֶת־כָּל־אֲשֶׁר לֶאֱלִימֶלֶךְ וְאֵת כָּל־אֲשֶׁר לְכִלְיוֹן וּמַחְלוֹן

כִּי introduces *what* they are witnesses of: "You are witnesses today *that* …" קָנִיתִי is the Qal perfect 1cs of קנה. Notice in the perfective conjugation with sufformatives that the III-ה reveals the original י of the root. It has coalesced as the thematic vowel in קָנִיתִי, but that is standard for many III-ה verbs. The perfective is best translated as an English perfect, "I have acquired." Although the actual transaction may not have been completed, Boaz states it as if it is already done. He has indeed completed the redemption of Ruth.

This clause takes a double direct object, expressing everything that Boaz has acquired. אֶת־כָּל־ introduces these direct objects. In both cases, כָּל־ is further modified by relative clauses, "All *which* [belonged to] Elimelech" and "All *which* [belonged to] Chilion and Mahlon." The doubled direct object phrases, along with the mention of all the men who died (Elimelech, Chilion, *and* Mahlon), suggest that Boaz is fully redeeming everything that belonged to Naomi *and* Ruth. The redemption that Boaz has sought is full and final.

מִיַּד נָעֳמִי׃

מִיַּד נָעֳמִי is a locative prepositional phrase telling the reader *from where* everything was acquired, but the phrase is idiomatic. Boaz did not literally redeem items from Naomi's hand. נָעֳמִי is the absolute noun in the construct package (מִיַּד נָעֳמִי) communicating an implied ל of possession, "from the hand of [*belonging to*] Naomi."

Ironically, the entire conversation about redemption began with Boaz proposing a portion of a field belonging to Naomi. Now he has redeemed everything that belonged to Elimelech, Mahlon, and Chilion "from Naomi's hand." Boaz not only has acquired these items from Naomi, but he also has freed her from the worry and bitterness of life without progeny. The land and family of these dead men is now in the hands of a mighty man of valor (אִישׁ גִּבּוֹר חַיִל) who will perpetuate the family name and provide for them as torah requires.

RUTH 4:10

וְגַ֣ם אֶת־ר֣וּת הַמֹּאֲבִיָּ֡ה אֵ֣שֶׁת מַחְל֡וֹן קָנִ֧יתִי לִ֣י לְאִשָּׁ֗ה לְהָקִ֤ים שֵׁם־הַמֵּת֙ עַל־נַ֣חֲלָת֔וֹ וְלֹֽא־יִכָּרֵ֧ת שֵׁם־הַמֵּ֛ת מֵעִ֥ם אֶחָ֖יו וּמִשַּׁ֣עַר מְקוֹמ֑וֹ עֵדִ֥ים אַתֶּ֖ם הַיּֽוֹם׃

ACCENT PHRASING

וְגַ֣ם אֶת־ר֣וּת הַמֹּאֲבִיָּ֡ה אֵ֣שֶׁת מַחְל֡וֹן קָנִ֧יתִי לִ֣י לְאִשָּׁ֗ה
לְהָקִ֤ים שֵׁם־הַמֵּת֙ עַל־נַ֣חֲלָת֔וֹ
וְלֹֽא־יִכָּרֵ֧ת שֵׁם־הַמֵּ֛ת מֵעִ֥ם אֶחָ֖יו וּמִשַּׁ֣עַר מְקוֹמ֑וֹ
עֵדִ֥ים אַתֶּ֖ם הַיּֽוֹם׃

וְגַ֣ם אֶת־ר֣וּת הַמֹּאֲבִיָּ֡ה אֵ֣שֶׁת מַחְל֡וֹן קָנִ֧יתִי לִ֣י לְאִשָּׁ֗ה

Ruth 4:10 continues all that Boaz has acquired in this redemption transaction. וְגַ֣ם is strongly additive, providing emphasis on Ruth. The additive גַּם ("moreover!") and the fronted direct object phrase (אֶת־ר֣וּת הַמֹּאֲבִיָּ֡ה אֵ֣שֶׁת מַחְל֡וֹן) make Ruth the highlight of this verse.

ר֣וּת is the head of the direct object phrase, and two appositional modifiers clarify who she is. הַמֹּאֲבִיָּ֡ה highlights once again her foreign status, and אֵ֣שֶׁת מַחְל֡וֹן indicates her widowhood. Boaz is completely unashamed to claim for himself this woman who is both a foreigner and a widow. He described her this way when proposing the redemption to the nearer redeemer (4:5), and now he rejoices that this is the exact same woman he has redeemed for himself. The repetition of these two appositional descriptors for Ruth suggests that Boaz did not deceive the nearer redeemer into thinking she was someone she was not. Boaz presented the redemption in an honest and fair way even though his plan to present the field before presenting Ruth proved to be effective.

קָנִ֧יתִי is a Qal perfect 1cs of קנה and translates as an English perfect as before, "I have acquired." When this is combined with the fronted direct object phrase, we get "And moreover, Ruth, the Moabitess, the wife of Mahlon, I have acquired." לִ֣י is the prepositional phrase marking advantage: "I have acquired Ruth … for myself." לְאִשָּׁ֗ה is the adverbial accusative of situation, marking Ruth's new status "*as* a wife." In context with לִ֑י, this adverbial accusative labels Ruth specifically as Boaz's wife.

לְהָקִ֨ים שֵֽׁם־הַמֵּ֜ת עַל־נַחֲלָת֗וֹ

Boaz continues his monologue by describing his purpose for redeeming Ruth using the same terms he presented to the nearer redeemer (4:5). Boaz continues to show that everything he presented to the nearer redeemer is now being completed *by him* in front of these witnesses. לְהָקִ֨ים is the Hiphil infinitive construct of קום + ל of purpose. Boaz has acquired Ruth "*in order to* cause to stand (or to perpetuate) the name of the dead (שֵֽׁם־הַמֵּ֜ת) concerning his inheritance (עַל־נַחֲלָת֗וֹ)." See 4:5 for details on these phrases.

וְלֹֽא־יִכָּרֵ֧ת שֵׁם־הַמֵּ֛ת מֵעִ֥ם אֶחָ֖יו וּמִשַּׁ֣עַר מְקוֹמ֑וֹ

וְלֹֽא־יִכָּרֵ֧ת is epexegetical (explanatory) and introduces a negative purpose clause explaining *why* the name of the dead should be perpetuated. As an epexegetical clause, the *vav* is translated as "that."[9] יִכָּרֵ֧ת is a Niphal imperfect 3ms of כרת and translates as a modal passive. Adding שֵׁם־הַמֵּ֛ת as the explicit subject, the clause translates as "that (וְ) the name of the dead *might* (modal) not *be* (passive) cut off."

מֵעִ֥ם is a combination of מִן and עִם ("from with") but translates simply as "from." אֶחָ֖יו is the object of the first prepositional phrase identifying the group from whom the name of the dead should not be cut off, "his brothers." A simple conjunctive *vav* (וּ) conjoins the two prepositional phrases, the second adding that Mahlon's name should not be cut off "from the gate of his place" (וּמִשַּׁ֣עַר מְקוֹמ֑וֹ). The logical relationship of the construct package implies a ב preposition, "the gate [located at] his place," an idiomatic way to speak of property. The combination of family (אֶחָ֖יו) and property (וּמִשַּׁ֣עַר מְקוֹמ֑וֹ) demonstrates the extent to which Boaz understood the gravity of this transaction. He is redeeming Ruth to perpetuate the name of the dead among his family *and* to protect Mahlon's property from those who

---

9. RJW §434.

would exploit Naomi and Ruth for unjust gain. Boaz's expression of these details exhibits his knowledge of the custom and torah, not his desire for personal gain.

עֵדִ֥ים אַתֶּ֖ם הַיּֽוֹם׃

עֵדִ֥ים אַתֶּ֖ם הַיּֽוֹם mirrors 4:9. Boaz reminds the elders and the townspeople that they are witnesses of this transaction today. אַתֶּ֖ם is the subject and עֵדִ֥ים is the predicate nominative, again fronted for focus. The article on הַיּֽוֹם is demonstrative, "this day," or "today." Having now reiterated the full redemption, Boaz again calls for the elders and the townspeople to testify as "witnesses."

RUTH 4:11

וַיֹּ֨אמְר֜וּ כָּל־הָעָ֧ם אֲשֶׁר־בַּשַּׁ֛עַר וְהַזְּקֵנִ֖ים עֵדִ֑ים יִתֵּן֩ יְהוָ֨ה אֶֽת־הָאִשָּׁ֜ה הַבָּאָ֣ה
אֶל־בֵּיתֶ֗ךָ כְּרָחֵ֤ל ׀ וּכְלֵאָה֙ אֲשֶׁ֨ר בָּנ֤וּ שְׁתֵּיהֶם֙ אֶת־בֵּ֣ית יִשְׂרָאֵ֔ל וַעֲשֵׂה־חַ֣יִל
בְּאֶפְרָ֔תָה וּקְרָא־שֵׁ֖ם בְּבֵ֥ית לָֽחֶם׃

ACCENT PHRASING

וַיֹּ֨אמְר֜וּ כָּל־הָעָ֧ם אֲשֶׁר־בַּשַּׁ֛עַר וְהַזְּקֵנִ֖ים עֵדִ֑ים
יִתֵּן֩ יְהוָ֨ה אֶֽת־הָאִשָּׁ֜ה הַבָּאָ֣ה אֶל־בֵּיתֶ֗ךָ
כְּרָחֵ֤ל ׀ וּכְלֵאָה֙ אֲשֶׁ֨ר בָּנ֤וּ שְׁתֵּיהֶם֙ אֶת־בֵּ֣ית יִשְׂרָאֵ֔ל
וַעֲשֵׂה־חַ֣יִל בְּאֶפְרָ֔תָה
וּקְרָא־שֵׁ֖ם בְּבֵ֥ית לָֽחֶם׃

וַיֹּ֨אמְר֜וּ כָּל־הָעָ֧ם אֲשֶׁר־בַּשַּׁ֛עַר וְהַזְּקֵנִ֖ים עֵדִ֑ים

וַיֹּ֨אמְר֜וּ is the Qal imperfect 3mp of אמר + *vav*-consecutive. With the 3mp verb, the subject now shifts to כָּל־הָעָ֧ם. כָּל־הָעָ֧ם is technically a singular, but as a collective singular, it communicates more than one, and hence the 3mp verbal form.[10] The subject phrase includes the verbless relative clause, אֲשֶׁר־בַּשַּׁ֛עַר. Since the antecedent of the relative is הָעָ֧ם (people, not things), the relative is translated "who" rather than "which." After supplying the English "to be" verb in the verbless relative clause, we get "who [*were*] at the gate." The ב on בַּשַּׁ֛עַר is locative, "*at* the gate." Notice also that the definite article ה has been supplanted by the ב preposition, but the ב retained the vowel pointing of the definite article (בַּשַּׁ֛עַר ⟵ הַשַּׁ֛עַר).

The *vav* on וְהַזְּקֵנִ֖ים is a *vav* of accompaniment, including an additional group of people to those at the gate. Those who are now "speaking" (וַיֹּ֨אמְר֜וּ) include those at the gate "*along with* the elders." The definite article (הַ◌) specifies that the narrator refers to "*the* elders" previously mentioned rather than a new group of elders that may have arrived or a generic group of community elders who have yet to be consulted.

10. RJW §229.

The final clause after the *ṭifḥā* (֖) is actually only one word (עֵדִֽים) and is the direct speech introduced by וַיֹּ֥אמְר֖וּ. It is terse and to the point. עֵדִֽים alone is just "Witnesses." However, in the context of the people of the city and the elders speaking, we get the complete clause "[We are] witnesses." Hebrew has an "echoing" style for question and answer, so when combined with the previous verse, where Boaz tells them they are witnesses, the group's answer here has the same echo, "[We are] witnesses."[11]

יִתֵּן֩ יְהוָ֨ה אֶֽת־הָאִשָּׁ֜ה הַבָּאָ֣ה אֶל־בֵּיתֶ֗ךָ כְּרָחֵ֤ל ׀ וּכְלֵאָה֙ אֲשֶׁ֨ר בָּנ֤וּ שְׁתֵּיהֶם֙ אֶת־בֵּ֣ית יִשְׂרָאֵ֔ל

יִתֵּן֩ continues the direct speech of those present at the redemption transaction. יִתֵּן֩ is a Qal jussive 3ms of נתן with the I-נ assimilated into the R2 ת (יִתֵּן ⟵ יִנְתֵּן). יְהוָ֨ה is the subject, and the jussive verbal meaning is determined by the context. Here the context is the people asking the Lord to bless Ruth, and so the modal request of the jussive is fitting: "*May* the Lord bless."

The direct object is אֶֽת־הָאִשָּׁ֜ה, marked by the accusative marker (אֶת־). הַבָּאָ֣ה is the Qal participle fs of בוא, and the definite article (הַ) functions as a relative particle, "who": "the woman *who* is coming."[12] The relative function of the participle further modifies הָאִשָּׁ֜ה. The durative aspect of the participle is appropriate ("is coming") since the decision to redeem has just now been confirmed and Ruth has not yet come into Boaz's house. Another option would be an inceptive meaning, "who is *about to* come."[13]

The next two prepositional phrases with the repeated כ give a comparison of qualitative resemblance.[14] Rather than the translation "give" for נתן earlier, we may now translate it as "make." The people are not asking the Lord to "give" Ruth an actual item "like" one that was given to Rachel and Leah. Rather, the clause (נתן + כ) communicates that the people are blessing Ruth to have the *same quality of matriarchy* as the mothers of the nation of Israel.

11. GKC §150n.

12. Compare this participle form to הַשָּׁ֫בָה in 1:22; 2:6; 4:3. Notice that the accent on the final syllable of this form (הַבָּאָ֣ה) clearly marks a participle.

13. RJW §214.

14. Wilch, *Ruth*, 161, who cites BDB, 1b.

אֲשֶׁר introduces the relative clause that further defines Rachel and Leah. בָּנ֤וּ is the Qal perfect 3cp of בנה, translated as a simple past, "built." Notice that the perfect 3cp of III-ה verbs attaches the vocalic sufformative (וּ) directly to the R2 (נ) of the root. שְׁתֵּיהֶם֙ is a resumptive subject, communicating that both Rachel and Leah are in view. אֶת־בֵּ֣ית יִשְׂרָאֵ֑ל is the accusative direct object. "Building a house" is idiomatic for building a family lineage. The townspeople and the elders ask God to make Ruth like these mothers of Israel and to perpetuate the family name of her deceased husband.

וַעֲשֵׂה־חַ֙יִל֙ בְּאֶפְרָ֔תָה

וַעֲשֵׂה is the Qal imperative 2ms of עשׂה + *vav*. The *vav* on an imperative is not consecutive in the same sense as a *vav*-consecutive imperfect or *vav*-consecutive perfect. A *vav* on an imperative is most often just connecting two imperatives together as a double command, but when it follows the jussive (יִתֵּ֨ן), it expresses purpose.[15] This purpose clause, along with the following one (וּקְרָא־שֵׁ֖ם בְּבֵ֥ית לָֽחֶם), is subordinate to the main blessing.

The structure of this discourse is a bit odd, but the townspeople ask God to make Ruth like Rachel and Leah, and then, subordinately, they command (wish/desire) Boaz (2ms imperative) to do/make חַ֙יִל in Ephrathah (וַעֲשֵׂה־חַ֙יִל). The idea of "making/doing חַ֙יִל" can be idiomatic for "to prosper." However, notice the same word used here, חַ֙יִל, that is used to describe both Boaz and Ruth in this book. Holmstedt comments (rightly, I think) that this clause (וַעֲשֵׂה־חַ֙יִל) is shorthand for to "make mighty men of character" who behave according to torah just like Ruth and Boaz.[16] In other words, the townspeople say, "Perpetuate your family name by making more people like you." The ב on בְּאֶפְרָ֔תָה is locative, indicating *where* the townspeople expect Boaz to עֲשֵׂה־חַ֙יִל.

וּקְרָא־שֵׁ֖ם בְּבֵ֥ית לָֽחֶם׃

וּקְרָא is another Qal imperative 2ms, this time of the root קרא. The *vav* again marks a subordinate purpose clause, to "call the name in Bethlehem."

---

15. *IBHS* §6w.
16. Holmstedt, *Ruth*, 203.

וּקְרָא־שֵׁם בְּבֵית לָחֶם is idiomatic for the perpetuation of the family name or even idiomatic for the name "to be renowned." בְּבֵית לָחֶם is locative with בֵּית לָחֶם parallel to אֶפְרָתָה in the previous clause. These place names recall 1:1–2, where the circumstances were not so pleasant. There, a famine drove this family of Ephrathites (אֶפְרָתִים; 1:2) *from* Bethlehem (מִבֵּית לֶחֶם; 1:1) to Moab. Now, upon returning to Bethlehem and gaining a covenant redemption, the townspeople seek to gain God's blessing in both אֶפְרָתָה and בֵּית לָחֶם.

RUTH 4:12

וִיהִ֤י בֵֽיתְךָ֙ כְּבֵ֣ית פֶּ֔רֶץ אֲשֶׁר־יָלְדָ֥ה תָמָ֖ר לִֽיהוּדָ֑ה מִן־הַזֶּ֗רַע אֲשֶׁ֨ר יִתֵּ֤ן יְהוָה֙ לְךָ֔
מִן־הַֽנַּעֲרָ֖ה הַזֹּֽאת׃

ACCENT PHRASING

וִיהִ֤י בֵֽיתְךָ֙ כְּבֵ֣ית פֶּ֔רֶץ
אֲשֶׁר־יָלְדָ֥ה תָמָ֖ר לִֽיהוּדָ֑ה
מִן־הַזֶּ֗רַע אֲשֶׁ֨ר יִתֵּ֤ן יְהוָה֙ לְךָ֔
מִן־הַֽנַּעֲרָ֖ה הַזֹּֽאת׃

וִיהִ֤י בֵֽיתְךָ֙ כְּבֵ֣ית פֶּ֔רֶץ

וִיהִ֤י continues the community blessing begun in 4:11. The *vav* is a simple conjunction because the vowel pointing indicates that וְ rather than וַ◌ּ was added to the beginning of יְהִי (וְיְהִי ⟵ וִיהִי). The verbal form then is jussive, not imperfective. בֵֽיתְךָ֙ is the subject, "And may *your house* exist." כְּבֵ֣ית פֶּ֔רֶץ is another qualitative comparison with כ like what occurred earlier with Rachel and Leah (כְּרָחֵ֤ל ׀ וּכְלֵאָה֙).

אֲשֶׁר־יָלְדָ֥ה תָמָ֖ר לִֽיהוּדָ֑ה

This relative clause modifies פֶּ֔רֶץ. תָמָ֖ר is the subject, and יָלְדָ֥ה is the Qal perfect 3fs of ילד. The ל on לִֽיהוּדָ֑ה indicates advantage or benefit. Tamar gave birth to Perez "*for* Judah."

מִן־הַזֶּ֗רַע אֲשֶׁ֨ר יִתֵּ֤ן יְהוָה֙ לְךָ֔

The next two מִן clauses indicate the source from which the blessing will come to make Boaz like Perez. In the first מִן phrase, Boaz's house will be like Perez's because of the offspring given by the Lord.

אֲשֶׁ֨ר modifies הַזֶּ֗רַע, specifying that the offspring given to Boaz and Ruth will be a gift from the Lord. יִתֵּ֤ן is the Qal imperfect 3ms of נתן. Context must determine whether this is imperfective or jussive, and here the hope of an actual future event leans toward imperfective, "The Lord *will* give." לְךָ֔ is the prepositional phrase indicating to whom the offspring will be given. The 2ms suffix refers specifically to Boaz but obviously should not exclude Ruth as a participant in the bearing of offspring as the next preposition מִן will suggest.

מִן־הַנַּעֲרָה הַזֹּאת׃

מִן is now used to specify from whom the children will come. The Lord will give the offspring, but the offspring will come "from this young woman" (הַנַּעֲרָה הַזֹּאת). Notice the agreement of the demonstrative pronoun הַזֹּאת with הַנַּעֲרָה to translate "this young woman." With an appositional descriptive noun, we would get "from the young woman, the this one," but that fails to accommodate the target language. "This young woman" is correct. Both the noun and the demonstrative adjective are fs *and* definite; hence, they agree in gender, number, and definiteness.

13 And so Boaz took Ruth and she existed for him as a wife and he entered to her. And
the Lord gave to her conception and she bore a son. 14 And the [towns]women said to
Naomi, "Blessed be the Lord, who did not withhold from you a redeemer today. And
may his name be called in Israel. 15 And may he exist for you as one who returns the
life (revives the soul) and as a sustainer of your old age, for your daughter-in-law, who
loves you, who she is better for you than seven sons, she has given birth to him." 16 And
then Naomi took the lad and she put him in her lap and she existed for him as a nurse.
17 And the neighborhood women called for him a name, saying, "A son was born to
Naomi." And they called his name Obed. He [was] the father of Jesse, father of David.

RUTH

4:13–17

13 וַיִּקַּ֨ח בֹּ֤עַז אֶת־רוּת֙ וַתְּהִי־ל֣וֹ לְאִשָּׁ֔ה וַיָּבֹ֖א אֵלֶ֑יהָ וַיִּתֵּ֨ן יְהוָ֥ה לָ֛הּ הֵרָי֖וֹן וַתֵּ֥לֶד
בֵּֽן׃ 14 וַתֹּאמַ֤רְנָה הַנָּשִׁים֙ אֶֽל־נָעֳמִ֔י בָּר֣וּךְ יְהוָ֔ה אֲשֶׁ֨ר לֹ֣א הִשְׁבִּ֥ית לָ֛ךְ גֹּאֵ֖ל הַיּ֑וֹם
וְיִקָּרֵ֥א שְׁמ֖וֹ בְּיִשְׂרָאֵֽל׃ 15 וְהָ֤יָה לָךְ֙ לְמֵשִׁ֣יב נֶ֔פֶשׁ וּלְכַלְכֵּ֖ל אֶת־שֵׂיבָתֵ֑ךְ כִּ֣י כַלָּתֵ֣ךְ
אֲשֶׁר־אֲהֵבַ֗תֶךְ יְלָדַ֙תּוּ֙ אֲשֶׁר־הִיא֙ ט֣וֹבָה לָ֔ךְ מִשִּׁבְעָ֖ה בָּנִֽים׃ 16 וַתִּקַּ֨ח נָעֳמִ֤י אֶת־
הַיֶּ֙לֶד֙ וַתְּשִׁתֵ֣הוּ בְחֵיקָ֔הּ וַתְּהִי־ל֖וֹ לְאֹמֶֽנֶת׃ 17 וַתִּקְרֶאנָה֩ ל֨וֹ הַשְּׁכֵנ֥וֹת שֵׁם֙ לֵאמֹ֔ר
יֻלַּד־בֵּ֖ן לְנָעֳמִ֑י וַתִּקְרֶ֤אנָֽה שְׁמוֹ֙ עוֹבֵ֔ד ה֥וּא אֲבִי־יִשַׁ֖י אֲבִ֥י דָוִֽד׃ פ

RUTH 4:13

וַיִּקַּ֨ח בֹּ֤עַז אֶת־רוּת֙ וַתְּהִי־ל֣וֹ לְאִשָּׁ֔ה וַיָּבֹ֖א אֵלֶ֑יהָ וַיִּתֵּ֨ן יְהוָ֥ה לָ֛הּ הֵרָי֖וֹן וַתֵּ֥לֶד בֵּֽן׃

ACCENT PHRASING

וַיִּקַּ֨ח בֹּ֤עַז אֶת־רוּת֙
וַתְּהִי־ל֣וֹ לְאִשָּׁ֔ה
וַיָּבֹ֖א אֵלֶ֑יהָ
וַיִּתֵּ֨ן יְהוָ֥ה לָ֛הּ הֵרָי֖וֹן
וַתֵּ֥לֶד בֵּֽן׃

וַיִּקַּ֨ח בֹּ֤עַז אֶת־רוּת֙

The primary narrative now resumes with וַיִּקַּח, the Qal imperfect 3ms of לקח + *vav*-consecutive of logical succession, "*and so* Boaz took Ruth." Remember that לקח often functions morphologically as a I-נ, so the initial ל assimilates into the ק (וַיִּקַּח ⟵ וַיִּלְקַח). בֹּעַז is the explicit subject, and אֶת־רוּת is the accusative direct object. To "take" (לקח) a woman in this respect is to marry her.[1] The next clause (וַתְּהִי־לוֹ לְאִשָּׁה) combines with לקח to create the idiom (cf. Gen 24:67). Boaz has not "taken" Ruth to a location. Rather, he married her.

וַתְּהִי־ל֣וֹ לְאִשָּׁ֔ה

וַתְּהִי is the Qal imperfect 3fs of היה + *vav*-consecutive, clarifying the idiom for marriage. Ruth is the implied subject of the 3fs verb, "and she existed for him (Boaz)." The ל on לוֹ is advantage; Ruth existed "*for* him." לְאִשָּׁה is the adverbial accusative of situation, communicating the status in which Ruth existed, "she existed for him *as* (in the status of) a wife."[2] The resulting translation is "Boaz took Ruth and she became his wife."

וַיָּבֹ֖א אֵלֶ֑יהָ

וַיָּבֹא is a Qal imperfect 3ms of בוא + *vav*-consecutive. The *vav* indicates temporal succession, presenting the next action after that of Ruth becoming

1. *DCH* 4:573–74.
2. *IBHS* §13z, 13ii.

Boaz's wife. Boaz is the implied subject of the 3ms verb (וַיָּבֹא). אֵלֶיהָ is a locative prepositional phrase. וַיָּבֹא אֵלֶיהָ is often idiomatic for an intimate encounter (Gen 6:4; 16:2; 30:3; Deut 22:13; Ezek 23:44; Prov 6:29). As the narrative moves forward quickly with this close chain of *vav*-consecutives (וַיִּקַּח ... וַתְּהִי ... וַיָּבֹא), the marriage has now been consummated.

וַיִּתֵּן יְהוָה לָהּ הֵרָיוֹן

וַיִּתֵּן is the Qal imperfect 3ms of נתן + *vav*-consecutive in temporal succession. The *vav* could possibly be understood as logical succession if we view conception as the logical result of sexual intimacy. However, since conception is not always the result of sexual intimacy *and* since the narrator is moving the action forward quickly, it is best to understand וַיִּתֵּן as temporal succession.

יְהוָה is the explicit subject and is theologically weighty. The townspeople knew that the Lord would give Boaz and Ruth offspring, and now the narrator confirms the truth that "the *Lord* gave to her (Ruth) conception." הֵרָיוֹן is the direct object. The phrase is mildly idiomatic ("to give conception") but communicates the intended idea ("to become pregnant") even if interpreted literally. "The Lord gave to her conception" simply means that she became pregnant.

וַתֵּלֶד בֵּן׃

וַתֵּלֶד is the Qal imperfect 3fs of ילד + *vav*-consecutive of temporal succession. Notice that the I-ו verb, ילד, loses the initial ו in the Qal imperfect and lengthens the preformative vowel (וַתֵּלֶד). Also notice that the *vav*-consecutive retracts the accent to the preformative, resulting in a *sĕgōl* as the thematic vowel (וַתֵּלֶד). בֵּן is the indefinite direct object.

All of these *vav*-consecutives move the narrative forward quickly, and while many of these verbal ideas are logically consequential to what precedes, the thrust of the narrative is to see the action moving forward quickly *in time*. In only one verse, the narrator outlines the result that the audience has been hoping for the entire book. The brevity of this narrative action adds to its force and excitement as the end result of God's covenant faithfulness *to* his people expressed through the covenant faithfulness *of* his people.

RUTH 4:14

וַתֹּאמַ֤רְנָה הַנָּשִׁים֙ אֶֽל־נָעֳמִ֔י בָּר֣וּךְ יְהוָ֔ה אֲשֶׁר֙ לֹ֣א הִשְׁבִּ֥ית לָ֛ךְ גֹּאֵ֖ל הַיּ֑וֹם וְיִקָּרֵ֥א שְׁמ֖וֹ בְּיִשְׂרָאֵֽל׃

ACCENT PHRASING

וַתֹּאמַ֤רְנָה הַנָּשִׁים֙ אֶֽל־נָעֳמִ֔י
בָּר֣וּךְ יְהוָ֔ה אֲשֶׁר֙ לֹ֣א הִשְׁבִּ֥ית לָ֛ךְ גֹּאֵ֖ל הַיּ֑וֹם
וְיִקָּרֵ֥א שְׁמ֖וֹ בְּיִשְׂרָאֵֽל׃

וַתֹּאמַ֤רְנָה הַנָּשִׁים֙ אֶֽל־נָעֳמִ֔י

וַתֹּאמַ֤רְנָה is the Qal imperfect 3fp of אמר + *vav*-consecutive, now shifting the subject to הַנָּשִׁים֙. The *vav*-consecutive is in temporal succession, moving the narrative forward. Ruth 4:14 shifts the focus of the conversation to the women of the city and Naomi. אֶֽל־נָעֳמִ֔י is the prepositional phrase that marks Naomi as the addressee of what the women are preparing to say.

בָּר֣וּךְ יְהוָ֔ה אֲשֶׁר֙ לֹ֣א הִשְׁבִּ֥ית לָ֛ךְ גֹּאֵ֖ל הַיּ֑וֹם

בָּר֣וּךְ begins the direct speech of the women, and again the community blesses the Lord for his provision (cf. 4:11–12). בָּר֣וּךְ is a Qal passive participle of ברך and is fronted for emphasis. The verbless clause carries an implied modal meaning, "*May* the Lord be blessed," or "Blessed be the Lord."

אֲשֶׁר֙ modifies יְהוָ֔ה and provides the characteristic of יְהוָ֔ה as to why the women are blessing the Lord. הִשְׁבִּ֥ית is the negated Hiphil perfect 3ms of שׁבת. The causative Hiphil means "to cause to cease." The negation indicates that the Lord did *not* "cause something to cease," and the accusative object (גֹּאֵ֖ל) is the thing that the Lord did not cause to cease. לָ֛ךְ is a ל of advantage because the Lord did not leave Naomi without a redeemer for her advantage: "who did not cause to cease *for* you." הַיּ֑וֹם provides the temporal context of the women's blessing, "today."

The Hiphil verb (הִשְׁבִּ֥ית) seems odd when translated literally. For the Lord "not to cause something to cease" implies that "he caused it to continue to exist." The גֹּאֵל is the object that continues to exist, and so, maintaining the negative verbal idea, we might say, "the Lord who has not left you without a redeemer today." Stated positively, the Lord provides a redeemer for Naomi today.

וְיִקָּרֵא שְׁמוֹ בְּיִשְׂרָאֵל׃

וְיִקָּרֵא is the Niphal jussive 3ms of קרא + conjunctive *vav*. The *vav* simply conjoins בָּרוּךְ יְהוָה with וְיִקָּרֵא. The jussive continues the modal nuance of the implied modal in the initial blessing (בָּרוּךְ יְהוָה ... וְיִקָּרֵא). The townswomen say, "May the Lord be blessed, *and may his name be called*." שְׁמוֹ is the subject now, and the antecedent of the pronoun (וֹ◌) is יהוה. With the Niphal jussive we get "And *may* (modal) his name *be* (passive) called." Like before, the meaning behind a name being called is that the name would be renowned, known, and perpetuated. בְּיִשְׂרָאֵל is a locative prepositional phrase communicating *where* the Lord's name will be renowned.

There is some ambiguity as to whose name is to be called. First, the name to be called could be Yahweh. The blessing begins in the previous clause with Yahweh as the clear name to be "blessed." If we disregard that the "redeemer" has been introduced between Yahweh and someone's name being renowned in Israel, the name that is to be called is the name of Yahweh. He has kept his covenant and demonstrated חֶסֶד to his people, and therefore the people desire to see his name made great in future generations in Israel.

Second, if the suffix (וֹ◌) refers to גֹּאֵל as its antecedent, the question is which גֹּאֵל, Boaz or the child? Throughout the story, Boaz has been referred to as the redeemer, and so this would seem the most obvious answer. However, the son of Boaz is also a redeemer—namely, of the family inheritance that he will perpetuate on. In this sense, the child will perpetuate the family name and thus "be renowned" in Israel. While all these interpretive options are possible grammatically, the most likely antecedent is Yahweh. Verse 14 seems to be set on reciting the blessing from the townswomen over Naomi, and that the Lord is the one who ultimately provided for Naomi suggests his name is the one to be perpetuated in Israel.

RUTH 4:15

וְהָ֤יָה לָךְ֙ לְמֵשִׁ֣יב נֶ֔פֶשׁ וּלְכַלְכֵּ֖ל אֶת־שֵׂיבָתֵ֑ךְ כִּ֣י כַלָּתֵ֤ךְ אֲשֶׁר־אֲהֵבַ֙תֶךְ֙ יְלָדַ֔תּוּ
אֲשֶׁר־הִיא֙ ט֣וֹבָה לָ֔ךְ מִשִּׁבְעָ֖ה בָּנִֽים׃

ACCENT PHRASING

וְהָ֤יָה לָךְ֙ לְמֵשִׁ֣יב נֶ֔פֶשׁ
וּלְכַלְכֵּ֖ל אֶת־שֵׂיבָתֵ֑ךְ
כִּ֣י כַלָּתֵ֤ךְ אֲשֶׁר־אֲהֵבַ֙תֶךְ֙ יְלָדַ֔תּוּ
אֲשֶׁר־הִיא֙ ט֣וֹבָה לָ֔ךְ מִשִּׁבְעָ֖ה בָּנִֽים׃

וְהָ֤יָה לָךְ֙ לְמֵשִׁ֣יב נֶ֔פֶשׁ

וְהָ֤יָה is a Qal perfect 3ms + *vav*-consecutive. The *vav* + perfect continues the previous verbal aspect and is a modal perfective, "and *may* he exist." לָךְ֙ is a ל of advantage. In this clause, the son born to Ruth is the referent, and he will be for Naomi's advantage. לְמֵשִׁ֣יב is a Hiphil participle ms of שׁוב + ל preposition and functions as the adverbial accusative of situation. This same construction was most recently seen in 4:13 (וַתְּהִי־ל֣וֹ לְאִשָּׁ֑ה) and communicates the "status" in which the referent exists. Here we get "and may he exist for you *as* (in the status of) one who causes to return the life." The idiom "to return life" does not refer to one who literally restores someone from death to life. Rather, it refers to one who brings vitality and joy.[3]

וּלְכַלְכֵּ֖ל אֶת־שֵׂיבָתֵ֑ךְ

וּלְכַלְכֵּ֖ל is a Pilpel infinitive construct כול + ל preposition. What grammars sometimes refer to as "additional verbal stems" are often the intensive stems (Piel, Pual, or Hithpael) of geminate or hollow roots (here כול).[4] So essentially the verb can be understood as a Piel infinitive construct with a morphological reduplication. Regarding meaning, think Piel, but possibly

3. Wilch argues that the term refers both to preservation of actual life and to restoration of vitality (*Ruth*, 169).

4. GKC §55f.

with an extensive nuance. Joüon notes that the Pilpel may "signify repetition of an action, often in quick succession."[5] This is not far from what Fuller and Choi call an extensive Piel.[6]

Syntactically, Holmstedt argues for a gapped, modal היה as in the first part of the verse.[7] If that is the case, then the infinitive makes better sense syntactically as an adjunct to complete the implied initial verb, "[And may he exist] *to sustain*." If we maintain the same meaning of the modal היה but drop the cumbersome translation, we get "And may he sustain." אֶת־שֵׂיבָתֵךְ is the accusative object and is idiomatic for old age.

Alternatively, the Pilpel infinitive may function as an epexegetical infinitive, explaining *how* the son will "restore the soul"—namely, *by* sustaining her old age. The Pilpel infinitive construct then would be translated as a gerund but also remains connected to the main verb הָיָה at the beginning of the verse. Here היה does not have to be gapped, but the infinitive simply follows from the main verb: "and may he exist for you as one who returns the soul, *even by* sustaining your old age."

כִּי כַלָּתֵךְ אֲשֶׁר־אֲהֵבַתֶךְ יְלָדַתּוּ

כִּי provides the ground clause for *why* the women speak these blessings over Naomi. כַלָּתֵךְ is the subject, and the relative clause further defines her as אֲשֶׁר־אֲהֵבַתֶךְ. אֲהֵבַתֶךְ is a Qal perfect 3fs of אהב + 2fs suffix, "who [she] loves you." Notice that with the suffix, the accent shifts to the R3 (אֲהֵבַתֶךְ), and therefore the vowel under the א reduces to a *shewa* (אֱ).[8] Being a guttural letter, the *shewa* must become composite (ֱ). The perfective is used here to communicate a past action displaying love that continues into the present. It does not refer to Ruth's love that existed at one point in the past and

5. JM §59c, n. 2. He cites I. Eitan, "La Répétition de la Racine en Hébreu," *Journal of the Palestine Oriental Society* 1 (1920): 174–77, and I. Yannay, "Augmented Verbs in Biblical Hebrew," *Hebrew Union College Annual* 45 (1974): 71–95.

6. *IBHS* §7c.

7. Holmstedt, *Ruth*, 207–8, citing WO §36.2.3g.

8. The disjunctive accent here is a doubled *pašṭā* (אֲהֵבַתֶךְ). The *pašṭā* is a postpositive, meaning that it occurs at the end of the word. If, however, the accent of the word falls on another syllable besides the last, the doubled *pašṭā* will mark the accented syllable (JM §15f).

now no longer exists. Hence, the present-tense translation is fitting: "your daughter-in-law, who *loves* you."

יְלָדַתּוּ is the Qal perfect 3fs of ילד + 3ms pronominal object. The morphology perhaps needs explanation. We would expect the 3fs Qal perfect with a 3ms suffix to look like this: יְלָדַתְהוּ. However, ה between the silent *shewa* and the final vowel often assimilates phonetically and hence disappears. Here the consonantal text reflects the loss of the ה phoneme, but since the Masoretes knew it should be there, they assimilated it into the ת. Once the ה assimilates, the vowel shifts to the ת.[9]

יָלְדַת + הוּ ⟵ יְלָדַתְהוּ ⟵ יְלָדַתּוּ

אֲשֶׁר־הִיא טוֹבָה לָךְ מִשִּׁבְעָה בָּנִים׃

אֲשֶׁר introduces a relative clause that further modifies כַּלָּתֵךְ (Ruth). The relative clause is a verbless clause with הִיא as the subject. הִיא is a retrospective pronoun indicating that we are referring to the "she" previously mentioned in the verse (כַּלָּתֵךְ). טוֹבָה is the predicate adjective, "who she (is) *good*." מִן on the numeral מִשִּׁבְעָה is comparative and, when translated along with the adjective (טוֹבָה), becomes "better than." As with many numerals, בָּנִים specifies the item numbered (numerable), "seven (in terms of) sons," or "seven sons." The ל on לָךְ is advantage. Ruth has looked out *for* Naomi's welfare and therefore is "better than seven sons *for*" her. The women of the town recognize that the Lord has provided offspring who will be a joyful blessing for Naomi in her old age, but they also know what a blessing Ruth has been for Naomi over the years. They see and rejoice in God's gracious provision for his people, particularly Naomi, the one who previously could not see the "comfort" that Yahweh was for her and could only reflect on her "bitterness."

9. JM §62d.

RUTH 4:16

וַתִּקַּ֨ח נָעֳמִ֤י אֶת־הַיֶּ֙לֶד֙ וַתְּשִׁתֵ֣הוּ בְחֵיקָ֔הּ וַתְּהִי־ל֖וֹ לְאֹמֶֽנֶת׃

ACCENT PHRASING

וַתִּקַּ֨ח נָעֳמִ֤י אֶת־הַיֶּ֙לֶד֙
וַתְּשִׁתֵ֣הוּ בְחֵיקָ֔הּ
וַתְּהִי־ל֖וֹ לְאֹמֶֽנֶת׃

וַתִּקַּ֨ח נָעֳמִ֤י אֶת־הַיֶּ֙לֶד֙

וַתִּקַּח is a Qal imperfect 3fs of לקה + *vav*-consecutive. The *vav* is temporally successive, moving the narrative to the point that Naomi acts as the child's caretaker/nurse. נָעֳמִי is the explicit subject, and אֶת־הַיֶּלֶד is marked as the definite accusative object.

וַתְּשִׁתֵ֣הוּ בְחֵיקָ֔הּ

וַתְּשִׁתֵהוּ is a Qal imperfect 3fs of שׁית + 3ms pronominal suffix + *vav*-consecutive in temporal succession to Naomi "taking" the child: "*and then* she put him." The ב on בְחֵיקָהּ is locative, indicating *where* she put the child—namely, at her bosom. This clause does not suggest that Naomi somehow became the child's wet nurse. Instead, חֵיק more likely refers to the bosom as a place of safety and security, as if a caretaker held a child tightly to her body for protection.[10]

וַתְּהִי־ל֖וֹ לְאֹמֶֽנֶת׃

וַתְּהִי is the Qal imperfect 3fs of היה + *vav*-consecutive in logical succession. Naomi put the child at her protective bosom "*so that* she might exist for him as a caretaker." לוֹ is a ל of advantage; Naomi's care was for the child's benefit. לְאֹמֶנֶת is a Qal participle fs of אמן. The verbal root literally means "to confirm or support." In this context, Naomi is "supporting" the

---

10. *NIDOTTE* 2:128–29.

child through protection and she is therefore his "caretaker." לְאֹמֶנֶת is the adverbial accusative of situation, indicating the status in which Naomi exists for the child: "and so that she might exist for him *as* (in the status of) a caretaker."[11]

11. The nature of Naomi's role may seem odd when using terms like "nurse" and "lap," which sometimes carry the idea of nursing at the breasts. However, אמן, when used as a masculine participle (אֹמֵן), refers to a foster father in Isa 49:23. The term can also refer simply to a guardian as in 2 Kgs 10:1 and Esth 2:7. So we should not jump to an odd sociological conclusion of the makeup of a family in ancient Israel. Rather, the verse portrays Naomi as a loving caretaker to the point of being a foster mother. She saw this child as her own provision from the Lord and loved him as such.

RUTH 4:17

וַתִּקְרֶאנָה לוֹ הַשְּׁכֵנוֹת שֵׁם לֵאמֹר יֻלַּד־בֵּן לְנָעֳמִי וַתִּקְרֶאנָה שְׁמוֹ עוֹבֵד הוּא
אֲבִי־יִשַׁי אֲבִי דָוִד׃

ACCENT PHRASING

וַתִּקְרֶאנָה לוֹ הַשְּׁכֵנוֹת שֵׁם לֵאמֹר
יֻלַּד־בֵּן לְנָעֳמִי
וַתִּקְרֶאנָה שְׁמוֹ עוֹבֵד
הוּא אֲבִי־יִשַׁי אֲבִי דָוִד׃

וַתִּקְרֶאנָה לוֹ הַשְּׁכֵנוֹת שֵׁם לֵאמֹר

Now that the child has been placed in Naomi's loving care, the townswomen confirm the name given to the child by Naomi and Ruth. וַתִּקְרֶאנָה is a Qal imperfect 3fp of קרא + *vav*-consecutive in temporal succession and continues the primary narrative. לוֹ is the prepositional phrase indicating to whom the הַשְּׁכֵנוֹת are talking. הַשְּׁכֵנוֹת is the subject, referring to the women of the city who have been talking in this portion of the narrative.[12] שֵׁם is the accusative direct object, or the "thing" they called. The idea of "calling a name" is that they actually gave him a name. לֵאמֹר is technically an infinitive construct of אמר with a ל preposition, but it is used so commonly to introduce direct speech that it can often be omitted in English.

יֻלַּד־בֵּן לְנָעֳמִי

יֻלַּד deserves some attention. The form can be a Pual perfect 3ms translated as the passive of the Piel, *or* it can be a Qal passive form. Older grammars call this a Pual perfect 3ms.[13] However, the meaning of the root ילד in the Piel is "to assist in childbirth," so the passive of that Piel meaning (i.e., the

12. Block argues that Naomi and Ruth named Obed but that the naming was a community event involving the townswomen in which they affirm the name given by the father and mother. Here the "neighbors" represent the community celebrating the birth of the child (Block, *Ruth*, 239).

13. E.g., GKC §52s.

Pual) is "to be assisted in childbirth." This meaning does not make sense in this context, "he was assisted in childbirth." Alternatively, the meaning of the root ילד in the Qal is "to give birth." Therefore, it is best to take יֻלַּד as a Qal perfect passive 3ms, "(he) was born."[14] בֵּן is the subject, and לְנָעֳמִי is the recipient of the benefit. The ל on נָעֳמִי suggests that the townswomen considered the child to belong to Naomi. This one who returned to Bethlehem "empty" has now been filled.

וַתִּקְרֶ֤אנָה שְׁמוֹ֙ עוֹבֵ֔ד

וַתִּקְרֶאנָה repeats the initial clause of the verse, but now with the specific name given to the child. וַתִּקְרֶאנָה is again the Qal imperfect 3fp of קרא + *vav*-consecutive in temporal succession. שְׁמוֹ֙ is the first object, and the second object is the more specific name עוֹבֵ֔ד.

The accent pattern may produce a mild element of suspense here on the specific name of the child similar to 2:1 when we first met Boaz. עוֹבֵ֔ד is delayed until the end of the clause, and the disjunctive accents provide a slight pause at each juncture. Here the main verb (וַתִּקְרֶ֤אנָה) is conjoined with the object (שְׁמוֹ֙). The *mĕhuppaḵ* (◌֤) combines with the *pašṭā* (◌֙) to form the verb-object combination, and then the *pašṭā* breaks the clause ever so slightly, but effectively, before the name is revealed with the *zāqēf-qāṭôn* (◌֔). The *pašṭā* (◌֙) is the near subordinate disjunctive accent in a *zāqēf* segment, but it does not always have to occur in very short segments. It would be difficult to prove, and caution must be taken when drawing conclusions about the accents, but it is possible that the accent pattern generates a slight narrative suspense before the name "Obed" is revealed. "And they called his name … Obed."

ה֛וּא אֲבִי־יִשַׁ֖י אֲבִ֥י דָוִֽד׃

ה֛וּא refers back to Obed. It is the subject of the nominal clause focusing our attention on Obed. The nominal clause is verbless, and so we have to supply the English "to be" verb, "He [*was*] the father of Jesse." אֲבִי־יִשַׁ֖י

14. See discussion in Wilch, *Ruth*, 172. For the Qal passive, see RJW §159b and associated references.

is the predicate nominative identifying who Obed was. אֲבִי דָוִד appositionally modifies יִשַׁי in genealogical succession. "He (Obed) was the father of Jesse, (who was) the father of David." Both construct packages (אֲבִי־יִשַׁי and אֲבִי דָוִד) carry an implied ל of possession logically, the sons "belonged to" their fathers.[15]

At the very end of the book, we now get the point of the narrative in Israel's historical story line. With the Davidic kingdom as a central structure in the history of Israel, we have just been given some details of David's lineage. For those hearing Ruth for the first time, this line would elicit a rather massive aha moment. The narrative is an incredible piece of literature, but when the connection is made to the Davidic kingdom, the story takes on a new level of significance for Israel. Without God's providence in the life of Naomi, Ruth, and Boaz, there would not have been a David and hence no Davidic kingdom.

15. Joüon calls this a "genitive of relation" (JM §129f C9).

[18] *[Now] these [are] the generations of Perez: Perez fathered Hezron,* [19] *Hezron fathered*
Ram, Ram fathered Amminadab, [20] *Amminadab fathered Nahshon, Nahshon fathered*
Salmon, [21] *Salmon fathered Boaz, Boaz fathered Obed,* [22] *Obed fathered Jesse, and*
Jesse fathered David.

RUTH

4:18–22

18 וְאֵ֙לֶּה֙ תּוֹלְד֣וֹת פָּ֔רֶץ פֶּ֖רֶץ הוֹלִ֥יד אֶת־חֶצְרֽוֹן׃ 19 וְחֶצְרוֹן֙ הוֹלִ֣יד אֶת־רָ֔ם וְרָ֖ם
הוֹלִ֥יד אֶת־עַמִּֽינָדָֽב׃ 20 וְעַמִּֽינָדָב֙ הוֹלִ֣יד אֶת־נַחְשׁ֔וֹן וְנַחְשׁ֖וֹן הוֹלִ֥יד אֶת־שַׂלְמָֽה׃
21 וְשַׂלְמוֹן֙ הוֹלִ֣יד אֶת־בֹּ֔עַז וּבֹ֖עַז הוֹלִ֥יד אֶת־עוֹבֵֽד׃ 22 וְעֹבֵד֙ הוֹלִ֣יד אֶת־יִשָׁ֔י וְיִשַׁ֖י
הוֹלִ֥יד אֶת־דָּוִֽד׃

RUTH 4:18–22

וְאֵ֙לֶּה֙ תּוֹלְד֣וֹת פָּ֔רֶץ פֶּ֖רֶץ הוֹלִ֥יד אֶת־חֶצְרֽוֹן׃
וְחֶצְרוֹן֙ הוֹלִ֣יד אֶת־רָ֔ם וְרָ֖ם הוֹלִ֥יד אֶת־עַמִּֽינָדָֽב׃
וְעַמִּֽינָדָב֙ הוֹלִ֣יד אֶת־נַחְשׁ֔וֹן וְנַחְשׁ֖וֹן הוֹלִ֥יד אֶת־שַׂלְמָֽה׃
וְשַׂלְמוֹן֙ הוֹלִ֣יד אֶת־בֹּ֔עַז וּבֹ֖עַז הוֹלִ֥יד אֶת־עוֹבֵֽד׃
וְעֹבֵד֙ הוֹלִ֣יד אֶת־יִשָׁ֔י וְיִשַׁ֖י הוֹלִ֥יד אֶת־דָּוִֽד׃

ACCENT PHRASING

וְאֵ֙לֶּה֙ תּוֹלְד֣וֹת פָּ֔רֶץ
פֶּ֖רֶץ הוֹלִ֥יד אֶת־חֶצְרֽוֹן׃
וְחֶצְרוֹן֙ הוֹלִ֣יד אֶת־רָ֔ם
וְרָ֖ם הוֹלִ֥יד אֶת־עַמִּֽינָדָֽב׃
וְעַמִּֽינָדָב֙ הוֹלִ֣יד אֶת־נַחְשׁ֔וֹן
וְנַחְשׁ֖וֹן הוֹלִ֥יד אֶת־שַׂלְמָֽה׃
וְשַׂלְמוֹן֙ הוֹלִ֣יד אֶת־בֹּ֔עַז
וּבֹ֖עַז הוֹלִ֥יד אֶת־עוֹבֵֽד׃
וְעֹבֵד֙ הוֹלִ֣יד אֶת־יִשָׁ֔י
וְיִשַׁ֖י הוֹלִ֥יד אֶת־דָּוִֽד׃

The final section has been considered together because the genealogy has the same pattern throughout lexically and syntactically. The pattern opens with the typical introduction to a genealogy, "[Now] these are the generations of …" וְאֵ֙לֶּה֙ is the subject, but it is looking forward to what information will come. הוֹלִ֥יד repeats throughout the genealogy and is the Hiphil perfect 3ms of the root ילד. The Hiphil communicates the idea of "causing to be born" and is often used in genealogies listing the fathers (e.g., Gen 11:27). The best translation of the Hiphil into English is "X fathered Y." Each Hiphil verb is followed by אֶת־ with a repetition of the person's name who fathered the next in line. The translation for this final section is "Now these are the generations of Perez: Perez fathered Hezron, Hezron fathered Ram, Ram fathered Amminidab, Amminadab fathered Nahshon, Nashon fathered Salmah, Salmon fathered Boaz, Boaz fathered Obed, Obed fathered Jesse, and Jesse fathered David."

GLOSSARY

absolute object The use of the infinitive absolute alongside another conjugation to communicate a strong assertion; "dying he will die" ⟶ "he will *surely* die."

accompaniment (*vav*) The use of the conjunctive *vav* that communicates "along with."

accusative The traditional term used in discussions of the direct object of the sentence. It is unmarked in Biblical Hebrew and may communicate the direct object or any of the adverbial accusatives.

additive (*vav*) The use of the conjunctive *vav* that communicates the addition of more than one object.

adverb A word that modifies a verb.

adverbial accusative A noun that is situated grammatically in the place of the accusative and most often communicates time, place, situation, and specification.

adverbial accusative of place A syntactical construction that modifies a verb with specific reference to the location.

adverbial accusative of situation A syntactical construction that modifies a verb by communicating status or the situation in which the verb occurs.

adverbial accusative of time A syntactical construction that modifies a verb with specific reference to time.

adversative A word or particle that communicates contrast between words or phrases.

agent The subject of a verbal clause or the subject of the verb in a nominal clause.

announcement The predicate of a nominal clause; the action or statement of existence attributed to the initiator of a nominal clause.

apocopation The morphological shortening of a word by dropping original consonant letters.

apodosis The "then" clause of a conditional ("if/then") statement.

apposition The syntactical construction where two nouns are placed side-by-side such that the second noun renames the first; "David, the king ..."

appositional modifier A word that further explains or provides specificity by renaming the word it is in apposition with.

aspect The nuance of verbal action that communicates whether an action is complete or incomplete as conceived by the audience.

asseverative A clause or statement that communicates a strong sentiment or statement.

assimilated *nun* The occasion when a נ occurs with a silent *shewa* and it becomes the letter beside it, resulting in a *dāgēš forte*.

assonance The poetic rhyming of vowel sounds.

attributive adjective An adjective that follows the noun it modifies and agrees in gender, number, and definiteness, giving a descriptive attribute to the noun.

causative The primary verbal nuance of the *Hiphil* in which the verbal action is initiated by the subject.

circumstantial clause An independent clause that is related to the main clause by communicating the circumstance in which the primary action occurs.

clause A distinct unit of grammar that consists of a subject and a verb.

closed syllable A Hebrew syllable that begins with a consonant and ends with a silent *shewa*. The closed syllable very often is a consonant-vowel-consonant (CVC) syllable.

coalesce The term used to describe the morphological phenomenon when a vowel and a *vav* or *yôd* combine into a new vowel.

cohortative The verbal conjugation that communicates volition or desire in the first person; "let me ... ," "may I ..."

collective singular A noun that implies a plural number of objects but is considered singular grammatically.

compensatory lengthening The morphological phenomenon when a vowel lengthens as a result of the rejection of a *dāgēš forte* in the following consonant.

complement A syntactical element of the sentence that is obligatory; most often a noun or prepositional phrases that are necessary to complete the sentence with clarity.

composite shewa A vocal *shewa* that is made up of a simple vocal *shewa* and the short vowel of the respective vowel class.

conditional clause A clause that expresses the circumstance(s) in which a certain outcome or effect will take place.

conjugation The element of verbal parsing that communicates tense, aspect, and potentially mood. In Hebrew, these conjugations are perfect, imperfect, imperative, infinitive, participle, cohortative, and jussive.

conjunction A word that joins two parts of a sentence together in a series, in a progression of thought, or in an adversative relationship ("but").

conjunctive accent An accent in the Masoretic system that joins two words together into a syntactical package.

construct The state of a Hebrew noun making the noun conjoined to the following word; translated with the preposition "of."

construct package The conjoining of two words in a Hebrew sentence, with one word in the construct state and the final noun in the absolute state. The package is translated with the preposition "of" between the two words.

copulative The "to be" verb in a sentence identifying the subject with the predicate; "David *is* the king." In Hebrew, the copulative verb is often implied and not explicit in verbless clauses.

definite article The word "the" communicating the specificity of the item a group. It is not just *a* book but it is specified/determined as *the* book.

demonstrative adjective A series of adjectives that communicate relative position in time and space; this, that, these, and those.

direct object The constituent in the sentence that receives the action of the verb.

direct speech The text within a narrative consisting of characters speaking to other characters.

discourse The name given to a series of sentences that are connected to create a broader narrative or argument.

disjunctive accent A Masoretic accent that indicates a relative level of "break" between two words or between segments of the sentence.

durative The verbal aspect indicating action happening and continuing in the present; most often associated in Hebrew with the participle.

epexegetical The syntactical function of a constituent that explains the word it is modifying, usually indicating manner and translated using the word "by" with an English gerund ("-ing" word).

explicative apposition An appositional construction in which the second noun explains the first noun by clarifying or identifying it.

factitive The function of the *Piel* that communicates the subject "making" something to be in a certain state. This most often occurs with verbs that are stative verbs in the *Qal*; in the *Piel* factitive, they become "to make ..." [whatever state of being the *Qal* stative verb communicates].

fronted/fronting When a constituent of the sentence comes before the verb for focused attention, especially when the verb is expected to come first.

geminate verb A verbal root in which the second and third root letters are the same consonant.

genitive The relationship between two words that primarily expresses possession. The genitive, while not marked in Biblical Hebrew morphology, is often communicated by the construct package and is translated using "of."

gentilic noun A proper noun ending with a *ḥîreq-yôd* to communicate nationality; "Israel" ⟶ "Israeli."

gerund An "-ing" verb that functions as a noun.

ground clause A clause that communicates the reason why a previous clause is true or happened. Ground clauses most often begin with "for" or "because."

guttural A Hebrew consonant that is articulated in the throat.

hapax legomenon A word or expression that occurs only once in a body of literature.

historic long vowel A vowel that is marked in combination with a *vav*, *yôd*, or *he*.

hollow root A verbal root that has a *vav* or a *yôd* in the second root letter position; for example, שׁוּב, שִׂים.

idiom A group of words that have a meaning that cannot be deduced from the meaning of the individual words.

improper annexation A function of the construct package that does not form one unit of meaning within the package.

indicative A mood of verbs expressing a simple statement of fact.

initiator The first noun in a nominal clause and therefore the subject of the nominal clause.

inseparable preposition A preposition that attaches directly to the front of a word.

interrogative A word or sentence that indicates a question.

jussive The mood of a verb that suggests a wish or desire in the third person.

ketiv The "written" consonants in the Hebrew text, as opposed to the *qere* that is to be read and occurs in the Masoretic marginal notes.

***lamed* of possession** A use of the *lamed* that communicates possession.

***lamed* of specification** A use of the *lamed* in which the word specifies the realm in which the previous noun occurs.

locative A grammatical construction that communicates location or direction.

logical succession The use of the *vav*-consecutive in which the implied meaning within the narrative communicates the purpose or result of the preceding sentence; "and so."

Masoretes The family in Tiberias who preserved the pronunciation of the text with the vowel markers and added the cantillation marks (accents).

monosyllabic Refers to a word that contains only one syllable.

morphology The term used to speak generally about the study of word forms in grammar.

nominal clause A clause that begins with a noun.

nominative The subject of a clause or sentence.

oath clause A clause that expresses a strong assertion, usually including a curse and/or consequences if a certain condition is not met.

object suffix The term used to describe a pronominal suffix attached to a verb in which it functions as the direct object of the sentence or clause.

open syllable A Hebrew syllable that begins with a consonant and ends with a vowel; often referred to as CV syllables (consonant-vowel).

paragogic *nun* A *nun* added to the end of a verbal form that does not change the fundamental meaning of the verb.

parallelism The relationship between two lines of text in which the second line echoes words or ideas from the first line in any number of semantic or logical relationships.

pausal form The form of a verb that displays a long vowel where a short vowel is expected. This is usually the result of the word having a heavy disjunctive accent.

phoneme A distinct unit of sound that distinguishes one word from another.

pluperfect A grammatical tense that communicates an event that happened in the past, but prior to another event in the past; usually translated with the helping verb "had."

possessive The grammatical concept that communicates ownership.

predicate The segment of a sentence that contains the verb phrase.

predicate nominative The name given to the noun when it occurs in the predicate position following a copulative verb.

preformative The letter(s) that occur before the verbal root to distinguish conjugation or stem.

preformative vowel The vowel that is associated with the preformative letter of the imperfect conjugation or one of the other preformatives of the derived stems.

preposition A word that attaches one word or phrase to another, as in "Ruth was *from* Moab."

prepositional complement The name given to a prepositional phrase when it functions as the complement of the sentence or clause.

prepositional phrase A construction that includes a preposition and any accompanying words.

pretonic Refers to the syllable that is directly before the accented (tonic) syllable.

pronominal suffix The use of a pronoun that is attached directly to the end of a noun or verb.

pronoun A word referring to a noun (the antecedent) that appears earlier in the discourse.

proper annexation A function of the construct package such that two words are combined to create one unit of meaning; for example, "the house of David."

propretonic Refers to the syllable that occurs two or more syllables before the accented (tonic) syllable. A word may have more than one propretonic syllables.

protasis The "if" clause of a conditional ("if/then") statement.

qere The suggested way to "read" a word in question. *Qere* was marked in the margin by the Masoretic scribes.

quiesce The phenomenon of a silent letter (usually *aleph*) that will cease to produce any sound in the word because it occurs with a silent *shewa*.

reflexive Refers to the action of the verb being performed *by* the subject as well as *to* or *for* the subject. Usually expressed by reflexive pronouns such as "himself" or "herself."

relative clause A clause that modifies a noun by clarifying it' meaning; "Ruth, *who was from Moab*."

segolate The name given to a noun that originally had one short vowel but has come in Biblical Hebrew to have the vowel pattern of two *sĕgōls* (two short vowels) and an accented first root letter.

silent shewa A type of *shewa* that has no vocalized sound but represents a lack of sound between two consonants, often creating a phonetic stop.

subject The constituent in the sentence that does the action of the sentence.

substantive Adjective describing a sentence constituent that functions as a noun.

sufformative The portion of a word morphology that comes at the end of the verbal root.

syntax The structure (word sequence) of a sentence.

temporal succession The use of the *vav*-consecutive in which the implied meaning within the narrative communicates the next verbal action in the narrative; "and then."

tense A category for describing the timeframe in which an action occurs in relation to the speaker.

thematic vowel The name given to the vowel associated with the second root letter of a verbal conjugation or stem.

tone The accented syllable of a word.

***vav*-conjunctive** The use of the *vav* to join two words together with "and."

verbal clause A clause that begins with a verb and focuses on the action of the narrative rather than the subject.

verbless clause A clause that does not contain a formal verb but implies a copulative verb between two constituents.

vocative Refers to one character in the discourse addressing another character directly.

weak verb A verbal root containing one or more consonants that do not morph according to normal patterns. These can include letters like *vav*, *yôd*, *nun*, or guttural letters.

Table of Masoretic Accents: Accents for Hebrew Prose

Disjunctive Accents					
	sof pasuq	*sôf pāsûq*	:		דָּבָר׃
Kings/D0	*silluq*	*sillûq*	◌ֽ		דָּבָֽר
	athnach	*atnāḥ*	◌֑		דָּבָ֑ר
Princes/D1	*segolta*	*sĕgōlta*	◌֒	postpositive	דָּבָר֒
	shalsheleth	*šalšelet*	◌֓ ׀		דָּבָ֓ר ׀
	zaqef qaton	*zāqēf qāṭôn*	◌֔		דָּבָ֔ר
	zaqef gadol	*zāqēf gādôl*	◌֕		דָּבָ֕ר
	tifcha	*ṭifḥā*	◌֖		דָּבָ֖ר
Dukes/D2	*revia*	*revîa*	◌֗		דָּבָ֗ר
	zarqa	*zarqā*	◌֮	postpositive	דָּבָר֮
	pashta	*pašṭā*[1]	◌֙	postpositive	דָּבָר֙
	yetiv	*yĕtîv*	◌֚	prepositive	דָּ֚בָר
	tevir	*tĕvîr*	◌֛		דָּבָ֛ר
Counts/D3	*geresh*	*gereš*	◌֜		דָּבָ֜ר
	gershaim	*geršaim*	◌֞		דָּבָ֞ר
	pazer	*pazēr*	◌֡		דָּבָ֡ר
	pazer gadol	*pazēr gādôl (qarnê parâ)*	◌֟		דָּבָ֟ר
	telisha gadol	*teliša gādôl*	◌֠	prepositive	דָּ֠בָר
	legarmeh	*lĕgarmēh*	◌֣ ׀		דָּבָ֣ר ׀

1. *Pašṭā* may occur as a doubled *pašṭā* (מֶ֙לֶךְ֙) if the accent falls on a syllable other than the final syllable. This is not a different accent, but since the *pašṭā* is a postpositive, it will occur at the very end of the word. The second *pašṭā* of the doubled *pašṭā* marks the accented syllable.

Conjunctive Accents				
munach	*mûnaḥ*	◌֣		דָּבָ֣ר
mehuppach	*mĕhuppaḥ*	◌֤		דָּבָ֤ר
mereka	*mêrĕkā*	◌֥		דָּבָ֥ר
mereka kefula	*mêrĕkā kĕfûlâ*	◌֦		דָּבָ֦ר
darga	*dargā*	◌֧		דָּבָ֧ר
azla (qadma)	*azlā (qadmā)*	◌֨		דָּבָ֨ר
telisha qaton	*teliša qāṭôn*	◌֩	postpositive	דָּבָר֩
galgal	*galgal*	◌֪		דָּבָ֪ר
mayela	*mayĕlâ*	◌֢◌֖		דָּ֢בָ֖ר

This table lists the disjunctive accents in order of relative strength or relative amount of disjunction between words or constituents. The older designation for these followed the idea of a monarchy with "Kings," "Princes," "Dukes, and "Counts" to illustrate that relative "power." Other scholars have used the designations of a "domain," and hence the D0, D1, D2, and D3 labels.

The summary of conjunctive accents below is adapted from Mark Futato, *Basics of Hebrew Accents* (Zondervan, 2020), 65. The conjunctive accents in the left column can be expected to occur immediately before the disjunctives listed in the right. This is not the whole picture of conjunctive accents, but it captures most of their occurrences.

SUMMARY OF THE PROSE CONJUCTIVE ACCENTS

Conjuctive Accent	**Group 1 Kings**	**Group 2 Princes**	**Group 3 Dukes**	**Group 4 Counts**
merecha	*silluq*	*tifcha*		
munach	*athnach*	*zaqef*	*revia/zarqa*	
mehuppach			*pashta*	
azla				*geresh*

Table of Masoretic Accents: Accents for Hebrew Poetry (Job, Psalms, Proverbs)

Disjunctive Accents					
	sof pasuq	*sôf pāsûq*	:		דָּבָר׃
Kings/D0	*silluq*	*sillûq*	◌ֽ		דָּבָֽר
Kings/D0	*ole veyored*	*ʿôle vĕyôrēd*	◌֫◌֥		דָּ֫בָ֥ר
Kings/D0	*athnach*	*atnāḥ*	◌֑		דָּבָ֑ר
Princes/D1	*revia gadol*	*revîa gādôl*	◌֗		דָּבָ֗ר
Princes/D1	*revia mugrash*	*revîa mugrāš*	◌֝◌֗		דָּ֝בָ֗ר
Princes/D1	*shalsheleth gadol*	*šalšelet gādôl*	◌֓ ׀		דָּבָ֓ר ׀
Princes/D1	*tsinnor*	*ṣinnôr*	◌֮	postpositive	דָּבָר֮
Princes/D1	*revia qaton*	*revîa qāṭôn*	◌֗		דָּבָ֗ר
Princes/D1	*dechi*	*dĕḥî*	◌֭	prepositive	דָּ֭בָר
Dukes/D2	*pazer*	*pazēr*	◌֡		דָּבָ֡ר
Dukes/D2	*mehuppach-legarmeh*	*mĕhuppaḥ-lĕgarmēh*	◌֤ ׀		דָּבָ֤ר ׀
Dukes/D2	*azla-legarmeh*	*azlā-lĕgarmēh*	◌֨ ׀		דָּבָ֨ר ׀

Table of Masoretic Accents: Accents for Hebrew Poetry (Job, Psalms, Proverbs)

Conjunctive Accents			
munach	*mûnaḥ*	◌֣	דָּבָ֣ר
mereka	*mêrĕkā*	◌֥	דָּבָ֥ר
illuy	*illûy*	◌֬	דָּבָ֬ר
tarcha	*ṭarḥā*	◌֖	דָּבָ֖ר
galgal	*galgal*	◌֪	דָּבָ֪ר
mehuppach	*mĕhuppaḥ*	◌֤	דָּבָ֤ר
azla	*azlā*	◌֨	דָּבָ֨ר
shalsheleth qaton	*šalšelet qāṭôn*	◌֓	דָּבָ֓ר
tsinnorit-mereka	*ṣinnôrît-mêrĕkā*	◌֥◌֘	דָּ֘בָ֥ר
tsinnorit-mehuppach	*ṣinnôrît- mĕhuppaḥ*	◌֤◌֘	דָּ֘בָ֤ר

BIBLIOGRAPHY

Arnold, Bill T., and John H. Choi. *A Guide to Biblical Hebrew Syntax*. 2nd ed. New York: Cambridge University Press, 2018.

Blau, Joshua. *Phonology and Morphology of Biblical Hebrew: An Introduction*. Warsaw: Linguistics Studies in Ancient West Semitic 2. Winona Lake, IN: Eisenbrauns, 2010.

———. *Topics in Hebrew and Semitic Linguistics*. Jerusalem: Magnes, 1998.

Block, Daniel I. *Judges, Ruth*. The New American Commentary 6. Nashville: Broadman & Holman Publishers, 1999.

———. *Ruth: A Discourse Analysis of the Hebrew Bible*. Zondervan Exegetical Commentary on the Old Testament 8. Grand Rapids: Zondervan, 2015.

Botterweck, G. Johannes, and Helmer Ringgren. *Theological Dictionary of the Old Testament*. 17 vols. Grand Rapids: Eerdmans, 1974–2020.

Brotzman, Ellis R., and Eric J. Tully. *Old Testament Textual Criticism: A Practical Introduction*. 2nd ed. Grand Rapids: Baker Academic, 2016.

Brown, Francis, S. R. Driver, and Charles A. Briggs. *The Brown-Driver-Briggs Hebrew and English Lexicon: With an Appendix Containing the Biblical Aramaic: Coded with the Numbering System from Strong's Exhaustive Concordance of the Bible*. Peabody, MA: Hendrickson, 1996.

Bush, Frederic William. *Ruth, Esther*. Word Biblical Commentary 9. Waco, TX: Word, 1996.

Campbell, Edward F., Jr. *Ruth: A New Translation with Introduction, Notes, and Commentary*. The Anchor Bible 7. Garden City, NY: Doubleday, 1975.

Clines, David J. A. *The Dictionary of Classical Hebrew*. 9 vols. Sheffield: Sheffield Academic Press, 1993–2016.

Cook, John A. "The Biblical Hebrew Verbal System: A Grammaticalization Approach." PhD diss., University of Wisconsin–Madison, 2002.

Davis, Ellen F. *Who Are You, My Daughter? Reading Ruth through Image and Text*. Louisville: Westminster John Knox, 2003.

Eskenazi, Tamara Cohn, and Tikva Simone Frymer-Kensky. *Ruth: The Traditional Hebrew Text with the New JPS Translation*. Philadelphia: Jewish Publication Society, 2011.

Fuller, Russell T., and Kyoungwon Choi. *Invitation to Biblical Hebrew: A Beginning Grammar*. Grand Rapids: Kregel, 2006.

———. *Invitation to Biblical Hebrew Syntax: An Intermediate Grammar*. Grand Rapids: Kregel, 2017.

Gesenius, Wilhelm, E. Kautzsch, and A. E. Cowley. *Gesenius' Hebrew Grammar*. Mineola, NY: Dover, 2006.

Hawk, L. Daniel. *Ruth*. Apollos Old Testament Commentary 7B. Nottingham: Apollos, 2015.

Holmstedt, Robert D. *Ruth: A Handbook on the Hebrew Text*. Baylor Handbook on the Hebrew Bible. Waco, TX: Baylor University Press, 2010.

Hubbard, Robert L. *The Book of Ruth*. The New International Commentary on the Old Testament. Grand Rapids: Eerdmans, 1988.

Hyman, Ronald T. "Questions and Changing Identity in the Book of Ruth." *Union Seminary Quarterly Review* 39, no. 3 (1984): 197.

Jepsen, Alfred. "Ama^{h} Und Schiphcha^{h}." *Vetus Testamentum* 8, no. 3 (1958): 293–97.

Joüon, Paul. *Ruth: A Philological and Exegetical Commentary*. Translated by Homer Heater. Rome: Biblical Institute Press, 2013.

Joüon, Paul, and T. Muraoka. *A Grammar of Biblical Hebrew*. Roma: Editrice Pontificio Istituto Biblio, 2003.

Kelley, Page H., Daniel S. Mynatt, and Timothy G. Crawford. *The Masorah of Biblia Hebraica Stuttgartensia: Introduction and Annotated Glossary*. Grand Rapids: Eerdmans, 1998.

Kittel, Rudolf, Karl Elliger, Wilhelm Rudolph, Hans Peter Rüger, G. E. Weil, and Adrian Schenker. *Biblia Hebraica Stuttgartensia*. Stuttgart: Deutsche Bibelgesellschaft, 1997.

Köhler, Ludwig, Walter Baumgartner, M. E. J. Richardson, Johann Jakob Stamm, and Benedikt. Hartmann. *The Hebrew and Aramaic Lexicon of the Old Testament*. 2 vols. Leiden: Brill, 2001.

Kutz, Karl V., and Rebekah L. Josberger. *Learning Biblical Hebrew: Reading for Comprehension; An Introductory Grammar*. Bellingham, WA: Lexham Press, 2018.

Lambdin, Thomas O. *Introduction to Biblical Hebrew*. New York: Charles Scribner's Sons, 1971.

Merwe, Christo H. J. van der, Jacobus Naudé, and Jan Kroeze. *A Biblical Hebrew Reference Grammar*. Electronic ed. Sheffield: Sheffield Academic Press, 1999.

Miller, Cynthia L. "Vocative Syntax in Biblical Hebrew Prose and Poetry: A Preliminary Analysis." *Journal of Semitic Studies* 55, no. 2 (2010): 347–64.

Moscati, Sabatino. *An Introduction to the Comparative Grammar of the Semitic Languages: Phonology and Morphology*. Wiesbaden: Otto Harrassowitz, 1964.

Pratico, Gary D., and Miles V. Van Pelt. *Basics of Biblical Hebrew Grammar.* 3rd ed. Grand Rapids: Zondervan Academic, 2019.

Price, James D. *Concordance of the Hebrew Accents in the Hebrew Bible*. Lewiston, NY: Mellen, 1996.

———. *The Syntax of Masoretic Accents in the Hebrew Bible*. Lewiston, NY: Mellen, 1990.

Sasson, Jack M. *Ruth: A New Translation with a Philological Commentary and a Formalist- Folklorist Interpretation*. Baltimore: Johns Hopkins University Press, 1979.

Saxegaard, Kristin Moen. *Character Complexity in the Book of Ruth*. Forschungen zum Alten Testament 2/47. Tübingen: Mohr Siebeck, 2010.

Schenker, Adrian, Natalio Fernández Marcos, Jan de Waard, Anthony Gelston, Carmel McCarthy, David Marcus, P. B. Dirksen, Y. A. P. Goldman, R. Schäfer, and Magne Sæbø. *Biblia Hebraica Quinta*. Stuttgart: Deutsche Bibelgesellschaft, 2011.

Tov, Emanuel. *Textual Criticism of the Hebrew Bible*. 3rd ed. Minneapolis: Fortress, 2012.

VanGemeren, Willem, ed. *New International Dictionary of Old Testament Theology and Exegesis*. Grand Rapids: Zondervan, 1997.

Waltke, Bruce K., and Michael Patrick O'Connor. *An Introduction to Biblical Hebrew Syntax*. Winona Lake, IN: Eisenbrauns, 1990.

Wilch, John R. *Ruth: A Concordia Hebrew Reader*. St. Louis: Concordia, 2010.

Williams, Ronald J., and John C. Beckman. *Williams' Hebrew Syntax*. 3rd ed. Toronto: University of Toronto Press, 2007.

Yannay, Igal. "Augmented Verbs in Biblical Hebrew." *Hebrew Union College Annual* 45 (1974): 71–95.

Yeivin, Israel. *Introduction to the Tiberian Masorah*. Translated and edited by E. J. Revell. Masoretic Studies 5. Missoula, MT: Scholars Press, 1980.

LEXHAM PRESS

TO LEARN A DEAD LANGUAGE, PRETEND IT'S ALIVE

Biblical Hebrew is more than vowel marks and *waws*. Teach your students how to read it for true understanding: like it's a living language with a unique personality.

Learn more at LexhamPress.com/Hebrew-Grammar